Accidental Chef

Accidental Chef

An Insider's View of Professional Cooking

Chef Charles Oppman

authorHOUSE®

AuthorHouse™
1663 Liberty Drive
Bloomington, IN 47403
www.authorhouse.com
Phone: 1-800-839-8640

First published by AuthorHouse   09/21/2011

ISBN: 978-1-4634-1471-9 (sc)
ISBN: 978-1-4634-1470-2 (hc)
ISBN: 978-1-4634-1472-6 (ebk)

Library of Congress Control Number: 2011911499

Printed in the United States of America

CONTENTS

In Memory of Carmen Oppman

Preface

"My wife said to take to her somewhere she'd never been,
so I showed her the kitchen."

Rodney Dangerfield

ACCIDENTAL CHEF IS the book that I have always wanted to read. It is essentially a narrative about the world of cooking and a wide range of subjects included in that world. This book is a tale about the restaurant world in America and how that world profoundly affects our lives. For instance, what is the restaurant industry's role in the prevention of food-borne diseases and is it fulfilling that role? *Accidental Chef* delves into this matter and explores environmental issues such as the overfishing of Atlantic bluefin tuna—prized for sushi and sashimi.

Because foreign fisheries continue to violate international catch quotas, the bluefin is headed toward extirpation. Until and unless quotas are honored, the bluefin population is inexorably headed the way of the North Atlantic cod—once at the brink of extinction, it is no longer a viable commercial food source. There is an in-depth discussion on a range of issues associated with *eco-gastronomy* in the section entitled *Green Food Matters*. One of the topics discussed in this chapter is the appalling abuse of factory-farmed animals—an issue that multinational agribusinesses are desperate to keep hidden in the shadows.

A book about the food world is a colossal topic, where should it begin and what topics ought to be included? It was a challenge for me to settle on the mixture of subjects that would appeal to you so I settled on those that I personally find either enlightening or entertaining or both. For example, as a veteran chef myself, I've always considered the subculture of the restaurant world a fascinating one so I've explored certain elements intrinsic in that culture that are largely unknown to the general public. For instance, since gender discrimination, sexual harassment and substance abuse are widespread in America's nearly 1 million food-service establishments, I have included these topics as part of the wider discussion about the restaurant world. Further, the restaurant business cannot be examined without discussing some of the scams that are perpetrated on unsuspecting customers in that business. For instance, in the chapter entitled *The Restaurant World According to America* I discuss how dishonest servers can use pocket-size electronic "skimming" devices to upload customers' credit card information (which is then sold to a third party) or how customers can be profiled and targeted for intentional overcharges. Eating out is not always the risk-free activity we assume that it is.

To understand the world of cooking you have to get inside that world. *Accidental Chef* takes you on that journey. You will be presented with an unembellished view of a cooking life, not as it's portrayed in many of the nonsensical reality shows on the Food Network. I share slice-of-life accounts with you so you can appreciate the rigors and demands of professional cooking. You will understand what it's like to cook in dilapidated, dangerous kitchens and the risks of working with people who suffer from chronic alcoholism and drug abuse. Cooking for a living is not the sexy world as it's often depicted by the media. It's a world of physical and emotional extremes. It was my world for twenty-five years.

While this book is comprehensive in scope, it is by no means an absolute treatment of the food and cooking. That would require an epic tome far beyond what I've accomplished in this work. Rather, my book is wide-ranging mixture of issues not generally found in books of this genre penned by other chefs. Most books written by chefs are usually restricted to their personal and professional anecdotes. I've largely avoided that. The story of my career is not that fascinating, but many of my experiences and the people I've encountered during my career are. You'll become acquainted with some of the more colorful characters I've known throughout my career. *Accidental Chef* is also a tale about food itself. Of course there is a recipe section replete with some of my favorite recipes. I've also touched upon food history and foods value as *objet d'art*. There is even a short tutorial about why couverture chocolate is tempered and how inexactitude during the process will ruin the appearance of fine chocolate. If not tempered correctly, chocolate will not have that beautiful luster we admire. It will be splotchy and dull an unappealing. Eye appeal is a critical element in the enjoyment of chocolate and most food for that matter. There is an axiom in the world of cooking: "One takes the first bite with one's eyes." Flavor is paramount, but presentation must be a close second. Many professional chefs have this backward.

~~~

Before becoming a chef, I worked in the fields of environmental and public health. Because of my keen interest in these areas and my culinary background I felt compelled to discuss some of the non-cooking issues of the food world that impact our health and that of our planet; the environmental risks associated with aquaculture, overfishing our oceans and the constant threat of food-borne disease. This last area seems always to be in the news. Spectacular public health emergencies—such as the massive fresh egg recall from two Iowa farms in 2010—offer opportunities to have social discussions about controversial issues related to our food production and supply systems. For instance, what is government's role in approving genetically modified animals sold for human consumption? Should society demand the irradiation of fresh fruits and vegetables to prevent epidemics of food-borne illness? This very question came into sharp focus during the deadly E. coli outbreak in Germany during the spring and summer of 2011. Questions such as these often spark vigorous public debate as they should; for it is through a healthy national conversation that effective public policy is created.

Regrettably, societal discussions too often become distorted or muted by powerful corporate interests whose financial and political agendas are threatened by changing the status quo. The successes of private enterprise and the public's health are not necessarily mutually inclusive. Influential interest groups often disregard public health or environmental concerns because these issues aren't factored into their business plans. Take veal calves as an example. Because of the inhumane treatment they receive and the appalling conditions under which they live, veal calves are exempt from animal abuse laws in beef producing states. Residents of these same states would be incarcerated if they treated their house pets in the same manner in which factory-farmers are allowed to treat veal calves. For decades the beef lobby has had its way with state legislatures. A similar situation exists in pig producing states such as North Carolina. Animal-rights groups have documented ample and irrefutable evidence of the monstrous abuse of factory-farmed animals yet the maltreatment continues unabated. Sections of *Accidental Chef* are forensic investigations of many of these contentious issues, which are necessary to stimulate debate and discussion.

~~~

This book has given me a platform to discuss something that has rankled me for years. It's the manner in which professional cooking is portrayed on television, especially by the Food Network. Through the endless supply of cooking reality shows there is an unrealistic, and often cartoonish, portrayal of what it means to cook for a living. This is because the networks and cable channels are more concerned with promoting their own ludicrous brand of *foodtainment* rather than with advancing the art of cooking. The Food Network is the worst of the lot. Most of its show hosts lack the requisite culinary skills necessary to teach others how to cook. To add insult to injury some time ago it began referring to its pitiable hosts as *chefs* when, in fact, few of them have even worked as professional cooks. They are not chefs or cooks. They're ordinary people impersonating professional cooks. I get really annoyed when the Food Network refers to Paula Deen as a *chef*. When I think of Paula as a *chef*, I recall Marlon Brando's famous line in *Viva Zapata*, "A monkey in silk is still a monkey." Just because she has a cooking show doesn't make her a chef. The same goes for food celebrities like Rachael Ray and Sandra Lee. If you believe this pair to be chefs then Al Sharpton and Jesse Jackson are preachers.

~~~

Above all I've tried to make *Accidental Chef* informative and entertaining. If you're not informed and entertained by this book then I have failed you. I hope I haven't. I think my book is informative because I've provided information on subjects we should all be familiar with if we are to contribute to eco-gastronomy. I think my book is entertaining simply because the world of cooking itself is interesting and entertaining. I share many of my experiences as a chef in New Orleans and a restaurateur in Alexandria, Virginia. I share both amusing anecdotes and sobering vignettes of a world hidden largely from public view. Here's a sample of what you'll find inside:

- In Appendix A entitled *The Food, the Bad and the Ugly* is about the public health aspects of the business of food. Trust me here, if you knew what I know you'd think twice before you grab a snack at your neighborhood food truck or hit those all-you-can-eat buffets. In this chapter I discuss the issues of food safety and how we can protect ourselves from food-borne illness. I reveal secrets chefs and restaurateurs would rather you didn't know. I also discuss foreign food production and how it impacts the food we eat.
- In *Food Network Fool Network* I talk about the current crop of criminally bad food shows available on cable TV, especially on the Food Network. With a dearth of culinary talent, the Food Network has become synonymous with what I call *karaoke cooking*, uninspired cooking demonstrated by people who have no business teaching others how to cook. The Food Network makes a mockery of the very thing it purports to advance—cooking.
- *The Big Easy* is the chapter devoted to the formidable food traditions, culture and history of New Orleans. How did the *po' boy* sandwich get its name? What role did African slaves play in creating gumbo? How did *jambalaya* come by its funny name? What's it like to be a cook in New Orleans? I answer these questions and many more in *The Big Easy*.
- I think *Requiem for a Café* is the most eloquent and poignant chapter in the book. It's the bittersweet story about the café I owned for fourteen years. Its name was Café Marianna—after my daughter. You'll have a front row seat to the life and times of an actual restaurant. I discuss the high times and the heartbreaks of owning a restaurant. If you've never owned a restaurant, you'll feel as though you have done so after you read *Requiem*.

I think there is something for everybody in this book. If you want to develop a fundamental appreciation for the scientific aspects of the cooking and food production (such as the basic science behind food-borne diseases), that awaits you in Appendix A, *The Food, the Bad and the Ugly*. And if you are concerned about the health risks associated with genetically modified (GM) salmon you can find a discussion on this highly controversial issue in Appendix B, *Green Food Matters*. I've included lengthy discussion about the health risks of importing food from Third World countries. These are issues that I believe we should all know and understand so we can better protect ourselves and become informed consumers. I would ask the reader to hang in there beyond the first few chapters, which deal primarily with how food fit into my family structure when I was growing up and what led me to become a chef. The subsequent chapters are devoted to the world of cooking and many of the crucial issues that are central to that world and how they affect our lives.

Me a Chef?

WHY I BECAME a chef is a story worth knowing only to the extent that anyone who is considering a career change might find inspirational. I went from hospital administration to professional cooking many years ago and have never regretted it. If I can make a successful career transition and succeed at it just about anyone can. Why did I do this? Not long before he passed away, the great comedian Bernie Mack appeared on the Tavis Smiley Show and was discussing his own career when he said, "Life is not a dress rehearsal." The funny man was absolutely correct. I knew intuitively then what Bernie Mack articulated so many years later.

When I launched my culinary career, learning from the best chefs meant learning primarily from Europeans. There was little choice; they dominated the culinary scene in America in those days. A few were good to work with, but most were arrogant jerks that seemed to take pleasure in condescending to their American subordinates. I once saw a French chef kick an American cook square in the *derriere* because the cook didn't make perfect diamond-shaped grill marks on a steak. The unfortunate cook committed the unpardonable sin making square marks. Yes, the marks should have been diamond-shaped, but was kicking the poor kid really necessary? There is no love lost between American and European chefs. I'm sure the situation has improved, but that's how it was in those early years of my career.

Thankfully, the Europeans have largely been supplanted by a veritable tsunami of talented, home-grown cooks. Americans have exploded onto the culinary scene in record numbers over the last decade or so. The popularity of cooking has compelled an entire generation to look at the culinary arts as a viable career option. Would-be chefs are abandoning white collar careers to pursue the culinary arts. There are many more training opportunities available today than when I started out. There are hundreds of privately-owned culinary academies as well as trade schools and community colleges offering a range of culinary courses. A tectonic shift has taken place in American gastronomy. There's a new and vibrant energy out there. Many of the talented young chefs are producing some cutting-edge cuisine never before seen in the American foodscape. And it's *not* only taking place in the large urban centers where we expect food trends to originate; it's happening in places like Austin, Toledo and Milwaukee. It's a magnificent time to be a chef in America.

~~~

Before you read any further, you would be well-advised to lower your expectations about this book. If you're expecting a great piece of literature you won't find it here. This book is replete with errors in punctuation and grammar. I'm a chef not an English major. I couldn't afford to have the entire book professionally edited. I had to self-publish this book because no reputable publisher would touch it with a ten foot pole. I thought it was a good idea to change the names of some of the characters, especially those whose portrayal is unflattering. I've also changed the names of some the restaurants and hotels where I've worked. Finally, I considered distancing myself from *Accidental Chef* by using a pen name. I briefly considered using "Sir Loin," but I decided to use my real name.

I hope you enjoy *Accidental Chef*.

Introduction

Two cannibals were staring at a bubbling
caldron when one asked:
"Have I ever told you how much
I hate my mother-in-law?"
"No, so just eat the noodles," The other
cannibal answered.

Louie Anderson

THIS BOOK IS the felicitous result of several of my deep passions—gastronomy, food journalism, cooking and eating. I especially like the eating part. Food is far more than mere sustenance for me. It represents sensual pleasure and an art form. Food fills our souls and enhances our lives. Food has the ability to elevate our moods. Have you ever noticed how people are awash with giddy euphoria over the prospect of eating foods they relish? This is a natural response. Food appeals to our senses and is scintillating. Many of us turn to food for comfort or to lift our spirits. Just as we have evolved as a species, so have our diets and food preferences. We've come a long way from our australopithecine ancestors who foraged for seeds and tubers on the savannahs of East Africa to today's connoisseurs of fine cuisine and practitioners of *molecular gastronomy*; the haughty, modernist term for food science.

Food is more than material that contains essential body nutrients; it can be transformed into artistic media. Blocks of ice can be deftly carved into intricate works of art. Chocolate and tallow can be shaped into handsome sculptures. Inedible oil and acrylic paints are replaced with cocoa powder, spices and food colorings. Common granulated white sugar is the most versatile of all edible media. It can be melted into a molten mass that can be blown like glass to create vases or fashioned into paper-thin flower petals and delicate figurines. An accomplished pastry chef can make pulled sugar look like the finest porcelain. A simple recipe of confectioner's sugar, water and gelatin is the perfect medium for wedding cake decorations like flowers and ribbons. The use of food to create works of art is limited only by the imagination of the food artist. And the best part of all is that the artists can snack on their rejects.

~~~

Throughout history food has played a crucial role in world events and has been used as currency. In his brilliant 2002 book, *Salt: A World History,* Mark Kurlansky tells how at times Roman soldiers were paid in salt, which was the origin of the word *salary* and the expression "worth his salt" or "earning his salt." In fact, the Latin word *sal* became the French word *solde,* meaning pay, which is the origin of the word *soldier.* The *gabelle*—the reviled French salt tax—was enacted in 1286 and remained in effect until 1790, immediately after the French Revolution began. The French Revolution itself was precipitated by famine, driven mainly by the rising cost of staples such as bread. Americans have only to consider our own tax on imported British tea to understand how food can catalyze an armed insurrection.

The indigenous people of the Pacific Northwest Coast practiced a festival ceremony called a *potlatch* where food items such as dried fish and flour were exchanged between tribes as a display of wealth. Chocolate was an important luxury good throughout pre-Columbian Mesoamerica. Purportedly, Montezuma II, emperor of the Aztecs when the Spanish Conquistadors arrived, drank no fewer than fifty cups every day of a chocolate beverage flavored with vanilla and spices. Cacao beans were commonly used as currency in Central American cultures. The Aztecs employed a bartering system in which one turkey, for example, might be valued at one hundred cacao beans or one avocado might be worth ten beans. When the Aztecs conquered a region where cacao grew, they ordered its people to pay them beans as a tax, or "tribute." These beans could well have been called *frijoles protectores.* In the Aztec and Maya empires, cacao beans were as valuable as salt and gold. In the 16th century the Conquistadors returned to Europe with cacao beans and as they say, "the rest is history."

So You Wanna Be a Chef

WHEN OSCAR WILDE famously said, "It's the sort of thing you like, if you like that sort of thing," he could have easily been referring to cooking. Cooking is the sort of thing you either like or don't, leaving little room for indifference. Some people have a passion for cooking while others abhor the very thought of preparing a meal. One thing is certain: if you want to cook for a living you should have an evangelical passion for it. If you've considered changing jobs to pursue cooking as a career you might want to think it over carefully before you tell your boss what he can do with your job. Many professional cooks can only hack it for a few years before they put down their spatula for good. Few cooks work until retirement age. The work is too stressful, too physically demanding and for too little pay. While many professional cooks regard their work as a calling, others consider it a life sentence. Which camp would you fall in?

There are two things that are required to make a successful chef. One is having a natural ability to cook and I can't remember the other one. You have to know how to cook in order to realize your full potential. Sure you can always get a job slinging hash at some mom and pop restaurant or you can get a job working for a national chain. But is this cooking or is it nothing more than assembling components to replicate a dish according to a prescribed formula. There is no creativity in this. Cooking is also called "culinary arts" for a reason. There is no limit to what you can achieve if you unleash your creative talents in the kitchen. But you must first learn to cook. The fundamental cooking techniques and culinary skills must be mastered.

With the explosion of cooking and food shows on TV in recent years, the public has come to have a distorted view of what it means to be a chef. Public opinion has been shaped by manufactured scenarios that have little to do with reality—professional chefs don't compete in ridiculous "foodtainment" scenarios like *Iron Chef America* or *Cupcake Challenge*. They're too busy honing their skills to become craftsmen. Even the title *chef* has been misapplied. For example, the Food Network refers to its show hosts as *chefs* when most of them have little or no professional training. Take Rachael Ray and Sandra Lee, for instance. They're good examples of talentless people, but are referred to as *chefs* by their adoring fans. Simply referring to someone as a *chef* doesn't make them one. I ride a motorcycle, but I'm not a biker.

~~~

Many would-be chefs believe that cooking for a living is a lark and a professional kitchen is some parallel universe where cooks spend their days piddling with recipes. This is not even remotely close to reality. Professional cooking can be dangerous, grueling work. Here's a typical scenario that can occur in many of the nearly one million restaurants across America:

It's another balls-to-the-wall Saturday night in the kitchen, halfway through a wicked dinner rush. As usual, everyone is running around with their hair on fire. One of your co-workers at the line carelessly splashes smoking hot grease on the back of your hand. You dash to the ice machine and plunge your hand into the ice cube bin in a futile attempt to minimize the tissue damage. Too late, your skin was fried within seconds of the hot grease coating your flesh. All you can do at this point is quell the pain. Now you've got a third degree burn. Within minutes the protective blister begins to form. You can't stand there all night with your hand in the ice bin—you need to get back to the line and cook. The orders are backing up and the waiters are clamoring for their food. The blister's ballooning by the second. Now it's the size of an egg. The head chef is wondering where the hell you are. He locates you and just glares.

"So you burned yourself, so what? Get your ass back on the line," he commands. "You can take care of your little burn after we get through all these orders." Unfortunately for you it's only 7 o'clock, and the rush won't begin to subside for at least another hour. Deal with it.

The head chef doesn't just want you on that line; he needs *you on that line. If the orders get backed up the owner will ask* him *what the problem is. You can bet he won't soon forget that you and your baby burn caused the problem.*

You return to your station. A busy kitchen is no place for wimps. The heat coming off the stove is excruciating. When you deglaze a sauté pan the plume of smoke and flame causes you to wince in pain. Tough, keep cooking. The other line cooks haven't much sympathy for you—they've all been through it. You have to gut it out or the other cooks will think you're a total pussy, and no serious cook wants that rep. You want to show them that you've got the right stuff. You work through the pain until the tsunami of orders subsides and you can tend to your injury. This is only the beginning of your ordeal. You have to cook with your blistered hand the next day and the one after that. You can't take off work because the restaurant doesn't offer paid sick leave. No work, no pay. These are the times that you wonder whether you've picked the right occupation.

This is the *real world* of extreme cooking. Make no mistake: a lunch or dinner rush in a busy commercial kitchen is a battle that is fought twice each day in most restaurants. The kitchen staff is caught in a relentless cross fire between and an unforgiving clock and an avalanche of food orders. The cooks are the front-line troops with no replacements. Cooks are tasked with producing dozens of orders simultaneously—soups, salads, appetizers, entrees and desserts. It all has to be synchronized so each course for each table leaves the kitchen in the correct order. It's all choreographed. It must be done with precision in a smooth, seamless flow. There's a thin margin for error. Mistakes mean repeats. Repeats can upset the delicate orchestration the head chef strives to maintain during the meal rush. This is why busy restaurants have an expediter whose role is to coordinate all the moving parts. He is a maestro of sorts. Professional cooking is not for the faint-of-heart. If you've never been through this gauntlet you can't appreciate the stress.

Meal rush in a busy kitchen can be an exhilarating experience, though. When you're in the heat of the moment, every nerve synapse in your brain and body is ramped up to nanosecond speed. The enhanced alertness gives you intensified powers of concentration. This translates into efficiency of motion. When you're in the *zone,* there is little wasted movement. There is no time for superfluous thoughts. To many cooks, the meal rush is the part of the job that they both loathe and crave. It's like rooming with a close friend who both excites you and drains your energy. You can only be around him for brief periods. Most ex-chefs will tell you that the adrenaline-stoked high of the dinner rush is addictive, but that it also comes at a price. This twice-daily encounter wreaks havoc on the body and spirit. Over a period of years it becomes increasingly difficult to summon the energy required to face each day. After ten or twelve years of this hellish work most cooks are depleted: bodies are broken, fortitude diminished. There are few old cooks in America's kitchens. Professional cooking is for the young.

Cooks are on their feet ten to twelve hours a day with few or no breaks. Many of us who have cooked as a career have only scars and varicose veins show for it. In a busy kitchen there isn't time to enjoy a leisurely lunch—cooks take their meals on the fly. They eat while they work. Have you ever tried to sauté with one hand while wolfing down a sandwich with the other? This is a way of life for a line cook. If you work in a private restaurant you're expected to work from the minute you punch in until the minute you punch out. The restaurateur wants to get his money's worth. If you cook in a hotel you'll fare slightly better. You might get a thirty minute lunch break, but don't bank on it. The work load is tremendous. Sure, in some cases union agreements stipulate that you're supposed to get breaks throughout the shift, but don't look to the hospitality workers' unions to enforce the contract. Most unions are corrupt, toothless tigers who will make a desultory attempt to ensure worker rights.

Work-related injuries are a common occurrence in an environment as hazardous as a commercial kitchen. If you're a cook in a privately-owned restaurant and you injure yourself you're pretty much on your own. You're expected to show up for your next scheduled shift. The chef has little sympathy for you. He needs warm bodies in the kitchen. If you aren't there then he has to do your work or pay someone else overtime to do it and he doesn't like that. What are you anyway, a candy ass? You can't work because you have a little cut or burn? And if you do miss work because of your injury don't expect to get paid—restaurants rarely provide paid sick leave benefits. Of course, if an on-the-job injury requires medical attention it will be covered under the state's Workers' Compensation law, but the owner won't be happy with you if he has to file a claim to recover the cost; it might drive up his insurance premium. Take care to not get injured too often because you'll become a business liability, which could cost you your job. The head chef might casually remind you that you are expendable and that there are five cooks who want your job. If the life of a professional cook sounds a bit Dickensian, that's because it is.

$$$

IF YOU STILL want to take the plunge and become a cook there are several routes you can take. You can attend a boutique culinary school such as the Culinary Institute of America (which calls itself the greatest cooking school in the world), Johnson and Wales or Cordon Bleu. If you go this route, expect to pay $25,000, $50,000 or even a staggering $100,000 for a four-year degree. It'd be a challenge to repay student loans on a starting pay of $10 to $12 per hour, which is the going rate for a rookie cook in most urban areas. It's not your credentials that matter; it's your performance in the kitchen. And finding a good-paying job has become increasingly difficult. Over the last few years culinary academies have churned out a record number of graduates, creating a glut of trained workers in an already tight job market. It's a simple matter of supply and demand: too many cooks vying for too few jobs. This suppresses wages. An academy graduate might eventually get a shot at a *chef de partie* position in a hotel after a few years experience. And if he does land a decent job he'll be working fifty to sixty hours per week for around $40 to $50 thousand. Attending a culinary academy does not make you a chef. This only comes with years of toiling in commercial kitchens. Calling yourself a chef because you've graduated from a culinary academy is like eating at an Olive Garden restaurant and claiming that you've eaten authentic Italian food. Uh, not really.

Many for-profit cooking schools have made fraudulent promises of employment upon graduation. The Department of Education is currently investigating such claims and lawsuits have been filed against for-profit culinary schools around the nation. For example, Cordon Bleu is in the process of paying a $40 million settlement from a California class-action suit, in which students said they were deceived by promises of lucrative employment which didn't transpire and were saddled with debt. Federal regulators are threatening to crack down on the schools that are eager to take students' cash, but aren't necessarily coming through with good-paying gigs upon graduation. Or schools will get a student as a Starbucks' barista and consider this a "culinary" position simply because it is in the restaurant industry. Those for-profit schools include a number of culinary schools around the country that are increasingly taking the heat. Several are embroiled in actual lawsuits.

Another route to becoming a chef is to attend culinary arts classes at a vocational institute or junior college. This is an inexpensive way get some basic training from professional instructors. With this route inexperienced cooks can get their foot in the door at a decent restaurant. A third way is to start at the bottom washing pots then advance to prep cook. Eventually they'll cook on the line, where the real action is: sauce making, grilling, deep-frying, sautéing, pastries—there's your education, my friend. There is nothing wrong with gaining experience by starting at the bottom. Many of the world's best chefs began this way. It just takes longer.

Only through years of intensive training can one become an accomplished chef. Attending a culinary academy is a jump start, but it can't replace the reality of performing under fire. Learning to make a *buerre blanc* in a cooking class isn't the same as having to make it while you're working on five other orders simultaneously. Meal rush in a busy restaurant can be a veritable *cookathon* where the cooks don't even have time to visit the bathroom until the mountain of orders is done. And many cooks get to go through this meat grinder twice a day since they have to work the lunch and dinner rushes. Welcome to my world.

So You Wanna Own a Restaurant

WOULDN'T IT BE fun to have your own restaurant? Do your friends tell you what a good cook you are and that you should open a restaurant? These are *not* your friends. You need to find a new set of friends, people who actually care about you. It's easy for them to encourage someone else to take a job that requires a sixty to seventy hour work week. They'd love to have a place to hang out. Your "friends" will be nestled in their beds when you're just counting the till. They won't be there when you have to work on your day off because a couple of employees are out sick. When your friends get the flu they can call in sick, but you don't have that luxury. Got the flu? Tough, get to the restaurant. The customers don't care, they just want their food. It's not their problem that you're sick. Think twice about having your own restaurant. Many restaurateurs were excited when their restaurant first opened only to suffer from serious buyer's remorse within a few years. In some cases it's better to enter the restaurant business uninformed and with a certain amount of naiveté. If you knew all the downsides and risks, you might not attempt it. Someone once said, "There is a reason we can't see beyond the horizon." They might have the restaurant business in mind when they said this.

Being a restaurateur is not like being employed. When you have a regular job you normally work a forty-hour week do what your boss tells you and everything is fine. As long as you keep your job paychecks are regular, vacations are guaranteed and you enjoy a fat benefits package. You do your time and one day it's all over, you're retired. It's all so predictable. A restaurateur's career is nothing like that. A forty-hour work week in the restaurant business is considered a part-time job. Income can be sporadic and is never guaranteed, you're at the mercy of the economy, the weather and competition. A vacation that lasts longer than a week is rarely possible because the business will implode if the boss is away too long. Your dream about retiring in Costa Rica may be just that, a dream. Owning a restaurant is one of the riskiest business ventures there is.

A common misconception about the restaurant business is that success is guaranteed if the owner is a good cook. In the first place, in very few situations is the chef also the owner. Even if he is a highly skilled cook, that's only a small part of what it takes to succeed. I've known master chefs—guys who could cook circles around me—who went belly-up when they opened their own restaurants. Either they lacked the requisite business acumen or they didn't understand that being the boss takes a certain amount of personal discipline. For example, the chef/owner can't bang his waitresses and bus girls. I knew a restaurateur in New Orleans who lost his successful restaurant because women refused to work for him. They were tired of his attempts to get them in bed.

A restaurateur does not *own* the restaurant; it's the reverse. Often the tail wags the dog, and the owner is never really off duty. He has an obligation to the clientele to ensure an optimal dining experience: consistently good food and service in a pleasant atmosphere. This is why we eat out. Consistency is key. If a customer enjoys a certain menu item—say, shrimp Creole—that Creole should be the same whenever he comes in, which is no easy feat in a business plagued by turnover. Consistency is a chronic problem with independently owned establishments, where a variety of cooks can produce various versions of the same dish. This is less of a problem with franchises.

It's not the customers' problem if the ice machine breaks down. They expect ice water with their meal. The diners don't care if one of your line cooks has a substance abuse problem (which happened at my café more times than I care to remember); they expect reasonable food value for their money. Many nights I thought I was done for the day only to have to return to work to deal with some crisis: toilet backed-up, AC malfunction, broken freezer . . . I know what it takes to restaurant alive; I did it for fourteen years.

There's more to running a restaurant than cooking and serving food. As a restaurateur you'll have an opportunity to study the human condition—that innate and irreducible part of us that makes us human. With experience you'll develop keen powers of observation. Unconsciously, you'll size up new customers as they walk through the door. You'll learn to profile customers by their dress and comportment. You'll discern the high-rollers from the skinflints. Servers are especially skilled at profiling new customers who are often referred to as "fresh meat." Just as bats rely on echolocation to find a meal, avaricious servers develop a sixth sense for targeting the big tippers or, in some cases, unsuspecting customers they can easily scam like drunks or high school kids out for dinner on prom night. You'll unwittingly form superficial judgments about relationships; you'll discern the solid marriages from those on life support. You'll learn the telltale signs of an unfaithful spouse. And observant restaurateurs can spot the hookers a mile away; they're the ones with eye-popping cleavage, collagen injections and exaggerated body work in all the right places. Your restaurant is a kind of social laboratory where human behavior is observed and analyzed. Oh, and one other thing: don't think for a second that your customers haven't sized you up as well.

Chefs: Solution or Part of the Problem?

THE WORLD OF cuisine is more than a buffet of flavorful dishes and exotic ingredients. Unfortunately, the business of food has a dark and sinister side. There are sectors of the world's food production systems that are associated with unspeakable human rights atrocities, where humans are nothing more than chattel labor. Take the cocoa industry, for example. According to a September 2010 report from The Payson Center for International Development at Tulane University, it appears that the cocoa industry does little more than pay lip service to the goal of eliminating child labor, forced labor and human trafficking abuses. The report underscores the lack of progress in voluntary self-monitoring programs adopted by the cocoa industry to address the problems of child and forced labor in West Africa, especially in the Ivory Coast and Ghana—who produce 40 percent and 15 percent of the world's cocoa, respectively. The average cocoa farmer earns 80 cents a day. The Tulane report makes it clear that the cocoa industry is not doing enough to address these problems and the world's largest chocolate manufacturers must do more to monitor their supply chains to combat child labor, forced labor and human trafficking.

In his muckraking book, *Fast Food Nation,* investigative journalist Eric Schlosser examines the insidious effects of fast food on societies worldwide, including its adverse health effects and its significant role in the epidemic of obesity currently sweeping the U.S. In the 2008 film documentary *Food, Inc.* Robert Kenner looks at the industrial production of meat, grains and vegetables and the economic and legal clout of the multinational food companies. Kenner explains how farmers around the world are often manipulated by corporations that sell "terminator" seeds, which produce sterile plants, forcing the farmer to buy new seed every season. *Food, Inc.* also highlights the overuse of petroleum-based pesticides and fertilizers that find their way into our sources of drinking water, creating another set of environmental health risks. The film shows us that while factory farming produces massive quantities of food cheaply, it also sets the stage for large-scale epidemics of food-borne illnesses such as the fresh egg recall involving two Iowa chicken farms during the spring and summer of 2010.

Another hard-hitting documentary is *The Cove*, a 2009 American film that shows actual footage of the annual dolphin slaughter in Taiji, Japan. The migrating dolphins are herded into a hidden cove where they are corralled with nets and speared to death by the locals from small fishing boats. The film highlights the fact that the slaughter occurs because of the insatiable Japanese appetite for whale meat and, of course, dolphins qualify because they are small, toothed whales. The consumption of whale meat (and shark fins for soup) is a good example of how a food preference can threaten the existence of a species. There are suitable seafood alternatives to dolphin meat. Not all dolphins are mutilated; some are captured and shipped to dolphinariums around the world. These horrific practices extend to killing sharks solely for their fins. Shark "finning" is big business in many Third World countries. According to National Geographic, 40 million sharks are killed annually for their fins. Shark finning has increased over the past decade largely due to the increasing demand for shark fins for Chinese shark fin soup and traditional cures.

No one can predict global food trends with any certainty. But we do know that the dynamic of food in modern societies is in a constant state of flux. We also know that mankind is doing irrevocable harm to wildlife habitats in its attempt to step up food production for an increasing global population. We are depleting the oceans of wild stocks and in some cases the situation has become acute. For example, at the rate we're harvesting East Atlantic/Mediterranean bluefin tuna it is only a matter of time before this species goes the way of the Atlantic cod, essentially fished to the brink of extinction. Once numbering in the hundreds of millions, Atlantic cod today are so few in number that the population lacks the critical biomass necessary for recovery.

The issue of agricultural animal welfare has garnered attention through the arts. In 2010, HBO dramatized the story of Temple Grandin, an autistic woman who overcame the challenges of her condition (she didn't speak until age four) to become an expert in the field of animal husbandry and a groundbreaking animal rights advocate. Despite the cattle industry's efforts to impede her research, Grandin's career and writings tackle the complexities of agricultural animal welfare from both philosophical and practical standpoints. She is noted for creating the *hug box*, widely recognized today as a way of relieving stress in animals housed in abattoirs. Her humane design for the treatment of cattle in processing plants won an award from PETA. Today, she is a professor at Colorado State University.

These critical social and cultural issues are among a range of challenges that the global community must grapple with in the 21st century. The responsibility falls mainly to the developed nations to take the lead. We must also call upon the burgeoning nations of Brazil, China, India and the countries of Southeast Asia to do their part, since they currently have the world's fastest growing economies and are playing an increasingly significant role in food production. These issues might appear tangential to the world of professional cooking, but in fact the opposite is true. Responsible fishing and seafood sustainability are at the very heart of what it means to be a chef. Chefs are end-users who must play a role in protecting species that are either under pressure or threatened with extinction from industrial fishing. These species are commonly referred to as "red-listed." This begs the question: why aren't celebrity chefs more engaged in *green food* issues such the welfare of agricultural animals or overfishing of our oceans? For example, why doesn't world-renowned Spanish chef Ferran Adriá champion a worthwhile cause such as reducing bluefin tuna quotas (especially since his own country often violates quotas by harvesting Mediterranean bluefin illegally) instead of promoting the latest fad in the culinary world—"molecular gastronomy"? Today's celebrity chefs have the power to make a difference by putting their fame to good use, but few do. If chefs are not part of the solution then they are part of the problem. They have skin in the game; this is their planet too.

Pleasure for Sale

WE CHEFS HAVE an expression, "You take the first bite with your eyes." This doesn't just apply to desserts; it pertains to many of our favorite foods. Food has the unique ability to titillate our senses. The sight, sound and aroma of a sizzling steak elicits a physical response. If you're at all like me you begin to salivate. We can even anticipate what that steak will taste like; its unctuousness, texture, juiciness and flavor. (Mother Nature even lends a helping hand to enhance our eating pleasure by replacing the taste receptors on our tongue daily.) The sheer anticipation of eating only intensifies both our appetite and desire to eat. If you're lucky, when you take a meal or a snack out you're purchasing a moment of exquisite and unforgettable sensory pleasure.

It's a pity that some regard food as mere sustenance. These poor souls are missing out on the boundless variety of gastronomic pleasures ripe for the taking. We have only to look to our neighbor to the south, Mexico, to find one of the planet's truly magnificent cuisines and an extraordinary culinary history. Mesoamerican gastronomy it is a product of thousands of years of evolution and is one of the world's most diverse and complex cuisines. Considered *la cocina de madre* or "the mother cuisine," Mexican cuisine has greatly influenced the food cultures of its smaller neighbors throughout Central America. Many ignorant American food critics confuse authentic Mexican food with Tex-Mex gobbledygook—created by Chicanos for the gringo palate. These so-called experts dismiss Mexican cuisine as simple fare revolving around beans, chilies, rice and maize. They fail to understand Mexico's food history and the depth and complexities of real Mexican food. Take the *mole* sauces, for example. Many food writers don't understand the nuances and complexities of these labor-intensive sauces. There are seven types of *mole* sauces, originating in the states of Oaxaca and Puebla.

Mexican cuisine has its roots in Olmec and Toltec cultures, and later in Aztec and Mayan societies. It was the Pre-Columbian cultures who introduced maize—growing in Mesoamerica by between 8,000 and 5,000 BC—to the world. The Spanish Conquistadors infused pork and Old World spices into traditional Mexican gastronomy. New dishes were born from this cross-cultural pollination. For example, prior to the arrival of the Conquistadors, the Aztecs consumed meatless tamales, but the Spanish incorporated the meat filling so familiar today. While other Latin

American countries have tamales, few have as many varieties as Mexico. Almost every region and state in the country has its own tamale specialty. Tamales are quintessential Mexican comfort food, eaten at breakfast, lunch and dinner. And they are the perfect street food; vendors serve them from huge, steaming, covered pots called *tamaleras*.

Today pork is considered an integral part of the Mesoamerican diet, but it wasn't until the Spanish explorers introduced the pig into the region that pork became a meat of choice. Wherever the Spanish gained a foothold, they brought along the pig. Pigs were easily domesticated and prolific. On his second voyage, Columbus brought eight pigs to Cuba and within twenty years the swine population had grown to thirty-thousand. Eventually, the uses for pork went far beyond tamale filling. Myriad pork dishes have evolved in Latin cultures such as *cochinita pibil* (slow-roasted suckling pig), *carnitas* (pulled pork barbecue) and *chicharrón* (fried pork rind or pieces of pork).

Thanks to Mexican food aficionados Diana Kennedy (often called the "Julia Child of Mexican cuisine") and celebrity chef Rick Bayless (America's current impresario of Mexican cooking), we have a better understanding of this food culture than ever before. They've succeeded in teaching us to understand and appreciate our neighbor's cuisine and cooking techniques. This knowledge engenders the creation of new dishes by exchanging the classic Mexican ingredients with others indigenous to North America.

Mexican cuisine is renowned and admired around the world for its uniqueness, tradition and cultural history. It has taken its rightful place among the world's great cuisines. Traditional Mexican food was recognized by the United Nations Educational, Scientific and Cultural Organization (UNESCO) experts, who met in Nairobi, Kenya in November 2010. The UN culture and education agency's mission is to consider candidates for its Representative List of the Intangible Cultural Heritage of Humanity in an effort to preserve the world's art forms and traditions considered under threat from globalization.

~~~

A perfect example of a poly-cultural food invention would be the iconic Louisiana dish known as jambalaya. This rice casserole was a result of the confluence of three disparate food cultures—French, Spanish and African—in 18th century New Orleans. The classic Spanish dish and precursor to jambalaya, *paella*, was introduced to Louisiana when Spain laid claim to New Orleans, long before the Louisiana Purchase. And, of course, rice was first known in Asia before being brought to the New World by the Europeans, adding another global influence to this dish.

Historically, there are two versions of jambalaya. Creole jambalaya originated in New Orleans where it was called "red jambalaya" because tomatoes were substituted for saffron. The Cajun version, sometimes called brown jambalaya, originated in Louisiana's rural, low-lying swamp country in the southwest part of the state where crawfish, shrimp, oysters, alligator, turtles, duck, boar and other wild game were readily available. Any combination of meats and seafood may be used to make jambalaya.

The etymology of the word "jambalaya" is an interesting one, but something of a mystery. While there is no consensus on the origin of the name, folklore has it that the word is derived from the combination of the French word "jambon" meaning ham, the French article "à la" and the word "ya," thought to mean rice in a West African tongue. Hence, according to the theory, the dish's name means "ham with rice" in a pidgin dialect. While the word is a mouthful, jambalaya is a delicious dish straight from Louisiana's Cajun country.

~~~

Accidental Chef is partly a narrative about the world of gastronomy and how it can enhance our lives. Like the weather, consider how much conversation is devoted to the subjects of food, eating and cooking. People never seem to tire of discussing new dishes, ingredients or places to eat. The world of gastronomy is in a constant state of flux. It's a world that is affected by a number of factors—the price of oil, economics, climate change, politics, religious and cultural traditions and farming practices to name a few. But no matter which direction the winds of change blow, there is one constant: food is the great equalizer. Eating and cooking transcends social and economic barriers. Whether you're a prince or a pauper it doesn't matter, we all have to eat and we all enjoy a tasty meal.

Chapter One

Home Schooled

"I come from a family where gravy is considered a beverage."

Erma Bombeck

I WAS BORN in 1949, the sixth child in a family that would become eight. For the first year of my life we lived in a low-income housing project whose austere brick structures looked more like military barracks than blocks of flats. Our parents eked a hardscrabble life; too many mouths to feed with too little money. My father did what he could; truck driver, welder, electrician. Our mother did her level best to make ends meet with scant resources. In those days there was no food stamp program; parents were responsible to feed their own or they didn't eat. Our mother bought potatoes by the hundred pound sack; beef, pork and poultry were luxuries. When we could afford it, our mother would send one of my brothers to the poulterer to fetch a couple of freshly-killed chickens. She wouldn't just roast the birds; that would be too extravagant. She boiled them first to make chicken soup and matzo balls; that would fill more bellies. She learned this quintessential Jewish soup from my father's mother, a Jewess who emigrated from Hungary *circa* 1913. As was the custom in those days, my grandparents' marriage was prearranged.

From Hard Work to Hard Times

EFFCTIVELY A SUBURB of Chicago, Gary, Indiana was once the beating heart of the nation's industrial heartland. In its heyday Gary was one of the most prolific steel manufacturing centers in the world. In tandem with Pittsburgh, Gary produced the steel required to build the armaments needed to defeat Nazi Germany. It's questionable that either city could have produced enough steel on its own to get America through the war effort. More recently, Gary is notable for its favorite son, Michael Jackson, and his charming family. The Jacksons escaped from Gary in the 1970s and never looked back. Can't say as I blame them; Gary has been a city in decline since the late 1960s. It's a classic example of urban decay American-style and a deep source of embarrassment and sadness for those of us who grew up in Gary. We remember our city as a vibrant and prosperous blue-collar community. Gary was a wonderful place to grow up.

Gary was created in 1906 as a company town for U.S. Steel, providing a constant supply of labor to work its Bessemer furnaces and rolling mills. After the WWII, Gary and its neighboring communities boomed—East Chicago, Hammond and Whiting. Unemployment wasn't something we ever discussed because it was never much of an issue. There were occasional lay-offs, but it was always temporary, the mills *always* rebounded. After high school you were expected to work in the steel mills. Everybody did. It was only natural. Our fathers and grandfathers worked in the mills. "If U.S. Steel was good enough for my generation then U.S. Steel is good enough for you," was a constant refrain throughout my childhood. It wasn't just the native Garyites who worked the mills, so did the immigrants and migrants. For thousands of immigrants from war-torn Europe, Gary represented a new start; for Americans from the Deep South, Gary offered the promise of a better life. Blacks flocked to Northwest Indiana where the mills represented opportunities at good-paying jobs. But they offered something more; a chance to escape the vestiges of the oppressive Jim Crow past. The mills were color blind; if a man was willing to work he could find work in the mills.

Gary's fortunes have risen and fallen with those of the steel industry. When the mills were hiring—and the mills were almost always hiring during my childhood—few were unemployed. All through my youth, working men could depend on the mills for a job, but that all began to change in the early 1970s when Gary entered a spiral of decline brought on by growing overseas competition in the steel and auto industries. This downturn caused the steel manufacturers—with U.S. Steel being the main one—to lay off workers in droves. Unemployment brought with it social ills. Crime increased, including rampant drug use and trade in illegal drugs. Gary's first black mayor, Richard Hatcher, was an unmitigated disaster.

Hatcher ushered in an era of unprecedented corruption, incompetence and malfeasance by city officials. Seeing their city crumble before their eyes, long-time residents fled to surrounding suburbs or left the area entirely for better employment opportunities.

U.S. Steel continues to be one of the world's major steel producers, but with only a fraction of its former workforce. While Gary has failed to reestablish a manufacturing base since its population peak, several casinos opened on the shores of Lake Michigan in the 1990s. Today, Gary faces enormous difficulties, staggering unemployment, chronic economic problems and perennially one of the nation's highest crime rates. For more than forty years Gary's downtown area has slid into a state of irreversible decrepitude. Businesses that once thrived have been boarded up for decades. Where a generation ago there was always hope for a brighter future, now there is only hopeless despair. Gary, Indiana has gone *from hard work to hard times.*

Home Is Where the Hearth Is

WHAT NOSTALGIA I have about my youth was largely due to the wonderful foods to which I was exposed. Northwest Indiana was a true melting pot. Immigrants brought their culture and cuisine of their native lands. Immigrants discovered dishes they'd only heard about, but never sampled. Greeks and Serbs grew partial to tamales and tostadas while Mexicans developed a taste for gyros and spit-roasted lamb. Gastronomic diversity is a prerequisite to becoming a well-rounded chef. I was exposed to a veritable smorgasbord of ethnic dishes from an early age—Polish, Mexican, Greek, Puerto Rican, Croatian and Serbian. Being exposed to these cuisines during my formative years would have a lasting impact and prove invaluable throughout my culinary career.

My own family's Canadian and European culinary traditions would have an impact on my approach to food. My mother's family, whose surname was Gervais, was French Canadians who immigrated to the States in the late 1920s. As a youngster, I was spellbound when Grandpa Gervais spun yarns about his days as a lumber jack when he was a teenager. His English was limited and he spoke with a pronounced French accent. As smoke from a hand-rolled cigarette swirled around his head, he'd tell a wide-eyed child tales of encounters with timber wolves and Indians in the wilds of Canada. Grandma Gervais made traditional north-of-the border dishes like pork and veal pie or *tourtiere*. I also have fond memories of her making crepes slathered with butter and strawberry preserves for my younger sister, Pam, and me. Those paper-thin discs of delight seemed to melt in our mouths.

My father's side of the family was Ashkenazi Jews from Hungary. I have no memories of these grandparents since both died when I was a small child, but their culinary influence survived them. My mother made typical Hungarian dishes such as fried bread, crullers (a fried pastry sprinkled with granulated sugar similar to Mexican churro), and chicken paprikash, beef goulash with spätzle. The delicious foods of my youth had a profound influence on my affinity for good food. My love of cooking and eating took root during these formative years.

~~~

Mealtime at the Oppman residence was not a place for amateurs. You needed sharp elbows to ensure that you received your fair share of food; there was only so much to go around. If you missed dinner you were forced to make yourself a bologna sandwich. Meals at our house were not like meals at Beaver Cleaver's house in the 1950s where the family leisurely picked at their food while they chatted about that day's events. Our table was more raucous, similar to a scene from a Marx Brothers movie. You had to eat fast so you didn't miss out. Our mother did her best to ride herd over her fidgety brood. She was a patient person, but the woman had limits. I recall one incident when one brother's incessant clamoring for food compelled our mother to crack his plate on his head.

My older brothers' appetites were the stuff of legend. Athletes all, they were all voracious eaters. I'd heard tales of dozens of eggs and stacks of waffles devoured at breakfast. I watched in awe as Paul polished off an entire chocolate cake and a half-gallon of milk. Bunny purportedly put away more than twenty White Castle burgers in one sitting. Granted, my brothers were real chow hounds, but they were all pikers compared to me. I hold the family record for eating the most food in one sitting. I vanquished my college roommate who dared to challenge me in a fried chicken eating contest. I devoured twenty-eight pieces of fried chicken—plus rolls, fries, salad and beer. That's about three and a half birds. My crestfallen competitor threw in the napkin at twenty-four pieces.

I could have claimed victory with twenty-five pieces, but I wanted to teach him a lesson. Take that Joey Chestnut!

Of our entire clan, I've always had the most intense relationship with food—a love affair that has contributed to a life-long battle with the scale. Around age seven or eight, I began to take a serious interest in cooking appointing myself sous chef to my mother. I willingly performed the menial tasks; peeling veggies, pitting fruit, washing-up. She would reward me by allowing me to lick the batter-laden beaters or give me with the first slice of freshly baked bread.

New Horizons

AS OUR FAMILY expanded, so did my culinary horizons. My oldest sister, Judy, married a first-generation Mexican. His family introduced our family to traditional Tex-Mex dishes. It was simple fare, but it was marvelous—tamales, refried beans, tacos, burritos and tostadas. This was my first introduction to Mexican cuisine and it made a lasting impression. I would also be exposed to authentic Mexican fare through the many Latino restaurants in and around Gary. My love affair with Mexican food survives to this day. A few years ago we went on a culinary excursion in Oaxaca, Mexico. We took cooking classes and sampled local fare, especially the *mole* sauces for which Oaxaca is famous. Many of today's top chefs dismiss Mexican cuisine as unsophisticated and banal. I couldn't disagree more. Mexico has given the world one of the truly great cuisines.

In the early 1980s, while I was attending chef school, my education about Mexican food would continue. My friend, Rudy Muñoz, helped to expand my Mexican food repertoire. Rudy, *mi hermano* (my brother), taught me classics such as *albondigos* (meatballs in beef broth), *menudo* (a type of tripe soup), and *migas* (a breakfast dish of fried *chorizo* with onions and crumbled and fried corn tortillas). Rudy and I have remained close friends since our chef school days. We still cook together. He left the culinary field years ago, growing weary of the stress and extreme demands of the work. Can't say I blame him; it is a grueling occupation not suited for the faint of heart.

My sisters-in-law also taught me some of their family dishes. Shirley, wife of my second oldest brother, Rick, also contributed my education. She introduced me to fried green tomatoes, a dish from her southern Indiana roots. I'm amused when I see fried green tomatoes on the menu of an upscale restaurant as if it's *haute cuisine*. Shirley also made gratin potatoes with ham. Kay, wife of my eldest brother, Doug, makes superb apple fritters and Swedish meatballs, both of which she served after my mother's funeral. My mother passed away in April 1964 at the age of forty-six. Her death was a crushing blow to our family and is still a source of deep sadness. My mother actually passed away in her tiny kitchen, the room where she spent countless hours doing one of the things she loved most—cooking.

~~~

My Uncle Howard and Aunt Bernice also contributed to my culinary home schooling. Aunt Bernice was Polish, which meant that autumn was that time of year to set up the meat grinder and make homemade kielbasa and of course sauerkraut. During my childhood people often made their own kielbasa or bought it fresh from local butchers, an endangered species today. Sausage would not be considered heart healthy cuisine, but with food this good no one cared.

I attended this rite of autumn to observe the sausage production. I enjoyed watching my uncle carefully grind just the right amount of lean meat and pork fat. "You have to get the right ratio of lean and fat to make juicy sausage," Uncle Howard would warn. "Nobody likes dry sausage." The pork, fat, and condiments were hand-ground before being injected into the casings. Uncle Howard used fresh pork shoulder or butt; more expensive cuts don't contain enough fat and collagen. You need fat and collagen for flavor, natural juice and texture. As much as anything, the sausage production was an opportunity for my uncle to socialize and drink beer.

My step mother, Mildred Arnold, also taught me many dishes I'd never seen before she came into our family. She was a country gal from rural Colorado. Mildred was also a natural cook. She taught me how to make chicken and dumplings, fabulous fruit pies, fried chicken, veal pocket and "city chicken." As did my mother, Mildred kept bacon grease in a coffee can on top of the stove—this was done in most homes when I was growing up—and used lard in her pie dough and for frying chicken. People don't often cook like this nowadays. We all know that animal fat isn't healthy for us, but any respectable cook will tell you that nothing imparts flavor to fried or sautéed foods like animal fat. In order of preference it is; duck fat, bacon grease then chicken fat. Also, like my mother, Mildred had a natural ability to season and could also create a tasty meal from leftovers. I never saw my mother or Mildred use a cookbook. They didn't need cookbooks; they cooked by intuition. This is how naturally gifted cooks perform once they've mastered fundamental cooking techniques and the art of seasoning. Not all cooks have the ability to work like this. I've worked with professional cooks who weren't as good as my mother and Mildred.

Cookin' for the Colonel

THROUGH OUT MY childhood I always hustled to make a buck. I washed cars, delivered newspapers, mowed lawns and shoveled snow. Self-employment was fine, but the time had come for me to move up to a real job. It was time to become employed and earn a regular paycheck so I applied at KFC. You were supposed to be sixteen to get a job in those days, but I lied about my age. I figured fifteen and a half was close enough. No one at KFC bothered to verify my age. Child labor and occupational safety laws weren't really enforced in those days. For instance, the potential for grease burns and explosions inherent in frying chicken with pressure cookers was acceptable at the time. Today these risks would be a violation of the Occupational Safety and Health Act, which didn't exist until 1970.

I was psyched about working at KFC. It was a new fast food chain in the Midwest and a lot of my friends were applying. It was my first professional cooking gig. I needed that job. I needed to earn my own cash and gain some independence from my father. More importantly, there was the matter of my love life. I'd never been on a proper date, but that was all about to change. Now that I was a working man, I was sure girls would flock to me once they discovered I worked at KFC. What girl could resist a chef?

My official title was Fry Boy. I even had a uniform—white shirt, white pants, white apron, and a white paper hat with a caricature of a little chicken stamped on it. The title and uniform gave me a sense of pride. I belonged to a team. My boss was a middle-aged Polish guy named Stanley Grabowski whose nickname was "Stosh." But of course I couldn't address him as Stosh to his face. I asked Stosh if KFC supplied name badges. He told me they did not. Starting pay was a buck ten per hour. Stosh explained my job duties.

"Chuck, here at KFC your title is Fry Boy and that means you will fry chicken and anything else that needs fryin'; French fries, onion rings, fish filets. You will also make craklin' gravy and mashed potatoes and whatever else Lester here tells you to do. Lester is your immediate supervisor and Lester answers to me. He's been with us for nearly a year now and knows how I want things done around here. Isn't that right Lester?"

"Actually, I've been here for three years, Mr. Grabowski. And I'm proud to say that it's been a pleasure to have you as my boss," Lester rejoined, with an obsequious tone in his voice.

"Why thank you Lester. Three years huh, maybe it's time we talk about a promotion. I'll have to check with Mr. Rich, of course." *What an ass kisser*, I thought. I'd always been good at wheedling my way into the good graces of most people, but Lester was good, really good. I knew that I could learn from this guy.

Lester didn't recognize me, but I sure knew him. His last name was Branson and I'd attended grade school with his younger sister, Sheila. In fourth grade I'd been in love with Sheila Branson, but I was too shy to make my feelings known. It was an unrequited love. Apparently, I made less of an impression on Sheila than I'd supposed, because Lester acted as if he didn't know me. Clearly, she never mentioned my name in the Branson home. No matter; that was all ancient history. That was then; this was now. Lester was my boss and I had to do what he told me. Stosh continued.

"Chuck, you also have to take out the garbage, collect trash in the parking lot, mop the kitchen, clean the toilets, filter the fryer grease, wash the pots and do whatever else Lester here tells you to do."

"Yes Sir Mr. Grabowski, will do. Whatever Lester tells me to do. I got it." I was determined to show Stosh that I was a go-getter and that I was willing to do whatever it took to climb to the top. I wasn't going to squander a magnificent opportunity like this. I knew that the fast-food business was the wave of the future and I wanted to ride that wave. Besides I liked working at KFC. It had perks. I could eat all the chicken I wanted and bread it the way I liked. I liked triple breading thighs, my favorite part.

~~~

I was determined to make something of myself at KFC. I poured myself into my work. I never missed and I was always on time. And I was a quick study. I did everything Lester told me to do. Within a few weeks, I was even keeping pace with Lester at the fry station. During the dinner rush I could kick it into high gear, making sure there was always plenty of fried chicken, French fries, onion rings and fish filets to fill the orders. I had grease burns all over my forearms, which I wore like tiny badges-of-honor. I wore short sleeve shirts to school hoping that girls might ask how I came by my burns. They might perceive me as a macho man. They didn't ask about my burns.

I remember the night I got my first raise. We were working at a furious pace one Friday night when Mr. Rich dropped in. Mr. Rich owned all of the KFC franchises in Gary, Indiana, all three of them. He stood motionless near the pot sink, just watching his cooks fry his chicken. It was unnerving, but I did my best to ignore him. I realized that this was an opportunity to impress the big boss. I picked up the pace; breading and frying like a whirling dervish. I wanted to show Mr. Rich that hiring me was a wise business decision and that I was worth more than a buck ten an hour. I wanted to show Mr. Rich that I had a future in the fried chicken business.

Stosh sidled up to Mr. Rich dutifully awaiting any orders that might come his way. It was then that I realized why Lester was such an accomplished ass kisser; he learned from Grabowski. Then I noticed Mr. Rich saying something to Stosh who promptly raced over to me.

"Chuck, I'm givin' you a raise. Startin' tomorrow you're gettin' ten cents an hour more. Now you're makin' a buck twenty." Stosh said as he gazed fawningly at Mr. Rich.

"Gee, thanks for the raise Mr. Grabowski." I knew that Mr. Rich had given me the raise and that Stosh was only the messenger. I would have thanked Mr. Rich myself, but Stosh told the fry boys that we were never to talk to Mr. Rich unless he spoke to us first. He didn't like us talking to his boss.

"Oh and Mr. Rich wants an order of chicken to go. Double breaded, breasts and thighs only. And make it snappy, Chuck. Mr. Rich is a busy man." Stosh seemed to find a set of balls when Mr. Rich was around. I guess he wanted to show Mr. Rich that he wasn't the sniveling lackey everyone knew him to be. *What a weasel*, I thought. It must have been demeaning for a man Grabowski's age to constantly grovel, but he didn't seem to mind.

"Sure, no problem; I'll get the order goin' right away. Double breaded, breasts and thighs only," I confirmed.

Stosh nodded as he scurried back to Mr. Rich's side. "I did just what you said boss, Stosh sniveled, "I told him about your chicken order and to make it snappy. And I told him that you're a busy man. I did everything you told me do to."

Holy shit, I thought, *a pay raise after only three months*. I couldn't believe it. I was moving up the ladder alright. I was one of the senior fry cooks at that KFC outlet. I had visions of supplanting Lester or maybe even Stosh someday. But it was not to be. After a few more months I had to quit my job. It was interfering with my sleep schedule. I wasn't getting enough shut eye and my grades were suffering for it. Some nights I wouldn't get to sleep until well after midnight and had to get up at six o'clock in the morning to get ready for school. I hated to quit that job. I liked the cash and my triple breaded thighs.

On the surface, my KFC experience appears to have been just a teenager's part-time job at a fast food joint. It would prove to be much more in the future. I didn't realize it then, but I was acquiring culinary skills and a working knowledge of a commercial kitchen that would be useful throughout my cooking career. I learned how to use commercial cooking equipment, kitchen operation, staff management, food prep and cooking skills, food safety and an appreciation for food replication.

Pigs' Tails 'n Hot Sauce

WHAT COULD PIGS' tails, usually dismissed as useless porcine offal, possibly have to do with a book about the world of cooking and gastronomy? Short answer is quite a bit. It was through pigs' tails—and a smorgasbord of equally tasty soul dishes—that I was introduced to a genre of cuisine completely foreign to me; soul food as it's cooked in the Deep South. And it was through this "new" cuisine that I was able to befriend a small group of black steel mill laborers who, as it would turn out, impacted my life to a degree.

My oldest brother, Doug, got me summer jobs working at Wisconsin Steel, located just outside of Chicago. Doug was a superintendent in the mill. One of his charges was the pit gang whose job was to clean the heating pits used to reheat massive steel ingots for processing in the rolling mill. Working in the heating pits was one of the hottest, filthiest jobs in the mill. It was the grungiest job I've ever had. The pit gang was an all-black crew except for one white guy—me. Other whites refused to do this crappy work because they felt that it was beneath them. So it fell to this handful of black laborers and yours truly. Since I was merely temporary summer help my brother gave me up to the *gang*.

Ostensibly, this was a summer job to earn extra money for college, but the job turned out to be more of an education. It gave me a front row view of the odious effects of racism in America. I was able to witness firsthand the genuine effects of school segregation. I was able to see the human toll of racism with my own eyes. It was an education unlike any I had received in college. There are no college courses that teach you how the world really works.

The crew consisted of Hank, the pit boss, Li'l Joe, who never took to me (Either because he resented nepotism or me because I was white.), Castro, the resident chef and incorrigible alcoholic, Fat Back, (Because on the nape of neck were rolls of fat.), Mr. Washington and Lunch Box. They all lived on Chicago's far south side.

I had a problem. Just because my brother got me the job didn't mean Hank and his boys had to accept me as a member of their group. Sure, they had to work with me, but they weren't bound to accept me. They could have ostracized me and I would have been powerless to do anything about it. What was I going to do, go crying to my brother? That was not an option. If they had shut me out those two summers would have been long and lonely indeed. For the first time in my life I felt what it was like to be the minority. It was uncomfortable being the outsider. Somehow I had to ingratiate myself to the group. It didn't matter that they were black, I wanted to befriend them. I understood that I had to show deference to them and that I was okay with being at the bottom of the pecking order. It was the natural order of things. But I had to ingratiate myself to them and food would be the bridge. I began bringing in fresh donuts a few mornings a week. This broke the ice.

It was their turn to reciprocate. Every Friday Castro generously brought a hot lunch for the gang. Apparently, he'd been doing this for years. Eventually, Castro offered me a plate of food.

That was it, I was accepted into the gang. I relished our lunches together. These were blue-collar workers and as such their conversations revolved around four basic topics; pussy, partying, food and booze.

I was all ears. I was by far the youngest member of the crew and listened with rapt attention to their salacious stories. I especially liked to hear about the blues clubs they frequented on Chicago's south side.

We lunched on corn bread, ham hocks and lima beans, greens, braised chicken feet, turkey necks, pork neck bones and rice, pork chops, pigs' tails and feet and chittlins. I wasn't crazy about the chittlins, they tasted nasty. But I devoured everything else. I'd never tasted food like that before. My mother and Mildred were a great cooks, but they never made soul food. I didn't know that random pig parts could taste so good. *White people didn't know what they were missing*, I thought. One of my favorites was pigs' tails and hot sauce. Chef Castro braised the tails until they were tender and the hot sauce was the perfect accompaniment. Castro was a damn good cook and I appreciated it. At summer's end I bought him a bottle of Crown Royal. If I was going to buy an alcoholic a gift why not make something he'll enjoy. Of course, I bought Hank a bottle too.

Hank and his boys were almost always in a collective good mood. Little in life seemed to bother them. I was too young to understand how they could be so happy given their life experiences. They seemed to dismiss all they had endured in the Jim Crow south. They had the ability to laugh at the smallest things. They seemed to laugh for the sake of it. I wondered, *why couldn't whites be this happy?* White folks just seemed to be more serious by contrast. I genuinely enjoyed being around these men. They treated me with respect as long as I did the same.

Over time I begin to recognize the vile effects racism had upon these men. I soon realized that they were all illiterate except for Hank, who could read and write a little. These were middle-aged men who couldn't even read a newspaper. They'd all been born during the late 1930s and early 1940s when Jim Crow laws legalized the institutionalized oppression of blacks, especially in the Deep South. They all hailed from the Mississippi Delta region, a bastion of southern racism. Eventually, most of them felt comfortable enough with me to reveal that they were illiterate. Every payday most of the crew would ask me to examine their paychecks to make sure they weren't shorted. They couldn't do basic arithmetic. It made me ashamed to live in a society that intentionally oppressed an entire race. At that moment I lost all respect for the Southern social structure.

Well into the 21st century, it still harbors a certain level of racism against minorities. After I finished college I moved to Atlanta where I saw firsthand the insidious effects that racism can have upon an entire culture.

Hank and his men weren't a bunch of shuffling darkies quick to wear a comic grin when a white man came around. They didn't go around talking like minstrel darkies, "*Yazzuh massah*" or "*Nozzuh bozz.*" Hank and his boys were hard-working, honest men trying to support their families back home. Although they were unsophisticated country folk, each man possessed an innate sense of dignity and pride. Their personal demeanor impressed me and I was a better person for having associated with them. Unfortunately, they were stuck in that filthy shit hole when I was able to return to college. I was afforded opportunities never available to them, but they didn't resent me for it. They accepted me for who I was.

After the second summer I never saw any of them again. Years later Doug told me that Castro had passed away, his liver gave out, and the gang disintegrated shortly after that. Hank took another job elsewhere at the mill. He didn't know what became of Fat Back, Lunch Box or Mr. Washington. Only Li'l Joe remained. Doug said the replacements weren't half the workers Hank's boys were.

I learned some valuable life lessons during those two summers. The most important lesson was forgiveness. If they could find it in their hearts not to hold an entire race accountable for what a despicable few had done, then I could forgive those who would wrong me in life. These men actually practiced one of the messages espoused by Martin Luther King, "Judge a man by the content of his character not by the color of his skin."

They accepted me even though I was as member of the society that had perpetrated so many wrongs on them and their people. They also taught me that personal integrity and high social station aren't necessarily mutually inclusive.

Unlike most of the summers of my youth, the two I spent at Wisconsin Steel are still vivid in my mind. Not only did I pick-up some valuable life lessons; I was introduced to an entirely new cuisine. I taught myself how to cook some of Castro's tasty dishes. I'm especially fond of the braised turkey necks, ham hocks and limas and of course pigs' tails and hot sauce.

Chapter Two

Accidental Chef

"You know my wife is a lousy cook. In our house, when she cooks we pray *after* dinner."

Rodney Dangerfield

THE YEAR WAS 1981. I was living in New Orleans when I found myself in a situation where I was forced to make two life-altering decisions. One would have been difficult enough for most people, but I had to deal with both simultaneously. The two decisions concerned my marriage and my career. Both were on the rocks. I had to decide whether I should quit my professional career—a career in hospital administration that I'd spent years building through professional and academic pursuits. I was fairly accomplished. I'd earned a respectable national reputation as an institutional environmental health and occupational safety specialist and was regarded as a national authority in the field.

I was published. I'd even earned a master's degree from the University of Minnesota. But what good was it all when I hated my work? I was suffocating in the corporate setting. I used to tell my friends, "My job wasn't the end of the world, but I could see it from my office." It wasn't just the work—I disliked the hospital industry in general because of the hypocrisy. The public façade is one of compassionate patient care, but behind the scenes hospital administrators are as ruthless and avaricious as their Fortune 500 counterparts. Administrators are concerned about patient care only to the extent that it generates profits and shareholders' dividends. With the national health care debate, the curtain was pulled back on what the health care industry is all about. We've seen how they charge obscene prices for medical supplies and medications as long as they can get away with it.

The other decision concerned my marriage of five years. It was over and we both knew it. Her name was Tessa. She hailed from London. She was a graphic designer in those days and I believe still is. The marriage didn't fail because we weren't compatible or ceased to be friends. It disintegrated for other reasons I'd rather not reveal. We remained friends for many years afterwards. She lives in Florida I believe. We've lost contact. You know how that goes. People mean to keep in touch but rarely do. I hope life has been good to Tessa. We enriched each other's lives.

I made the decision to change careers and seek a divorce in one fell swoop. But what kind of work was I going to do? I knew that I had to take advantage of this opportunity. A person doesn't get the chance to change careers every day. I decided to pick a profession that I genuinely wanted to do. I knew that I had to choose an occupation that was a natural fit.. The board room was a bad fit. I wouldn't make that mistake again. This time it would be different. I'd become a chef. I'd always a natural affinity for cooking and knew I possessed innate culinary skills. It only made sense.

~~~

Cooking is my calling. The late Sonny Terry, the legendary blues harmonica player, once said, "You don't pick the blues, the blues pick you." It's the same with cooking. The passion to cook is in your blood or it isn't. It can't be manufactured. Becoming a professional chef was not some quixotic adventure; it was serious business. I was thirty-two years old when I decided to become a chef. While not exactly over the hill at that age, building a new career from the bottom becomes increasingly difficult as the years slip by. I didn't view my age as an obstacle, instead I regarded my maturity as an asset. In all probability this would be my last shot at another career so I had to make the most of it. Chinese culture accentuates the value of time, and appreciates that missed opportunities are gone forever. They have a proverb: "A piece of time is as valuable as a piece of gold, but a piece of gold cannot buy a piece of time." The sooner I began my new career the better. I knew that I had a steep learning curve and that I had to throw myself at it. One big advantage I had was that I was living in New Orleans. What better city in which to launch a culinary career?

~~~

Becoming a professional chef wouldn't be just another run-of-mill job. I'd already had plenty of them. Most jobs were just for the money, while a few offered an education. I took something away from each experience, a bit of knowledge, a new skill, a valuable contact—some intangible that would be useful in the future. Here's a partial list of experiences: altar boy, newspaper delivery boy, gas station attendant, toy store stock boy, health inspector, furniture deliverer, grocery bag boy, car wash and parking lot attendant, construction laborer, restaurant inspector, convenience store cashier, chicken fryer, windshield wiper plant stock boy, steel mill laborer, hospital administrator, hardware store stock boy, bus boy, Naval corpsman (in 'Nam), college student. How could these experiences prepare me to be a chef? I learned the importance of being on time, to be responsible for my actions and how to get along with others. I also learned how to manage people, a skill that would come in handy when I was a hotel chef and also when I had my own restaurant. Professional actors employ a device they call "sense memories," these are life experiences that they file away at the back of their mind, so that later they can recall the appropriate memory to use as a tool to act a part convincingly. I did the same thing, I called upon my previous work experiences when the situation warranted.

Becoming a chef would be nothing like any job I'd done before. For the first time in my life I'd be a craftsman, a food artist of sorts. The very prospect of becoming a chef was exciting. And it's a good thing, too, because cooking for a living is not a stroll in the park. Cooking is tough, demanding work. The hours are long and the working conditions can be unpleasant. Commercial kitchens can be cramped, hot and even dangerous places. Too often coworkers suffer from drug abuse or alcoholism. Some are even on the run from the law. Every cook has a story. I wish I had a dollar for every time I've heard, "Oh I'm not planning on cooking for a living. This is just a temporary gig to earn cash." Cooking was always a pit stop during their journey to another career; an actor, a pilot, a teacher. For me cooking *was* the destination.

She Had Me at Pâte Brisée

IT WAS ANOTHER sultry New Orleans summer afternoon. With nothing particular to do I thought I'd watch a PBS cooking show. It happened to be Julia Child. She was making a *béchamel* sauce for a cheese *soufflé*. I remember thinking, *what's so hard about that?* I'd seen my mom make white sauce dozens of times. Next, Julia made pie dough, except she called it *pâte brisée*. I'd never heard pie dough called that. Again I thought, *so what's the big deal? This is just pie dough.* She gave it a French name, but to me it was still just pie dough.

I realized that my mother and I had made many of the things Julia made during my childhood. I thought, *wait a minute, I can make this stuff.* I began watching Julia's shows regularly. By watching her I came to understand that a fairly complicated dish is only the sum of its parts. This was the essential lesson I learned from Julia. Looking back I realize that Julia was not a professional cook at all. However, she was an accomplished home cook who had the unique ability to demystify intimidating French dishes. She popularized French cookery for the masses. What she demonstrated I practiced. Small successes increased my confidence. I was hooked. I watched her show as often as I could. Julia demonstrated some the basic cooking techniques and methods my mother and stepmother had taught me as a child and teenager.

~~~

In no time at all my fascination with cooking shows grew beyond Julia. I began watching Graham Kerr and a then-new series called *Great Chefs of New Orleans*. One of the first episodes featured chef Warren Le Ruth who owned a swank restaurant in Algiers, Louisiana, located on the west bank of the Mississippi directly across the river from New Orleans. (Within a few years I would cook at Le Ruth's. Few people have ever heard of him, but Chef Le Ruth was one of the first great American-born chefs.)

I became obsessed with cooking shows. I took notes. I recorded them. I replayed shows to master certain skills; making an omelet, boning a fryer, filleting a flounder. Before we parted, I experimented on Tessa, a very willing volunteer. I would try to replicate the dishes I'd learned from the cooking shows. Some of my attempts were absolute disasters—our cat wouldn't touch them. No matter, I was determined to pursue a culinary career.

I was changing as a person. I was going through an emotional growth spurt. I became consumed with cooking. I'm reluctant to use that over used word "epiphany," but I don't know how else to describe it. At some point I decided to chuck the hospital gig and become a chef. It just seemed right. None of this was planned. I didn't have some well thought-out plan to become a chef. It all just happened by accident, which is why I think it's fitting to refer to myself as an *Accidental Chef.*

The Le Coq Culinary Academy

I KNEW THAT I wanted to become a chef, but how was I supposed to make this happen? I had no idea where to begin. I didn't know any chefs and the only thing that I knew about the restaurant world was that it was the world you entered when you wanted to eat out. With no professional experience, who would hire me? I needed to get trained; I needed to enroll in a cooking school. At that time there were only two cooking schools in New Orleans. In fact, you could probably count on both hands the number of schools in all of America. In the early 1980s few Americans considered pursuing a culinary profession. The Europeans dominated the culinary scene in the United States. Americans were usually relegated to jobs like short order cooks, prep cooks, bus boys and servers. And there were very few female chefs—the Europeans, especially the French, didn't want females in their kitchens. That's all changed and for the better.

I didn't want to start out washing pots and climb the proverbial ladder to becoming a chef. That would take too long. At thirty-two I was no spring chicken and I knew I needed to jump-start my career if I was going to make something of myself. Attending a cooking school seemed like the quickest route to where I wanted to go. The only cooking school I could find in the yellow pages was a place called the Le Coq Culinary Academy. When I called the academy to get directions the voice of the person on the line sounded soft and effeminate. I also detected a slight lisp.

When I arrived at the address I was confused. I knew I was at the correct address, but I stood in front of a private residence on Prytania Street. The house was a few doors down from the Prytania Theater, an artsy movie house where you can buy mixed drinks and beer. That's what I love about New Orleans. *Why was there a cooking school in a residential neighborhood,* I asked myself? The house was an enormous antebellum shotgun camelback. They're called camelbacks in New Orleans because of the second level, the camel's hump, at the back of the structure. Wide colonnaded porticos wrapped around three sides. Badly weathered whitewash peeled from the clapboard façade. Weeds had taken over the expansive front and side yards. A rusty wrought-iron corn stalk fence leaned toward the street. I was shocked by the dilapidated state of the old house and briefly reconsidered keeping the appointment, but I'd traveled all the way across town so I decided to go through with it.

I pressed the doorbell button, there was no response. Again I pressed the button, still nothing. I banged the tarnished doorknocker, a solid brass ring with the face of a gargoyle mounted on the door. Still there was no sign of life so I decided to let myself in. After all it was supposed to be a place of business, so why shouldn't I just enter? The hinges of the massive wood door groaned as I struggled to force it open.

The anteroom felt cool and damp, a welcome relief from the withering heat outside. Sunshine streamed through the grimy windows creating diaphanous shadows throughout the space. The feel of the space reminded me of a Val Lewton movie—the 1940s Hollywood producer famous for macabre cinema and an innovative use of shadows and grey tones. Strands of spider silk stretched from the window mullions to the large and dusty chandelier where a perfect spider web had been constructed. The eight-legged architect lay motionless at the center, ready to pounce on any unfortunate victim that became enmeshed in its lair. It was eerily quiet—too quiet for my liking. I reconsidered leaving when suddenly the silence was broken by the murmur of voices coming from within the house. Just then a small man materialized. He entered the foyer through a pair of tattered, paisley curtains that served as a makeshift room divider. The curtain material looked like the heavy embroidered drapery I'd seen in *Gone with the Wind*. The little man bore a striking physical resemblance to Truman Capote. He cradled a blonde Yorkshire terrier who seemed completely disinterested in the goings on.

"Bon jour, cher, I'm Chef Marcelle Dupree, but please just call me Marcelle. Welcome to Le Coq Culinary Academy. I must apologize for the doorbell. We've been meaning to have it repaired, but we've been so busy with the culinary academy and all. I'm sure you understand. And you must be Charles. And this is my sweet little Coquette," he said, thrusting the pooch toward me as if I was supposed to pet the creature. I didn't.

"Yes, I'm Charles. I believe we spoke on the phone," I said, a bit nonplused by the situation.

"Yes, it was me you spoke with. I'm charmed to meet you."

With a wave of a hand the milquetoast little man beckoned me to follow him through the curtains. Marcelle's manner of affected speech even resembled Capote's, complete with the lisp.

We entered a living room at the center of the premises. The walls were adorned with faded Mardi Gras posters and velvet portraits of Louis Armstrong and Fats Domino. An enormous tabby lay coiled on a beach towel in a corner. The creature was oblivious to the humans in the room. A half-dozen or so people were lounging about on two threadbare sofas. They stopped talking when we entered the room. They seemed annoyed that Marcelle and I had interrupted their conversations. It must have been their muffled voices that I heard earlier in the foyer. Several were smartly dressed in black chef jackets while the others wore outlandish clothes that would do nicely at a Mardi Gras costume ball. Marcelle deposited the Yorkie in its bed where it remained for the duration of my visit.

The group displayed forced, lifeless smiles suggesting that my appearance was not wholly appreciated. They were an odd assortment. One guy wore a Mohawk-style haircut and far too much eyeliner. Another man's arms were covered with tattoos from wrists to neck suggesting that his entire torso was inked up as well. His seatmate's hair was dyed purple and resembled the spiky coat of a hedgehog. Another woman wore black lip gloss and had a mane of ebony hair that cascaded down her back. She looked like a voluptuous version of Morticia Addams. I'd been accustomed to seeing these kinds of misfits in the French Quarter, but they seemed out of place in a professional cooking school. I began to think that I'd made a huge mistake by even making the appointment in the first place. How was I to know that I'd wind up at a freak show?

"Students, this is Charles," Marcelle said, "He might be joining our little family. Let's give Charles a very warm Le Coq round of applause." Only Marcelle clapped; the others just sat there motionless leering at me. Judging by the vacuous expressions on their faces, they couldn't have cared less about what Marcelle had to say or that I was present. The entire class looked me over as if they were undressing me. I felt uncomfortable. The guy with the Mohawk even winked at me. I swear he was coming on to me.

"I'm going to take Charles on a short tour of the premises, but before we begin does anyone have anything they'd like to say to Charles?" Marcelle said, as they all continued to sit there as if they were catatonic. Then the guy with the Mohawk raised his hand.

"Hi there my name is Henri. I just have one question for Charles. Charles, are you married?" Henri snickered inciting the others to do the same. Naturally, the question made me feel uncomfortable. I looked to Marcelle, appealing for his intervention.

"Now Henri, don't be so cheeky," Marcelle admonished, "After all, Charles is our guest and hasn't decided whether he'll attend Le Coq. Now if there are no further questions I'll show Charles around." Henri seemed pleased with himself that he'd gotten a rise out of the group.

"Oh, before I forget, Vivian please melt the Vermont cheddar for the fondue au fromage," said Marcelle, with another swirling hand gesture, "And Devaugh you're in charge of the croutons. I want Charles to sample the special Le Coq cheese fondue."

Once we began the tour, the students returned to their conversations, squawking like a murder of crows. Vivian ignored Marcelle's instruction to melt the cheese, which convinced me that they were not there to learn cookery; it was more of a venue for these freaks to socialize. The woman with the purple hair snorted at something the tattoo boy said. When her mouth was open I noticed several silver studs embedded in her tongue, which made her sound as if she had a speech impediment. The studs impaired her ability to form words. At that very moment our eyes met. She glared at me disapprovingly as if to say, *You are not one of us. You are not wanted here. You do not fit in. You should leave.* If those were her sentiments, the feeling was mutual. It was at that moment I knew that I couldn't possibly work with this collection of deviants. Sure, I wanted to be a chef, but if that meant attending school with these lunatics I'd find another line of work. I would have left at that precise moment, but I didn't want to appear impolite so I decided to suffer through the remainder of the tour. I noticed the cat was roused. It was swiping at a huge cockroach that is so common in the Deep South. It taunted the bug before it pounced and devoured it.

Marcelle showed me the bar area where they taught *mixology*, the then-trendy term for bartending. He emphasized that Le Coq possessed all the special glassware for all the specialty drinks. The mixology portion of the curriculum seemed to be a great source of pride for Marcelle, but bartending wasn't a skill I wanted to acquire. I wanted to learn cooking. I listened to what he had to say and asked an occasional question pretending to be interested. I really wanted to get out of there.

Just then I noticed a short, thick-set man descending the staircase from the upper level—a part of the house that I thought could have been the former slaves' quarters. Antebellum homes in New Orleans often featured slaves' quarters on the upper level or in a separate building at the back of the property. The man bore a strong facial resemblance to Marcelle, but that's where any physical similarity ended. He was wearing a black chef's jacket and one of those floppy hats that professional chefs won't be caught dead wearing. Suddenly, the screech of an old woman's voice came from the upper level.

"And don't forget my bawks (Barqs soda) and Moon Pie, dawlin'. And if we outta Moon Pies gimme a cherry Hubig's pie, sweetie! And put some ice in my glass. You know I like my cold drinks real cold, yeah."

The man halted his descent as he noticed Marcelle and me. "Okay mama, I won't forget and I'll be up with your snack and cold drink directly." The short man rolled his eyes in exasperation, and directed his next comments to Marcelle. "Cher, mama's gonna be the death of me, yeah. You just wait and see. Moon Pies, Bawks, Hubig's. Mama always callin' me fer some damn thing."

Marcelle introduced us.

"Charles this is my brother, Hercule. Hercule, this is Charles. You know, the prospective student I told you about," Marcelle said, gently placing a hand on my shoulder.

"Oh yeah, so you be Charles. How ya doin'? Welcome to Le Coq. Don't mind our moma upstairs, she old and fussy." Hercule made a circling motion with his finger pointed at his head suggesting that his mother was mentally ill. Hercule chortled.

Hercule decided to participate in the tour before fetching the old woman's snacks. The siblings gave me their spiel about the advantages of attending the Le Coq Culinary Academy. They went on to tell how they'd both cooked at Arnaud's and Commander's Palace as teenagers, which must have been many decades earlier since they both appeared to be in their fifties. I pretended to listen intently as Marcelle explained how I would be eminently qualified to be a chef in New Orleans if I were to graduate from the Le Coq. At that point, I couldn't have cared less where the Dupree brothers had worked. I wasn't about to attend any school with those perverts I met earlier. And the Dupree brothers and their mother reminded of the movie *Psycho*. This was all too weird for me.

"In da Quarta dey always needin' bartendas," Hercule chimed in, trying to remain relevant to the tour.

"No Hercule, it's mixologists. We train mixologists. We mustn't refer to our students as bartenders anymore. That's so 60s," Marcelle intoned, as pulled me aside and whispered.

"Please excuse Hercule's earthy manner. He's not as unsophisticated as he seems. Really, he isn't."

We wound up the tour in the kitchen. The walls were grimy and it was dimly lit. The counters were covered with residential kitchen gadgets—a food processor, a blender, a toaster oven. It was clear that the Le Coq was a total scam. It was meeting place for the dregs of society to meet and do whatever it was that they did. I'd seen enough of Le Coq. I'd already made my mind up that I wanted no part of that farce. I told Marcelle and Hercule that as much as I would have liked to have stayed for the fondue au fromage, I had to leave for another appointment. I just wanted to get away from that mental institution.

I drove home completely deflated. My first attempt at finding a culinary program was a total bust. Not only did I not find a cooking school, my visit to the Le Coq Culinary Academy left me feeling somehow unclean. I thought a hot shower might wash away the lingering feeling of unease and discomfort I got from spending time with the Dupree family and those weirdo students. I know my feeling was an overreaction, but I was unnerved by it nonetheless. The whole thing was a waste of my time. There had to be a decent cooking school somewhere in town—after all, New Orleans was one of the premier food cities in North America.

Finally, The Real Deal

EVENTUALLY, I DISCOVERED that a real culinary program did exist in the Big Easy. It was part of the Delgado Community College, which is located next to City Park. It was a vocational program called Les Chefs de Cuisine de La Louisianne—it went under in the late 1990s. It had been in operation for only a year or so before I enrolled. There were two full-time instructors, Chefs Gary Darling and Mark Fitch. The program would eventually relocate to the University of New Orleans, which had a fully equipped commercial kitchen facility, a large dining room and an auditorium. It was better equipped and more modern than the Delgado facility.

The Board of Directors included Chef Paul Prudhomme. The world hadn't yet heard of Chef Prudhomme, but it soon would. In the early 1980s he was a big deal in Louisiana, especially in New Orleans and in Cajun country where he was from. Chef Prudhomme's involvement with this program gave it credibility and stature. I didn't have second thoughts; I enrolled immediately. I went in for a perfunctory interview. Possessing five senses were the only prerequisites necessary for getting in. The program was just getting started so they weren't picky about whom they admitted.

Gary Darling was a So Cal ex-pat. With a shock of wavy blonde hair, he reminded me of some 1960s surfer dude. He was an accomplished chef who'd held several premier chef positions around New Orleans. Darling was recognized as New Orleans' Chef of the Year in 1983. In surfer parlance Darling was one *bitchin'* cook. He was a member of an elite club of American born and bred chefs who began the movement to supplant the old guard European chefs who had dominated gastronomy in America for most of the 20th century. He taught garde manger, charcuterie, hot food, table service, etc.

Fitch hailed from Manchester, England. Just in his middle twenties, he was already an accomplished pastry chef and a master baker. He taught the pastry students, of which I was one, all aspects of bread baking and pastry production. Darling and Fitch were not ordinary chefs; these guys were superb craftsmen with a natural ability to teach. They were two of the top chefs in North America at the time. We were fortunate to have them as instructors. They transformed raw apprentices into decent cooks who could hold their own in most kitchens anywhere in America. Our cooking school was excellent. The tuition was low and the students received a first class education.

My culinary school was a three-year program. Culinary students attended school one day a week while they worked a full-time job at a property of the school's choosing, a local hotel or restaurant. Each school day consisted of basically two things: classroom lecture and creating actual dishes in the kitchen under the supervision of the instructors. We also practiced by creating lavish meals for volunteer diners, of which there was never a shortage. We just needed warm bodies to feed. These practice sessions were useful because we learned how to create and execute a menu, work as service staff and prepare a wide range of cuisines. The number of guests could range from five to fifty. The experience of cooking for large groups would prove to be invaluable later in my career when I would open my own café and cater large events.

The culinary program offered the students a choice between a regular cooking course and basic pastries. I began doing the regular cooking curriculum, but switched to pastries within a few months. The cooks just seemed to be less hip and less talented. It became clear that anyone with taste buds and the olfactory sense of a German Shepard could become a cook, but pastries required enhanced skills. Pastries demanded a sense of design, style and a tactile facility. I also didn't care for the stress of line cooking and working in a hot, chaotic environment. Plus some of the regular cooks were absolute cretins and difficult to work with. The pastry shop was different. It was more serene, more pacific. I've always said that pastry-making is to regular cooking what cabinet-making is to carpentry. A pastry cook can easily become a regular cook, but the reverse is far less likely.

Most culinary programs are primarily classroom-based with a short internship. My culinary school took the opposite approach: we were in the classroom less and in professional kitchens more, where the real learning takes place. In the hotels and restaurants we were supervised by experienced professional chefs who taught us hands-on cooking. The hotels and restaurants could just use us as chattel labor, the chefs were required to actually teach us culinary skills. That was the deal. The property got an enthusiastic employee for a pittance, but they were obligated to teach us how to cook.

Things were changing fast for me. I had a new pad, a new gig, and was on the track to a new career. I wasn't making as much money as I had before, but my quality of life had improved immensely—I was finally doing what I wanted to do. Still, this was just the beginning, and I knew that the Le Coq Culinary Academy was only the first of many strange places that my career as a chef would take me. In the world of commercial food-service, I still had a lot to learn.

The Channel

SINCE I EARNED so little I was forced to take an apartment in a very low-rent section of New Orleans so I moved into the Irish Channel. The Channel is bordered by Magazine Street to the north, First Street to the east, Tchoupitoulas Street to the south (and the Mississippi River just beyond) and Toledano Street to the west. The Irish Channel was originally settled largely by Irish immigrants in the early 19th century. The whites had long since been supplanted by blacks. When I moved in the hood it was almost all black. My landlady and I were the only white folks in our part of the community. It didn't matter to me as long as my neighbors didn't mind having me live amongst them. I came to know my neighbors. They accepted me. I guess they figured if I was living with them I was either *not* a racist or too stupid to know the difference. They liked me and I developed a genuine affection for them. They protected me. They took me under their wing. I lived there for four years and never had a problem. I could bicycle or walk through my neighborhood anytime of the day or night and no one ever hassled me. During the wee hours the brothers from our part of the Channel (outsiders were not welcome even if they were black) would gather under the street corner light sipping wine from a bottle that was swaddled in a brown paper bag. They didn't need the bag. It struck me that the bag thing was an important part of their subculture. It's just what they did and they were adamant about it. It was as if the bag was a point of propriety. When I'd bicycle home late at night they'd always offer me a swig from the bag. I always accepted. Refusing their offer might have insulted them. I always had to be mindful of the fact that I was an outsider in their community and a minority at that.

Living in the Irish Channel had a singular and unique benefit, I could grow my own pot. My landlady's backyard was surrounded by a tall wood fence that provided privacy from prying eyes. My landlady was okay with my crop as long as she got her share of the harvest. I didn't have to worry about getting busted by the NOPD—cops rarely patrol black neighborhoods. I grew several bumper crops of very good, organic weed. At harvest time I hung the plants upside-down in our laundry room for a few days to allow the THC to drain into the leaves for maximum potency. New Orleans has the perfect climate for growing pot. I produced much more than I needed for personal use so I sold it at work. I sold pot to fellow cooks, security guards and the maintenance crew. I earned enough cash to pay my rent for a few months after each harvest.

Changing careers and starting at the bottom again can be challenging. The early days as an apprentice cook were difficult. I don't know how I would have fed myself if I hadn't been working the hospitality industry. There was one bright spot. I knew that I'd have two hot meals every day I was scheduled to work. I could count on getting breakfast and lunch on those days, but I also had to eat on my days off. The hotel was my salvation. For a time, I pinched food from the hotel. Racks of lamb, beef filets, butter and chocolate fit nicely into my back pack. Security at the Lafitte Hotel was lax and no one cared about petty theft anyway. Most of the cooks pilfered from that hotel. It was easy to get through security. All I had to do was give the guards a few pastries now and then and they'd turn a blind eye when I passed through security. When you're forced to take care of yourself you make do somehow. You might have to resort to things that you wouldn't ordinarily do, but you do what is necessary.

Chapter Three

The Big Easy

"Leave the gun, take the cannolis."

Clemenza
The Godfather

EVERY FEW YEARS I feel compelled to return to New Orleans. I do not have a choice; I have to get my fix of great food and rekindle my love affair with the one city that never completely gets out of your blood. Like a first love, it's the one you can never get out of your mind. My most recent visit was in summer of 2009. I was delighted to find the city well on its way to recovery from the devastation caused by hurricane Katrina. One area I felt bound to inspect was the French Quarter, the beating heart of the Big Easy. I wandered its streets and back alleys early in the day, before the thermometer rose. The Quarter was a beehive of activity, tourists and locals alike were crammed into and cafés, bars and shops. Jackson Square was as busy as I'd ever seen it. It all seemed so familiar, just as I remembered it when I lived there. A National Park Service guide recited the history of the Pontalba apartments—America's oldest condos that ring the square—to a gaggle of disinterested tourists. Buskers entertained passersby and vendors hawked their wares in the shadow of Saint Louis Cathedral whose bells chimed a reassuring message that New Orleans is back on its feet—like an indomitable prize fighter who refuses to stay down. Fortunately, the French Quarter was spared from a juggernaut named Katrina when large sections of the city were underwater. What would New Orleans be without the Quarter?

My brisk stroll through the French Quarter worked up an appetite for a plate of Café du Monde's melt-in-your-mouth beignets and a cup of chicory café au lait. For the uninitiated, beignets (pronounced *ben-yays*) are deep-fried fritters or as I once heard a French Quarter carriage driver describe them as, "doughnuts that ain't got no holes." Beignets are made by deep-frying squares of yeast dough until they puff up and turn golden brown. They're smothered with confectioner's sugar and served piping hot with a cup of delicious chicory coffee. This is quintessential New Orleans.

There was one problem. A serpentine queue meandered in front of the New Orleans' landmark. The line appeared to be at least a thirty minute wait. There was no way I was going to endure the mid day heat for coffee and pastry no matter how good they might be. So I decided to do the next best thing. I went around to the side of the café where I could watch the Café du Monde cooks making beignets through a viewing window. If I couldn't eat beignets at least I could watch them being made. This proved to be a bad idea. Watching the beignets being fried and sugared sharpened my appetite all the more. I could resist no longer so I hopped in line. The wait was worth it, even in the oppressive heat. Café du Monde is open 24/7 except when the occasional hurricane washes over the city. Seeing this most famous of all beignet shops crowded was more reason to believe that New Orleans was on the mend.

~~~

During my stay, I also visited parts of the city that were hardest hit by Katrina. I visited City Park, which had been several feet of water. It now resembled an antediluvian New Orleans. There was no indication that the nation's second largest public park had temporarily become part of Lake Ponchartrain during the storm. The park looked just as I remembered—sleepy lagoons and stately oaks dripping with Spanish moss.

Suddenly, I heard the familiar whistle of the antique miniature trains the park operates as a children's ride. As it rumbled toward me I heard the gleeful squeals of the train's pint-size passengers. As the tiny train chugged out of sight I realized that it represented another comforting sign of the city's return to normalcy. I also checked to see if the remaining one of a pair of Dueling Oaks survived the hurricane—the other oak fell in the 1940s. The Dueling Oaks served as the designated spot where colonial Creole gentlemen defended their honor. In his *History of Louisiana*, Alcee

Fortier states that, "On a Sunday in 1839 ten duels or more were fought at the oaks." Duels were outlawed in 1890. The Oak was still there standing straight and tall unfazed by Katrina. It would take more than a little wind and rain to down this giant.

Despite its remarkable recovery, there are still pockets of the city that had not fully recovered such as the Upper 9th Ward, the part of town that received the heaviest flood damage from Katrina. A few blocks below the French Quarter, the Upper 9th remains largely a barren wasteland. The landscape is acre upon acre of nothingness. Outlines of brick foundations are all that remains in vast stretches of this once vibrant blue collar community. But even here there is reason for hope. Long-time residents are returning to their neighborhood and newcomers are taking advantage of the depressed real estate market. They are buying property at bargain basement prices and building new homes or refurbishing existing structures.

Thanks to concerned celebrities like Brad Pitt, founder of Make It Right Foundation green houses have begun sprouting up throughout the Upper 9th. These modernistic structures seem oddly out-of-place, bearing no resemblance to the classic "shotgun" style homes for which New Orleans is famous. No matter; they represent a rebirth, a new beginning. The Make It Right Foundation is slated to construct one-hundred and fifty homes. If more celebrities lent their star power to the reclamation effort perhaps the process could be expedited. Government at all levels has failed the Jewel of the South, but especially at the national level. President Bush failed to deliver on his promise. He stood in Jackson Square and swore "do what it takes" to rebuild the city. When the disaster was no longer newsworthy Bush's commitment to rebuild became just another hollow public pronouncement by an unconcerned politician. New Orleans was irrelevant. It was only after Obama became president that federal money flowed into the city. Obama made good on Bush's promise.

When a city rebounds from being battered the way New Orleans has, it says something about its people. It speaks to their character and will to survive. New Orleanians' intense and undying devotion for their city has carried them through this tragedy. Sadly, an estimated one third of New Orleans' former residents are scattered across America because of Katrina. As of March 2009 the population of New Orleans topped 300,000 representing slow but steady growth.

New Orleans French Market, Est. 1791.

Cafe du Monde, New Orleans landmark, has served beignets
and chicory coffee since 1862.

Commander's Palace, located in the Garden District,
has sated sophisticated diners since 1880.

The Napoleon House was offered as refuge to the exiled Emperor in 1821.
Its muffulettas are some of the best in the city.

Situated on Rue Royale in the Vieux Carre, the Court of
Two Sisters offers Creole cuisine at its finest.

Central Grocery is home of the original muffuletta sandwich. Est. 1906.

Known as the "Queen of Creole Cuisine," Leah Chase
opened Dooky Chase in 1941.

~~~

To work as a chef in New Orleans is a glorious thing; you're not just cooking in some nondescript restaurant in an uninspired city that has no connection to American food history. When you cook in the Big Easy you become part of a rich culinary tradition. Louisiana and New Orleans is where American gastronomy began. Nowadays, some food journalists might dismiss New Orleans' cuisine as provincial; too rich, too stodgy, too yesterday. And at some level they correct; New Orleans has clung tenaciously to its culinary traditions. But it's precisely because New Orleans has remained connected to its roots that it continues to be one of the world's premiere food venues. Trends come and trends go, but New Orleans' food remains a constant. This isn't to say that today's chefs have not succeeded in applying modern interpretations to traditional because they have. But what about San Francisco, Las Vegas, New York and Chicago you ask? Sure, these are exceptional food towns, but none can match New Orleans' food history, tradition or reputation.

New Orleanians adore cooking and eating; it borders on religion. I've never seen people so connected to their native food. For centuries, gastronomy has been at the heart of Louisiana society and culture. New Orleans' cuisine is the delicious result of poly-cultural influences—primarily French, Spanish and African—melded together long before there was a United States of America. Each culture contributed its unique ingredients and cooking techniques, which resulted in America's first true regional cuisine.

New Orleans has time-honored culinary traditions that are followed ardently. We've all heard of the tradition of King Cakes during the Mardi Gras season, but there are other food traditions. For example, red beans and rice is often served on Monday; traditionally laundry day when housewives put on a pot of red beans since it required little attention and they could tend to their chores. Throw in onion, garlic, spices and fat back and *voila,* they had dinner. I can't imagine New Orleans' cuisine without pig flesh. Some form of porcine product in most of the traditional dishes. (This helps to explain why Louisiana ranks fourth in obesity in America, closing in on Alabama for the third spot. Mississippi is the reigning king of cellulite.) We have the Spanish to thank for this since the Conquistadors introduced the pig to North America during the mid 16th century during their conquests of Mesoamerica. The Spanish were twice in possession of New Orleans during the 18ᵗʰ-century giving them an opportunity to have a deep and lasting impact on the city's culture including its food preferences.

~~~

It wasn't until I moved to Louisiana that I'd heard of po' boys, jambalaya, gumbo or soft shell crabs. I was raised in northern Indiana where the cuisine can be fairly banal and uninspired except, that is, for the ethnic foods. I had no idea of the decadent delights that awaited me in New Orleans. It was as if I'd left a culinary backwater and walked into a veritable cornucopia of new flavor sensations. I believe that is was the exposure to this sensational world of food that sparked the desire to become a chef. I can't imagine being inspired to become a chef if I'd moved to say Kansas City or Minneapolis.

In short order I embraced fabulous new dishes such a trout amandine, bread pudding and étouffée. Probably the most eye-popping discovery was the soft shell crab. I didn't know that the entire animal could be eaten during the molting stage before a new shell forms. The first time I munched one of these crunchy crustaceans was at the River Bend Restaurant—no longer in business—located where St. Charles and Carrolton Avenues intersect. I was amazed at how delicious this deep-fried delight tasted especially with clarified butter and toasted almonds and served with remoulade sauce. I was hooked. I still am. When they're in season—April through October in the Mid-Atlantic states—I cook them at home. Soft shells are popular in the Washington, D.C. area too. I sold thousands when I owned my café.

For Hoosiers, dessert usually means fruit pies or layer cakes. In New Orleans, dessert means warm bread pudding with bourbon sauce, bananas Foster and chocolate pecan pie. I had my first taste of pecan pie at the Camellia Grill, still located at the river bend where St. Charles and Carrolton Avenues meet. It was an experience I won't soon forget. Camellia Grill has been in operation since 1946. The all-black wait staff is nattily attired in their white waist jackets and black bow ties. Serving the customers is as much theater as it is table service. The waiters dazzle diners by twirling flatware like tiny batons and singing while they work or as one waiter called it, "shucking and jiving."

Sandwich Royalty

ANY DISCUSSION ABOUT New Orleans' food is obliged to include a pair of American sandwich legends; the muffuletta (pronounced muff-uh-let-uh) and the po' boy. Both creations are authentic sandwich royalty. Other famous sandwiches just don't stand up; the Rueben, corned beef on rye, BLTs or French dips are not in the same league with muffs or po' boys. John Montagu, the Fourth Earl of Sandwich, couldn't have dreamt how popular this most elemental and delicious way of eating would become. Nor could he have known that a version of his *sandwich* would become synonymous with New Orleans' cuisine and culture. The po' boy is quintessential street food.

Muffs and po' boys are New Orleans' signature sandwiches and each has an interesting history. Take the muffuletta, for example. It originated at Central Grocery over 100 years ago. Central Grocery is located on Decatur Street and is still in operation. While its name is a mouthful, the muffuletta is truly a workingman's sandwich that was created to satisfy the Italian workers who labored in the French Market during the late 18th century. A round loaf of crusty bread is layered with Italian meats, cheeses and marinated olive salad. Central Grocery still sells them. In the heart of the French Quarter is the eponymous Napoleon House—offered as refuge for the exiled Emperor in 1821—where muffs are also sold. The Napoleon House serves them warm and they're the size of a hub cap. One is enough for four. I think they're the best in the city.

As the story goes the name *po' boy* was coined during the four-month long streetcar workers' strike of 1929. Hungry strikers were given free sandwiches from sympathetic sandwich shop owners, Clovis and Benny Martin. As the story goes, a lone striker approached the Martin's sandwich shop when someone said, "Here comes another poor boy." The name stuck, but was quickly shortened to "po' boy." The sandwich wasn't created during the strike; it just received a new name. A po' boy is a crunchy, sliced baguette filled with fried seafood, beef, ham or turkey or pretty much anything that fits. Po boys are not just stuffed loaves of bread. The key ingredient that distinguishes po' boys from other subs and sandwiches is the French bread. It's has a tender crumb or interior and a crunchy crust that crackles when you bite it. Po' boys and muffs were the original version of street food that is so popular today.

~~~

The story of how Louisiana cuisine evolved is a two-part one. Part one has to do with the Cajuns who first entered the New World as French Catholics, settling in Acadia, Canada's Nova Scotia and New Brunswick today. During the mid 18th century they were exiled by the British overlords for their religious convictions. These French Canadians had essentially three choices; leave Canada, convert to the Church of England or be executed. Beginning in the 1750s, many Acadians escaped British persecution by making their way south along the Atlantic seaboard. Many swung around to the Gulf coast where they took refuge in the alligator-infested swamps of southwest Louisiana. The word Acadian was eventually shortened to "Cajun." Deep in the swamps they lived off the land. Native species such as turtle, alligator, crawfish and game found their way from the sweet water bayous into Cajun kitchens. Combined with European spices and cooking techniques, these indigenous foods evolved into an entirely new cuisine, which eventually spread to neighboring regions of the Deep South including Alabama, Mississippi and Texas. America's first authentic cuisine was born—Cajun food.

The second half of Louisiana's food saga involves the Creole cooking that was the result of poly-cultural influences of the French, Spanish, Italian, Native Americans, Africans, Haitians and other ethnic groups. The Creole cooks, most of whom were black, cooked in the homes of the wealthy Creoles. The position of domestic cook was highly esteemed and the best paid position in the household. Domestic cooks had to learn how to cook a variety of foreign cuisines, but the developed their unique spicy, home-style method of cooking that was distinct form Cajun cooking. This is how the Creole genre of cooking was born. In doing so they unintentionally introduced common European culinary influences. Their foods tended to be richer with sauces from the French, sausages from the Germans—which inspired quintessential Louisiana sausages such as andoullie and boudin—rice and spices from the Spanish and desserts from the Italians and French. Creole cooking began in New Orleans and tended to be more sophisticated and complex than Cajun cooking—it was city cooking as opposed to country. Nowadays the lines between Cajun and Creole cooking are blurred so most people refer to both genres as Louisiana cooking.

The slave ships delivered Africans to the port of New Orleans and to its kitchens. African contributions came in the form of spices, peanuts, vegetables, legumes and various uses for tomatoes. The slaves introduced *gombo*—Americans called it okra—as a flavoring and thickening agent (because of its mucosanguineous quality) for soups and stews. The Africans might have also introduced sassafras bark, or *filé*, and bay leaf; both key ingredients in gumbo. The Choctaw Indians have also been credited with introducing filé, which they sold at the old French Market, which is still in operation. This is where the townsfolk and early restaurateurs could purchase produce, seafood, poultry, beef and pork. While the French Market is mainly a tourist attraction where vendors hawk cheap jewelry and T-shirts, customers can still buy fresh produce and pastries. Today's French Market is a shadow of its former self.

Part-Time Gigs

BEFORE I WAS promoted to pastry sous chef at the InterContinental I was only making around $4 per hour. It was hard to make ends meet even though I had only myself to support. To get by I resided in a low-income neighborhood, the Irish Channel. I bought a bike and took public transportation, but I still struggled so I was forced to take part-time jobs. I also wanted these part-time gigs so that I could acquire new skills from other pastry cooks and chefs. I put myself on a career fast track so I could learn a lot in a short amount of time. I sought out the best places to work.

<u>Four Seasons Pastry Shop</u> Before closing its doors in the late 1980s, the Four Seasons Pastry Shop was a fixture in the French Quarter since the 1960s. It was located across the street from the elegant Royal Orleans Hotel. The Four Seasons was one of the finest pastry shops in the city and offered a variety of European-style pastries and breads. The French Quarter location was the retail outlet. The production facility was located in the Upper 9th Ward, which flooded during Hurricane Katrina. I bicycled to the production facility after working my regular shift at the Royal Lafitte Hotel. I worked alone in the evenings.

It was a small operation with only a two-man daytime crew, Herman and Yan. Herman, a German immigrant, was a middle aged man and a true child of the Third Reich, literally and figuratively. Literally, because, given his age, he was a small child during Hitler's reign of terror. Figuratively, because he could be bombastic and dictatorial just like the Fuehrer. Herman was a cross between Colonel Klink and Herman Göring, he could be ditzy and affable at times, but he also had a vicious mean streak. Yan, a Czech immigrant, was Herman's assistant. Yan and I jokingly called Herman the "Nasty Nazi."

Consistent with perception of the Aryan personality profile, Herman reveled in *schadenfreude*—deriving pleasure from pain and misery that befalls others. Herman enjoyed tormenting Yan and took particular delight when ridiculing him about the Prague Spring—when the Soviet Army invaded Czechoslovakia in 1968. Herman found amusement in the anemic Czech resistance to the Russian tanks as they rolled through the capital effectively unabated. Herman intentionally insulted Yan when I was present. Yan felt that had to endure Herman's gibes because he was new to America and considered himself fortunate to have a job. While Herman's verbal assaults were intolerable, his behavior got worse, much worse.

I reported for work one afternoon to find Yan in the backyard behind the pastry shop. He was sitting on a milk crate with his face buried in his hands. When he looked up I could see that eyes were flushed from crying. He told me that Herman had just slapped him a few minutes earlier. I was speechless, but not completely surprised. I knew Herman had a vicious temper, but I didn't think that he was capable of this. I decided to quit right then and there. I told Yan to call me about a pastry position that had recently become available at the Columns Hotel in the Garden District. A few weeks later I began dating a cocktail waitress who worked at the Columns. She told me that they had recently hired a Czech pastry cook. Since there weren't too many Czech pastry cooks in New Orleans, I knew that it had to be Yan. I was glad that he escaped from Herman's concentration camp.

Le Ruth's Located in Algiers—directly across the Mississippi from New Orleans—Le Ruth's was one of the finest restaurants in the city during the 1970s and 1980s. The owner, Chef Warren Le Ruth, was one of the premier chefs in the city and appeared in an early episode of PBS's *Great Chefs of New Orleans* series. He specialized in Continental cuisine. I wanted to work for him to learn about *haute cuisine*. This was before I decided to redirect my career to specialize in pastries. I worked at Le

Ruth's while I worked full-time at Stephen and Martin's on St. Charles Ave. I took the Algiers ferry and bicycled to Le Ruth's. It was worth taking the job just to ride the Algiers Ferry to cross the river. While there was always some drunk on the ferry that served as entertainment, I enjoyed the ride across the Big Muddy.

I admired and respected Chef Le Ruth, but I didn't care for his sons, Lee and Larry, both of whom were younger than me. They were accomplished cooks and far better than me at that point in my career. I didn't like them because they were insolent brats who disrespected their father. I wasn't raised that way so I loathed that sort of conduct. Chef Le Ruth was a kind-hearted, gentle man who found it difficult to stand up to his sons' strong personalities.

I didn't quit because I couldn't handle the work. Actually, I was a quick study and learned whatever they threw at me. I was allowed to work the line shortly after being hired. Allowing me to work the line was testament to my progress and ability. In a top notch kitchen you're not allowed to work the line until the chef decides you're ready.

The Le Ruth's were an extremely organized family. I'd often wondered whether they suffered from OCD. Every slotted spoon, every whisk, every pair of tongs had to be hung on its assigned hook. It was a misdemeanor if any tool was hung on the wrong hook. I got the efficiency part because organization in a busy kitchen is paramount, but their style was way out of my comfort zone. It was too stifling for my personality. I can't obsess over small stuff like that. I need to have fun when I cook at home or at work. My personality is more suited to a kitchen like Chez Helene's where everyone's chattering away and the radio is dialed to a soul station. I just didn't fit in at Le Ruth's. It wasn't anyone's fault; I just didn't fit into their system. It was my problem not theirs—it was Chef Le Ruth's kitchen. In the restaurant business you either get on board or get out. I thanked Chef Le Ruth for giving me the opportunity to work there. He understood and told me that few cooks fit in his kitchen. I could believe that.

There was one thing I did appreciate about Chef Le Ruth's kitchen—the chef's table. The "chef's table" is a European tradition where the head chef dines with the underling chefs and their sous chefs early in the evening before dinner service. This is a vestige from the *chefs de partie* system practiced in the old country. There is even a pecking order at the chef's table where the highest ranking chefs sit nearest the head chef who is prominently seated at the head of the table. In a large hotel there might be a dozen or more chefs dining together. The purpose of the chef's table is to promote *esprit de corps*. When men break bread together they are more likely to perform as a cohesive unit. At Le Ruth's we were only four since it was such a small restaurant. Still, I found this tradition remarkable since it's a part of culinary history; a commodity unknown to American cooks at the time. However, no amount of food or tradition would endear me to Chef Le Ruth's incorrigible sons. I was elated over the prospect of never setting eyes on the pair again.

Chez Helene As I discuss in the chapter entitled *Soul Kitchen*, for a short period of time I worked at Chez Helene, one of the most famous restaurants in New Orleans over the last half of the 20th century. The owner, Chef Austin Leslie, specialized in Creole cuisine. For two months I worked twelve-hours per week without pay. This sounds crazy I know, but I decided to put myself on the learning fast track when I was a novice cook. The only way to increase your cooking skills and food knowledge is by working with as many good cooks as you can until you gain the skills you need to become an accomplished pro yourself. There's no short cut to success in the culinary world. Culinary schools are a good starting point, but nothing replaces work experience. It was a mutually beneficial arrangement—Austin got free labor and I learned a ton. Sadly, Austin Leslie passed away from health problems related to diabetes that were exacerbated as a result of Hurricane Katrina. All that's remains of Chez Helene is its concrete foundation. Austin was given a jazz funeral; a high honor bestowed on few New Orleanians. This was testament to how much Austin was loved and respected by the community. New Orleans remembers it own.

The City That Care Forgot

New Orleans was a wonderful place to learn to become a professional cook. I didn't move there to become a cook, but that's what I became by the time I left there and headed back North. Living in New Orleans can profoundly change a person. The culture and society of New Orleans is like none other on the planet earth. If you live there for any length of time, you will be a different person from that which you were when you arrived. You will fall in love with the city on the river. You'll become enamored of the sights, the sounds, its people. You'll grow to love the grand oaks in Audubon and City Parks, Mardi Gras parades, street cars rides, hurricane parties and fried oyster po' boys. You'll become attached to New Orleanians. Unlike the residents of other cities in the Deep South, New Orleanians welcome and embrace outsiders. For a short time in the 1970s I lived in Atlanta where it soon became clear that I was not welcome there primarily because I was a "Yankee." Georgians harbor a deep-seated resentment for losing the Civil War, which I find odd since they began the conflict in the first place. If they chose to, New Orleanians would have every right to dislike outsiders, especially northerners since the city was captured and occupied by Union forces until the conflict was settled in 1865.

I even found race relations in New Orleans to be different, almost nonexistent at times. There isn't the racial tension that exists in other major American cities, Chicago, Washington, D.C., New York, Dallas or Detroit. I had numerous friends who were black. We socialized together. They invited me to house parties where I was often the only white person there. If it didn't matter to them, it didn't matter to me. As I said earlier, I lived in the Irish Channel, an all-black neighborhood, and never had one bit of trouble.

I'm not suggesting that New Orleans isn't without its faults, because it has plenty. It has one of the worst public school systems in the country. I've lived in cleaner cities and the streets are pocked with pot holes. Perennially, it ranks as one of the most dangerous cities in the U.S. In recent years it's often difficult to distinguish between the criminals and the NOPD, well known for its nepotism, brutality and corruption. Louisiana and New Orleans in particular, has redefined political corruption. Former Governor, Edwin Edwards, 84, has just completed a 10-year sentence in a federal penitentiary for racketeering riverboat licenses. No matter, his friends and cronies all honored him at a welcome home roast at the Monteleone Hotel in the French Quarter in 2011. New Orleanians can reason any event into a party—impending hurricanes and corrupt politicians. That's another reason why I love the Big Easy.

Chapter Four

Blackened Blues

"Never lift more than you can eat."

Miss Piggy

OFTEN REFERRED TO as the "Jewel of the South," New Orleans is famous for its music and food. The musical legends are legion: Fats Domino, Louis Armstrong, Robert Parker, Ernie Kado, Professor Longhair . . . More recently, prodigious talents like the Neville and Marsalis Brothers, Harry Connick Jr., Dr. John, Allan Toussaint, Champion Jack Dupree and James Booker have kept New Orleans in the lime light.

New Orleans has also produced some exceptional culinary talent. A few are nationally renowned—Paul Prudhomme, Cajun cuisine impresario and owner of K-Paul's Louisiana Kitchen, Susan Spicer of Bayona and mega-celebrity Emeril Lagasse who is actually a Massachusetts ex-pat. And there are countless numbers of lesser known chefs who have contributed to New Orleans cuisine to make the city a gastronomic legend.

Make no mistake, Chef Paul Prudhomme introduced Louisiana cooking to the world and altered the manner in which the public viewed American chefs. Through his celebrity he convinced would-be chefs nationwide that Americans can cook as well as the Europeans who had dominated the culinary scene in America up until that point. This was a tectonic shift in commercial gastronomy in America. Prudhomme's reputation spread far and wide. The wealthy were clamoring for his services; he took his show on the road and did catering jobs in New York, San Francisco and elsewhere. The man is a master of his cuisine. Craig Claiborne wrote, "Paul Prudhomme is the greatest practitioner of Louisiana cooking."

No longer regarded as provincial swamp food cooked by backwoods recluses, Cajun cooking took America by storm. It became wildly popular. Chefs from California to New York scrambled to learn how to cook this *new* cuisine, but few got it right. They didn't understand that they couldn't just buy a Cajun cookbook and think they could replicate dishes that took generations to perfect. Cajun cooking isn't elegant or sophisticated, but it's a nuanced cuisine that explodes with flavor. Unless you're from southwest Louisiana, you have to be taught how to cook Louisiana food by Louisiana cooks. That's what I did; there are no shortcuts. And Prudhomme spawned the culinary revolution. It wasn't some poodle of a French chef from Manhattan or some pampered prima donna from Hollywood who ignited America's first food movement. It was a then-little known chef straight from the Louisiana bayous, Paul Prudhomme who hailed from Opelousas, Louisiana, the heart of Cajun country. Too little credit has been given to Chef Prudhomme for his contribution to American gastronomy. There were other influential chefs at the time such as Alice Waters, Jeremiah Tower and Jean Louis Palladin, but none was as influential or transformative a figure as Chef Paul Prudhomme.

Cajun Crazy

BEFORE THE CAJUN cooking craze swept the nation, I happened to be working as a rookie line cook at an upscale restaurant called Sal and Mario's or S & M as we called it. S & M was located in the heart of the Garden District on St. Charles Avenue, one of the most beautiful tree-lined boulevards in America. No longer in business, S & M was New Orleans' first high-end Creole restaurant. It was attached to a one of New Orleans' most popular hipster bars. You couldn't get into the place on a Friday or Saturday night. If you couldn't get laid there, there was little hope for you.

Paul Prudhomme popularized the *blackening* method of cooking. I doubt whether he discovered this way of cooking, but he presented it to America. Blackening is when cuts of meat or seafood are rapidly seared by the extreme heat of a red-hot cast iron skillet. Basically, two things take place during blackening; surface sugars are caramelized to the point of nearly becoming burnt and interior juices are sealed within because they don't have time to escape. Cooking takes place so rapidly, there literally is no time for juices to exude and evaporate as happens with conventional cooking methods such as roasting, grilling or sautéing. Interior marbled fat melts and cannot escape; the liquid is trapped within by the exterior crust. For the consumer this all results in an explosion of flavors.

I dreaded working weekend nights at S & M in those days because I knew that we would be cooking massive amounts of blackened steaks and fish, primarily redfish. I could look forward to inhaling smoke and getting my hands roasted for an entire shift. All the hair on the back of my hands got singed off. When the oil-laden fish fillet or meat is dropped into the smoking hot skillet, there is literally an explosion of smoke and flame. It only takes a few close encounters with heat this intense to learn the necessary safety precaution—use a long pair of tongs. The problem is that during the heat of dinner rush you don't have time to use tongs, you just use your bare hand.

We might have served two or three hundred covers, one fourth of them would be blackened redfish, keeping four skillets belching out smoke and flames throughout the dinner rush. While the blackening craze began with redfish, it soon grew to include beefsteaks, pork chops, scallops, shrimp and catfish. If it could be blackened, it was. Blackened redfish appeared on the menus of nearly every restaurant in New Orleans. So much redfish was being harvested from the Gulf, the wild stocks were being depleted to the point that marine biologists were concerned that the species could not recover. The federal government stepped in and invoked strict harvest limits and threatened a complete moratorium if the redfish didn't recover in sufficient numbers. Without government intervention the red fish might not have recovered as a sustainable species as has happened to the Atlantic cod. The situation was slowly becoming an environmental catastrophe. But within a few years the redfish did bounce back, thanks largely to the catch limits.

When the rest of the country caught the Cajun cooking fever, blackened foods and other Cajun dishes appeared on menus everywhere. Overnight America had thousands of "Cajun" chefs. The problem was that most of them had no idea how to cook Louisiana food. These wannabes thought all they needed to do to make a food item "blackened" was to dredge it in fiery spices and sauté it in hot oil until the food was, well, blackened. This is absolutely wrong. Blackening doesn't mean scorching food until it's an unrecognizable chunk of charred animal protein. These shoemakers also thought that if it was a Cajun dish that it must be tongue-scorching hot so they would heavy up on the cayenne and black pepper. They presumed, correctly, that their customers wouldn't know the difference and few outside of Louisiana did.

To blacken any food correctly, the item is coated with spices and butter or dipped in a mixture of vegetable oil, clarified butter and/or olive oil with spices and herbs. Once coated with this mixture, the excess oil is allowed to drain off the food item, which is gently laid into an extremely hot cast iron skillet. *Gently* is the operative word here. The last thing you want to do is to toss the food item into the skillet. This will result in a back splash of flaming hot oil and scorch anyone who happens to be nearby. Blackening became all the rage in New Orleans. People were even trying to blacken food in their homes, which proved to be an unwise decision for most. A friend of mine tried to blacken a steak at home, which resulted in him having to repaint his kitchen. I can imagine that the NOFD was called out on many occasions during the height of the blackening craze.

Oh No She Didn't

WHEN I FIRST began cooking at S & M I learned quite a bit, primarily because I knew so little to begin with, but as time passed I increasingly learned less to the point where my experience became diminishing returns. Even the head chef taught me so little after six months or so it wasn't worth remaining at S & M. The head chef, some guy named Brian Delafose, was basically a glorified line cook who had worked his way up from pot washer. This is laudable, but when a cook, any cook, has only worked at only one property his culinary knowledge is restricted to the cuisine at that particular establishment. This was the case with Delafose; his culinary knowledge was limited only to the cuisine at S & M. This is not a good situation for a rookie cook who needs to learn as much as possible in a short time period.

I disliked working at S & M for other reasons. Delafose was a weak chef who had little control over the service staff. A head chef must have control over the servers; otherwise they run amuck creating headaches for the kitchen staff, especially the cooks. The kitchen is the chef's domain and he must maintain authority at all times. Delafose allowed the waiters to argue with the cooks, verbally assault each other or even swipe each other's orders. He also showed favoritism to a few pet waitresses, one being his girl friend, Annette DuBrûlée. The coquettish Annette resented being a waitress; she felt that serving others was beneath her. But she had little choice; she had no other marketable skills that any of us knew about. Annette refused to do any of the tasks that waiters are required to do before lunch or dinner service—set tables, vacuum the dining room, polish flatware and clean wine glasses. While her coworkers readied the dining room for dinner service, Annette sat on her ass filing her nails, chomping gum and reading tabloids. It was only when the owner of S & M, Mr. Delafose Sr. (father to the Brian), dropped by that she sprang into action. Nobody's fool, the buxom Annette beguiled the old man with her feminine charms. It was obvious that he was smitten.

Before anyone else could, she'd promptly fetch the Mr. Delafose Sr. his usual Sazerac. She made sure to display her cleavage and offer a toothy grin as she set the drink in front of him. The little vixen shamelessly ingratiated herself with the old fool in order to enhance her standing in the restaurant. The other employees loathed the little wench, but they were powerless to do anything about her. Everyone blamed Delafose for the disharmony in the back and front of the house. I learned from this experience. You learn from the failings of an incompetent boss. You learn what not to do when you're in a position of authority.

An ugly incident occurred one evening during the dinner rush that illustrates my earlier point about Delafose's utter lack of control. It was a busy Saturday night and, as usual, the waiters were bickering over food orders. A black waiter, named Oscar, and Annette got into a dispute over an entrée. Annette called the Oscar a "nigger" and, true to form, Delafose turned a blind eye to the incident. He pretended to not hear the epithet and walked out the kitchen. Oscar was powerless to do anything and had to accept the insult. He knew that he would find no justice by pleading to Delafose for justice. At first I was incredulous over what had happened, but I could deny it, happen it had and right before my eyes. I don't know why I was so shocked; I was in the deepest part of Deep South and in a state where the institution of slavery was most heinous because sugar cane was the most laborious of all crops. Appalled at what happened, I began chastising Annette in front of the other employees. Predictably, the vamp complained bitterly to Delafose who demanded that I apologize to his girl friend. It was then that I took the opportunity to give Delafose two week's notice. I can stomach a lot and I usually mind my own business, but this was too much. I couldn't work in a kitchen where racism was tolerated. Jim Crow was ancient history. By the time I left S & M Delafose had a situation on his hands. When the other blacks heard about the incident with Oscar and Annette they became irritated with Delafose. Who could blame them? They began a work slowdown. They would do their jobs alright, but as slow as possible. They would feign illness or manufacture some other bogus reason to justify their slow pace. Delafose couldn't fire the whole lot, they comprised over half the kitchen staff. I learned from Delafose's mistakes. You can learn what not to do when in a position of authority. He was a deplorable boss.

Mentors and Misfits

The Mentors

THERE WAS AN upside to working at Sal & Mario's. I got the chance to work with a couple of great cooks who taught me a ton about cooking. One guy was a New Orleans' native whose name was Big Mike. I never knew his last name. He never attended a chef school. It didn't matter; he was a superb cook. Big Mike taught me sauce-making, how to work the fry station and some classic New Orleans dishes. He was a far better cook than Delafose and everyone knew it, including Delafose himself. He implored Big Mike to show him how to cook certain dishes. Big Mike was reluctant to teach Delafose anything for two reasons; he wasn't hired to teach Delafose and he disrespected the man. Chefs aren't obliged to share their culinary knowledge, but they usually will if there is mutual respect.

S & M was only a part-time gig for Big Mike. His full-time job was saucier at Antoine's where he is currently the executive chef. To be the head chef at Antoine's is a big deal in a city with more than its share of superb restaurants. During my visit to New Orleans in 2009, I stopped by Antoine's to pay my respects to Big Mike. We reminisced and he gave me the skinny on the post-Katrina food scene in the city. In a smallish city like New Orleans the chef community is tight; chefs know who's working where and which restaurants are struggling. Big Mike told me that a lot of chefs lost their restaurants during Hurricane Katrina. Many left and never returned while others refused to leave and salvaged what they could to reopen their restaurants. I expressed my appreciation to Big Mike for all he'd taught me at S & M. It's important not to forget your mentors; they help to mold you into a professional. It was good seeing Big Mike again. As I walked back to my hotel it occurred to me that I still didn't get his last name. I'll guess I'll always remember him as Big Mike.

My other mentor at S & M also took me under his wing and taught me a fair amount about Louisiana cooking. He went by the name of Baptiste. I often refer to cooks as *old school*, but this guy was the real deal. Baptiste was a broken down, old quadroon man who'd been cooking since the late 1940s. Evidence of a punishing life was etched in his grizzled face. Basptiste seemed to harbor a deep sadness. The man rarely smiled. Growing up in Southwest Louisiana during the Jim Crow era could not have been pleasant for old Baptiste. We all respected him as a man and for his wealth of culinary knowledge, especially Cajun cuisine. He knew more about cooking than any of the other cooks, certainly me. I don't believe he'd ever had any formal schooling. I'm sure he was illiterate. A deep scar that ran down one side of Baptiste's face. Rumor had it that he received the gash during a dice game in the French Quarter. Rumor also had it that the old man was mighty fond of drink and that he was a hellion in his younger days. Maybe there was something to the alcohol rumor because Baptiste would go on an occasional bender, not reporting to work for days.

Baptiste spoke French and English with a heavy Cajun accent. I recall when he taught me how to deep fry shrimp. I already knew how to fry shrimp from chef school, but out of respect I feigned ignorance. He went through the whole breading procedure then dropped the shrimp into the fryer. Then he launched into what seemed to be a familiar tutorial.

"First you coat dee swimp *comme ça*. Den juss drop 'em in dee oil." He demonstrated the breading procedure with a handful of shrimp and dropped them into the deep-fat fryer. The shrimp sank to the bottom, but bobbed to the surface within a few minutes. The old man just stared at the fryer as the other shrimp reappeared one by one. I imagined that he'd repeated this same frying procedure a thousand times before. I wondered why he wound up in New Orleans. Maybe he moved here to cook for wealthy whites in the Garden District. Or maybe he cooked the riverboats or one of the French Quarter gumbo shops. Who knew? None of us knew anything about Baptiste's personal life. He was somewhat of an enigma.

"When dee swimps be done dey float like dis here, *cher*. Den you pull dee swimp out da greeze *tout suite*," intoned Baptiste as he plucked a couple shrimps from the hot grease with his bare fingers. I was stunned. *Why did he do that*, I thought. He could have just as easily lifted the shrimp out of the grease with a pair of tongs or by raising the fry basket. Obviously, he used his fingers purely for effect.

"*Regardez mon ami*, how da swimp be nice, gold color, yeah."
Apparently, the expression on my face revealed my utter astonishment.

"What dee matter, *cher*? You look like you seen one dem ghost, yeah.
The old man guffawed and muttered to himself in French.

"You tink dis little bit greeze too hot for Baptiste old fingas? No *mon ami*, deeze fingas been in plenty tings moe hotter den dis here greeze."

Dipping his bare finger in the hot oil seemed like a crazy thing to do, but Baptiste was making a statement. He wanted me to know that I could never be the cook he was. If that's what he was thinking, he was spot on. If dipping my fingers in smoking hot oil was a rite of passage, then I'd never make the grade and that was fine with me. I also think that by shocking me, he derived some perverted entertainment at some level. I did notice a rare smile come over his face as he pulled out the shrimp. At least one of us got something out of the cooking lesson. I really liked the old guy though. As weird as the lesson was, Baptiste was taking the time to teach me something he thought I should know and I appreciated that.

The Misfits

ALTHOUGH I LIKED working with Big Mike and Baptiste, they were only part-timers, which meant I had to spend more time cooking with Delafose and his cadre of mediocre cooks. It wasn't just that the others weren't very good cooks; a few of them were downright frightening. There was this Haitian cook named Toussaint. He reminded me of Snoop Dogg, lanky and boney with gold-capped teeth. Toussaint chattered constantly, mostly gibberish to himself. While I rarely got into a conversation with Toussaint, on one occasion he told me about the Tonton Macoutes—the murderous paramilitary thugs who kept the brutal dictator François "Papa Doc" Duvalier in power. Toussaint described the reign of terror under the Tonton Macoutes and how members of his own family disappeared for reasons unknown to him. When Toussaint was a boy, his father was pulled from their home in the middle of the night never to be seen again. Toussaint never did reveal what infraction his father committed. Although I felt sorry Toussaint childhood experiences, it didn't overcome my unease when he was around.

It didn't take long to for me realize that Toussaint had mental issues. He wasn't quite yell-at-pigeons-on-a-park-bench-crazy, but his nonsensical ramblings and odd behavior made me feel uneasy. I was afraid that some little thing could set him off and who knew what he was capable of doing? This wouldn't be a problem in most work settings, but we were in a commercial kitchen where there are plenty of lethal weapons at hand. I even imagined the headlines in the *Times Picayune* newspaper, **COOK WHACKS COWORKER with CLEAVER.** Everyone stayed clear of the Haitian. Even old Baptiste warned me to stay out of his path, "Dat boy ain't right, no. He be tetched in da head, yeah," Baptiste warned. "He believe in voodoo and gris gris and all dat religion mumbo jumbo. Dat boy ain't right, no."

Then one day Toussaint just up and disappeared. It's not unusual for restaurant people to just quit without notice. They vanish for one reason or another and you rarely see them again. The hospitality industry is very transient, which is why you don't bother to make friends at work. It was the same when I was in Nam, I didn't develop a relationships. What was the point, I reasoned, they might not be around tomorrow. When you work in restaurants and hotels you do your job and you mind your own business. You punch in, you punch out. But Toussaint's sudden disappearance was extraordinary because he'd been working at S & M for a few years, a fairly lengthy employment by industry standards. He'd even taken up with Velvette, a middle-aged negress who worked the salad station. She was a portly, toothless hag who reminded me of Aunt Jemima. She even wore the head scarf. Velvette was a jolly woman and when she laughed her gold-capped teeth would sparkle. The restaurant world seems to spawn the unlikeliest personal relationships.

Someone said they heard that Toussaint had been murdered. They said that they saw on the news that a black man who fit Toussaint's description was fished out of the Mississippi near Algiers Point. No one knew much about Toussaint's personal life. If Velvette knew anything she didn't let on. Like a lot of cooks in New Orleans, Toussaint was just another drifter. He never mentioned a family or mentioned his past. I was never told what actually happened to him and I didn't inquire. Velvette was morose for weeks afterwards. She never mentioned Toussaint's name again. The jovial spirit had gone out of her. I hoped that he hadn't come to a bad end, but to be honest I was glad Toussaint was gone.

~~~

I especially didn't like working with a particular evening cook named Vladimir; who we called Vlad for short. How does a Russian immigrant wind up cooking in New Orleans? Vlad illustrates an inescapable truth about the world of cooking—that it attracts people from across the social and national spectra. People come to the world of cooking for a variety of reasons; some cook because they have no other marketable skills. These are usually the ones who remain line prep cooks or mediocre line cooks. They don't aspire to become a skilled chef. Others become cooks because they love it; cooking is their calling. This was not the case with Vlad. He was content to do only enough to keep his job.

When we were introduced, Vlad pointed his clenched fists directly at my face to display the tattoos on the tops of his fingers. Why he thought this necessary I have no idea. The letters on one hand read *V-L-A-D*, the other read *C-O-O-K*. The body art looked like the *artist* was on an acid trip when he inscribed them onto Vlad's finger; the letters were slightly crooked and different sizes. I thought the whole fist display thing was pretty bizarre, but I guess he was making a statement about some self-perceived bravado. Vlad was the spitting image of Luca Brasi from the *Godfather* movie. Luca was the Guido who made a heart-felt speech in Don Corleone's office on Connie's wedding day. Vlad even wore a buzz cut like Luca.

This was one Ruskie who really made me nervous. He struck me as the kind of guy who enjoyed mutilating cats when he was a kid. He made it clear that he was not the kind of a guy you crossed. Vlad was a dark, brooding personality. He kept to himself. After working with Vlad for a few weeks I discovered that he had a serious alcohol problem. As we were breaking down the kitchen one night late one I entered into the walk-in refrigerator where I caught Vlad gulping vodka straight from the bottle. I didn't even know that he had it stashed in the walk-in. Alcoholics are clever at hiding hooch. He glared at me as if to say, *One word about this and I'll kick your ass.* If he was concerned about me telling anyone, he needn't have been. I didn't want any trouble. In the restaurant business you come across all sorts of screwed up people and they're not always paragons of virtue. You learn to deal with it because it's the nature of the business. You mind your own business and there's no problem. It's the natural order of things in the cooking world.

I never mentioned the incident to anyone. Vlad's alcohol problem wasn't any of my business. As long as his drinking on the job didn't endanger me, I couldn't have cared less. Vlad was typical of many New Orleans cooks with a substance abuse habit. It's not as if cooks in other cities don't suffer with these sorts of personal demons, it's just that it's ratcheted up to another level in the Crescent City. Cooks with addictions can usually get some kind of work, enough to eke out a living and support their habit. They float from kitchen to kitchen. Cooks like Vlad eventually wind up slinging hash in some shithole diner making burgers and fries. No professional cook wants to do that kind of dead end work.

~~~

Here's an example just how pervasive alcoholism is in the hospitality industry. If you're ever creeping around the French Quarter around six o'clock in the morning you might notice groups of men and women gathered at the hotel loading docks. They're there to get hired as *day laborers*. These are the people who wash pots, clean kitchens and empty the garbage in the swanky hotels we stay at. In many urban centers, day laborers are part of the invisible under belly of the hotel business. Day laborers are to the hotel business in New Orleans what the Funk Brothers (the legendary studio musicians who were essential to Motown's success) were to Motown—invisible and underappreciated, yet critical to the success the operation.

Day laborers get paid cash at the end of the day for that day's work. Many of these wretched people are incorrigible alcoholics. After work they make a beeline for some sleazy bar at the back of the Quarter or on Tchoupitoulas Street near the river and drink up most of what they earned that day, saving just enough to sleep in a flop house. One guy I knew slept in a chair because it was only five bucks per night, half the price of a bed. Their only hot meal of the day is often the one they get in the hotels' employee cafeterias. These are broken people who hold little hope of turning their lives around. The day laborers I came to know seemed resigned to their plight. When they depart this earth they're usually buried at Potter's Field.

The health care plans offered by many companies include treatment benefits for employees who suffer from a substance abuse. Not so in the hospitality industry. While hotels might offer some pathetic health insurance benefit, the restaurants routinely offer far less or nothing at all. Employees receive an hourly wage and that's about it. Sure, employees are guaranteed workers' compensation if they get injured on-the-job, but little more. If an employee has an addiction problem, he's pretty much on his own. He won't receive professional treatment for his illness. It's not part of the "health insurance" plan, if there is one. If he misses work a few times he's 86'd. The industry appears to be stuck in a time warp when employers could exploit workers with impunity. There is little incentive for employees to remain at a particular property for any length of time. They are made to feel as chattel whose job is to clean, cook and serve. This is one of the reasons why the industry is so transient in nature. Employees need to be valued as human beings. The hospitality industry just doesn't get that.

Adieu Nouvelle Orleans

AFTER ABOUT SIX months at S & M I recognized that it was time for me to leave. I could barely disguise my disdain for Delafose and continuing to work at S & M was reaping diminished educational returns. I was learning less and less as the weeks dragged on. When you're in the training phase of a culinary career you have absorb as much as possible from the best chefs in a short amount of time. When you're not learning new culinary skills, cooking techniques and recipes, you're not advancing your career. You have to go where the learning is. But it's important to be selective about who to learn from. Like any craft, you'll only be as good as your mentors. Even though the chef school stipulated that I was to remain at S & M for one full year, I requested an early transfer to another property. I had to get out of S & M. But I didn't want to go to another restaurant. I didn't feel that I was cut out for line cooking. It was too stressful, hot and dangerous and I didn't like working with some of the alcoholics and lunatics that wind up as line cooks. I was attracted to pastries so I requested that the school arrange an apprenticeship in a hotel pastry shop. I was granted a transfer to the Royal Lafitte Hotel, located in the French Quarter. I went from the frying pan into the fire. My new boss would be a Limey named Oswald Crookshank who would turn out to be one of the vilest people with whom I would ever have the displeasure of working. The maxim rang true, "Be careful what you wish for; you just might get it."

Chapter Five

Soul Kitchen

"New Orleans' food is as delicious as the less criminal forms of sin."

Mark Twain

TO LARGE DEGREE, New Orleans is defined by its restaurants. A handful are fabled establishments that have sated diners since the 19th-century with Creole *haute cuisine* while others have made their mark by serving traditional New Orleans' fare like red beans, gumbos and po boys. Early in my culinary career I worked at one such restaurant, a very special one. Its name was Chez Helene. She wasn't much to look at. Chez Helene was a white clapboard structure in a nondescript residential neighborhood. I think it was someone's home before it was converted into a restaurant. All that remains of the place now is its concrete foundation. The venerable place fell victim to the wrecking ball shortly after Hurricane Katrina.

Chez Helene was located a short distance from the French Quarter, in the Tremé neighborhood. Tremé remains an important center of the city's African-American and Creole culture, especially the modern brass band tradition. This neighborhood and its residents have been portrayed in recent years on the very successful HBO series *Tremé*. Chez Helene was a family-owned operation—a black family affair. To my knowledge, I was the only white person to have ever worked there. The white chef establishment in New Orleans in the early 1980s dismissed Chez Helene as an unsophisticated soul food shack; a black eatery catering to a black clientele in a black neighborhood. Truth be told, they were pretty much right, but what they failed to recognize was that Chez Helene was quickly becoming one of the most popular restaurants in the city. The restaurant became so popular that it was the inspiration for the 1987 sitcom *Frank's Place*.

Big Funk

HIS NAME WAS Austin Leslie, but those of us who worked in his kitchen called him Big Funk; "Big" because he was built like a Saints linebacker and "Funk" because the man had soul. Austin Leslie was the owner and chef of Chez Helene restaurant, which he'd taken over from his aunt Helene in 1975. Austin's culinary prowess took the business to heights of which aunt Helene could have only dreamt. Celebrities visiting New Orleans routinely stopped at Chez Helene. It didn't matter that Austin hadn't attended a formal culinary school or didn't know the first thing about refined *haute cuisine*, the man could flat out cook New Orleans fare. His kitchen wasn't much to look at either. It was cramped, four was a crowd. He worked with same dilapidated equipment he inherited from his aunt. But his kitchen had that one intangible that very few commercial kitchens possess. Big Funk's kitchen had a thing called soul. And his food was made with a feeling that a blues musician could understand. Austin's food was foremost about the flavor. If a customer wanted a heart-healthy meal, Chez Helene was not the place. If a customer wanted petite portions and food that was artfully presented Chez Helene was also not the place. Big Funk's signature dishes were Big Easy staples—fried chicken, bell pepper stuffed with shrimp and ground beef, shrimp and smoked sausage gumbo, crawfish *étouffée* and shrimp Creole. Everything was garnished with persillade, finely chopped parsley and garlic. It's a small attention to detail, but persillade adds another flavor dimension to most savory dishes.

Food people who are knowledgeable about New Orleans' cuisine credit Austin with redefining a genre of cuisine—Creole-Soul. New Orleans gave us Creole cuisine, and the Deep South gave us soul food, Big Funk married the two. It was like merging two musical genres, say country and blues. It doesn't matter which one came first, what was important was the fact that they was a crossover. This was facilitated by the fact that both cuisines, like both genres of music, share common roots in—African and European culinary influences.

I worked at Chez Helene as a part-timer while I had a full-time job Sal and Mario's. As previously mentioned, S & M was an upscale restaurant in the haughty Garden District. I worked at Chez Helene for no pay. I know this sounds crazy, but at that time I was a novice cook who was desperate to learn authentic New Orleans cuisine. When you're a rookie cook it is imperative to learn from other skilled cooks who are willing to teach you. Big Funk was the man; he was one of the premier black chefs in the city. I got the better end of the deal because, since I was a novice, my contribution to the kitchen was limited to doing menial task such as prepping vegetables, frying pork chops and cutting up chickens. Big Funk didn't need to tutor me, he wanted to tutor me. I think he took me on as an apprentice because he felt compelled to pass on his culinary knowledge to an eager student. And I'm sure, like all good chefs, he had a healthy ego that became inflated when he had the opportunity to show off his culinary skills. I learned an enormous amount in the few months I worked there. I learned cooking fundamentals and how to make classic New Orleans dishes. But I learned more than just cooking. I learned how to operate a professional kitchen; organization and purchasing, work assignments and staffing. I felt comfortable working at Chez Helene. I liked the relaxed, laid back atmosphere. Like any creative endeavor, I realized that cooks perform best when they're having fun. The radio was always dialed to a soul station and there was constant chatter about the things cooks love to talk about; women, sports and cooking.

I got to know Big Funk like few other white cooks in New Orleans ever did. He wanted everyone to have fun in his kitchen, but he expected us to get the job done too. It was his kitchen and there was no doubt that he was in charge, but he also cared about the people who worked with him. I remember the morning I sliced my finger nearly to the bone. Austin took me to the emergency room and paid the medical bills. He wasn't obligated to do that. No other chef would have done that for me. Big Funk was an unconventional chef. He never wore a *toque blanc*, the traditional stove-pipe chef's hat. Instead, he sported his trademark sea captain's cap and gold necklaces.

One Bad Ass Chef

AUSTIN LESLIE WAS not a man to be trifled with. Apparently, the beer delivery man wasn't aware of this. I recall one morning when the beer man got cheeky with Big Funk. I'm not sure exactly how it started, but it seems the deliveryman didn't drop the beer where Austin told him. I happened upon the brouhaha when I walked from the kitchen into the adjoining lounge to get a coke. The lounge was a dank, dark room that reeked of cigarette smoke and stale beer. As I entered the dimly lit room I saw the deliveryman, also a black man, standing at the door behind his empty dolly.

"Next time you put the fuckin' beer where I say to put," Austin barked. "This is my restaurant. Got dat?" I knew Austin had a temper, but I'd never seen it unleashed like this before. The deliveryman muttered a barely audible response. I thought, *oh oh, this is not good.*

"What mother fucker?" You got somethin' else to say to me? Bring yur punk ass over here and tell me again soze I can hear ya. I'll knock you out bitch."

For a quick second the deliveryman considered Austin's invitation, but thought better of it. He wisely backed through the door with his dolly in tow. The screen door slapped shut behind him. It was at that point I decided that I didn't need that coke that badly so I crept back into the kitchen unnoticed. I don't think Austin even knew that I had just witnessed the brouhaha. From the kitchen, the other cooks and I could hear Big Funk continue his rant to an empty lounge.

"This is my damn restaurant. No jive nigger gonna tell me shit. I'll whoop his black ass next time he come here."

After he completely vented his anger he returned to the kitchen to continue cooking the pot of gumbo he'd begun prior to the beer man's arrival. No one said a word. We all pretended to be lost in our work. No one wanted any part of that situation. That morning I witnessed a side of professional cooking that I had not anticipated. It wasn't something that I was used to at work as a hospital administrator in my previous career. And my chef instructors at culinary school somehow failed to mention that I should be prepared for on-the-job brawls.

After witnessing the lounge incident, it was clear that Chef Austin was not a man to be trifled with. I understood that it behooved me to follow Austin's instructions explicitly. It didn't matter that he wasn't paying me; he was the chef, and I was a lowly apprentice. That was the natural order of things. I now knew that Austin could morph into a real bad ass whenever he needed to and I did not want any part of that shit. He was a real-life "Top Chef" not like those pussies on TV who rant and rave for effect.

Soul Gumbo

ANOTHER MEMORABLE MOMENT at Chez Helene is one that I have come to think of as my "chicken-cutting episode." Austin told me to cut up a case of fryers—to be used for fried chicken orders. When you cut up chicken—also called "jointing"—the carcass should be cut at the joints producing eight pieces per bird or ten pieces if you halve the breasts. Austin asked me if I knew how to joint fryers and I told him that I did. I lied. I told him that because I didn't want to appear to be a complete culinary idiot. Besides, I thought, *it can't be that difficult to cut up a fryer.* I'd seen my mother do this at home dozens of times. I proceeded to mangle about half the case of chickens before Austin discovered what I'd done. He exploded.

"What are you doing? You told me that you knew how to joint a chicken. Now how I'm gonna to serve this here chicken you done cut up all wrong? Damn Chuck! That ain't what I told you to do." he barked in his baritone voice.

"But I just . . ." he cut me off in mid sentence.

"But nothing, Chuck! That ain't what I told you to do. I told you to joint 'em not butcher 'em. Now gwan home and when you want to listen to what I tell ya come on back."

Big Funk was really pissed off. He only called me by my first name when he was annoyed with me, most of the time he jokingly called me "white boy". This didn't offend me because I knew that he didn't mean mean it as a racial epithet. It was more a term of endearment. There was no racial tension at Chez Helene, at least none that was palpable. I felt comfortable there. I developed an affinity for Austin and his family. As for the chicken thing it might seem like no big deal, but Chez Helene was famous for its fried chicken. Any chef or restaurateur will tell you that food must be consistent even if it's something as simple as fried chicken. Chez Helene's customers expected the pieces of fried chicken to be the same size as the previous time they had it. I should have known better from my KFC days.

As he was chastising me I knew better than to answer back. The rest of the kitchen staff conveniently disappeared during the tirade. They weren't about to come to my rescue. Undoubtedly, they had incurred Big Funk's wrath themselves and wanted no part of this situation. Nope, the token white boy was completely on his own. As a form of punishment, Austin wouldn't let me touch a fryer for an entire week, which was, effectively, a demotion. It was his way of instilling in me the importance of food replication. He could have terminated our relationship, but he didn't do that. Instead, Austin took the time to teach me a valuable cooking lesson. Most chefs wouldn't have bothered. Eventually, he softened and one day he tossed me a couple of fryers.

"Now cut 'em right this time. Cut 'em like I showed you," he warned. Now that I was back in boss man's good graces, I made sure to cut fryers correctly from then on.

The morning kitchen crew consisted of Uncle Sydney, Helene's brother, Glenn, Austin's nephew, a pot washer and me. Uncle Syd's main jobs were to make the corn bread muffins, cook the collard greens and the red beans and smoked sausage. He was old and sluggish; I think Austin kept him on because he was family and to keep the old man active. Glenn's jobs were to make the stuffed bell peppers, cook the étouffée sauce and work the fry station. One of the reasons Austin's fried chicken was so good was because he fried the chicken in lard. It's not the most healthful cooking fat, but lard imparts a flavor unlike any other cooking fat. There was no mystery to Chez Helene's fried chicken. It was seasoned with salt and white pepper and breaded in the usual manner: flour, egg wash, flour, and then deep-fried. The lard must have been the secret for his great-tasting chicken.

Gumbo had to be made every day since it was one of the most popular menu items. We made about five gallons a day. One of my primary jobs was to prepare all the ingredients for the gumbo, which included dicing celery, bell pepper and onion. In Louisiana, these vegetables are referred to as the "Holy Trinity" because they flavor just about every Cajun or Creole dish ever invented. Austin believed in doing things the old-fashioned way, even to the point of inefficiency. There wasn't a microwave in the kitchen. He scoffed at me when I suggested that a food processor could chop the vegetables for gumbo in just seconds.

"I didn't have none of those fancy gadgets when I was comin' up, no indeed. We did everything by hand. Looky here, I been cooking like this since my whole life and I don't see no sense in changing now. All them gadgets is just plain nonsense."

"Yazzah boss man, y'all knows best." I replied, mimicking how an uneducated Southern black might talk. He accepted my ribbing in the same vein I accepted his when he called me "white boy," poking fun at racial stereotypes. We had a good rapport. That's one of things I liked about working in New Orleans and Chez Helene in particular, the racial tension was almost imperceptible. How many other cities in America could a white person live in an all-black neighborhood? I did when I lived in the Irish Channel.

Oh well, so much for my attempt to modernize Chez Helene's kitchen, I thought. Austin and his family took me under their wing. They were kind and generous. Everyone took the time to share his cooking knowledge. It was like attending my own private cooking school. At Chez Helene I learned the basics of New Orleans cuisine. When I owned my own café, I reproduced the dishes I had learned there. My customers absolutely devoured them. And why not, they were Austin's dishes. My café was renowned as one of the most authentic New Orleans-style restaurants in the Washington, D.C. metro area.

Making the gumbo was a two-man job at Chez Helene. I did all the grunt work and Austin cooked it. He added the spices and made the seasoning adjustments. He wanted his soup to be consistent. Customers expect a certain dish to taste the same every time they go to a particular restaurant no matter how much time has elapsed between visits. There are two ways to ensure consistency; follow a recipe—something most professional cooks loathe—or designate certain cooks to make particular dishes. At Chez Helene, gumbo wasn't gumbo until Big Funk said it was gumbo. He religiously added great lumps of ham fat for flavor, which, at the time, I thought was unhealthy. One day I proceeded to fish the fat out of the pot and he happened to catch me in the act.

"What you doing? Why you pulling dat ham fat out my gumbo?"

"Because it'll make it too greasy." I reasoned. By the expression on his face I knew that was the wrong answer.

"Too greasy! You don't know what you're talkin' 'bout. That fat gives soul to my gumbo. No fat, no soul, no soul, no flavor. Got it white boy? Now put dat ham fat back in da pot." he directed.

At the time I thought Austin over reacted to the ham fat thing, but many years later when I opened my own restaurant I realized that he was absolutely correct. When my reputation was on the line I often chastised my cooks for varying from the recipes and cooking methods I had established. A consistent product is just smart business.

Fin

AFTER THIRTY YEARS in business Chez Helene closed its doors in 1995. Austin attempted to take advantage of his fame and embarked on a series of failed business ventures. He even tried to open a second restaurant in the French Quarter, which also went bust after a year or so. Nothing panned out and he wound up cooking at other restaurants, such as Jacques Imo's, a currently popular café. Make no mistake: Austin Leslie's reputation put Jacques Imo's on the map in New Orleans, a city where it's difficult to distinguish yourself from the thousands of other restaurants. Where Austin Leslie cooked the public followed. It must have been painful for Austin to suffer such an ignominious end to such a remarkable career.

Tragically, Big Funk died in 2005 within weeks of Katrina striking the city. Like many Katrina victims, Austin was stranded for days in his home attic to escape the floodwaters. His situation was made even more serious because Austin suffered from severe diabetes. He was finally rescued and taken to the Convention Center where his condition deteriorated further. He was eventually evacuated to an Atlanta hospital where he died from complications from his disease. Chef Austin was honored with a jazz funeral in October 2005. This extraordinary gesture was high praise indeed for the man known as the "Godfather of Fried Chicken."

Chez Helene wasn't just another New Orleans "greazy spoon" serving pedestrian soul food. It was much more. Among the pantheon of legendary New Orleans' restaurants, Chez Helene stands out as one of the city's most notable during the second half of the 20th-century. Austin Leslie managed to master a cooking style that was unique to New Orleans. This was no easy feat. He was one in a long line of distinguished black cooks whose approach to and respect for cooking have deep cultural roots. Big Funk taught me a lot about cooking and helped to shape me as a professional cook. I'll always cherish the memories of my time at Chez Helene and be grateful for everything Big Funk taught me.

Chapter Six

Happiness Is a Warm Bun

"My wife has sex with me for only one reason. She uses me to time an egg."

Rodney Dangerfield

THERE ARE FEW things in the world of gastronomy more attractive than a tray of perfect baked goods. When I was a baker and I'd pull a sheet pan of croissants from the oven a deep sense of pride washed over me. Like a fine perfume, the scintillating aroma wafted into bakery. Croissants are the most laborious of all yeast breads. The process begins with regular yeast bread dough. Next, the time-consuming procedure of folding layers of butter between the dough must be done. This process gives croissants their flakiness. The final stages are rolling, cutting, shaping, proofing and baking. A lot of work, but it's worth it. A handsome tray of Danish or scones brings the same sense of pride and accomplishment. I know a bit about baking, I was a baker at the Lafitte Hotel in the French Quarter for an entire year early on in my culinary career. That's when I learned the fundamentals of professional baking. Although I had my sights set on becoming a pastry chef, I knew that learning to bake was a prerequisite to that goal. Any good pastry chef will agree that you have to pay your dues in the bakery before you can move on to sophisticated pastries. You need to learn how to make cookies, tarts, cakes, quiches, yeast breads, quick breads, pies and laminated products—*lamination* is the process of layering fat between thin layers of dough to obtain flakiness. Croissants are an example of laminated dough. An accomplished baker is a highly-skilled craftsman.

~~~

The history of bread goes back to Upper Paleolithic Europe, around 30,000 years ago. Early forms of bread were created about the same time modern man was painting caves in Southwestern France. Cereals and bread became a staple food during the Neolithic, around 9,000 years ago, when wheat and barley were among the first plants to be domesticated in Mesopotamia. The first bread produced was probably cooked versions of a grain-paste, made from roasted and ground cereal grains and water, and may have been developed purely by accident when water and grain flour were combined. The earliest breads were unleavened. Loaves and rolls have been found in ancient Egyptian tombs. In the British Museum's Egyptian galleries you can see actual loaves which were made and baked over 5,000 years ago. Wheat has been found in pits where human settlements flourished 7,000 years ago. Bread, both leavened and unleavened, is mentioned in the Bible numerous times. The development of leavened bread can also be traced to prehistoric times. Yeast spores are ubiquitous in nature, including on the surface of cereal grains, so any dough left to rest in a warm place will become naturally leavened.

Baking and pastry-making flourished in the Roman Empire. In about 300 BC, the pastry cook, or pastillarium, became a respected occupation in Rome. Pastries were considered a decadent taste treat and often made for special celebrations. And what ancient culture loved to celebrate more than the Romans? It seems they could reason any occasion into a party. Pastries were often cooked for large banquets, and any pastry cook who could invent new types of tasty treats was highly regarded. Around 1 AD, there were more than three hundred pastry chefs in Rome, and Cato wrote about how they created diverse foods, and flourished because of those foods. The Romans baked bread in an oven with its own chimney, and invented mills to pulverize grain into flour. Apparently, being a Roman baker was not without risks, especially if you were Julius Caesar's baker. Caesar had his baker thrown into chains for serving substandard bread. And on another occasion, according to Suetonius Tranquillus, the Roman historian, Caesar had the unfortunate baker put in irons for serving him one kind of bread and his guests with another.

Bakers and pastry chefs even have their own patron saint, Saint Honoratus or Saint Honoré. How many crafts can make this claim? Legend has it that in the year 1400 Parisian bakers established their guild in the church of Saint Honoratus and in 1659 Louis XIV decreed that on the 16th of May every baker observe the feast of Saint Honoratus. A special pastry was created in his honor, the Saint Honoré Gateaux. The French version is a base of short dough or puff pastry with a ring of pâte à choux and eight to ten profiteroles are dipped in caramel and attached at the top of the ring. With a star tube, Chantilly cream is piped in the center of the ring. The choux ring and buns are filled with liqueur-flavored pastry cream. The Italian versions—of which there are four—are essentially a large vol-au-vent filled with cake and liqueur-laced, chocolate and plain or Chantilly cream that is alternately piped in the center of the puff pastry base. The pastry cream-filled profiteroles are dipped in hot caramel and attached to the top of the wall of the vol-au-vent.

Clearly, the world of gastronomy has come a long way from the time when our ancestors in the Fertile Crescent (the modern-day countries include Iraq, Syria, Lebanon, Jordan, Palestine and Israel), often considered the cradle of civilization, began farming Neolithic founder crops about 9,000 BC. Founder crops consisted of cereals such as wheat, rye and barley and pulses (the edible seeds of various crops) such as peas, chickpeas, lentil and bitter vetch. Once regarded as only life-sustaining sustenance, food has evolved into culinary art forms and has become the subject of modern scientific investigation. Long forgotten food trends of centuries past have been replaced by modernist cuisine. However, there is one constant in cooking. No matter how much culinary trends vacillate, cooking fundamentals never do. A roux is made the same way today as it was in the 16th-century. Puff pastry is made by using the same techniques when it was invented in 1646 by French pastry cook Claudius Gele. When one masters the basics cooking techniques and culinary skills one can master any cuisine.

Little Shop of Horrors

IT WAS FIVE o'clock in the morning, the time my work shift began at the Royal Lafitte Hotel pastry shop. I worked there as an apprentice baker. As I opened the door a woman whizzed past me as she exited the shop. I recognized her. She was Wanda, the night room service waitress. Wanda wasn't much of a looker: she was fat, slovenly and pushing sixty. My immediate thought was *why is Wanda even here right now?* The answer became clear once I entered the shop. As I entered the shop I noticed

Dwayne Tolliver, my coworker, zipping up his fly. I didn't need Bill Clinton to explain the situation to me.

"Please, tell me that you did *not* just get a blowjob from that old skank," I asked Dwayne, in utter disbelief.

"Yep, shore did," Dwayne replied, with a rich country drawl. His grin said it all. Dwayne was mighty pleased with himself.

"But Wanda, of all the women in this hotel? And did you have to get sucked off here in the shop? We bake here." I couldn't believe that Dwayne had just had sex in our pastry shop. And I also couldn't believe that anyone would let room service Wanda touch their penis. Who could know where Wanda's mouth had been? I think the hotel just yanked her off the back alleys of the French Quarter because they needed a warm body as a room service waiter.

Strange things can happen in hotels during the night shift, especially in a city like New Orleans, a city known for hedonism and debauchery. On the graveyard shift in most hotels there are few supervisors around. The dregs of the hotel work force prefer to earn their living at this ungodly part of the day.

"Hey, a blowjob's a blowjob ain't it, pal? And what's the big fuckin' deal about gettin' some head here in the shop anyhow? And why do you care so much? Now c'mon get your ass in gear, we gotta get some shit done 'fore chef gets in," Dwayne commanded, terminating further discussion about what had just occurred.

Dwayne misconstrued my comment. I wasn't making a moral judgment about his romantic interlude with Wanda. Who was I to judge what consenting adults did? It was just that I didn't think our pastry shop was an appropriate place for their moment of passion, as it were. What bothered me was that the shop is where we made food for the hotel guests. Perhaps my days as a health inspector clouded my judgment. I guess I missed the "it's okay to get a blow job in a pastry shop lecture" during my training. I don't know why was so surprised at what happened; this was New Orleans after all. What puzzled me was that Dwayne couldn't comprehend why I was so shocked at his dalliance with Wanda. He responded as if I was overreacting to some very trivial matter. As my career progressed, I would learn why Dwayne found my reaction unwarranted. Eventually, I would discover that sex amongst employees is commonplace in the hospitality industry. It's absolutely pervasive. Employees don't routinely have sex in

America's restaurant kitchens—although this does happen—but it's there where they fraternize.

~~~

Becoming a chef in the early 1980s was different than it is today. Today it's a career choice made by people who have a variety of options. When I made a career transition, people became cooks because they had few other employment options. Professional cooking attracts the deviants and down-and-outers—the Dwayne Tollivers of American society, if you will. Today many people leave lucrative white collar jobs (which is precisely what I did when I changed careers) to get into mainstream cooking. This sea change has come about because public perception of professional cooking has changed. Where the public used to see cooks as life's losers, they now see professional cooking as a hip, trendy and even a sexy career path. This evolution has grown out of the absolutely astonishing explosion of food and cooking in mainstream media.

Please, Not Again!

I ASSUMED THE incident with Wanda and Dwayne was a singular event. I was wrong. A few months later I reported for work at the usual time only to discover Dwayne sprawled out on our work bench. He had a towel stuffed with ice cubes over an eye. I thought, *what is it this time?* I really did not want to hear his story, but felt obligated to ask.

"Well, I was just a-sittin' there in Pat O's (Pat O'Brien's) mindin' my own business and this dick comes behind me and sucker punches me fer no reason. Bastard knocked me clean off the stool. I think I done broke my dern back too." I'd worked with Dwayne Tolliver long enough to suspect that there was more to the story so I pressed him for details. He groaned as he rose to an elbow.

"Well, goll dang it how was I supposed to know that I was buying that dick's wife a drink? She kept makin' eyes at me all night. What was I supposed to do? Her husband whacks me and then the bouncer throws me out in the dern street. I'm never going back to Pat O's again," he intoned, as if the nightclub were in some way responsible for the mêlée. By now Dwayne's eye had swollen completely shut and turned a deep shade of purple.

"Dwayne," I said, "the chef can't see you like this. He'll have a fucking fit and you're in no shape to work." Dwayne jumped off the table to view his reflection in the door of the stainless steel refrigerator.

"Dang it, no wonder I cain't see, I look like a dang Chinaman." He gently caressed his puffy eye.

"How you gonna explain your eye to the chef?" I asked. "You need to get your ass out of here and pronto. The chef will be here any minute. I'll take care of our work today and I'll think of some bullshit story to tell him." Dwayne nodded in agreement. He grimaced from the pain in his back as he bent over to pick up his backpack.

"I owe ya one, pal," he huffed, as he hobbled through the shop door. As promised, I told Crooks some bullshit story. I said that I found Dwayne puking when I reported for work. He knew I was lying, but let it go. The next day he explained that his black eye was the result of walking into his bathroom door when he was sleep-walking. No one believed him, but he didn't care. At least he didn't get into trouble.

Dwayne Tolliver's life appeared to be a pathetic syndrome of untoward recurring events: the same stupid decisions invariably resulted in the same stupid outcomes. Unfortunately, his bad decisions weren't restricted to dealings with women; the consequences of other wrong-headed decisions reverberated in other areas of his life. For example, he often lamented about getting ripped off in minor drug deals. It didn't occur to him that when you associate with riffraff bad things are bound happen. He also complained about living in a barren apartment, devoid of furniture—all he owned was a mattress and a used black and white TV. It didn't occur to Dwayne that if he didn't spend so much money on drugs he might have been able to afford a few sticks of furniture.

Dwayne's life resembled the life of a character in *Groundhog Day*, the 1993 movie starring Bill Murray. Murray played the part of TV weatherman Phil Connors, who finds himself repeating the same day over and over again. Connor's repetitive, egregious behavior toward people produces the same unfortunate results: damaged relationships. It's only when Connors reexamines his life and priorities that he's able to break the cycle of self-destruction and cultivate healthy relationships. Connors realizes that he brought his problems upon himself. He even falls in love with Andie MacDowell's character. When I saw *Groundhog Day*, it was as if segments of Dwayne Tolliver's life were being replayed on the big screen. Dwayne was like so many that I've met throughout my culinary career:

deeply flawed people who can never seem to get their lives on track for one reason or another. I had a particular affection for Dwayne and hoped that he turned his life around. After I left the Royal Lafitte I never saw Dwayne again so I guess I'll never know.

Crooks

OF ALL THE characters I've encountered during my twenty-five year career, there was one guy in particular whom I'll never forget. He was the pastry chef at another upscale hotel in New Orleans. The Royal Lafitte. His name was Oswald Crookshank. He was from England. Crookshank had dual personalities. He could be charming one moment and the next nastier than Dick Cheney. Crookshank possessed every flaw in the human character. He was dishonest, unscrupulous, crude, unsanitary, irascible and disrespectful. Did I mention unscrupulous? He had an affinity for profanity. At times he cursed so much I actually wondered if he suffered from Tourette's syndrome.

There are two kinds of chefs in this world: those who lead by example and those who lead by the lash. Crookshank, or Crooks, as we affectionately called him, preferred the lash. It was better suited to his personality. I don't think he knew another way to manage people. I reckoned that he was probably abused and mistreated back in merry old England when he was trained as a young baker. European chefs are not known for their gentle approach to personnel motivation. Working with this guy was my Vietnam, and I've served in Vietnam. He was that bad.

We'd never know what would send him into a rage, and he was prone to mood swings. Sometimes he'd arrive at work in a foul mood, usually from having a row with his wife before he left home. He'd often warn us: "I'm in a sour mood today mates so I'm givin' you lot fair warnin'. Just do what I tells ya and there won't be no trouble 'round 'ere."

Like everyone else in the shop, I received the occasional verbal insult from Crooks. I recall one time in particular time when I'd screwed up rolling croissants—I wasn't making them in perfect crescent shapes. Crooks launched into an absolute tirade, but this time he was more aggressive than usual and his verbal attack was more vicious. As I rolled the croissants he stood right next to me and began screaming. The veins on his neck bulged. His mouth was within inches of my ear. I could feel his warm, tobacco-tainted breath on the side of my face. It was all I could do to ignore him and continue working as if he weren't there. This only served to infuriate him further. As he began walking away, he wheeled around and unleashed another fusillade of insults.

"I'm the chef 'ere. You're just a fuckin' wanker. You're nuffin but a lowly apprentice. Understand me mate?"

"Sure, whatever you say Sir Loin," I answered, in an insolent tone. Of course, I knew that would drive him over the edge. It was entertaining to watch him come undone. He sidled next to me again and resumed his rant. Spittle sprayed from his mouth as he screamed at me.

"I don't want to hear no more from you, cheeky bastard! I'm warning you for the last time. You fuckin' Americans don't when to keep your mouths shut. It ain't that way back in England. We minded the chef, we did. What you need is a good throttlin'."

Crooks had the very unsanitary habit of smoking cigarettes while he prepared food. I recall one incident when he was mixing a forty-quart mixing bowl of chocolate mousse with an unwashed arm, while a cigarette dangled from his mouth. He did this so often we became inured to it, but this time I noticed the ashes dropping directly into the mousse. I had to say something.

"Chef you just dropped your ashes in the . . ."

"Bollocks! I know what I done. You think I'm blind? Mind your own fuckin' business! Besides, them little bit of ashes ain't gonna 'urt no one. Trust me mate, they won't even notice. Probably add some flavor, I expect." Crooks chortled as he continued mixing the mousse.

There's one thing you have to understand about Crooks: the pastry shop was his little fiefdom and he wasn't about to allow some impudent rookie cook challenge his authority. He was trained in the traditional European *chefs de cuisine* system (a skill-based hierarchical system with the executive chef at the top) where the chef is the undisputed master. In this system the chef is never challenged. Americans have difficulty following orders blindly so there was a constant clash of cultures between the Europeans and the Americans, especially when we began to supplant them in the 1980s. The Europeans knew their era of culinary dominance in the U.S. was coming to an end and they did not like it.

In a previous occupation I was a restaurant inspector, so I was fairly well versed in food sanitation practices and I was pretty sure that cigarette ash in food was a health code violation. I couldn't believe what I had just seen. I didn't even know how to react. My coworkers were completely unfazed by the spectacle. Apparently, as long as they weren't eating any of that mousse it didn't matter to them.

As time worn on I developed a visceral dislike for Crooks and considered quitting, but reconsidered. I refused to allow him to chase me out. Besides, there was no guarantee that I wouldn't encounter another Crooks-type at the next property. As unbearable as Crooks was, I had to admit that I was learning a lot. I was just a rookie and needed to learn as much as I could, even if it meant having to endure him. Acquiring more advanced culinary skills was the only way I would improve my lot. When you're a raw rookie you're not in a position to choose your mentors. You have to learn from anyone who will take you on. I was also learning from the other guys in the shop: the sous chef, Dwayne and even the other apprentice, Troy, who was attending chef school with me. Even he was more advanced than I was. It's just something you have to go through. Every decent chef I've ever known has had to pay dues.

Crooks the Black-Hearted

FOR CROOKS TO be a total dick was one thing, but I discovered that he was also a cheat. I can tolerate a lot, but not dishonesty. It was discovered that Crooks was complicit in a scheme to ensure that his then-apprentice would be awarded first place in a culinary competition. Although I was not working in Crooks' shop yet, I was a contestant in the same competition. Thanks largely to Crooks I was cheated out of first place and was awarded second place behind Crooks' protégé, a So-Cal transplant named Troy.

A professional culinary competition is an official contestant where food art or show pieces are entered for judging by highly-trained chefs. The entries are rated according to specific criteria: craftsmanship, originality, degree of difficulty, etc. One criterion is that the showpiece must be constructed with edible media. The rules allow for minimal use of inedible material, which must be used for structural purposes only. There are separate classes for apprentices and experienced chefs. The American Culinary Federation (ACF), the national governing body whose basic mission is to advance the art of cooking in America, sponsors these competitions, and supplies the chef judges.

The ACF competition in which I was robbed was held in Atlanta while I was working at another restaurant. Troy also entered the contest.

He made a gorgeous showpiece—at least we thought he'd made it. It was a beautifully painted parrot inside of a white sugar cage that protected the bird. The judges couldn't physically examine the parrot. If they had they would have discovered that the parrot wasn't made from sugar at all. It was made of plaster, a clear violation of the rules.

My showpiece was a pastillage (also called gum paste) lighthouse complete with blue icing to resemble the ocean and sugar boulders at its base to represent a rocky coastline. I'd worked hard on my showpiece to give it extraordinary detail. A small team of apprentices, including Troy and me, traveled to Atlanta with our showpieces for a regional competition. We were accompanied by Mark Fitch, one of our instructors from chef school in New Orleans. When the big moment of judgment arrived, Troy won first place and I was awarded second. I wasn't happy about losing, but accepted it and congratulated Troy on his victory.

Then something unexpected happened. By sheer accident Troy's showpiece was accidentally knocked over and completely destroyed. The sugar cage was in pieces and the parrot was exposed. Unfortunately for Troy, chef Fitch happened to be there and began helping Troy collect the pieces off the floor. When he picked up the parrot he realized that it was too heavy to have been made from sugar. With a key, he scratched the surface to taste the white, powdery interior. This confirmed his suspicion that the bird was made from plaster. It was too late to do anything about the judging, since the show was over and the judges had left the hall. Officially I got the blue ribbon, second place.

Troy immediately confessed to what he'd done and that Crooks was complicit in the plot. The entire time I worked with Crooks he never mentioned the incident. I'm sure he wanted to forget it. He never apologized, and I don't believe he felt any compunction for his role in the gastro-crime. That incident served as a window into Crooks' deeply flawed personality.

Et Tu Crooks?

JACQUES COUSTEAU, THE iconic explorer, ecologist, scientist and filmmaker, has always been one my heroes. He was speaking at Tulane University and I had to be there. This was a once-in-a-lifetime opportunity and I wasn't going to miss it. But I had a problem. He was speaking during the afternoon when I was scheduled to work. No problem, I'd just call in sick from work so I could make the Cousteau lecture. I didn't miss work unless it was for a good reason, but this was Cousteau and he was a good reason.

As he walked onto the stage Dr. Cousteau was greeted with a standing ovation. He clasped his hands and waved them above his head in a triumphant gesture as he paraded around the stage like a rock star. He spoke about ocean ecology and global pollution. He discussed water pollution, the environmental risks of aquaculture and overfishing our oceans. He talked about global warming and climate change long before these terms were popularized. It was a great speech and it was worth missing work to hear it.

The next morning I was cooking myself breakfast in the main kitchen when I heard a voice behind me.

"So, how did you like Cousteau?" I didn't need to turn around to see who it was. I recognized the voice. It was Yves, the executive sous chef. Judging by the tone of his voice he was pissed. Hoping he would go away, I ignored him and kept frying my ham and eggs. He didn't go away. Yves raised his voice to nearly a scream.

"So, you were seek yesterday, huh? But not so seek to listen to Cousteau? Geet out of my keetchen!"

"But, chef what about my ham and—"

"Geet out God damneet! *Maintenant!*" His face turned red and his eyes bulged. As I scurried toward the door I could hear him swearing at me in French. I don't know what he said, but it couldn't have been flattering.

I realized what had happened. I'd made the mistake of telling one of my coworkers that I was going to the Cousteau lecture. Obviously, the Judas ratted me out to Yves. I was banished from the kitchen for weeks. I had to stay out of sight until Yves calmed down. He had a long memory. I never discovered who threw me under the bus. I don't care how much trouble it caused me, it was worth it hear one to the greatest scientists in modern history. I'd do it all over again regardless of the consequences.

~~~

Crooks never did mend his ways. He remained irascible and vile until the very day I left to take a job at the InterContinental Hotel. I'm sure he was just as glad to see me leave as I was to get out of his shop. To him I was a royal pain in the ass because I wouldn't just take his insults lying down. There was no love lost between us. The last time I saw Crooks was at the Westin Hotel located on Canal St., where he was the pastry chef at the time. I'd heard he left the Royal Lafitte, but I didn't know where he had gone. Crooks hurt his back and his executive chef asked my executive chef at the InterContinental to lend him a pastry cook to fill in for Crooks. I got picked.

I'd been filling in at the Westin for a week or so when I happened to run into Crooks near the executive chef's office. He'd come by to collect his paycheck. We hadn't seen each other for several years and were surprised by the chance encounter. It felt uncomfortable because of our tumultuous relationship at the Lafitte.

"What you doing' 'ere mate, we 'ard up for pasty cooks or summit?" He chuckled at his own lame joke. I didn't respond for a few seconds. My silence was meant to inform him that I was no longer his apprentice.

"No Oswald. I'm here because you can't work. I'm replacing you until you return." The expression on his face said it all. He was shocked that I was now capable of doing his job. In his wildest dreams he never thought that I could replace him.

"Crikey, mate you're doin' what? You're fillin' for me? Bollocks! Fucking 'ell, I never would 'ave thought that a cheek like you could do my job."

I cut him off in mid-sentence. "Well I guess you're the only one who feels that way. I've been here for a week now and I'm doing everything you were before you hurt your back. And your chef likes my work, so I'll be here until you come back."

Crooks was speechless. This was the first time I'd seen him at a loss for words. He couldn't come to grips with the fact that I was now skilled enough to replace him. It was only a few years earlier that he was screaming at me for the slightest infraction. My skills had improved a lot since those early days. Of all the pastry cooks in New Orleans, I was probably the last one he wanted to fill in for him. For some reason he felt compelled to apologize for his unforgivable conduct at the Lafitte. He launched into an apology of sorts.

"Listen mate, no 'ard feelings for what I done when we was at the Laffite. What I mean is, me being the chef and all I 'ad to run the shop like I seen fit. It weren't nuffin personal, mate."

"Forget about it Oswald."

"I ain't such a bad bloke, really I ain't. It's just that—"

"I said forget it Oswald. I gotta go. I need to get back to the shop. I've got two wedding cakes to get ready."

Our brief encounter would have been easier for Crooks had I disclosed the resentment I harbored toward him for the way he treated me in the past. If I'd done that, he could have felt justified his reprehensible behavior at the Royal Lafitte. He might have reasoned that I'd deserved his insults all along. I wasn't about to let him off that easily. I supposed that he actually felt a twinge of guilt after our brief exchange. I didn't think he was capable of feeling compunction for any personal transgression. He remained planted in front of the office as I sauntered back to the pastry shop—*his* pastry shop. I never saw Crooks again. The last I heard was that he'd returned to England. I guess there is such a thing as professional justice.

Chapter Seven

Oh Chef! My Chef!

"I love Thanksgiving turkey; it's the only time I see natural breasts in LA."

Arnold Schwarzenegger

AFTER I SERVED my time at the Royal Lafitte Hotel I was obligated to move on to another property in order to fulfill my chef school's academic requirement of working one year each at three different properties. After the Lafitte, and a few part-time gigs, I had acquired enough skills to advance to a more challenging position and work under a more experienced pastry chef. There was only one pastry chef in New Orleans who I wanted to work with. His name was Gilles Waché, who was arguably the best in the city, making him one of the best in North America at the time. He was the pastry chef at the InterContinental Hotel located in the Central Business District of New Orleans. I couldn't get away from the Royal Lafitte fast enough. I'd had it with Crookshank and I hungered the opportunity to be trained by someone of Waché's caliber.

Since I was still in school, I applied for a pastry apprentice position. I had to get this job, but just submitting an application didn't guarantee that I'd get the job; I had to massage the process. At that time the InterContinental was a brand new property and wasn't opened yet. I knew there were dozens of applicants for only a few openings in the pastry shop and my application would just get tossed in the pile with the others. I couldn't allow that to happen. My plan was to show chef Waché how badly I wanted that job. I would do this through persistence. I stopped by the shop twice a week to ask if he would hire me. Each time he told me the same thing in his broken English, "No, I hab job, come back." And so it went for a month or so. It was always the same, "No, I no hab job, come back." I wouldn't allow myself to get discouraged. I wasn't giving up until he hired me or told me that the position had been filled.

Chef Waché finally relented. I might have worn him down, but then again, did I? I've often wondered. He might have wanted to hire me all along, but wanted to see how much I really wanted to work under him. Chef Waché came from the old school where cooking was a craft that took many years to master. Chefs from his generation expect you to show that you will be a serious student if they agree to take you on. It's sort of a game they play. He knows a lot and he knows he knows a lot and he isn't about to share a career's worth of knowledge with just anyone off the street. You had to show him that you were hungry. He could afford to be picky because he had a stack of applications to choose from. I also knew that most of the other candidates were better qualified than I. I think the game changer was my persistence.

You might be wondering why I so desperate to work with Chef Waché? Was he some sort of pastry deity? Well, yeah, pretty much. He was the best pastry chef in a city full of good pastry chefs. Learning my craft from Chef Waché would be like learning to play blues harmonica from Little Walter Horton. You know that you'll never be as good as he is; you just hope some of his magic rubs off. I knew that if I could hang with him for a few years, my career would be solid. I could master enough skills to work pretty much wherever I wanted and even be pastry chef of my own shop someday. This all came true. I later moved to Washington, D.C. to take the job of pastry sous chef at the renowned Willard hotel. Thanks to Waché's tutelage, there wasn't much that my new boss could teach me. I worked at the Willard for two years and resigned because I wasn't getting along with the pastry chef. As an enticement to get me to stay with the chain, I was offered the pastry chef job at the then-new InterContinental in Atlanta. I declined and went out on my own.

Pâtissier

THE CHEF LEARNED his craft within the traditional European *chef de cuisine* system—a hierarchical pyramid system—where young apprentices are essentially indentured servants and they have to work their way through the system to become chefs. Apprentices often had to work long hours for little or no pay. If this sounds as if this is a theme out of a

Dickens' novel that's because it very well could have been. Sometimes these lads were physically abused by their mentors. They might be cuffed about the head for some infraction in the kitchen. If a lad failed at academics, he would most likely be thrust into a trade. If a boy chose to be a chef he would serve an apprenticeship in hotel, a privately-owned restaurant, bakery or pastry shop. He would probably live on premises. The large hotels usually provided dormitories. In a private enterprise, a boy's *patrone* would be responsible for his training, care and supervision—a sort of surrogate parent who, effectively, adopted a boy. Of course, the boy's family had to agree to the arrangement.

Since I was still enrolled in chef school, I had to hire in at the InterContinental as an apprentice, which meant that my wage was predetermined. I was paid $4.50 per hour, up from the $3.50 I earned at the Royal Lafitte. There was a contract between the property and my culinary program. The deal was that if a property would hire an apprentice cook at a lower than market pay rate, the property had to guarantee employment for one year. It was a good deal for the property since they would get a motivated employee at a bargain price.

Being an apprentice means you have to do all the grungy work that no one else wants to do. One of the jobs that everyone loathed was filling sorbet glasses for banquets. I hated this job. I would have rather had a root canal than fill sorbet glasses. I had to fill hundreds of glasses with a large pastry bag and star tip (or nozzle). Of course, this had to be done in a freaking walk-in freezer that was set at about 10ºF. It's a sloppy job that I had to do with my bare hands. My hands would get so cold the only way I knew I had fingers was because I could see them. Somebody had to do this shit! But I didn't mind as long as long as I continued to work under Waché. My pastry skills were improving dramatically. Gilles Waché was the polar opposite of Crookshank. He taught by example, not by screaming like a maniac.

~~~

After my final year as an apprentice cook I satisfied the culinary school requirements and I graduated from the program I was promoted to second cook then first cook the following year. The difference between the two positions is mastering more challenging skills and increased responsibility for shop operation. Pay raises came with promotions, which enabled me to move out of the Irish Channel to the Garden District section of New Orleans where I was promptly burglarized. Within a month of moving into my new digs burglars broke in and ripped off my stereo system, TV and jewelry. How ironic, after living in an all black neighborhood for five years with no problems, I moved to a more affluent part of the city and got burglarized within weeks.

Eventually, I got promoted to the sous chef position and was put on salary. My promotion was made possible because the sous chef resigned. I was elated to see that jerk leave. He was a graduate of the Culinary Institute of America which he thought entitled him act superior to the rest of us. He thought he was God's gift to the pastry world, but was far from it. And the way he resigned was shameful. He only gave Chef Waché the minimum two weeks' notice. I know that's the customary amount of time, but you don't leave your mentor in a lurch like that. Waché taught that ingrate everything he knew about pastries and he repaid him like that. Oh well, at least it paved the way for me to become the sous chef. I was ready for the job anyway.

Being assistant pastry chef might not sound like a big deal, but it really was. I was working at one of the top-rated hotels in North America, in one of the premier food cities in the Western hemisphere. Even though I wasn't as seasoned as he might have liked, Chef Waché didn't give me the promotion because of my good looks; I busted my ass to get it. I'd worked hundreds of hours for no pay just so I could learn my craft.

From the first I was always eager to learn new skills. If the chef was doing something I didn't know, I would work with him after my regular shift. Off the clock, I would observe him as he worked, take notes and fetch tools like an operating room nurse. I was a dutiful subaltern. I worked with him so often I began to anticipate what tool he needed and deliver it, unbidden. This sounds like I was trying to suck up to him, conduct not entirely beneath me, but these old school guys will take the time to teach you if you show them that you're eager to learn. Chef was kind of my personal tutor. This is the best way to advance your career. Having one-on-one mentoring from a master chef is better than any degree from any culinary school anywhere.

He taught me chocolate work, specialty cakes and how to work with edible media—such as *pastillage* (also called gum paste), pulled sugar, marzipan . . . Chef taught me pastry fundamentals such as how to temper couverture, which is premium coating chocolate with a high percentage of cocoa butter (32-39 percent) and liquor (more than 70 percent). This is a very exacting and delicate procedure of heating-cooling-reheating chocolate, which requires a special thermometer for the uninitiated. But by working with him so often I learned how to temper just by dabbing a bit of the melted chocolate to my lip in order to sense the precise temperature. This can only be done with many hours of practice, but the results are worth it. If couverture is tempered correctly, it has a beautiful luster and snaps when bitten. If this tempering process is done incorrectly the chocolate presents a splotchy surface called fat or sugar bloom when it cools. It didn't matter what chef Waché was doing; if it was a skill I didn't know I was there.

My eagerness to learn created some friction between the sous chef and me. I couldn't have cared less. I wasn't there to be his friend. I was there to learn a craft and begin and continue a career. My after-hours lessons paid off. My skill level increased to the point where Chef Waché began to assign me more challenging tasks such as decorating wedding cakes. This was huge. He wouldn't have entrusted me with this unless he had confidence in me. He didn't bother to ask his lazy sous chef because he didn't have the skills.

~~~

Chef Waché had an unwavering respect for classic desserts no matter the country of origin. Here's an example—a painful one for me at the time—of how he introduced me to the concept of classic desserts. When I was still a pastry cook I thought it might be fun to show the chef my creative side so I suggested that I replace the filling of a classic dessert. I asked the chef if I could change the filling of a *Paris Brest Gateaux* from classic hazelnut filling to a chocolate filling. (This dessert is named in honor of the famous 1,200k Paris-Brest-Paris bicycle race. Its shape is a circular tube that's supposed to represent a bicycle tire. It's made of *pate choux* and *must* be filled with hazelnut-flavored pastry cream *only*.) As soon as I asked him if I could use the chocolate filling, he stopped what he was doing, turned toward me and just glared. Words weren't necessary; I got it that he disapproved of my suggestion.

His mostly bald head turned a rose color and the arteries on his neck bulged. (For a second I imagined that Napoleon might have looked like this when he was about to scream at someone.) Oh shit, this is not good, I thought. I pretty much knew what was coming next so I braced myself.

"No, God damn eet, if you shonge zee feeling eets no more a *Paris Brest*," the little Frenchman barked, his voice rising.

"You American, you always want shonge tings. Shonge zeece, shonge zat. No respect for zee old way," he yelped, as he sent his spatula flying across the marble counter top.

"But chef I was just gonna . . . ," I defended, but he wouldn't allow it.

"*Arrêt*! Don't say somesing more," he warned, as he raised his hand to stop to indicate that the conversation was over.

I thought it was wise to keep my mouth shut; I just nodded in agreement. I could only stand there like a whipped dog. I had to let him chew my ass out. It was his shop and that was that. We returned to our work. He resumed making chocolate truffles while I finished making the hazelnut, not chocolate, Paris-Brest. He muttered to himself in French for a few minutes more. I didn't need a translator to understand what he was pissed off. He wouldn't speak to me for the remainder of the shift. I got it; you don't modify the classics. I just didn't think he needed to launch into a Code Red to make his point. I had to allow him to chastise me and couldn't respond in any way. Waché was trained in the rigid European system in which you never, ever challenge the chef. Even if the chef is wrong, he's right. His authority reigns supreme. This is why American cooks often refer to the French head chefs as the "Bull Frogs."

I got his point about classic desserts. You do not alter them. If you modify the tail fins on a '57 Chevy what do you have? I don't know, but it's not a '57 Chevy. It's the same with classic desserts. As my career progressed I realized that the chef was absolutely correct. Classic dishes are classics for a reason; they celebrate significant people, places or events. Renowned chef José Andrés crystallized the importance of culinary tradition in an interview with mega-celebrity chef Eric Rippert when he said, "You cannot cook *avant-garde* cuisine without respecting and understanding culinary tradition." To paraphrase, you cannot know where you are going in gastronomy if you don't know where you've been.

Half-Baked Baker

BAKERS ARE A peculiar breed. They lead a semi-solitary existence living at the fringe of society. Bakers seem to feel comfortable to make their living in the shadows when the rest of the world is sound asleep. I've worked with many bakers over the course of my career, but none as challenging as Radcliffe Smyth II. He was my coworker and the baker at the InterContinental Hotel in New Orleans. He was a big man, easily tipping the scales at three-hundred pounds. Radcliffe could be both acid-tongued and amiable. He could be annoyingly verbose and pedantic. He wasn't demonstrably asocial yet it was clear that he was uncomfortable around people. Probably a good thing when you're occupation requires you to be alone for prolonged periods of time.

Being a hotel baker was difficult for Radcliffe. Professional baking is a respected craft. It's the kind of job that requires a modicum of culinary and organizational skills, qualities sorely lacking in Radcliffe's personality. Hotel bakers must get all their work done before well before the restaurants open for breakfast. To accomplish this, a baker needs to be efficient with his time. There was little about Radcliffe that was efficient. Countless times I had to help him finish his work so he could punch out on time. I had to make sure he left work on time. I was the pastry sous chef, and technically Radcliffe's boss, so I was responsible for his performance. If he didn't get his work done I'd hear about if from the chef. Fair or not, the sous chef is responsible to make sure that everyone else gets their work done.

My take on Radcliffe was that he was the ne'er-do-well son of a highfalutin New England family. His father was an international financier and sister was a law professor at some Ivy League university. He had every advantage growing up; private schools, maids, cars. He'd never struggled. So how does a guy from an elitist family wind up in a dead end job in New Orleans hotel? Radcliffe was living proof that the world of cooking attracts an unlikely assortment of characters.

Radcliffe made it clear that he considered himself intellectually superior to the rest of us in the shop, which made him all the more insufferable. He was a victim of own his own obnoxiousness. He became an object of derision. He'd annoy otherwise indifferent people by making condescending or surly comments purely for effect. Radcliffe seemed to derive pleasure in provoking a response, even a negative one. Even the lowly banquet waiters—considered by most to be one of the lowliest positions in a hotel—slung personal insults at him. When they arrived at the shop to collect breakfast pastries for catering events they couldn't resist an opportunity to attack Radcliffe. They might say, "Radcliffe, you so fat if you wear a Malcolm X t-shirt a helicopter will land on yo' big ass." Darnell, a black waiter, was especially brutal on the baker. One morning he said, "Radcliffe, you so fat when you back-up yo' pager starts beepin'."

Radcliffe suffered from a chronic case of garrulousness. After being virtually alone for most of the night, he was starved for attention so he would attempt to chat-up anyone who would oblige him. Here's an example one morning's conversation.

"Chuck," Radcliffe asked, as he rolled triangles of dough into croissants with his short, pudgy fingers, "Did you know that I have a second career? Well, it's more of an avocation really." Radcliffe loved to start random conversations first thing in the morning when I was still half asleep.

"No, I didn't know that Rad and I'm not sure I want to know, but I have a feeling you're gonna tell me anyway," I replied, as I began preparing my desserts for the hotel's restaurants.

"Please do not address me as Rad," he requested. "I've asked you this repeatedly. My given name is Radcliffe."

"Sure whatever tubby."

"Anyway, I dabble in phrenology," Radcliffe revealed, wagging a raw croissant at me as if he were conducting a lecture. At that moment his ill-fitting spectacles slid to downward to the tip of his nose and when he pushed them to their proper position he left a trail of flour on the top of his nose. This happened daily.

"You mean you feel the bumps on peoples' heads so you can figure out something about them."

"That's the basic premise, a layperson's way of describing the science of phrenology," Radcliffe intoned, as he finished arranging the croissants on the tray.

"And you plan to do what exactly with your new-found talent?" I asked.

"Well, I haven't really had a chance to practice on anyone and I was going to ask you if you would allow me to . . ."

"To practice on me, right."

"Yes, that is if you don't mind in the name of science."

"Are you outta of your freakin' mind?" I barked, "I'm not lettin' your doughy, fat fingers touch my head."

At that point I walked out of the bakery cutting off any further conversation on the subject. Ignoring Radcliffe was the only sure way to put a stop to his incessant blathering. Since I refused to talk to Radcliffe, he turned his attention to Lightnin', our black pot washer. Lightnin's real name was Wilson. I gave him that nickname because he worked at a glacial pace. I borrowed the nickname from the 1950s sitcom *Amos 'N Andy*. Lightnin' was the name of the show's slow, dim-witted janitor. I know it was discourteous, but the name fit perfectly and Wilson didn't seem to mind.

"Good morning Lightnin', my good man. May I ask you a question?" Radcliffe asked. Without waiting for Lightnin's consent, he continued.

"Which JFK assassination conspiracy do you embrace?" Radcliffe inquired as Lightnin' was filling the pot sink with hot water.

"Assassa what?" Lightnin' responded.

"I didn't say *assassa* Wilson. I asked you who do you think killed JFK?" Radcliffe sniffed.

"Yeah, I knows who kilt him. It was dat dude who shot him from da uh, uh . . . da *greazy nolt*." Lightnin' had the charming habit of using malapropisms. He couldn't be bothered to probe his mind for the precise word or phrase he needed to express himself so he'd pluck out the first utterance that sounded similar to what he wanted to say. In this particular instance *greazy nolt* was phonetically close enough to *grassy knoll*.

"Ha, I can't believe that you're so dumb Wilson," Radcliffe said nastily. "It's not *greazy nolt* it's grassy . . . oh never mind. What's the point? I give up." Radcliffe was becoming aggravated in his another useless attempt to have a serious conversation with Lightnin'. This happened routinely.

"Why don't you let Lightnin' be?" I interjected. "You know he doesn't know what you're talkin' about. You know he didn't even finish high school." Occasionally I had to step in and shield Lightnin' from Radcliffe who was perfectly capable of being an arrogant prick. Just then Lightnin' pointed at the window that looked out on to St. Charles Avenue. He brought our attention to a violent summer shower.

"Dam, look at dat *tarantula* rain," Lightnin' remarked.

"It's not a *ta-ran-tu-la* rain Wilson, it's a *tor-ren-tial* rain," Radcliffe scolded and guffawed as shook his head disapprovingly.

"A *ta-ran-tu-la* is a type of arachnid Wilson. "Do you know what an *a-rach-nid* is?"

"Look snow flake," Lightnin' snapped angrily. Radcliffe had gone too far. He'd infuriated the normally nonchalant Lighnin'. "Why don't you stop flappin' yo' fat lips you fat mother fucker and kiss my black . . . ?" Lightnin' stopped in mid-reply when he noticed the chef had arrived. The chef disapproved of idle chatter in the shop. The chef preferred that the shop operate with quiet efficiency. I was glad the chef was there. It forced Radcliffe to shut his pie hole and stop pestering Lightnin' and me.

Besides being a chronic aggravation, Radcliffe presented other problems for the shop. Occasionally, he would just vanish. He'd go missing for two or three days at a time. We had no idea where he'd gone. We knew little about Radcliffe's personal life. He didn't really discuss it. He didn't mention having any friends. Like most bakers, he was somewhat of a recluse in the outside world, preferring to keep his own company. We did know that he didn't have a home phone. His mother might call asking if we knew where he was. I had to speak with her because the chef spoke English with marginal proficiency. Radcliffe's mother spoke with a pronounced upper crust New England accent befitting her social class. She sounded like the female version of FDR. Eventually, Radcliffe surfaced spewing some cockamamie story that a personal emergency demanded his abrupt disappearance. Nobody bought it. We never discovered Radcliffe's whereabouts. Lightnin' took pleasure in accusing him of getting involved in some kinky sex adventure,

"I knows where you been. You been bangin' some blow up dolls in yo' apartment, ain't it? You a freak, you fat cracker." Radcliffe never responded to Lightnin's taunts suggesting that there might have been a glimmer of truth in the allegations. I didn't really want to know. Normally going AWOL was grounds for automatic dismissal, but the chef was reluctant to axe him. Hotel bakers don't grow on trees, even ham-handed buffoons like Radcliffe Smythe II.

As my culinary career in New Orleans came to a finish I realized that there was a singular advantage to have worked with deeply flawed personalities like Radcliffe, Dwayne, Crooks, Vlad, Toussaint and Herman the German. I was grateful that I was not like them. Associating with misfits whose lives are virtual train-wrecks makes you feel pretty good about your own life by contrast. I came to view my occupation as a kind of real-life *Jerry Springer Show* where my coworkers' shocking lives were on display for me to observe and learn from. Working with these characters was a sort of bizarre theater and I had a front row seat. You get to know a lot about a person when you're cooped up in a kitchen with them for forty hours a week. They weren't dangerous people, well, except for Vlad. There were just being who they were and that was the disconcerting part. I understood why they were cooks. They could function in few other occupations. They had no other marketable skills. Why do so many oddballs seem to wind up as cooks or bakers? They probably asked the same question about me.

Hotel Perks

WHEN WAS HIRED at the InterContinental I had no idea that certain perks came with the job. Other than the fact that I was working under a top notch pastry chef in the person of Chef Waché, I originally considered my job to be an unremarkable position in a hotel pastry shop. I couldn't have been more wrong. Working at the InterContinental had benefits that went beyond learning a trade and the employee benefits package. There were intangible benefits that weren't explained during the new employee orientation lecture.

Smoking Lounge

ONE OF THE perks I enjoyed the most was that I could smoke pot at work. Yes, that's what I said, I smoked pot at work! Before I was promoted to pastry sous chef I worked the evening shift, which I did for two years. I worked alone so no one else was privy to my extracurricular activity. Some nights I was busy with banquets or had to do a lot of *mise en place*—prep work for the daytime crew. But there were many nights I had little to do. These were my *Reefer Madness* nights. This was in the early 1980s, one of the heavy pot-smoking periods of my life; college was the other. Once I got my work done, I could relax by lighting up a joint in my smoking lounge—the walk-in refrigerator. It was the perfect place; the walk-in was off limits to other employees. It was in a secluded area and the odor didn't linger because air was cooled and conditioned. And on certain nights before I punched out, I would make myself a few mixed drinks. A pastry shop needs to have an assortment of booze on hand for making desserts and sorbets—white and dark rums, gin, vodka, whiskey and bourbon. All

I needed was some mixers and I got those from room service. I was partial to rum and tonics with lime. Occasionally, I over indulged. One night I collided with a car. I was on my bike. The car won.

Paying It Forward

DURING MY TIME at the InterContinental I was involved with an event that would change me as a person. This event was one of the most rewarding times of my life and probably wouldn't have happed if not for the kind assistance of the InterContinental Hotel. The hotel management helped make it possible by allowing me time off to do interviews for radio and TV. Here's the story.

I was waiting for my ride to chef school. I was enjoying a second cup of coffee and taking one last hit off of a joint before my friend arrived. I was watching the news when they aired a piece about the brutal famine in Horn of Africa and Sudan. I was shocked at the sheer scale of human devastation. The images on the TV moved me to tears. As I sat there in a semi-stupor I wondered whether there were any local fundraising efforts to help those wretched people.

My friend still hadn't arrived so I thought I'd make a few phone calls. I immediately called the TV station and asked for the anchorman who reported the story. His name was Alec Gifford of WDSU. I asked him if he knew of any upcoming famine relief events. He didn't, but suggested I call the Public Relations Director at Catholic Charities and to use his name when I called. When my buddy arrived I told him to go on to school without me. The world of cuisine could do without me for a day. I was on a mission.

When told the contact at Catholic Charities that I wanted to do a fundraiser for famine relief, he embraced the idea and offered to assist with the services of his office. During our brief conversation we formulated a general game plan. He was a real pro and knew exactly whom to contact at the various media outlets. The first person he called was his counterpart at the local Red Cross chapter. Catholic Charities in New Orleans is very influential organization in a city that is half Catholic. With Catholic Charities fully committed, the effort gained instant credibility; individuals and organizations were eager to participate. By that afternoon we had assembled an ad hoc committee who met at the Red Cross office. I was astonished at the speed the whole thing came together; from an idea to action within hours. As I sat in the meeting I couldn't help being amazed by what was taking place. I'm convinced that if I hadn't been high I wouldn't have come up with the idea at all. Don't let anyone tell you that all drugs are always harmful. I don't advocate drug use, but in rare situations they can take us beyond ourselves and enable us to accomplish extraordinary things.

The committee delegated me to be the official face and voice of the event. The Red Cross scheduled a series of appearances for me on the local television and radio stations. They also arranged for the Times Picayune newspaper to do an article. The manager of the Cherry Blossom, one of those enormous paddle wheelers docked at the Mississippi, offered the ship as a venue for the event. We seemed to be gaining momentum by the hour—even the Mayor's office was willing to assist. We were able to get Aaron Neville and Erma Thomas as headliners for the show. In New Orleans, to have Aaron Neville and Erma Thomas on the same bill is huge. They're living legends. Even though Erma Thomas was from the 1950s, she's still a big draw in a city known for musical talent.

Each member of our committee was assigned different tasks. Besides being the spokesman for the event I was responsible getting the hospitality community to supply all the food and beverage as well as the cooks to work the function. This was a big job and I didn't have a clue to how I was going to do this, but I promised to get it done. I became obsessed with this venture. It literally consumed my life for a month or longer. I began by asking my chef school to donate food and supply student manpower. The students were more than happy to volunteer. They even came in on their own time to make jambalaya, fried chicken, red beans, gumbo . . . I also went to restaurants asking for food donations. Most were willing to help out. The InterContinental Hotel's manager could not have been more helpful. He personally guaranteed me that the hotel would do its part to promote the fund raiser and to take time off for the effort if I needed to.

The big day arrived. Unfortunately, unseasonably cold weather stifled attendance, but we still had a decent turnout. Everyone had a great time. We raised nearly $20,000. Ernest "Dutch" Morial, the then-mayor of New Orleans—he served from 1979 to 1986 and passed away in 1989—addressed the crowd. He presented me with a key to the city.

The fundraiser brought much favorable publicity to the InterContinental. Largely because of it, I was awarded Employee of the Year honors. The award included a one week, all expenses paid vacation for two at any InterContinental in North America, including Maui. Of course, I picked Maui. Airfare and meals were included. I can't imagine that I received that honor for being an exemplary employee. Nevertheless, I'd never been involved with anything like that before and it felt great. I was proud of what we accomplished. I took a gal I was dating, Anne-Marie Gordon, who would eventually become my wife and mother to Marianna, our lovely daughter. We had a great time in Maui.

The bottom line was that we gave the Red Cross a substantial amount of money for famine relief. It was thank in no small part to the InterContinental. It's times like this that restore your faith in humanity. It was incredible how many people gave of themselves for this effort. I'll always be grateful to the InterContinental and all those people who worked with me on this event.

Lagniappe

IN NEW ORELANS, a *lagniappe* means to receive an unanticipated small gift, which applies to this tale. Even though this particular event wouldn't be considered a perk, it was a benefit I didn't anticipate receiving. When I was promoted to the pastry sous chef position at the InterContinental I was placed on salary. I typically worked 55 to 60 hours each week. However, I was told I didn't receive overtime pay because I wasn't a *manager*. Being ignorant of the labor laws, I didn't object. I worked in this capacity for around two years. Eventually, I discovered that it was not being a manager according to the criteria set forth by the U.S. Department of Labor, which made me eligible for overtime. Suspecting a chance to wring some cash out of the InterContinental I filed an anonymous complaint with the DOL's Wage and Hour Division. They said that they'd investigate and get back to me with the results. In the interim I was transferred to the Willard Hotel in Washington, D.C. and forgot about the entire matter, believing nothing came of my complaint. Eventually, I received a check for $1800 for all the back pay I was due. No one ever knew that I was the whistle blower.

Au Revoir Nouvelle Orléans

IT WAS 1986 and I'd been living New Orleans since January 1979. I felt it was time to move on. I was ready to return north. I missed the change of seasons and all that the North had to offer culturally. I also knew that I would not advance beyond the pastry sous chef position at the InterContinental because chef Waché had no intention of leaving. When I learned that there was pastry sous chef position open at the Willard Hotel in the nation's capital I applied for it. It was time to embark on another adventure.

My life changed in fundamental ways during my time in New Orleans. I met Anne-Marie Gordon who would accompany me to Washington, D.C. and eventually become my wife and mother to our beautiful daughter. While I lived in the Big Easy I made a complete career change, going from hospital administration to the world of cooking. I advanced from raw rookie cook to a reasonably skilled pastry chef who could hold his own in most pastry shops. I fell in love with a city and became enamored of a new career. I would not have thought it possible to become so attached to a city, but then, New Orleans isn't just any city. I've never really fallen out of love with New Orleans. She still tugs at my heartstrings from time-to-time. Every revisit rekindles my relationship with the city on the river. It isn't possible to erase from my mind the images of Spanish moss dripping from stately oaks at Audubon Park, the streetcars rumbling up St. Charles Avenue, the magnificent food, Mardi Gras or the French Quarter.

Mostly, I'll remember the people I worked with. I'll always be grateful to the men who helped to shape my career: Big Mike, Baptiste, Big Funk, Mark Fitch, Gary Darling and a few others. My time at the InterContinental was especially important to my career. Chef Waché generously shared his culinary knowledge with me. He also taught me how to manage a pastry shop. I was sorry to leave Gilles behind. I'll always be indebted to that little Frog. The last I'd heard, he left the InterContinental to open a pastry shop in Gretna, Louisiana, a community on the west bank of the Mississippi River directly across from New Orleans. I can't say I blame him for getting out of the hotel business; eventually I would do the same and start my own business. I hope life has been good to all those who made a mark on my career, even crusty old Crooks.

~~~

During a 2009 visit to New Orleans I decided to visit Café du Monde for a plate of their delicious beignets and chicory coffee. Of all people,

Lightnin' was waiting tables there. It had been nearly fifteen years since I'd seen him, but he still looked pretty much the same as I had remembered him. He recognized me as soon as he laid eyes on me and broke into a wide grin. I asked him for a table in his section so I would be able to chat with him. As he delivered my pastries and coffee we took the opportunity to catch up.

"So when did you leave the InterContinental?"

"Shoot I been gone nigh on eight years," Lightnin' said. There was a discernable sluggishness—even slower than I remembered—in his countenance suggesting that a lifetime toiling in restaurants and hotels had taken a toll on his body and his spirit.

"After ya'll quit I worked in da pastry shop fer a while den I transferred to to da main kitchen. I didn't want to work with dat crazy mother fucker Radcliffe no mo'. He too freaky man."

"So how long have you been working here?"

"Goin' on 'bout six months now, Lightnin' reported. "It ain't too bad; I make good money offen da tourists mostly." I noticed he was wearing a wedding ring.

"Lightnin' are you married now?" I asked, glancing at his ring.

"Yep, and I got two baby girls," he answered, proudly.

"That's great bro. I'm happy for ya."

"Yep, I was proud papa when dey was born, yeah," he continued. "And I even hep da doctor cut they *unbiblical* cord."

"You mean the umbil . . . Forget it, it's not important. Lightnin' I gotta to run. It was good seeing ya again pal." We hugged and I departed. The next time I get to New Orleans I'll make it a point to stop by the Café du Monde to see if Lightnin' is still working there. I hope he is.

Chapter Eight

Requiem for a Café

"Is Rosie O'Donnell fat or what? Her favorite food is seconds."

Joan Rivers

THE STORY OF Café Marianna—the restaurant I owned and operated for fourteen years—might be more meaningful if I begin towards its end, a few years before I sold the place. Perhaps you'll get a better sense of the character of the café and what it meant to those of us who worked there. I'll start with a tragedy that befell Café Marianna several years before I put the place up for sale. The tragedy was the death of one of my cooks, Tim Grey. Losing Tim was a sock in the gut for everyone. I knew that Tim was well liked, but it wasn't until after he was gone that I appreciated just how much he meant to his coworkers.

It was a sleepy Sunday morning in Alexandria, Virginia. I drove to work on auto-pilot; my mind was fixed on the work ahead of me that day. As I pulled in behind the café I noticed two of my waiters, Chris and Kent, standing out back. I'd seen them out back dozens of times before; they were always animated with laughter, but this day they weren't. They were just standing there starring at the ground. Chris was taking a drag on a cigarette. I got a bad feeling. As I parked my van I got a closer look at the pair. Chris's eyes appeared flushed from crying. They both wore doleful expressions. I knew this could not be good. I didn't want to ask what the problem was, but I had no choice. When you own a restaurant everything is your business.

"What's up dudes?" I directed my question at both of them.

"Timmy's dead," said Chris in a wavering voice.

His words had crushing weight. I was absolutely stunned. *This cannot happening*, I thought. I had just worked with Tim the night before and we all had a few beers at the end of the shift.

"A friend of Tim's family called and said that he was hit by a car last night near his apartment. He was crossing Rte. 1 to buy beer at the 7-11," Kent said, his voice also trembling.

I knew where Tim lived and was familiar with that particular stretch of highway. It's a busy, ill-lit thoroughfare on the far south end of town. Apparently, the driver couldn't see Tim because he was wearing blue jeans and a dark hooded sweatshirt. She hit him doing forty or fifty. The family friend said that he didn't suffer long; he died en route to the hospital. At least there was a shred of solace in this horrible event.

Tim Grey was in his early thirties. He was single and lived with his mom. He'd been working at the café for four or five years. Everyone liked the guy. He was good-natured and generous to a fault. Tim loved a good laugh. And just like that, he was gone. My immediate concern was for his mother, Mrs. Grey. She and Tim were extremely close. Tim was her youngest son and she doted on him. No matter how old a child becomes, it remains the parents' little one forever. Everyone at the café knew Mrs. Grey. When she brought Tim to work she'd often stop and chat with the kitchen staff. Mrs. Grey raised her sons on her own. Her husband abandoned her when Tim was just a kid. A parent's worst nightmare is to bury a child. The loss must have been unbearable for Mrs. Grey. She was inconsolable at the funeral.

After talking with Kent and Chris I entered the café. It was obvious that the other employees were also distraught. A few of the waitresses and bus girls had been sobbing. Everyone milled about in a daze. Their faces were vacant and expressionless. It reminded me of 9/11 when everyone moved like automatons. On that unforgettable day people spoke only when they had to and when they did it was in hushed tones. The cafe was uncharacteristically quiet. My kitchen was normally a bustling, cheerful place, but that morning there was only silence.

Sunday was usually TV day. We had an old broken-down television with a coat hanger for an antenna, and on Sundays we watched the Redskins or the Orioles. The Latinos, rightfully, claimed the TV during World Cup. That morning, however, the set was off.

The sight of the dark television was a reminder of our grief. Tim and Chris were huge Redskins fans and could easily goad Kent into making ill-considered wagers. Kent's Achilles heel was that he bet with his emotions and Chris and Tim knew this about him. When they won, and they usually did, they'd tease Kent mercilessly. But it was harmless humor. Chris normally worked as a waiter, but wanted to cook Sunday brunch to pick up extra cash. At least that's what he told me. I think he just wanted to work with Tim. They played like a pair of otters when they cooked together. That was fine with me. Laughter indicates that people enjoy working together.

Since the cafe experienced very little turnover, most of my staff had worked with Tim for several years. Friendships sprouted; relationships deepened. We all genuinely cared for one another. The café was more than a place to earn a living; it was a second home for most of us since we spent so much of our lives there. But for several of the El Salvadorians the café was the only family they had in America. We did a Christmas gift exchange every year. Significant events were always acknowledged—birthdays, high school graduations, births . . . I recall one of Tim's birthday celebrations. I treated him to an evening at his favorite strip club. He wanted to invite Chris, Kent and Jorge, the El Salvadorian pot washer. Tim loved to watch pole dancers. We guzzled beer and caroused until we got kicked out—Jorge swears he didn't know that you aren't allowed to touch the dancers.

I asked Mrs. Grey if she would let me host the post-funeral luncheon. We had a good time, just as Tim would have wanted. I made sure that his favorite food was on the buffet: Buffalo wings. Mrs. Grey offered to pay, but I wouldn't accept it. A few days later I found Tim's work shoes in the storeroom and hung them in the kitchen. They remained there until I sold the restaurant.

After Timmy's death, Mrs. Grey stopped by the restaurant occasionally just to say hello. Her synthetic smiles belied her deep sadness. No one at the café really recovered from Tim's death. Losing Tim was more than losing a coworker. Years later I ran into Mrs. Grey at a local hotel where she worked as a restaurant hostess. We were genuinely happy to see each other. We shared a heartfelt embrace and made idle chatter for a few minutes. Neither of us brought up Tim's name. I felt that our chance encounter dredged up unpleasant memories so I thought it best to cut my visit short. Somehow I think Mrs. Grey preferred that as well. I never saw Mrs. Grey after that day in the hotel.

In retrospect, I considered Tim's death as an omen of sorts. His passing and a succession of subsequent untoward events compelled me to sell the café. A restaurant can be thought of as a metaphor for life. There are moments of unimaginable joy matched by heart-wrenching pain. Inevitably, the day arrives when you realize that it's time to move on, time to close the doors and begin a new chapter in your life. It just feels right in your gut.

When Café Marianna ceased to exist it was morphed into something completely different. The building still stands, but the menu, décor, ambience, and spirit are gone. It was a special place for those of us who worked there, and if it still exists, it's in our stories and memories. So here are a few of those precious memories: incidents and events that can only take place in a family restaurant. Incidents in the life of a café.

Taking a Chance on a Dream

MOST CHEFS DREAM of owning their own restaurant. Very few ever get the chance. The odds are stacked against them. In the first place it's tough to get venture capital. Banks are reluctant to give start-up money to a chef, no matter how good a cook he might be. Lenders understand that a restaurant is risky business. Another route is to do what I did: invest your own seed money and slowly expand the business as the situation dictates. It's critical to have a substantial cash reserve to get through the start-up period. Someone once said, "You can't jump a chasm in two leaps." This holds true for restaurant start-ups. You can't make a partial effort because there is usually no second opportunity.

My café was located in the Old Town section of Alexandria, Virginia, a fifteen-minute drive from Reagan National Airport. The demographics were perfect. It was nestled in a residential area and within walking distance of many high-income households. It was situated within walking distance of the Potomac River and the bike path that runs from D.C. to Mount Vernon. The building itself was a yellow clapboard structure on a corner lot, dating to the early 1950s—admittedly not much to look at, but it had one asset essential to any restaurant: character.

I named the café after my daughter, who was about two and a half years old when it first opened. Café Marianna was only supposed to be a neighborhood coffee shop serving homemade pastries—croissants, brioche, scones, Danish—which I would make at a production bakery I also owned in another part of town. I had recently sold a luncheonette that I'd owned for several years and wanted no part of full-blown restaurant operation. I wanted to get back to my culinary roots: breads, desserts, wedding cakes and pastries. After all, I was a classically-trained pastry chef with more than a decade of experience.

I opened Café Marianna in the autumn of 1992. It was not a lark; this was serious business as I had a family to support. My professional future was tied to the success of the café. Failure meant crawling back to some hotel pastry shop and being treated as chattel labor once again. The prospect of this happening impelled me to succeed. I'd spent too many years working with condescending Europeans and social deviants in restaurants and hotels and I wasn't about to return to that situation anytime soon. Having my own place meant I could control whom I worked with. Plus, I came to resent the restaurateurs and hotel managers who profited from my skills. It was high time for me to reap the financial fruits of my own hard work.

I opened my restaurant on a shoestring budget compared to what most restaurateurs shell out. The proceeds from the sale of my sandwich shop provided seed money for the café. I didn't spend more than $50,000 on everything: build-out, equipment, food supplies, dining room furniture . . . Many restaurants spend fifty grand on dining room furniture alone. I bought used equipment when I could—sinks, refrigerators, tables. Used restaurant equipment can usually be picked up for a dime on the dollar and some of the stuff is almost new since many restaurants fold within the first couple of years. We didn't have a state-of-the-art POS computer system that automatically prints out a copy of the food order in the kitchen. I bought a cash register for two hundred bucks from COSTCO. I figured it was one less thing to malfunction and I could always get a replacement if the register broke down, which it did every year or two. Thanks to COSTCO's generous return policy I only paid for one cash register in fourteen years. Abusing the retailer's return policy bothered me at first, but eventually I reckoned that if I didn't do it, somebody else would.

Rather than hire an expensive architect or restaurant design consultant, I designed the kitchen myself. It wasn't a complicated process. I measured the kitchen area and purchased equipment to fit its designated space. I converted a small room adjacent to the kitchen into a bakery. It was tight, but large enough to accommodate a floor mixer, flour bins, a work bench and Alberto, the diminutive Bolivian pastry cook I eventually hired. It wasn't fancy, but it got the job done. My kitchen and bakery were not state-of-the-art by any means, but it all worked out.

~~~

Business was slow the first month or so, but word spread fast that there was a new restaurant in the neighborhood and it wasn't long before things picked up. There was a large office complex within walking distance that provided me with a built-in customer base at lunch. But my new customers wanted more than a coffee shop. They clamored for a full lunch menu: sandwiches, salads, soups and desserts. I wasn't prepared for that kind of food or that volume. It was supposed to be a pastry shop, not a restaurant. Any savvy businessman adapts to market conditions, though, and that is exactly what I did. I wanted a coffee shop, but the customers wanted a café—and you know what they say about customers. Ultimately I was there to earn a living, not resist what my patrons wanted. And I knew that I only had a certain amount of time to turn my place into a café. You only get one chance at a new customer. If they're not satisfied they'll go elsewhere.

Once I began serving a full lunch menu, business really zoomed. We were getting slammed at lunch. I could barely keep pace with the business. As soon as I could I hired waiters and cooks, which isn't as easy as it sounds. It's a chore to find the right individuals: people who are honest, dependable and possess a good work ethic. People with those qualities don't grow on trees in the restaurant business. Hiring cooks and servers is akin to the joke about divorce settlements being like a gold mine—sometimes you get the gold and sometimes you get the shaft. You never know what you'll get until they've been on the job for a few months. You're lucky if your new hires don't have some sort substance-abuse issues.

I made my choices, rolled the dice, and we were all surprised to watch our business steadily increasing. After a few months, I knew that I had lightning in a bottle. I'd tapped into a burgeoning micro-market that more experienced restaurateurs had dismissed as an untenable location. No one else considered putting a restaurant in a dilapidated lumber yard. I saw opportunity where they saw failure.

~~~

The location did have its drawbacks, though. During harsh winters, rodents came indoors to escape the cold. My pest control service kept their populations in check, but didn't eliminate them. They can never be eliminated. I remember a busy Saturday night when one of our winter residents decided to make a public appearance. The restaurant was packed when Fauvia, one of my bus girls, pulled me aside.

"*¡Jefe, tenemos un ratoncito!*" Although my Spanish was marginal at best, I got the *ratoncito* part. We had a mouse somewhere in the dining room.

"Fauvia, please speak English," I said. Her English was better than my Spanish, and I didn't want any miscommunication. I knew I had a full-blown emergency on my hands.

"We hab a leetle mouse."

"Where?"

"By *la mesa ocho*, table eight."

"Oh shit!" I exclaimed. "Why me, why tonight when we're packed to the rafters?"

"What the hell are we gonna do?" I asked Fauvia, as if she was somehow obligated to help me solve this dilemma. It was her problem only to the extent that she'd get *nada* for tips if the customers caught sight of that *ratoncito*.

"*No sé, jefe*. I mean I don't know boss," Fauvia responded, as she shrugged her shoulders.

This was a crisis that demanded action. If anyone saw our "leetle" friend the word would spread like wildfire and the restaurant would become helter-skelter. The entire dining room would clear out within a matter of minutes. Worse yet, most of the customers would expect dinner on the house. Plus, the wags eating at Café Marianna that night would take delight in spreading the word that my restaurant was infested with rodents. And of course I'd have the Health Department to contend with afterwards, since someone was sure to call them. I had to do something, and I had to do it fast.

I nonchalantly cruised by table eight, and noticed its inhabitants with dismay. *Of all customers, it had to be the O'Briens*. Mrs. O'Brien was a prolific gossip and would take delight in telling her cronies about the mouse. The bad news was that Fauvia had told the truth: there was a mouse there all right. The good news was that it was dead: belly-up directly underneath Mrs. O'Brien's chair, legs pointed skyward like tiny toothpicks.

I formulated a plan to create a diversion. I'd pretend to stumble near the table and drop a few dishes. Before the customers could realize what was happening, I'd drop to my knees and scoop up the mouse carcass with a napkin. The plan went off without a hitch and, accordingly, Fauvia followed behind me with the broom, sweeping up the shards of shattered dinner-ware. I apologized to the O'Briens for my clumsiness. They were none the wiser. Crisis averted! Chalk it up to quick thinking, decisive action, and teamwork.

~~~

The interior of Café Marianna was not a thing of beauty like the swank, high-end restaurants in D.C. The kitchen was open to the dining room, separated by pastry showcases and a bar that seated eight. The customers enjoyed watching the bustle of a hard working kitchen. The dining room was filled with an eclectic and random mixture of tables and chairs purchased from Goodwill or the Salvation Army. Our flatware, dinner-ware, glassware and coffee cups were a total mishmash. When you ordered a cup of soup that's exactly what you got: a cup of soup in a coffee mug. Café Marianna had an *Alice In Wonderland* feel about it. It was a whimsical place unlike any restaurant I've seen before or since.

The walls were adorned with Marianna's grade school artwork, which she occasionally sold. The ceiling was festooned with Mardi Gras beads, garlands and mobiles to distract one's eye from the unsightly acoustical tiles and fluorescent lights. A fire truck pedal car from the 1950s and a 1940s snow sled were suspended from the ceiling. I encouraged my artistic customers to display and sell their art at the café. I wasn't interested in a consignment arrangement; I just thought they should have a venue to display their work. I felt their creations enhanced the dining room. Café Marianna was a retreat for its regular patrons. They were encouraged to while away the afternoon sipping wine with friends or get lost in a book. No customer received a check until he or she asked for it. One man told me, "When I come in here it feels like an old pair of slippers." (At least it didn't smell that way.)

The service staff became familiar with the food and beverage preferences of the regulars. While they perused the menu their favorite beverage would be delivered, unbidden. This level of rapport engendered a dedicated customer base, the life blood of any small business.

Café Marianna featured al fresco dining for thirty on its patio. It was an attractive spot with wrought iron tables and chairs and canvas umbrellas with floral designs. The floor was comprised of flagstone pavers surrounded by English boxwoods. I planted a small garden off the patio where I grew an assortment of organic herbs for our own use: chives, rosemary, thyme, cilantro, basil, and so on. A 19th century Hoosier stood at the front door, which is where we kept the menus and displayed the gingerbread house I made every Christmas. All in all, Café Marianna was a homey, comfortable place where customers could escape life's tribulations for a moment.

I made it a regular practice to hire the homeless. They helped out by washing pots or doing other kitchen chores for a few weeks or months until they could find a better-paying job. One guy remained with us for three years. They were usually good success stories, but not always. I had to fire one homeless guy because he kept sneaking wine on the job or showing up for work with a snoot full. A person should be warned only so many times. Commercial kitchens are dangerous enough without being hammered.

I supplemented my income by selling t-shirts and cookbooks. I wrote and self-published the *Café Marianna Cookbook*, which included family recipes and many I'd used at the café. I commissioned my then-pot washer, Greg Coles, to do the illustrations for the cookbook. Greg was a truly gifted artist who was exceptionally good at portraits. Greg also designed the artwork for the t-shirts I sold at the restaurant. The slogan read: "I Got Sconed at Café Marianna." I sold many hundreds of cookbooks and t-shirts.

Salmon Surprise

WHEN I OWNED Café Marianna, it was my habit to always personally inspect seafood deliveries for accuracy and product freshness. For a brief period I bought fresh fish from a certain seafood wholesaler in Arlington, Virginia. I recall one incident when this particular vendor delivered an order of salmon filets. When I opened the container I detected a faint odor of laundry bleach. Experienced chefs, like experienced sommeliers, have a highly developed sense of smell. I removed all the filets from the container. They had put the bad filets at the bottom and the fresh ones on top, hoping no one would smell the bleach or root around in the container.

Fresh fish should be completely odorless. If it smells of anything it should be the ocean breeze. If it's a whole fish, the eyes should be clear, not opaque, and the gills should be ruby red. If it's a salmon filet the flesh should be the familiar orange-red color and not pale in appearance like these filets were. I realized immediately what the vendor was trying to pull on me. The filets had gone off and in an attempt to mask that unmistakable odor of bad fish they immersed the filets in a solution of water and bleach and placed them at the bottom of the container hoping I wouldn't notice. In the restaurant world there are a relatively few food wholesalers that are unscrupulous. They'll do anything to make a buck, even if it means pawning off unsafe product on an unsuspecting customer. And there are equally dishonest chefs and restaurateurs who will knowingly buy unsafe product at a discount. These bottom feeders don't mind, they aren't eating it.

These shysters are well aware that's it difficult for the public health authority to prove unequivocally that it was a particular vendor's product that caused an outbreak of food-borne illness. Food-borne disease is difficult to trace back to the source of an outbreak because the evidence may no longer exist; it might have been consumed or simply thrown away, ending the investigation. Obtaining a sample of the suspected tainted food is fundamental to any epidemiological investigation. Symptoms of food poisoning typically manifest between twenty-four and forty-eight hours after ingestion. However, the onset of symptoms from food intoxication, ingesting a chemical contaminant, can happen as little as thirty minutes after ingesting the tainted food. Sadly, too often public health authorities can only surmise responsibility for an outbreak based on circumstantial evidence, and rarely is the guilty restaurateur held accountable.

I opened the second box of salmon filets. It was the same song, second verse: this time they'd used a pine-scented disinfectant to mask the putrid odor. Again, they'd placed the bad fish at the bottom of the Styrofoam container. Of course, I sent the fish back, but that wasn't the end of it. I reported this purveyor to the Arlington County Health Department, who assured me that they would immediately inspect that facility and monitor them in future. I didn't tell the vendor that I was going to call the health department, as this would have given him time to get rid of any bad product before the inspectors arrived.

Fortunately, I caught these scumbags in the act and did something about it, but how often had this same vendor gotten away with selling bad seafood to other restaurants? Not all restaurateurs are able to physically inspect their fresh seafood or poultry deliveries. In large food service establishments, deliveries are merely dropped at the loading dock and someone signs for them. The head chef is not going to leave the kitchen and go out to the loading dock to inspect every seafood delivery to ensure that it's fresh. He doesn't have the time. The vendors know the delivery is not likely to get a thorough inspection, so they risk mixing in bad seafood with the fresh. If they can slip in a bad filet here and there they can easily get rid of a great deal of otherwise unsellable product.

The "Best Of" Contest

DURING THE SUMMER of 2000, the Washington, D.C. Fox affiliate had a contest for the "Best of D.C." in the metropolitan area. Each week Fox viewers could e-mail in their vote for their favorite bakery, coffee shop, restaurant, hair salon, etc. The winners were announced each morning. When I learned of the contest I was determined to win, but I couldn't simply leave it in the hands of fate. I needed to improve my chances. I asked everyone who I knew had a computer to e-mail in their votes for Café Marianna. I asked customers, employees and family members. I must have voted a hundred times.

My tenacity paid off. Café Marianna won the "Best Restaurant" category. No one was more surprised than I. Even though I did my best to fix the outcome I never thought we had a prayer, given how many great restaurants there are in the D.C. area. Winning this contest was huge for business. To get advertising this good you'd have to take out a whole page ad in the Washington Post. The venerable Palm Restaurant came in second. The Palm is the polar opposite of my little joint. It's a sophisticated establishment where politicians meet to make decisions that affect our lives.

The television station sent out a reporter and a cameraman to do a piece on the café. They arrived at lunchtime and it could not have been a more perfect day. The weather was gorgeous so we were absolutely packed inside and on the patio. The reporter interviewed several customers, one of whom was a good friend of mine so she happily raved about Café Marianna—of course, she hit me up for a free lunch afterwards. They interviewed me as well and shot some footage of the dining room and patio. Right after the piece aired we were overwhelmed with business. For more than a week there was a queue at lunch. The boon in business was short-lived, but really helped to put us on the map—and won us legions of new customers.

Those Special Customers

IF YOU DEAL with the public long enough absurd shit is bound to happen, especially when alcohol is thrown into the mix. It's inevitable. You can never predict who's going to walk through the door or how they'll behave, especially once they get liquored up. It's not always fun or pleasant at the time, but these episodes make for good conversation through the years. Here are a few of the more memorable incidents.

Cooks Have Feelings Too

AT CAFÉ MARIANNA the customer wasn't always right. If they misbehaved or were rude I usually did something about it. The café was my little fiefdom and I ran it the way I saw fit. In any restaurant the moral tone is established by the management. It decides what acceptable conduct is on its premises. This brings to mind the gumbo incident. It was at the end of another busy lunch when one of my waitresses came to me.

"The guy at table two said the chef should be shot for his gumbo." Now, I learned to make gumbo from one of the best chefs in New Orleans, so I know my gumbo is awesome. It was by far the most popular soup I offered—we sold a minimum of ten gallons each week. No one ever complained about my gumbo. People bought it by the quart to take home. As I approached the table I thought, *why is this guy in such a bad mood?* No matter what his problem was, I couldn't allow this guy to slam my cooking and get away with it.

"Which one of you said I should be shot for my gumbo?" I asked, with arms akimbo. I'm a large man and standing there with my tall chef's hat on I must have appeared an imposing figure. Neither gentleman responded, but I knew who had made the comment because one of the customers was a regular who had always been delightful.

"Well, was it you?" I asked, staring at the newbie. The vacant look in his eyes suggested that his crocodilian brain was searching for an intelligible response. I enjoyed watching this little prick squirm. He was about my age, mid-fifties. He wore a long scraggly beard. He reminded me of that codger in the first *Home Alone* flick—you remember, the old guy next door who eventually befriends Macaulay Culkin's character.

"I just meant that the gumbo was too thick for my taste," the man said, apologetically.

"Have you ever cooked in New Orleans?" I asked, giving him a glare that could have melted a frozen margarita.

"Well, no, but—"

"Well, but nothing. I attended chef school there and cooked all over the city, and you're gonna tell me that my gumbo sucks?"

"I just meant that—"

"If you don't like my gumbo, fine, that's your prerogative, but don't tell my waitress that I should be shot," I barked, as I continued to stare him down.

Suffice to say I never saw that guy again. I felt sorry for the regular customer who was embarrassed by the whole incident. The next time he came in he apologized for his buddy's comment.

I know that I'm not in the same league with chef Eric Rippert, but like most professional chefs, I go to great lengths to get the food right. Most chefs will tell you that they cook for themselves and not to suit the customers. If we didn't do that, we would be serving steak and baked potatoes all the time. Cooking is a personal thing—if you denigrate the food you denigrate the cook. Call it arrogance or over-sensitivity, but I could not and cannot allow such an attack to go unanswered.

At Least I Didn't Ask, "So How's Tricks?"

HAVE YOU EVER wondered why *hookers* are called hookers? Story has it that Joseph D. Hooker, Union General during the American Civil War, had a fondness for the prostitutes who trailed his army. When the situation permitted the "Hooker Girls" were invited into headquarters to service him and his officers—hence the name *hooker*. But I digress.

Café Marianna was a family restaurant. I didn't offer a "happy hour." A happy hour brings a nice cash flow, but it also brings a lot of trouble through the door: drunks, fights, barflies. Another reason why I didn't want a happy hour was because it can attract prostitutes. Remember, my cafe was located a few miles from Washington, D.C., not the most wholesome city on the East Coast.

Because my place was quiet and out-of-the-way, a handful of hookers regularly brought their johns in for dinner or drinks. You don't have to be a gumshoe to spot the prostitutes: they come in with a different guy every time, they drip with sex appeal, and they're dressed to accentuate their curvaceous bodies. All in all, I didn't mind having them come in. They didn't cause trouble and their customers spent lavishly and were generous tippers. We gave the hookers nicknames. Ladette was our favorite, though. With Hollywood good looks, she brought in clients who were more elegant and polished than the other hookers'. Ladette came in two or three times a month. I would chat with her when I could. She was sweet and affable. I often wondered what compelled her to choose hooking rather than pursue a more conventional career. But then who knows why any of us wind up doing what we do in life? We all have a story, I suppose.

Ladette must have surmised that I knew she was a hooker. After all, she brought in a different man every time she came into my joint. She seemed to like bringing her clients to Café Marianna. I think she felt comfortable with us. We weren't judgmental and treated her with the same level of respect as all our regulars—though I do recall one embarrassing conversation when I committed a monumentally stupid gaffe. Ladette's client had gone to the bathroom so I sauntered over to her table just to say hello.

"How ya doin' Ladette, I haven't seen you for a while," I said, glancing at her very stunning cleavage. I don't believe she minded; it was displayed to be appreciated.

"Good Charles, really good. Yeah, it's been a while since I been in ain't it," she replied, as her fingers sensuously circled the rim of her champagne flute. Ladette bore an uncanny resemblance to the character played by Fran Drescher in the sitcom *The Nanny*. She was a buxom, attractive brunette who turned men's heads whenever she walked into my place. I'd often wondered about what it would be like to spend the night with Ladette. I knew it would never happen, but what was the harm in fanaticizing?

"So how's business?" I asked. As soon as I uttered those words I realized what a moronic question it was. *What was I thinking?* Talk about Freudian slips. I just asked a prostitute how business was going. Why didn't I just say: "So Ladette, how many johns you banged since the last time you were in?" For a moment all the oxygen was sucked out of the room. She stared at me, not quite sure how to respond. I expected her to say: "Fuck you Charles, you dumb shit," and stomp out, but she didn't. What she did, after a beat of silence, was giggle into her champagne glass like some ditzy high school girl. Clearly, she was amused by my unintentional *faux pas*. I was relieved that she wasn't offended. "Ladette, I'm so sorry. I didn't mean it the way it came out."

"That's all right sweetie. I don't mind. I know you didn't mean nothin' by it. You always been nice to me and my boy friends." She giggled again and sipped her champagne. *What a good sport,* I thought.

Her client returned to the table.

"Welcome to Café Marianna sir. I was just chatting with your charming lady." I had to pretend as if I weren't well acquainted with Ladette.

"We need another bottle of Mumm," the john told me, caressing Ladette's hand. "And make it extra dry this time if you have it. No *brut*."

"Very good sir," I replied. "Mumm extra dry it is." Since my café was such an informal place I didn't normally address male customers as "sir," but I thought I'd make an exception in this case. I wanted Ladette to feel as if she warranted preferential customer service.

"We're ready to order."

"Very good sir, I'll have your waiter come over directly," I said, as I executed a half bow and backed away. Ladette gave me a reassuring wink that everything was copacetic even after my unseemly question. Hookers are all right in my book.

The Biker Wedding

MY LANDLORD DIDN'T much care how I made the rent; he just wanted his cash every month. I wasn't in a position to be selective about my customers. Money is money. My customers came from both ends of the social spectrum. I made a wedding cake for the daughter of Antonin Scalia, the Supreme Court Justice. At the other end of the spectrum was the unforgettable Biker Wedding. We were on-site making preparations for the reception when we heard the thunderous roar of dozens of motorcycles as they pulled into the parking lot. It sounded like Rolling Thunder had just arrived. Some were in suits, others were wearing their riding leathers. These were some hard-core bikers. Quite a few were ZZ Top lookalikes.

I knew that this was not going to be a run-of-the-mill wedding reception. The nuptials took place in the grassy back yard. The bride and groom rode up on their Harleys where they remained seated throughout the ceremony. The JP even sat on her bike as she conducted the wedding. After they got hitched the handsome couple cranked up their bikes and spun out, ripping tire tracks in the lawn. The party was on.

They came to get their groove on and that's what they did. I thought I'd brought enough beer. Not even close! I learned that bikers prefer Budweiser. They chugged down the three cases of Bud I'd brought and ignored the fine assortment of premium foreign beers I provided. When the groom complained that they were "gittin' low on Bud," I told him that his guests hadn't even touched the foreign beers I'd brought.

"Me and my boys ain't drinkin' that 'furrin' pisswater. We need more Bud and pronto, Chuck," he replied, as if Heineken and Becks were inferior to the NASCAR devotee's beverage of choice. Hey, it was his wedding. If he wanted more Bud then more Bud he got. Besides, I didn't really want a bunch of rowdy bikers pissed off at me, so I made a quick beer run to the nearest Safeway and grabbed a few cold cases.

Another memorable moment of that evening came when the best man complimented me on the pâté we served on the buffet.

"Hey cooky, them little slices of meat loaf was damn good!" he exclaimed. "And I like them little pickles too." By *little pickles* I think he was referring to the imported cornichons I served with the pâté. Hey, I'm just glad he enjoyed the food.

The beer emergency, the ceremony and the pâté comment weren't the only memorable moments that night. As bikers are prone to do, they got liquored up, which can lead to amorous behavior. Around 1 A.M. one of my cooks and I were taking out a load of trash when we heard the unmistakable sound of love-making in a garden near the rear entrance. Curious to know who it was, I kept an eye out from the kitchen to see who emerged from the shadows. After a few minutes a fat biker chick emerged, trailed by my pâté devotee. Apparently he found a dish that he liked as much as my "meatloaf."

It was a great wedding. Other than mopping up the occasional puddle of vomit, my staff and I had a good time. It was entertaining to say the least. Before the revelers rode off into the night the groom paid the balance due: $3,000. He was so pleased with Café Marianna's services that he gave us a $500 tip. All cash! I love bikers!

Bikers' Ball

I'LL NEVER FORGET this next story. It was a crisp October afternoon and I was enjoying a beer on the patio when two bikers rode up on Harleys. Both were dressed in full leathers. They sat at a table near the door that offered a bit more privacy since it was tucked in a nook while the rest of the dining room was essentially an open room.

When you own a restaurant you learn to distinguish the married couples from those who aren't. The married couples are easy to spot: they pretty much ignore each other. I've seen married couples sit through an entire meal without exchanging a word. These bikers were definitely not married. They were having far too good a time. They enjoyed a leisurely lunch and a bottle of wine and then another. They started getting touchy-feely, which was okay at first, but I began to get concerned when he started fondling her under the table. I'm all for couples having a good time, but there are lines of decorum that should not be breached in public. A restaurant is not exactly the ideal place to engage in sexual activity.

After the biker wedding experience I wondered, *why is it that bikers give new meaning to the phrase "Public Displays of Affection?"* Not wanting this situation to spiral out of control, I instructed my waitress to give them their check. I thought the interruption might have a chilling effect on their *tête á tête*. Wrong! They paid their check and simply relocated behind the café where they continued their carnal exhibition. By now the entire staff, including myself, was jockeying for position at the rear window to catch a glimpse of the spectacle. I had no idea that biker leathers could be ripped off that fast.

The charming couple chose a grassy strip of real estate just beyond my dumpster and off my property, which left me powerless to intervene. They seemed to be completely oblivious—not that it would have mattered—to the fact that they were entertaining passersby and the entire Café Marianna staff. We watched without shame; after all, it wasn't every day that we got to see our customers having intercourse. I couldn't believe it—another biker couple banging away outdoors. True children of nature!

Fat Woman Throws Menu

IT WAS AN unusually busy lunch and I was on the verge of a meltdown trying to work through all the orders. Luis, one of my waiters, came into the kitchen to ask how much he should charge for an off-menu seafood salad. I answered his question and he reported back to the customer, an extra-large woman who sat alone at a table near the kitchen. My café had an open kitchen so I could see her arguing with Luis. She wagged her finger at him. *This is not going to go well*, I thought. Luis returned to report that the woman was upset about the price and wanted to talk with me. I told him to tell her that the price was firm and that I was too busy to visit with her.

"Luis, I don't have time for this shit. Tell her that this is not negotiable and if she doesn't like it she can order something else or leave."

A few seconds later the woman stood at the kitchen opening, glaring at me.

"Hey, are you the owner?" she demanded. "I want to talk to you. And I want to talk to you right now." She spoke loud enough to get the attention of the customers at the nearby tables. They continued eating while they watched the drama begin to unfold.

"I'm sorry, but as you can see I'm kind of busy right now. If you'll give me a few minutes I'll stop by your table," I said, in an attempt to pacify the oaf.

"No!" she barked. "I want to talk to you this instant. The price for that salad was outrageous!" She waved the menu at me.

"Lady, the price for the salad is what the waiter told you, fourteen bucks. Now excuse me, I have orders to get out." My patience was wearing thin.

"You son of a bitch, I'm never coming here again!" she screamed, and threw the menu directly at my head.

I ducked like George Bush did when that guy threw his shoes, and the menu sailed through the kitchen and landed in the deep fat fryer. Fortunately, no one got splashed by the shower of hot oil.

The audience of lunch patrons caught its collective breath. After a tense moment, the hefty woman pivoted and began to waddle toward the door. I yelled after her, "Get your big, fat ass out of here and keep it out!" The customers who had witnessed the episode broke into applause. The leviathan crashed through the dining room, careening off other customers as she bulled her way to the exit. Needless to say, she never returned.

Last Call

IN RETROSPECT, I believe that September 11, 2001 marked the beginning of the end for Café Marianna. The disaster in itself was devastating enough, but the ensuing years saw a succession of setbacks that became increasingly difficult to overcome. I can take a punch as well as the next guy, but repeated blows take a toll after a while. I can't say exactly when, but at some point being a restaurateur ceased to be fun. It just seemed like one tragedy came on the heels of another, and it became harder to recover each time. The spate of unfortunate events took a collective toll on the morale of the staff and me. The café wasn't just about making money. Café Marianna had always been more than just a place to work; it had always been an enjoyable place that felt like home. Once running the restaurant ceased to be enjoyable, what was the point of it all? Eventually I began thinking about selling the place. Tim Grey's death was a major factor that led to the eventual sale of Café Marianna, but there were other events that contributed to my decision to call it quits. Here are a few.

9/11

MOST OF US remember where we were and what we were doing on the morning of Tuesday, September 11, 2001, and I'm no different. I was at my café making a pot of shrimp gumbo for lunch. When I heard the news I wasn't sure what to do. This was one of the few times in my life I felt utterly helpless. I decided to close the café for the rest of the day and was in the process of calling the employees when Richard, one of my evening cooks, called to tell me that the Pentagon had just been hit. Since the café is only a few miles from the Pentagon, I raced to the back door to look in that direction. Sure enough, a plume of black smoke was billowing from the horizon. Now I was really rattled: this was way too close for comfort. I collected Marianna from school and headed home.

On the way home I stopped at the grocery store. It was usually bustling and noisy, but on that day it was totally subdued and eerily silent. People spoke in hushed tones. I thought I'd better gas up. There too, everyone seemed almost zombie-like. People were actually civil toward one another, not something I was accustomed to in the D.C. area. Not only were drivers not aggressive, they were even courteous. Police cruisers were racing in all directions with sirens blaring. The clear blue sky was devoid of commercial air traffic. Only fighter jets screamed over the Capital. Reagan National was shut down.

Hopefully, 9/11 was a once-in-a-lifetime catastrophe. It was so devastating that the effects lingered for months. People were reluctant to leave their offices for lunch or venture out in the evenings. "Go out!" our leaders told us. "Go shopping, go to restaurants. Show them you aren't afraid." The people didn't listen. They *were* afraid.

A pall fell over the entire region. My business was severely affected. Both lunch and dinner business nearly evaporated. This continued for weeks, then months. The very survival of the café came into question. Eventually, the Small Business Administration offered low-interest loans for small businesses, a financial lifeline. I applied for and received an $80,000 loan. I needed it to survive. I had no choice—I had twelve employees to take care of and my own responsibilities to manage. I'm still repaying that loan.

D.C. Snipers

DURING SEPTEMBER AND October of 2002, Washington, D. C., Maryland and Northern Virginia were beset by sniper attacks. Eleven people were killed and three others critically injured in random locations throughout the metropolitan area. The snipers succeeded in paralyzing the region. Citizens only left their homes when absolutely necessary. People had to go to work, but they didn't have to eat out. and they didn't—at least not at my place. No one knew where the snipers would strike next. My lunch business suffered since few customers would leave the safety of their offices. My dinner business virtually disappeared, because the snipers were primarily targeting victims after dark. I had to cut employees' hours. My own income suffered.

This nightmare continued for about a month. The snipers were finally apprehended in late October, but the psychological affect lingered for months even through the holiday season, which is usually a busy time for the cafe. It wouldn't be until the following spring that business began to pick up. John Allen Muhammad, the older of the two snipers, was put to death in November 2009. Lee Boyd Malvo is serving a life sentence without parole in Virginia.

The Economy

THE STATE OF the economy has everything to do with the success and survival of a restaurant. America experienced two recessions during the life of Café Marianna: one in the early 1990s and another in the early 2000s. Recessions are difficult enough for most businesses, but they are especially hard on restaurants. Eating out is a luxury. People have to buy groceries, health insurance and gasoline, but they don't have to dine out. And if they do eat out it is not likely to be at full-service restaurants; it's mostly at fast-food joints. During recessions some of the first businesses to go under are restaurants and those that do manage to survive just limp along until things improve. This can take years. Keeping an independently-owned restaurant afloat during the lean times is a tricky proposition. Austerity measures must be implemented: employee hours cut, no raises, periods of no pay for the owner. Servers often quit because they aren't making any money.

The last years of the café's life were good ones. The housing bubble drove an unbelievable period of prosperity. Business boomed at Café Marianna. However, my sense was that the high times could not last forever and that it was only a matter of time before it all came tumbling down. It did not take Nostradamus to predict that an economy built on a house of cards would tank at some point. I decided to sell the café before that happened. Events proved me right when it all began to come undone in 2008, two years after I sold the place. Had I remained in the saddle I doubt that I could have survived the deep recession that enveloped the nation.

Closing Time

THERE WERE OTHER events that were less catastrophic, but still took a collective toll on of us who worked at the café. The net effect of all the negative events moved me to seriously entertain the prospect of selling the place. Plus, I wasn't getting any younger and I couldn't see myself running a café for many more years. Operating a restaurant is a young person's job. It takes a tremendous amount of energy. The main factor in my decision was my daughter. I was a single parent and Marianna lived with me. At the time she was a sophomore in high school and I felt I needed to be at home more to monitor her life. We've all heard the stories about internet perverts and young girls. I just didn't feel comfortable not being home every night. The café was still a very profitable operation and if I was going to sell, I wanted to do so ASAP. This way I could get top dollar.

After weighing all these factors I put the café up for sale, and closed the deal in August of 2006. The couple who bought the place were experienced hotel chefs, but had no experience running a private restaurant. Being a hotel chef brings little to the party where running a café is concerned, so I knew they had a steep learning curve. One of the new owners was a frog, which must be why they renamed the café *Bastille*. Of all the dreamy French names they could have selected, they named it after a prison. I get the historical significance of the Bastille, but to name a restaurant after it . . . that wasn't working for me. But it was their restaurant now—they could call it "Roach Motel" if they wanted to.

The new owners made it clear that they weren't interested in the Café Marianna's customer base, which had taken me years to develop. They wanted a more "sophisticated clientele." How stupid was that? When you buy a business the last thing you want to do is discard the existing customer base. That's part of what you buy, so you don't have to reinvent the wheel. In business parlance it's called *good will*. This superior attitude hurt them in the short term. They made the start-up harder than it needed to be. My customers were devoted to the café, and it was their loyalty that carried me through the lean times. I liked my customers as people. Through the café I developed some wonderful and lasting relationships. If it weren't for the café, I wouldn't have met my life partner.

The new owners also didn't like the appearance of the café, so they completely remodeled the interior. I got that. The interior was never very attractive, but at least it was distinctive. Now the place looks like every other restaurant in D.C: austere, stark and devoid of personality. It just isn't the same as the old Café Marianna anymore. The customers were sorry to see it sold. I continue to run into former customers in public who sometimes chastise me for selling the place.

The last day that I legally owned Café Marianna I threw one helluva barbeque. It was open to anyone who had ever been associated with the café: family, friends, customers, employees and their families, salesmen, deliverymen, vendors . . . I even invited Ladette and a few other hookers who came in regularly. Over two hundred people showed up. I hired my nephew to grill chicken, burgers and hot dogs. I served a full buffet with salads, jambalaya and fried chicken. There was plenty of cold beer and wine. I drank more than I should have. Most had a good time, but not all. My employees didn't seem to enjoy themselves. They only attended out of a sense of obligation. They didn't want to be there. One of my cooks, Ricky LaSalle, sat quietly alone in a state of near catatonia. He just stared into space. Ricky was one of the first cooks I'd hired. He'd stood by me through thick and thin. I was involved in some of his life's significant events; his marriage to Olivia (a former waitress of ours) and their baby's baptism among them. I knew that I was disrupting people's lives by selling, but I had to move on with my life too. My employees didn't know the pressures of being responsible for everything—bills, food, service, success and failure. It all fell to me. That kind of responsibility wears on you.

I had a guest register at the front door where people could record their thoughts about Café Marianna. Some of the comments were heart-felt, especially the ones that mentioned significant personal experiences associated with the café—first dates, marriage proposals, wedding rehearsal dinners, baby showers and birthday parties. Many customers were saddened by my decision to sell the place; a few were moved to tears when they said their final farewells. One of the last tasks that day was to give each employee a $500 going-away gift. I did this to help tide them over until they found new jobs. Selling the café was a difficult decision because it meant that our little family was breaking up, and I've always felt a twinge of guilt over that. But it was also difficult because I was leaving a piece of myself. At some level it was a personal loss.

~~~

Shortly after I sold Café Marianna I stopped by the restaurant for lunch. I didn't recognize my waitress. She seemed polite enough, but there was something absent from her countenance. There was a certain iciness about her. No smiles, no warmth, perhaps a reflection of the new owners. There was usually a friendly rapport between my customers and my servers. I sensed none of that. This was just another restaurant now. You order your food, you eat, you pay, you leave. It was all very matter of fact. For some ridiculous reason I thought that she ought to recognize me as the previous owner. I didn't consider myself just another customer, but I guess that's what I had become. For a moment I was offended, but quickly dismissed that childish thought from my mind and focused on what I was going to have for lunch. I settled on the sautéed salmon with mesclun and Dijon vinaigrette. After mulling over the wine menu I ordered on a bottle of Sonoma Cutrer, a California chardonnay to which I'm partial.

As I sat at table two (the same table the amorous bikers shared) sipping wine and waiting for my food, memories of the café flooded my brain. My thoughts took me back to the very beginning, before the café was a café. It was an empty shell, offering nothing more than a glimmer of hope for a brighter future. I recalled all I had endured to even get the place open— permits, contractors, hiring staff. I scratched and clawed to get that place off the ground, but I did it and was beholden to no one. I could picture myself standing on the ladder mounting the Café Marianna sign above the front entrance. It was a moment of immense pride.

Random memories continued to stream through my head. I recalled trying to console the young woman who sat at table three sobbing because she'd been stood up by her dinner date. I chuckled at the thought of Lars Anderson asleep and drunk in a snow drift. Sadness washed over me as I reflected on Tim's tragic death and the pall that hung over the café afterwards. In a flash my spirits were lifted when I replayed Marianna's birthday parties that we celebrated at the café. I remembered the Sponge Bob and Barney cakes I'd made. I smiled inwardly as I recalled the fat woman throwing a menu at me narrowly missing my head. I was amused at the image of Fauvia and me collaborating to collect the mouse carcass from underneath Mrs. O'Brien's chair. I even reflected for a moment on the whores who frequented the café, especially Ladette. Like frames of an old movie, a collage of memories flashed before my mind's eye.

While I was lost in my thoughts a half an hour had expired and my food still hadn't arrived. I thought, *Jesus Christ how long does it take to sauté a freakin' piece of salmon and throw a salad together? A simple order like this would not have taken this long at Café Marianna.* Feeling no love for the new owners, there was nothing they could have done to please me. I realized that my attitude was being juvenile, but I couldn't help it, my feelings were genuine.

I was on my third glass of chard. The effects of the alcohol put me in an introspective mood. For the first time I regretted selling the café. I was suffering from a case of seller's remorse. I knew selling was the right thing to do at the time, so why was I experiencing these feeling now? I'm usually so cocksure about my decision-making, but at that moment I wondered if I'd made a mistake. I realized that I had difficulty coming to grips with the finality of it all. I didn't anticipate that it would be so hard to let go. I rationalized that I'd made a pile of cash off the sale, but even that knowledge didn't alleviate my childish envy. I admitted to myself that I was jealous of the new owners. I've never liked them personally, but that wasn't the issue. They now owned what was mine for so many years. My domain was now theirs. Money changed hands and documents were signed. In a flash my restaurant was no longer mine. What I had worked so hard for was now someone else's. Relationships were terminated.

Maybe the alcohol had corrupted my brain. I began to sulk. I felt resentful that the new owners were now restaurateurs and I wasn't. I began to miss things I never imagined I would. I yearned for the exhilaration of the dinner rush. I wanted the kudos my customers lavished upon me and my staff for the good food that we all worked so hard to get right year after year. Mostly, I pined for the exceptional people with which I had the pleasure of working all those years. I missed their friendship and companionship. My food finally arrived. The salmon wasn't hot and the greens weren't fresh so I sent the plate back. The waitress seemed miffed. *Tough sweetie, deal with it*, I thought. I chugged the last glass of wine knowing that after I paid the check I was going home for a nap and the new owners weren't. There was some solace in that.

Even today, some five years later, there are moments that I still miss Café Marianna. I appreciate what it brought to my life. That totality of the restaurant experience taught me to understand that everything in this world has a preordained life—even cafés.

Chapter Nine

The Restaurant World According to America

"I like children, fried."

W.C. Field

THE DINING PUBLIC seems blithely unconcerned about the sanitary conditions of the kitchens in America's restaurants. We assume that chefs and restaurateurs make sure their kitchens are in compliance with all the latest Health Department ordinances. We feel secure in the knowledge that chefs and their kitchen staffs conscientiously follow food-safety practices to ensure that the food they prepare is always safe for us to eat. If you believe these things to be true then you also believe that Jesse Jackson and Al Sharpton are real preachers. And blindly trusting the restaurant industry to protect you from food borne disease—commonly called food poisoning—is tantamount to trusting Wall Street with your financial wellbeing. I don't know about you, but I don't have much confidence in either institution to look out for my welfare. It's foolhardy to suppose that the Health Department is all we need to stand between us and a deadly outbreak of food poisoning. This is an unrealistic expectation. Health Departments cannot possibly monitor the nearly one million food-service establishments in the United States. While public health officials do their best, many restaurants slip through the cracks and serve food that can send us to the emergency room. This is the unvarnished truth that many Americans merrily choose to ignore. There are 48 million cases of food borne illness every year in the United States. While there is no way to determine exactly how many cases are caused by restaurants, it is a known fact that eating out is riskier than eating at home because at home we have more control over safe food-handling practices.

The distressing truth is that many restaurant kitchens are unfit as food preparation facilities and food handlers often ignore—due to casual indifference and/or lack of knowledge—food sanitation practices when preparing our meals. While these transgressions might seem egregious from a public health perspective, they occur with shocking regularity in America's restaurants. The genesis of this public health dilemma is usually the profit motive. Let's be realistic. Restaurateurs are in business to make money and there is little some won't do to realize that end. Here are a few specific examples to illustrate this point. More than 60 percent of restaurant workers in America do not receive paid sick leave benefits, forcing unwell employees—who may be experiencing diarrhea and/or vomiting—to report for work because they can't afford to lose the income. It is estimated that one restaurant worker in ten reports for work when ill. This is especially true with the service staff that relies on tips for the bulk of their income. Other than the health care industry, I can't think of a business where a healthy work force is more critical. You will read more on this issue in Appendix A, *The Food, the Bad and the Ugly*.

Here are a few more troubling examples of how restaurateurs increase their profits. You know those little foil-wrapped butter chips your waiter delivers with your bread? The disturbing truth is that they may not be discarded after a one-time use as required by Health Department codes. Some restaurants collect and melt all the partially used butter foils—they re-serve the unopened ones—in a large pot. They heat the foils to melt the unused butter. They strain out the foils and run the oil through a cheese cloth to remove unwanted matter such as bread crumbs and, in some instances, cigarette ashes. The clarified oil is used for sautéing or making sauces such as Hollandaise. The restaurateur rationalizes that a penny saved is a penny earned. And you know that uneaten bread you left on the table? It doesn't go into the garbage like it's supposed to by law; it's used for croutons, bread crumbs or bread pudding. Shocked are you? Don't be. This stuff really happens. I know. I've seen it dozens if not hundreds of times. For decades I've been on both sides of the restaurant business. Before I became a professional chef thirty years ago, I was a restaurant health inspector, inspecting thousands of food-service establishments. I don't mean to be alarmist, but you need to know what can and does happen behind the scenes in some of America's restaurants. I'm very choosy about where I eat out.

~~~

Here are some actual examples of just how unsanitary commercial kitchens can be. Early in my career I worked in a French Quarter hotel whose pastry shop was situated below ground level—not where you want to be in a city that is already below sea level. With every heavy rain storm the shop's floor drain would back up, flooding the shop. The storm water would be two or three inches deep each time. No matter. We still had to produce pastries, wedding cakes, breads and whatever else was needed for the hotel's guests. It might be a matter of hours before the water drained from the shop. Here's another gem. I had a job at an upscale restaurant in the Upper Garden District of New Orleans where for a very short time I had a part-time job making desserts. I was dumbstruck when I first saw my pastry shop. It was a garage that had been converted into a "pastry shop." There were holes in the screen door; there was an unfinished concrete floor and no AC. It was a constant battle to keep the flies off the butter cream and sponge cake. It was impossible to make delicate desserts in the sweltering New Orleans heat. I hated to quit that gig. The ten bucks per hour cash was pretty good money in the early 1980s, but I couldn't work under those conditions. How could a place like that have been approved by the Health Department you ask? It wasn't. Remember, this was New Orleans, a city known for corrupt civil servants. Some Health Department inspectors, who typically earn a meager salary, are eager to take a few hundred bucks to look the other way.

When doing research for this book I came across an article in a local newspaper that I thought would better illustrate my point about restaurant employees not following food-safety practices. The Washington, D.C. Health Department made a series of surprise weekend inspections in March 2010. The Washington Examiner reported that hundreds of D.C. restaurants—many of them upscale establishments—were guilty of numerous health code violations. Some of the violations were critical in nature, such as a barehanded cook observed "preparing desserts with open cuts/sores on fingers" and other cooks seen "using the same pair of tongs on raw and cooked food." It's not the kind of thing we want to read about, but this is the reality of the restaurant business. Unfortunately, these kinds of occurrences are only the tip of the iceberg. This particular D.C. bust happened to get publicized. The public usually doesn't get wind of the restaurants that are guilty of far more serious violations. I wish this was the exception rather than the rule, but the sad truth is that this sort of thing is a common occurrence, we just don't know about it.

Chefs and restaurateurs know that Health Department inspectors come around once in a blue moon as it is, and they almost never show up on weekends, so the chance of getting busted is remote. Even if they do get hit, it's not that big of a deal. The establishment is given ample time to correct the violations before being re-inspected. Once they pass muster, it's back to business as usual, and unsafe food-handling practices prevail once again. Old habits die hard. Everyone lets their guard down because they know they won't get inspected again for six months or so. However, a restaurant will get inspected more often if its violations are of a critical nature like signs of rodent infestation.

Certainly a restaurant can be closed through a court order for repeated serious health code violations that present a public health emergency, but this is rare. I've seen this cat and mouse game played out throughout my entire career. To be fair, many restaurants are fastidious about kitchen sanitation and safe food-handling practices. Those aren't the ones we need to worry about. It's the establishments who won't spend the time or money on kitchen sanitation, training employees in safe food-handling techniques or pest control that we need to be concerned with.

America's Restaurants

DINING OUT IN America is in a state of flux. Eating out isn't what it used to be. The dining public has become more sophisticated and demands more from restaurants and chefs than ever before. The current evolution in the restaurant business reflects larger societal trends, underscoring the fact that American diners are becoming increasingly interested in what's on their plate, how pure it is and where it comes from. Sustainability and nutrition are becoming key themes in our nation's nearly one-million restaurants (nearly 5 percent of which, by the way, are Chinese restaurants). These trends were reflected in a survey of chefs nationwide. In late 2010 the National Restaurant Association (NRA) conducted its "What's Hot" survey of more than 1,500 professional chefs—all of whom are members of the American Culinary Federation(ACF)—that is touted to be a reliable prognosticator of the hottest trends on restaurant menus in 2011. "The annual 'What's Hot' chef survey is one of the industry's most anticipated and oft quoted culinary forecasts, largely due to the credibility of its respondents—professional chefs that work in some of the nation's finest dining establishments and educate the next generation of chefs in culinary institutions," said Hudson Riehle, senior vice president of Research and Knowledge Group for the NRA.

One of the most encouraging statistics was that 83 percent of respondents indicated that sustainable seafood would be one of the "hot trends" in the culinary scene in 2011. The top 10 menu trends for 2011 are locally sourced meats and seafood, locally grown produce, sustainability as a culinary theme, nutritious kids' dishes, hyper-local items (restaurants growing their own produce or raising their own livestock), children's nutrition as a culinary theme, gluten-free/food allergy-conscious items, back-to-basics cuisine and farm-branded ingredients.

The validity of the survey itself raises some questions. Is the sample randomly distributed to give an accurate representation of culinary professionals across the nation? ACF chefs are the "Ivory Tower Grads" of the American culinary scene and might not have their pulse on what is happening on Main Street America. ACF chefs work in our large urban centers mostly, especially on the coasts, so their prognostications may not be an accurate bellwether of coming trends. This could mean that the results are skewed and, therefore, not representative of national trends. Are the respondents merely reporting the trends or are they helping to shape them? Only time will tell how accurate the survey is.

The restaurant industry is big business. According to the results of an NRA survey, the nation's restaurants are strong contributors to the national economy, with industry sales representing 4 percent of the U.S. GDP and employees comprising nearly 10 percent of the U.S. workforce. Its total economic impact exceeds $1.7 trillion, as every dollar spent in restaurants generates $2.05 spent in the overall economy. The restaurant industry is the nation's largest private sector employer with 12.8 million employees. The restaurant business is critical to the structure of the American economy. As American jobs are exported, the restaurant industry takes on increased economic importance. The health of the restaurant industry is a leading indicator of the health of the U.S economy.

The Trends

THE NRA STUDY mentioned earlier also confirmed what many of us have known for some time: Americans' dining habits are undergoing a fundamental shift toward more sophisticated cuisine. We have become more demanding diners creating a market for restaurants and chefs that can deliver a higher level of cuisine. While there is, and always will be, a market for traditional fare, gastronomes are also demanding innovative approaches to our cuisine. Creativity is part of America's DNA, so it only follows that our creative genius should be applied to gastronomy. We no longer have to go abroad for a fine dining experience; we can get it right here in North America. Las Vegas is a good example of a venue that has gone from all-you-can-eat buffets to a smorgasbord of exquisite restaurants run by highly-skilled professional chefs. But there is a price to pay for the haute cuisine in the desert and I mean that literally: in 2010 the average meal in Las Vegas, at around $45.00, was the most expensive of any city in America.

Chefs around the country are producing cutting edge cuisine in the unlikeliest of places. In cities not historically known for good food, such as St. Louis, Austin, Denver and Minneapolis, young chefs are creating incredible cuisines. They're using ingredients native to their locales. Chefs of the Mid-Atlantic States can serve rockfish and oysters from the Chesapeake. Chefs of the Upper Midwest can serve wild-caught northern or walleye pike cheeks. Chefs of the Deep South utilize crawfish and alligator. Chefs are buying local to reduce the carbon footprint—food typically travels 1,500 miles to get from farm to plate—and to support local and regional economies.

Americans have also become more discerning about the source of their food. We are in a more enlightened era of eating. Increasingly, diners want to know where their food comes from and whether the producer is operating in an eco-responsible manner. Consumer demand is being felt in the market place; retailers like Whole Foods Company are getting greener by selling free-range poultry and beef raised on all-natural feed without the use of growth hormones. Walmart has announced that it will increasingly offer more locally-grown produce and set produce suppliers' standards such as environment, occupational health and safety, employment practices, etc.

Another sea change in the restaurant industry is the use of social media—Facebook, Twitter, Yelp, Foursquare—as marketing tools and to facilitate professional development. According the National Restaurant Association, more than 8 out of 10 restaurateurs report that social media will be more important to their business in 2011. Industry experts predict that this trend will only continue to grow.

Mobile food trucks (this is not exactly a new food-service concept; mainstream media just thinks it is) and pop-up restaurants have been popular for some time and will continue to be a sizzling trend in urban centers for the foreseeable future. Food trucks offer a unique venue for consumers' point of access to restaurants and a means for entrepreneurs to grow their businesses. This food truck mania now has its own national website where foodies can find their favorite mobile vendors by metropolitan area: www.foodtrucklocator.com. I'm not surprised at all the hoopla over moveable eateries. It all makes sense. Transience has long been a hallmark of American society, so it's only natural that we would develop an appetite for these meals-on-wheels eateries. No doubt about it; it's an exciting time to be in the food business—whether it's harvesting it, making it, cooking it and, yes, even writing about it. I hope you are as excited about this gastro-revolution as I am.

High on the Job

SUBSTANCE ABUSE HAS always been a problem in the restaurant industry and continues to be pervasive. A recent study by the Substance Abuse and Mental Health Services Administration states that 18.7 percent of restaurant workers used illicit drugs at least once in the month preceding the survey it conducted. That's nearly 1 in 5 workers. The study also states that 15 percent of restaurant workers are heavy alcohol users. Only the construction industry has a higher rate of alcohol abuse. Collectively, the number of crack fiends, potheads, speed freaks, alcoholics and pill poppers might even be higher. Does the restaurant culture attract these kinds of personalities, or does it set the stage for addiction? I worked with a guy who downed a six-pack every day before punching in. One of the cooks at my own restaurant was hauled away by the police during the dinner rush. There was a battery warrant out for his arrest. He'd been in a fight that resulted from his drug-induced belligerent behavior. He was a good cook, but the lifestyle of the restaurant world got the best of him.

If you cook for a living, rest assured that you *will* work people who have substance-abuse problems. You *will* work with people who are working under the influence of drugs or alcohol, which compromises your safety. You *will* work with people who will try to sell you drugs.

The restaurant lifestyle is conducive to substance abuse. Think about it: restaurant workers perform under tremendous pressure, work insane hours and often have a pocket full of ready cash at the end of a shift. At most restaurants where I've worked, cooks and servers routinely meet at their favorite watering hole to unwind. And the problem is only getting worse. Now, do you still want to be a chef? If you do, go for it, but don't say I didn't warn you.

America's Restaurant Worker

IN THE RESTAURANT world only the strong survive. It's a dog-eat-dog culture where kitchen staffs and service employees are secure in their jobs only as long as they pull their weight. There's no room for laggards. The restaurant business is the most essential of zero-sum games—one worker benefits where his counterpart fails. It all comes out in the wash. Employees are interchangeable parts in America's food mill. If a $10 per hour cook does not to perform up to expectations, he'll be replaced by another $10 per hour cook of roughly equal skill level. By replacing one cook with one of an equivalent skill level the food quality remains the same. The customer is none the wiser. The same applies to servers, bus people and managers. By doing this the restaurateur maintains equilibrium and his business survives another year. These incessant staff exchanges are the life blood of the industry. There is an inexhaustible supply of willing workers.

Taking a chance on a restaurant is one of the riskiest of all small business endeavors. According to the National Restaurant Association the odds of a new restaurant surviving its first three years are slightly better than 1 in 3. In a business where it is common for profit margins to be dangerously thin, the independent restaurateur has to carefully consider each and every expenditure. Can he afford to provide an employee benefits package? Should he advertise? Should he pay servers less than minimum wage if state law allows? These decisions directly affect the bottom line and the restaurateur's personal income. It takes more than being a skilled chef to make a restaurant succeed. Many good chefs have become restaurateurs only to fail because they lacked the requisite business acumen. Owners of chain restaurants don't live so close to the edge. They have the support of the mother ship to assist them with advertising, advice and logistics. When you strip away the business side of a small business you are left with the human factor. The success of a restaurant boils down to the quality of its people, not only the workers but the customers as well.

~~~

I can hardly write a book that explores the hospitality industry in America and not discuss the people who are at the very center of that industry—Hispanic workers. Hispanics are the great underclass in America's $604 billion a year restaurant industry. They represent a large portion of the nearly 13 million restaurant workers in America. Hispanics work in every facet of the restaurant industry. They cook, wash pots, park cars, wait tables, manage and own food-service establishments. It hasn't always been like this. Historically, non-Hispanics did the menial tasks in America's restaurants, but that's all changed. With a population that has swelled to more than 50 million, Hispanics have supplanted other population groups who have done these jobs in the past. Non-Hispanics are reluctant to do restaurant work so the Hispanic immigrants are more than happy to fill the void. They are the latest wave of immigrants to call America their home. Mexicans and Mesoamericans are the Irish, Italians and Jews of the early 20th-century.

Pick a cuisine and Latinos are cooking it—French, Italian, Asian, American. I recently went to one of my favorite French cafés in Alexandria, Virginia, where I live. It's my habit to thank the chefs when the situation permits, so after a superb dinner I knocked on the kitchen door to do so only to discover that two Hispanic cooks had prepared our food. There wasn't a Frenchman in sight, yet they produced impeccable French fare. I wasn't surprised. In fact, I expected to see Hispanics in the kitchen. Most Hispanic cooks are not graduates of hoity-toity culinary academies. They don't need to attend cooking school; they learn on the job. From personal experience, I believe Latinos have a natural facility for cooking. It just makes sense. Hispanic cooks, especially Mexicans, are inheritors of one of the world's great culinary traditions. Mexican cuisine is renowned and admired around the world for its uniqueness, tradition and cultural history. It has taken its rightful place among the world's great cuisines. In 2010 traditional Mexican cooking was included by the United Nations Educational, Scientific and Cultural Organization (UNESCO). Food is an extremely important aspect of Latino culture, so it only follows that they would have a natural affinity and respect for cooking.

Without Hispanic labor the restaurant business would be virtually paralyzed in many parts of America, especially in the urban centers located in the southern tier of states. Hispanics displayed their collective muscle on May 1, 2006 when they staged the Great American Boycott. The one-day work stoppage affected schools, hospitals and businesses across the nation, especially those in the hospitality industry. Many restaurants and hotels in the Washington, D.C. area were affected and some restaurants had to close for the day. And this happened with the participation of only a fraction of the Hispanic workforce. Clearly, without the Hispanic labor force, it would be extremely difficult to operate food service establishments in the U.S.

No Papers, No Problem

IN AMERICA'S RESTAURANT universe turnover is unbridled. Itinerant cooks and servers drift from restaurant to restaurant seeking better working conditions or the prospect of earning a few more bucks. Employees come and go with more frequency than Larry King's wives. If an owner needs another server, cook, pot washer or bus boy he only has to get the word onto the street and *voilà*—eager applicants will materialize at the restaurant back door in no time flat. In conventional business parlance an employee search is called "human resource recruitment," but I dubbed it my *Latino Grapevine*. I only needed to tell my Salvadorian waitresses in the morning that we needed a bus person and I'd have one by that afternoon. My Salvadorian cooks also kept the kitchen fully staffed with line cooks, prep cooks and pot washers. There was no need to spend money on traditional advertising.

No papers, no problem! When I hired a Latino I didn't want to know their immigration status. I told them that I needed documents to prove American citizenship—driver's license and social security card, voter registration. If they didn't have the docs when I hired them, they'd produce them in short order. For one hundred bucks they could lay their hands on forged documents that were indistinguishable from the real McCoy. It wasn't my responsibility to determine whether their documents were authentic. I didn't ask how they came by them. I didn't care. It wasn't any of my business. I just needed something to show ICE in the event I got busted.

We're all well aware of the illegal immigrant issue. Few sectors of the American economy have felt the impact of illegal immigrants more than the restaurant industry. Many misinformed Americans believe that illegals are *taking* jobs that Americans are willing to do. News flash: *Few Americans are willing to do menial restaurant work, but illegal immigrants are happy to.* I gave up putting ads in the newspapers for kitchen help. There was rarely a response. I had no problem finding illegals who were more than willing to do the work as long as I paid them a fair wage.

Many restaurateurs fail to treat illegal immigrants with even a modicum of respect. Many exploit illegals because they know that they have no recourse. They treat them like they're sub humans—no work breaks, no food and below-market wages. What are they going to do, call the cops? Illegal immigrants have the same needs and aspirations everyone else does. Not only is it immoral to exploit illegal workers, it is bad business. The secret sauce of restaurant success is employee loyalty. This reduces turnover—the Achilles Heel of any small business. Any business is only as good as its employees. When you respect *all* of your employees by paying them a decent wage and treating them with dignity, they're likely to remain loyal, not pilfer and elevate their performance. Treating them well is the right thing to do. The Latinos that worked at Café Marianna were fine people for the most part. It was an honor to work with them.

Sexual Harassment and Gender Discrimination

WHILE JAMIE OLIVER is obsessing about nutrition in schools—which is a good thing—a much more sinister aspect of the food business exists. If you're a female in the restaurant industry a completely different career might await you. Be prepared to work in a hostile environment—one that treats females as second class citizens. Odds are good that you'll be a victim of sexual harassment and/or gender discrimination at some point in your career. The glass ceiling is firmly in place. Many times I've seen women get passed over for promotions they were qualified for. The situation has improved, but discrimination is still with us in subtle, yet tangible ways. Commercial kitchens are replete with chefs and cooks that mistreat females with impunity. How can they get away with such behavior? Because they can in a male-dominated work setting where too often females are defenseless targets. I've seen this egregious conduct first hand. I've worked in New Orleans restaurants where female cooks and bartenders were coerced into having sex with the chef or manager in order to keep their jobs. I nearly came to blows with my boss when I was the pastry sous chef at the Willard Hotel in Washington, D.C. over the way he mistreated our female pastry cook. It should come as no surprise that he was French who, generally speaking, don't believe that women have a place in a professional kitchen. If a woman complains to the head chef or restaurateur that some guy keeps feeling her up in the walk-in refrigerator, her complaints are likely dismissed as female histrionics. Besides, it's her word against his.

Female immigrants—legal and illegal—in America's restaurants are often the targets of sexual harassment and sometimes even physical assaults. These crimes may be under reported because victims tend to not report incidents out of fear, shame, lack of information about their rights, poverty, cultural and/or social pressures, language barriers and, for some, their status as undocumented immigrants. The Southern Poverty Law Center, in its report *Injustice on Our Plates,* states that 80 percent of female farm workers in California are sexually harassed. (While farm workers are not strictly considered part of the restaurant industry, they are part of the food production system that supplies restaurants.) Additionally, a study conducted by the University of Southwestern Louisiana stated that 42.4 percent of the female restaurant workers indicated they have felt sexually harassed while at work. Over 70 percent (71.4 percent) of respondents in the same study indicated that in their opinion sexual harassment is more acceptable in the restaurant industry than in other industries.

Females are not warned during a job interview that they might be groped or their career advancement stymied. The designer culinary schools fail to mention to female applicants that they will battle sexual harassment and gender discrimination throughout their careers. They don't want to scare them off—they need the tuition. Women are shocked when they are thrown into a situation where their male coworkers don't conduct themselves like professional gentlemen. So how can this still be happening today you ask? It all sounds so yesterday, right? Simply put, professional cooking is dominated by males who believe that females are not their professional equals. Many cooks are simpletons who won't respect female co-workers for no other reason than the fact that they are females. Homosexuals get the same treatment, especially by Latino cooks who hail from cultures where gays have historically been objects of derision and discrimination.

Female workers in the restaurant industry are often victims of discrimination when it comes to equal for pay for equal work. According to a 2009 study conducted by the New York Restaurant Opportunities Center minorities and women who work in New York City's high-end restaurants do not have equal salaries, positions or experiences as white men who work there Only about 54.5 percent of the minority restaurant employees said that they had the same interview and employment opportunities in the restaurant industry as their white counterparts. The study also stated that the average salary of female employees was 21.8 percent lower than the average salary of white employees. Therefore, these female employees paid "gender tax." As women try to secure restaurant jobs that could provide them with higher wages and job stability, they face sex discrimination in hiring, promotions, and compensation. A University of Pennsylvania study found that in 68 of New York City's most expensive and elite restaurants, roughly one-third of these restaurants do not hire women for server positions even though there was an available pool of female servers.

Why would anyone—regardless of gender—subject themselves to the abuse and stress of restaurant life for so little money? Short answer, cooking gets in your blood. Many professional chefs feel that they are destined to cook for their life's work. Any die-hard cook will tell you that cooking chooses you, not the reverse. I'm one of those guys. I cooked for nearly twenty-five years and can't imagine having done anything else. I tried corporate gigs and was suffocated by meetings, memos and corporate politics. I obtained a master's degree in environmental health from the University of Minnesota. It didn't really matter in the end; I wound up where I should have been all along: in the kitchen. Sure, finishing grad school was an accomplishment that I'm proud of, but my true calling is cooking. I come alive in a bustling kitchen. I feel a deep satisfaction when I make a perfect anything. The site and fragrance of a tray of perfectly baked croissants gives me a sense of accomplishment that I never felt in the board room. There is nothing like the immediate reward of cooking. But cooking is not for the faint of heart. It's demanding and challenging, but if you were born to cook you will not resist the allure of the kitchen. If you genuinely love to cook, reach for that dream.

Cooks and Servers, The Eternal Conflict

IF YOU'VE EVER worked in a restaurant you'll know that servers and cooks share an innate dislike for each other. Ill feelings are always palpable. Servers do not hold cooks in high regard. If you ask a server his opinion of restaurant cooks he's likely to say, *I wonder when cooks stopped eating ants off a stick.* Servers are convinced that cooks are mere culinary cretins who lack the mental agility to wait tables. Now, if you ask a cook his opinion of servers he's likely to say something like, *Servers only began to walk upright about the same time restaurants were invented.* Despite this natural disharmony theirs is a symbiotic relationship—they need one another to survive. I was watching a nature show the other day about the relationship between grizzly bears and wolves in Yellowstone. The show illustrated how the two carnivores coexist within an uneasy relationship, yet seems to understand that their interdependence is mutually beneficial. It occurred to me that a cook and server have a similar—albeit slightly more evolved—relationship. While the grizzlies (the cooks) and the wolves (the servers) dislike each other intensely both species begrudgingly share the same territory (the restaurant) in order to feed on the same carcass (you, the customer). They are willing to do this because sharing their kills enhances the odds of survival of their respective species. It's the natural order of things that has served both species well for tens of millions of years. This real-life drama plays out in America's restaurants millions of times every day.

Servers generally earn more than cooks, which generates an enormous amount of resentment. A good waiter in a high-end establishment can knock down $300 or $400 bucks (and more if he's able to bilk more cash out of his ~~prey~~ customers) in a single shift. Cooks never make that kind of money. They toil long hours in hot, dangerous kitchens for $10 to $14 per hour. It's no wonder there is a conflict. However, on balance the cooks are more indispensible to the success of a restaurant. Ultimately, it's the food that brings customers marching through the door. When was the last time a friend suggested taking a meal at a particular restaurant because the service was outstanding? The dining public will tolerate mediocre service if the food is worth it. I know I will.

The kitchen is the cooks' fiefdom and servers know this. If a server has the temerity—or the stupidity—to challenge the cooks on their turf, he's inviting trouble. Cooks have an arsenal of ways to get even with servers who are disrespectful. Line cooks can *accidentally* misplace a ticket or move it to the end of the queue. Conversely, cooks have pet servers who get preferential treatment. The sycophant needs an emergency order, no problem. He needs to add something to an order, no problem. This elevated status can be achieved in many ways. I've worked at New Orleans restaurant, called Sal & Mario's, where certain waitresses (and female bartenders) were only able to keep their jobs by having sex with the manager.

When they can, cooks will usually blame a server for a mistake with the food order. Cooks take delight in making servers wait for their food or refusing to make food exchanges hoping this will result in a reduced gratuity. To hell with customer service, it's more important to punish the server, they rationalize. Cooks will refuse to make food exchanges; servers return the favor by blaming any mishaps on the kitchen when at all possible. Think about it. When was the last time you heard your waiter take the blame for anything that went wrong with your meal? To do this would jeopardize his tip. It's just easier to blame the group that isn't present to defend itself. If the customer asks for a food exchange the server might say: "I've tried to get the kitchen to substitute home fries with French fries, but they won't do it," when the truth is that the server couldn't be bothered to even make the request. These sophomoric spats are part of daily life in America's restaurants and it's not likely to end anytime soon.

Life's Losers?

LIKE BAKERS AND night watchmen, waiters and waitresses are children of the night. Most of us have been tucked in bed for hours when servers are just punching out. They reside in the shadows of the restaurant world. They're nocturnal creatures whose lifestyle makes it difficult, if not downright impossible, for them to maintain a relationship with *regular* people who live nine-to-five lives. For this reason, servers lead a quasi-incestuous existence in that they're *almost* forced into relationships with their own kind. It just makes sense since they work similar schedules and share a common lifestyle. Only a server can genuinely commiserate with another server about the tribulations and challenges of waiting tables. Servers have to hang around until the last of the late diners decides to ask for the check, which might be midnight or one o'clock in the morning in some restaurants. Anybody want to be a server in Spain?

Fair or not, many people regard waiters and waitresses as life's losers who don't have what it takes to enter the mainstream of society and carve out a real career. They lack ambition and shun responsibility. They're an odd breed of people who exist at the fringe of society. Whatever the case may be one thing is certain; waiting tables is a young person's occupation. Servers are on their feet for eight to ten hours a day and often have to carry heavy trays of food and buss pans full of dishes. They come to work when they're ill because restaurateurs rarely offer sick paid leave benefits. No work, no pay. Servers seem content to live a precarious hand-to-mouth existence.

The relatively few dishonest servers out there are adept at the art of the mini-scam. If you make the mistake of dining out on a major holiday (please don't) or, worse yet, Mothers' Day—the one day of the year you're guaranteed subpar food and service—your server might make a shameless play to secure a *sympathy tip*. One way they do this is by offering some cockamamie story about why they're working that particular day. You'll hear snow jobs like,

"My brother's serving in Afghanistan so I'm working today to save my vacation days so when he comes home my mom and I can spend time with him." or

"I'm working Mothers' Day this year because my mom recently passed away so I'm working today to keep my mind occupied."

Cabbies also make these pathetic attempts to wheedle tips out of their fares, especially at vacation venues like Las Vegas. *Make a buck any way you can is the server's credo even if it means hustling trusting customers now and again. What's the harm? If a customer is wealthy enough to dine out he won't mind paying a bit more in the way of his meal or gratuity. I'm entitled to it; I work hard and am underpaid and underappreciated.* Thieves can rationalize their conduct in many ways to exonerate themselves. No one begrudges a server for hustling to make an honest living, but there must be limits to how low they'll stoop to swindle a pigeon out of his money.

~~~

Let's briefly revisit the bear-wolf analogy. Servers possess a primordial canine survival instinct that allows them to turn on each other in a New

York minute. Just as wolves will gnash their teeth and nip at one another over a fresh kill, servers will do what's necessary to ensure that they get their fair share of the tables, especially the big tippers. While they all squabble over the most generous customers, the senior server (the alpha wolf in the pack) usually lands these Big Kahunas. Once the alpha server has hit his financial target (sated himself on the prime parts of the kill), he allows the less-senior servers to fight over the remainder of the carcass. The restaurant business is an every-man-for-himself world. When I first opened Café Marianna the waiters pounced on customers like wild dogs on a defenseless fawn. They were overly eager to start earning tips to the point that they were becoming avaricious. I had to install a system to bring some order to the situation, so I divided the dining room into sections. Each station had an equal number of seats. The waiters had to rotate amongst the stations taking a different one each shift. Plus, I made them pool their tips and divide the booty at the end of each shift. This worked pretty well. It reduced server backbiting, but didn't eliminate it entirely. It can never be eliminated entirely. In New Orleans servers can really be vicious and will do pretty much whatever it takes to make a buck. I worked with a waiter at the InterContinental Hotel in New Orleans who would have sold the Red Cross to Dracula if he thought he could profit from it.

If the servers are the wolf pack in our imaginary apex predator relationship, the bartenders are the jackals of that world. Just as the jackal is an equal opportunity scavenger, bartenders are indiscriminate when it comes to the swindle. A clever barkeep has dozens of ways to rip off both the restaurateur and the customer. They give away free drinks to elicit generous tips, under-ring the correct price and pocket the difference, claim a phony walk-out and keep the cash, charge customers regular prices while ringing happy hour prices and claim returned drink and pocket the money. It's more difficult for bartenders to cheat with a monitoring and control system, but these systems are expensive and few bars have them.

Of course, the vast majority of servers, bartenders and restaurateurs are honest working class stiffs just trying to make an honest buck, but still there are those who will take advantage of unsuspecting customers. Many servers have a repertoire of scams they can employ to fleece a restaurant's patrons. Sometimes even the manager or the restaurateur is in on the scam. Servers can do things like add a house tip to the food and beverage total, duping the customer into adding another gratuity. They will also "unintentionally" over charge for beverage or food items. A common scam is to add food items you didn't order, hoping you won't notice. In *Appendix C, I* offer an extensive list of the common scams perpetrated by dishonest servers. With more than 100 million Americans dining out every day, there is ample opportunity to bilk the dining public.

~~~

You may not realize it, but when you dine out you are entering into a short-term business relationship with the restaurateur and his dining room staff. You're buying a *food product*—it just happens to be edible. In some respects buying a meal is like buying an automobile. If your *food product* is defective and the service is subpar you are entitled to lodge a complaint and refuse to pay until it gets resolved. When you take your car to the dealer to get serviced you expect to pay the agreed-upon price for the parts and labor. If you're dissatisfied with either or both aspects of said transaction you will, or should, complain or withhold payment until you're satisfied. It's the same when dining out. You're paying your hard earned money for a *food product* that is commensurate to its relative cost and for reasonably good service. If you're not completely satisfied with your *food product* you should send it back to the kitchen and keep sending it back until they get it right. Chefs are professionals and must be held to a certain standard. The same goes for servers—bad service, bad tip. By demanding excellence you'll elevate the restaurant's performance in general, which will benefit the next customer. I mention all this because Americans still haven't reached the point where we demand excellence from restaurants. We're still intimidated or we worry about the cooks or servers spitting on our food if we send it back, even if it's for a legitimate reason. We accept cold French fries, overcooked steaks and mediocre service without a whisper of a protest. Sure you can make your dissatisfaction known by leaving a 5 percent tip, but that only punishes the server. What about the indifferent cooks? Remedies range from complaining to the manager to returning egregiously bad food to the kitchen and refusing to pay for it. The kitchen will get the message. The notable author and philosopher Ayn Rand once said, "In a democracy, people get the government they deserve." The same applies to the dining public and America's restaurants. If we don't demand excellence who will?

~~~

A few of the servers at my café, Café Marianna, had the distasteful habit of referring to new customers as *fresh meat*. Clear evidence that some servers view restaurant patrons as living, breathing instruments of currency—a means to make rent, buy groceries and do whatever it is that servers do when they're off duty. To this end, servers want to maximize their earning potential. One way to do this is by having efficient bus people working their tables. The faster servers can turn over tables the more customers they can run through, thus increasing tips. They can't be faulted for this, but too often greedy servers only want the Heisman trophy winner of busboys.

Two of my waiters were constantly whining about the slow pace at which one of my bus people worked. The bus person in question was, Paz Alvarado, who claimed to be fifty years old, but I don't believe she was a day under sixty. The waiters, Kent and Chris, exhorted me to fire Paz and replace her with a younger, more efficient person.

"We want to talk to you about Paz," Kent said, interrupting me as I was calculating the payroll.

"Sure, what's up?" I said, as I continued with the payroll.

"We think you should get rid of Paz and hire someone younger who can work faster and handle the work load," Chris continued, "We always have to help her bus our tables and it slows us down."

"Yea, I know she's slow," I agreed, looking first at Kent then Chris.

"We know some bus people at another restaurant," Kent said, as they nodded in unison. I was getting irritated by what amounted to throwing Paz under the bus, a faithful coworker with whom they worked for nearly eight years. I had no intention of firing Paz, but I wanted to hear them out.

"Oh really, you guys want me to can Paz and you'll replace her just like that," I replied, snapping my fingers.

"Yep," they both answered simultaneously as a sense of self-satisfaction wafted over them.

"Okay, let's do this," I said "but you guys have to help me. Okay?" They glanced at each other and nodded again in mutual agreement.

"Sure what do you want us to do boss?" Now they were calling me *boss* since they presumed they'd won me over.

"First of all, I'm *not* gonna to tell Paz she's fired. You guys are gonna tell her. And you guys have to explain to her why she's being fired after being a model employee here for the last eight years," I said, my voice rising. "And I want you two to tell me how this old lady accepts the news. Then after you fire her, you guys are gonna find me a replacement. I want a Paz clone. I want someone who is as honest, dependable and punctual as she is," The pair began to back away.

"Wait I'm not done, I said. "If Paz's replacement doesn't work out you two will be responsible to find another replacement and another and another until you guys find me another Paz. If you guys can't find me someone as good as her you two will take turns busing tables until we find a keeper."

They just stood there in silent contemplation. Astonishment washed over their faces. They slunk away and never brought up the matter again.

Paz Alvarado was more than a bus person. She was the Latina matriarch at Café Marianna. She was old enough to be grandmother to some of my other employees. They all respected Paz. In Latino cultures, the elders are paid a certain amount of respect. Admittedly, Paz worked about as fast as continental drift, but I couldn't fire her. An employee's ability to work fast isn't the sole or most important criteria when estimating their value and contribution to a business. Because Kent and Chris had no management experience, they couldn't understand that there are criteria other than speed—leadership, punctuality, affability and honesty. Another reason why I couldn't fire Paz was that working at my joint was a part of her very existence. We were like family and she knew that people at Cafe Marianna cared for her. She felt like she was part of something. She was a lonely old woman who lived alone. What would she do to keep herself busy? Who would hire a sixty-year-old bus woman? She would have sat in her apartment and wasted away.

One of the reasons that restaurants don't survive in America (according to the National Restaurant Association 61 percent fail within the first three years) is because the owners fail to understand the importance of the employer/employee relationship. Employees have to know that they're valued as people and feel secure in their jobs. They don't realize that disloyalty breeds chronic turnover, which necessitates training new hires. Turnover leads to subpar service. Plus, regular customers like to see the same dining room staff so they can establish a relationship. Familiar faces in the front of the house indicate that the restaurant is being well managed.

My customers used to comment that my employees seemed *happy*. That's because they were. Many restaurateurs treat their employees like chattel labor. They hire and fire people as if they were interchangeable parts in a food production factory. They don't understand that their cooks, servers, pot washers and bus people have to support themselves and their families, both here and in their countries of origin. Loyalty is a two-way street. I know a thing or two about loyalty. I'm a life-long Cubs fan.

The Cooks

WHAT'S THE DIFFERENCE between a cook and a chef? The short answer is not much. The term *chef* is bandied about by people who have little understanding of what the term really means The Food Network refers to its show hosts as *chefs*. Rachael Ray is not a chef. Paula Deen is not a chef. Nigella Lawson is not a chef. They're not even cooks in the professional sense. Just because they prepare some lame meals that most home cooks could throw together does not make them *chefs*. It's similar in the world of professional cooking. There are cooks and there are cooks—some are better than others. There are chefs and there are chefs. The title of *chef* and the ability to cook are not mutually inclusive. I've worked with "chefs" who didn't have the culinary skills of many line "cooks" I've worked with. You'll recall when I worked at Sal & Mario's in New Orleans the head chef was a deplorable cook, but he held the title of *chef*. He assumed the title only because he was in charge of the kitchen; it had nothing to do with his culinary prowess. Some of the cooks he supervised could cook circles around him and he knew it, but it didn't matter, he was technically the chef. Examples of real chefs are Eric Ripert, Paul Prudhomme and Hubert Keller. These are consummate professionals who have earned the right to be called *chef*. Compare them to a Paula Deen or a Sandra Lee, who are also referred to as chefs, and you immediately understand that there is a difference.

The world of professional cooking often attracts the dregs of society and the lowest of the low can be those who cook for us. I know this first-hand because I am also a cook and former restaurateur. Cooks often have checkered pasts. Many are on the run—from the law, an ex-wife or some untoward event from their past. Cooks lead a nomadic life. They're the Bedouins of the culinary world, always on the move, floating from kitchen to kitchen, city to city. A skillful cook can always find work.

Culinary skills and cooking techniques can be applied to a diverse range of cuisines. It's often merely a matter of becoming familiar with the ingredients, how they're assembled and in what combinations.

In years past, when a man failed at pretty much everything else in life his career options were limited to selling Amway products, insurance or automobiles. As a last resort he could become a cook. That's what I did. These losers usually didn't aspire to becoming a respected chef in a four-star restaurant, but they could eke out a living at a Cracker Barrel restaurant. Some people take to cooking like a duck to water and become extraordinary professionals. A relative few even open their own restaurants. Most never become exceptional. To many, professional cooking is a wondrous odyssey rife with sensation and creativity. To others cooking seems an interminable sentence of drudgery and hard labor, a way in which to earn a buck. These are the cooks who are content to do their time at chain restaurants like Olive Garden, Chili's or TGI Fridays where cooking is devoid of creativity and done by formula. This isn't cooking; this is merely assembling food. There is a difference.

Demon Rum

IF AMERICA'S RESTAURANTS enforced a *zero tolerance* policy for drugs and alcohol, you would have a difficult time finding a fully-operational restaurant. An inordinate number of restaurant workers suffer from drug and alcohol abuse. A 2002 to 2004 survey conducted by the National Survey on Drug Use and Health states that full-time food service workers ranked third amongst all occupational categories with 12.1 percent of the population ages 18 to 64 abusing alcohol within the month prior to the survey. Illicit drugs were used at a rate of 16.6 percent for this same population for the same time period. Food service workers in general—and cooks in particular—suffer one of the highest rates of illicit drug and alcohol abuse of all occupational categories. By industry, full-time food service workers aged 18 to 64 ranked number one and four for illicit drug and alcohol dependence, respectively. These statistics are frightening indeed when you consider that commercial kitchens are hazardous work environments.

Over the fourteen years I owned Café Marianna I had to fire servers, cooks and pot washers for alcohol abuse. I remember a pot washer named Sydney I had to let go because he was drinking on the job. Sydney was honest, dependable and a good worker. He'd been with Café Marianna for several years during which time he remained as sober as a judge. Because of alcohol Sydney lost everything: career, home, marriage, children. I hired Sydney from the homeless shelter. He was doing fine. He moved out of the shelter and into his own flat. He'd even begun a serious relationship. He seemed to be on the road to recovery until he began showing up to work drunk. Sydney began returning to work for the evening shift after he'd been drinking. I warned him that the kitchen was a dangerous place and he was going to hurt himself or someone else. He apologized and said he wouldn't do it again, but, of course, he did. The situation worsened. We caught him drinking on the job. When he thought no one was looking, he'd fill up a Styrofoam cup with wine and sip from it while washing pots. That was the last straw. Sydney had to go. He pleaded for his job, but you can give a man only so many chances.

I fired four waitresses for showing up shit-faced for the evening shift. I fired a French cook who guzzled a six pack in his car before every shift. He became belligerent and got into a fight with our pot washer who couldn't speak English. I wasn't there when it happened, so I called him at home and fired him. He was plastered when he came to collect his last paycheck. I could go on, but you get the idea: alcoholism is ingrained in the restaurant culture. It affects the workers in diners and high-end establishments. Alcoholism is a major underlying cause for reduced productivity and countless lost man-hours from work-related injuries like falls, cuts and burns. Even restaurateurs are prone to abusing alcohol. I've done this myself more than once. Wine tastings were part of the job. More than a few times I got hammered sampling wines. All those little sips add up to a lot of wine and *voila*, before I knew it I was three sheets to wind. Plus, when you host a wine tasting the wine vendor leaves all the opened bottles behind. I took them home and continued the tasting in front of the TV. Not a good habit to get into.

Part of the problem is that alcohol is so accessible in the restaurant business. Here's an example. I was eating dinner at a casual restaurant a few weeks ago in Alexandria, Virginia where I live. I sat at the counter so I could watch the cooks work in the open kitchen. It's a form of entertainment for me. During the hour I sat there I watched my waitress sneak wine while the manager and coworkers were occupied elsewhere. She'd guzzle a cup of white wine from a coffee cup when she was convinced no one was watching. But I was watching. She must have drunk nearly an entire bottle. How much wine had she consumed before I'd arrived and after I'd gone? Obviously, the woman had an alcohol problem and it was only a matter of time before someone discovers her problem and she gets fired. In most other businesses an alcoholic can pursue treatment through the employee health plan, but that's rarely an option in the restaurant business since so few restaurants provide health care benefits. Alcoholics in the restaurant industry are merely fired and left to their own devices. They drift from job to job. The really incorrigible ones wind up homeless. Not a pretty scene is it? Think about this the next time you dine out.

~~~

Occasionally, the customers brought their alcohol-related problems into Cafe Marianna. I could usually handle the situation without much turmoil. But I recall one customer who became a persistent problem. His name was Jackson Pepper. Jackson was an alcoholic. I'd run into him occasionally at the local health club. His face was often cut and bruised, suggesting that he'd been in a bar room brawl or tangled with his girl friend. Jackson usually visited Café Marianna at lunchtime when the dining room was full of twenty-something women. He'd slam down three or four vodka and tonics, which morphed him into a ladies' man, at least in his mind. Once he felt emboldened, he'd send drinks over to a table of females following up this generous overture with an introduction of himself. Jackson's lame attempts at pitching woo invariably resulted in laughable failures. Jackson became a pest. Women were beginning to complain. I had to intervene so I told the staff to not serve him any alcohol. This annoyed Jackson.

"What's the idea of not serving me, Charles," Jackson asked, incredulously.

"Jackson, you're a nice guy and all, but women are complaining about you hitting on them all the time."

"Hittin' on 'em. Hell I'm was just tryin' to be sociable," he replied, in self-defense. At that point I was not only convinced that Jackson had an alcohol problem, but I also suspected he had mental health issues. I say this because one day in the locker room at the health club Jackson and I were chatting and I asked him what he did for a living. He told me that he couldn't discuss it because he worked as an *undercover* agent for the federal government. Yeah right, I thought, I'm sure the FBI would hire an alcoholic who shows up to work with a mangled face as if he's been worked over in an alley. Sure, Jackson was the consummate spy catcher. Al-Qaeda would have a field day with him protecting us.

"This is a family restaurant, Jackson," I said, "and you're harassing some of the women and I'm getting flack for it. I'm gonna lose business."

"I'm gonna sue you," Jack threatened.

"Uh, wrong Jackson," I fired back. "According to the law a restaurateur can refuse to serve any customer if they're getting out of control and you've been getting out of control."

And that was it. Jackson didn't come in for a while either in protest or out of embarrassment. Eventually he surfaced and would stop by to have lunch. He knew better than to order any alcohol. He was pleasant enough and all was forgotten. Eventually, Jackson just disappeared and we never saw him again.

~~~

Then there was the impecunious Lars Anderson, a regular who enjoyed getting plastered at Café Marianna half a dozen times a month. He could never afford a meal, but managed to have enough cash in his pockets to get hammered with. Lars was a regular guy who, after a few drinks, would lament about failed relationships. I didn't mind Lars drinking beyond his limit because he lived just across the street and would harmlessly stumble home. We all liked Lars; he was part of the Café Marianna family. He was a happy drunk unlike many who can become boisterous and mean-spirited. There were two memorable incidents involving Lars. The first was when he plopped into a snow drift on the café patio. We discovered him as we were locking the front door. Lars managed to embed himself face first into the drift. He'd been there for well over an hour. He was sound asleep when we plucked him from the drift and escorted him home. The second incident was the night Lars mistook a city parking enforcement vehicle for a taxi. It was a slow night, which allowed us time to watch Lars climb in and out of the parking vehicle's rear seat. We knew exactly what had happened. Lars mistook the vehicle's rooftop emergency light for a cab's sign light. He made his way back into the restaurant and asked us to call him a cab, which we gladly did.

A mixture of people and alcohol often results in untoward incidents. Some will be serious and unseemly while others will be benign and entertaining. It's just part of the restaurant culture and the drinking public. Not all alcoholics drink themselves into a mind-numbing stupor like Ray Milland's character in *The Lost Weekend,* the 1945 flick illustrating the ravages and depths of alcoholism. Many are subtle drinkers who drink and drink without causing a ruckus. Restaurants love these kinds of drunks because they represent a very substantial, yet almost invisible cash flow—requiring little or no labor. A restaurant makes a significant portion of its income from booze. Take a bottle of wine, for example. A restaurateur will typically mark up a bottle two and a half to four times depending on the varietal, the vintage, customer perception of the quality and the wine's scarcity. Of course, the restaurateur has to estimate just how much he can charge his clientele based on their spending habits. Rest assured, he will charge as much as he can get away with. Such is the nature of the restaurant business.

~~~

Restaurant people are a misunderstood lot. They're often the odds and ends of society, the remnants that don't seem to fit in anywhere else. Restaurant workers don't always start out wanting to be restaurant workers. Many of us who wound up in the business started out in a completely different field. I'm a perfect example, I've got college degrees and had a respectable career, but I wound up in the hospitality industry in the end anyway. I remember having this same discussion with a customer at my café. I told her that when I was in graduate school I never thought that I'd say, "You want that with fries?"

Restaurant people are often vastly underappreciated. The next time you're deciding what to have for dinner consider that the guy who will cook your meal might have begun work at seven o'clock that morning and he won't get off until long after you're home in bed. He does this because very often he has to, he can find no other work. Most people would condescend to the cook's situation and rationalize that he should have acquired marketable skills. He's a cook because of his own shortcomings. It's his fault that he's doing what he is. What most people don't understand is that more often than not being a cook, a server or a busboy is not a choice; it's a matter of necessity. Because life isn't kind to everyone many have to seek employment in the restaurant industry. I would encourage everyone to consider this the next time they dine out and perhaps we might treat restaurant people with a bit more respect.

Restaurant Scams

The vast majority of servers and restaurateurs are honest people, but not all. There is tiny fraction that is perfectly willing to rip off unsuspicious customers. They do this in a variety of ways. They are so adept at perpetrating scams it is often difficult to detect a scam. And some scams are perfectly legal. It's a matter of the unsuspecting customer not knowing that he is being had. I have listed some of the more common scams that are perpetrated in America's restaurants:

Some servers are skilled at bilking a "sympathy tip" out of a customer. For example, a waiter might *happen* to mention that he's working a holiday because his brother is serving in Afghanistan and he's saving his days off so he can celebrate with his family upon his brother's return. This is a common scam for people who rely on tips for a living. This particular scam is not unique to the restaurant industry, cabbies use this one too.

Examine your check. Large parties are often unaware that a gratuity has been added to the bill and they tip on top of it. Servers "facilitate" this error by *forgetting* to inform the diners that the *house* tip has already been added. They might write the house tip on the backside of the check or add it to the food and beverage total. This scam occurs more frequently at vacation venues where the servers know they'll never see you again. The gratuity for large parties should be printed on the menu, but isn't always. This is a common deceptive practice. Some owners take a portion of the tips when this happens.

A server might tell you that the credit card machine is malfunctioning to impel you to pay cash. They pocket the cash and discard your check. The restaurant loses here.

Examine your check to make sure that you aren't paying for drink or food items you didn't order. Also check to see if the server over charged you for any food or beverage items that you did order. Make sure the dollar amount matches the prices stated on the menu. Once the sales transaction is completed and you leave the restaurant it will be difficult for you to claim that you have been overcharged.

Servers have been known to commit credit card fraud scams. When you give the server your credit card they upload your unique credit card information with a "skimming" device. They can sell your credit card information to a third party. Protect yourself by scrutinizing your monthly credit card statement for unauthorized charges and report any irregularities to your credit card company. Don't forget, you will need your credit card receipt as proof in a dispute.

Examine your monthly credit card statement. Waiters and managers have been known to "pad" the tip when processing the credit card charges. They're hoping you won't notice, or don't remember, the *error* on your credit card statement. Dishonest servers might ask you to sign the credit card in pencil so they can change the tip amount after you leave. This also occurs more often at vacation venues. A friend of mine got scammed like this in Las Vegas—a $20 tip became a $200 one. Usually, they won't try to scam for this large of an amount because it's more noticeable. Fortunately, in my friend's case the credit card company alerted him and rectified the situation, but don't depend upon the credit card company to protect you, they don't monitor customer charges like they used to.

If you can, keep an eye on the bartender. Bartenders will pour a fraction of the alcohol in your drink than they're supposed to especially in those specialty drinks with the little umbrellas. They know you won't be able to taste the alcohol anyway because the booze is overpowered by sweet, syrupy ingredients such as grenadine and soft drinks.

Who makes a good target? Servers who engage in scams often profile customers—man trying to impress his date, a customer in a hurry, a businessman with a group of clients, elderly people. A drunken customer is not likely to dispute, or even notice, overcharges and may not remember what he ordered when he sobers up. Customers who are attempting to impress others usually won't dispute a bill out of fear of embarrassment. Another favorite target is teenagers out on a date, say, dinner after the prom. These types of customers are often easy targets. The unscrupulous server or restaurateur calculates that it is worth the risk. Even if the scam is found out, they can claim it was a mistake and adjust the bill.

Protect yourself from these scams. If possible, observe the waiter or bartender closely, make sure that they are giving you what you are buying, don't let them order for you, select what you want and not what they suggest, check the bill carefully and make sure that it's accurate, pay with a credit card (it's more difficult for the waiter to scam the restaurant) and always examine the bill before you sign the credit card receipt. Keep the credit card receipt and the itemized food order, if provided. These may be your only proof if a subsequent dispute arises. Always use a pen and check to see if the tip has already been factored into the total cost of the food and beverage. And write the tip amount so that it cannot be changed. As stated above, at the end of the month look over your credit card bill and make sure that there are no unknown charges.

A Diners' Need-To-Know List

IF YOU HAVE waited tables you'll probably know that there are a number of factors that can make or break a dining experience. There are a number of Do's and Don'ts of which diners should be aware. Diners need to understand that they have a responsibility to be polite and respectful. Servers can be vindictive if they're mistreated, so think wisely about sending food back for an illegitimate reason. And don't disrespect your server. There are ways servers can get even by subtly sabotaging your dinner experience. The following list is a Diners'-Need-To-Know list. By following these suggestions, and being aware of possible risks, your dining experience can be enhanced and trouble-free:

Be punctual for your reservation. Think of your dinner reservation as a business meeting. When you're late everyone else at the meeting has to wait for your arrival. They have other meetings (customers) to attend to. When the table is not occupied the restaurant is losing income. Be considerate.

Understand that menus are constructed to maximize profits. For example, dollar signs will not appear before the dollar amount and the price numbers may be printed in very small font. This is all by design. Keeping the concept of money as abstract as possible makes spending less threatening. Some high-end restaurants omit pricing completely. They know that few people will ask the prices to avoid appearing cheap. Cooking schools teach menu design.

Don't be chintzy by asking for water, lemon, and sugar so you can make your own lemonade. Remember, they get a low hourly wage (the Federal legal minimum for servers is $2.13/hour) and live off their tips. Plus, servers often have to share their tips with the bus boys, bartenders and/or hostesses. Tip at least 15 to 20 percent.

Unless it's for health reasons, don't ask the kitchen to create a special meal for you. This annoys the cooks because you're forcing them to make an off-menu dish and this can upset their workflow. They're likely to just throw it together to get it done so they can move onto the next order. Have you ever tried to get a special order in a Chinese restaurant? Good luck with that, they usually refuse.

If you return food, make sure that it's for a legitimate reason—over-spiced, cold food, not what the menu stated, wrong order—and be respectful to your server when you make this request. We've all heard of stories about cooks or servers spitting on food. This is extremely rare, but it does happen. I know, I've seen it. While this is totally inexcusable, this sort of thing only happens when a customer's conduct is beyond egregious.

If you don't care for your meal, inform your server immediately so they can return it to the kitchen and order something else. They will almost always remove it from the bill. Don't eat half the meal and then tell your server you don't like it. A restaurateur is not going to fall for this.

Treat your server with respect. Remember, he can make or break your dining experience. Never snap your fingers to get your server's attention or bark his name across the room.

Remember, your server is a sales person. They're trained and instructed to sell you as much as possible. This is how they make their living and the restaurateur wants increased sales. There are books and seminars available where servers are taught the art of "suggestive selling." Forewarned is forearmed.

Servers are usually not allowed to tell customers about menu items that they consider inferior. Also, servers are instructed to recommend dishes that the chef wants to push. Sometimes the chef wants to get rid of food that is not as fresh as it should be or maybe he got a great deal on a particular food item. You might want to question what the server is pushing.

If your server tells you that the desserts are homemade, be skeptical—very few restaurants make their own desserts or bread. The next time you go to COSTCO don't be surprised to see a few of your local restaurateurs or chefs in the next line next to you stocking up on desserts.

If possible, avoid eating out on major holidays—especially Mothers' Day and Easter—and prime time on weekends. The sheer volume of customers pretty much guarantees that you'll receive inferior food and subpar service. Cooks rush to get the orders out and speed breeds mistakes. I've seen cooks drop food on the floor and slap it right back on the plate or they'll drop it in the deep-fat fryer first to "cleanse" it. It takes too much time for them to start the order all over again and that will disturb the work flow they are trying to maintain. If you do dine out on these heavy volume days, go early to increase your chances of getting a decent meal and snappy service.

Very few restaurants offer paid sick leave so employees tend to show up for work even when they're ill. A busboy or server with a family to support isn't going to miss a weekend or holiday shift, and miss an opportunity to earn big tips, just because he has diarrhea or is vomiting. Their fortitude is laudable, but these people are handling your food. If it's obvious that a server or busboy is ill, notify the manager. Not that he'll act on your complaint; he needs warm bodies in the front of the house. Plus, he won't be eating any food they might have handled.

If you want to linger long after you've finished eating, that's fine, but increase your tip. Waiters need to turn over tables as often as possible in order to serve the greatest number of customers during their shift. If you see that others are waiting for tables, leave when you're done so others can enjoy a meal too.

Avoid showing up just before closing time. I can tell you from personal experience cooks hate this. They're are tired and want to clean up the kitchen and punch out. They'll slap your entire order together all at once. Your entrée will be sitting under a heat lamp while you're still eating your salad.

If you've established a rapport with a certain server during previous visits ask to be seated in his section. Be generous with your tip and you'll get more attentive service. Your waiter can be your guardian and make sure the kitchen prepares your order correctly. A server who is familiar with your food preferences can ensure that your meal is prepared the way you like it.

Do not lose sight of the fact that when you eat out you're entering into a short-term purchase agreement with the restaurant. Don't forget the age-old legal doctrine of *caveat emptor*—Buyer Beware! Again, the vast majority of restaurateurs and servers are honest people trying to make an honest buck, but there are exceptions. After reading this you might be wondering why even risk eating out? True, there is a certain amount of risk, but the risks can be greatly minimized if you know the DOs and DON'Ts of dining out. It's simply a matter of being aware of what can go wrong and taking precautionary measures to prevent unfortunate incidents. As long as you're mindful of the risks, there's no reason you can't have a pleasant dining experience.

Chapter Ten

~~Food Network~~ *Fool Network*

"My wife is a terrible cook. She made us dinner last night and even the garbage disposal threw up."

Rodney Dangerfield

IS IT POSSIBLE that the ~~Food Network~~ Fool Network is waging a war on gastronomy in America? Some of its pathetic cooking shows suggest that it's on a mission to obliterate all that is decent about cooking America. The Fool Network show hosts aren't real cooks at all; they impersonate them. Take Patrick and Gina Neely, hosts of *Down Home with the Neely*s. If bad cooking was a criminal offense the Neelys' would have been fugitives from the law since their show began. Their show is more like a culinary crime scene than it is a cooking demo. The Neelys cleverly distract us with their playful banter and cutesy kitchen antics while they assemble with absolutely horrid dishes.

It isn't enough that the Neelys are pathetic cooks; they inflict additional pain upon their audience by giving it glimpses of their personal life. This tactic seems to work like a charm. For a while they had me convinced their marriage was made in heaven. I find it difficult to fight back the tears when Gina Neely gazes at her man with fawning admiration. Patrick responds with gestures of equal approbation. This is a marriage tailor-made for the kitchen where too many chefs often spoil the broth. But not in the Neely kitchen. And it's all I can do to maintain my composure when we're shown still photos of some of the soppy moments in their personal life.

Ms. Neely has fallen in love with the camera. She cannot resist winking at it and supplying toothy grins in a shameless attempt to curry favor with the audience. Patrick does his part by pretending to be a soul food cook who knows his way around a kitchen. Just because he's black doesn't mean he can cook soul food. Patrick is a worse cook than his pitiable wife. He bombards us with ersatz country slang like *y'all this* and *y'all that*! Patrick, please lose the phony chawbacon colloquialisms. You're not foolin' anyone.

Try as they might to convince us that they are a pair of exceptional home cooks who missed their calling, the Neelys are absolutely wretched cooks. Don't misconstrue what I say, they seem like genuinely nice people, but if I wanted to watch a cooking show with genuinely nice people I'd replay Jacque and Julia reruns. At least there I'd learn something.

~~~

The Neelys are not the only determined to sabotage good cooking in the homeland. There are other Fool Network operatives who are just as sinister and committed to snuffing out the American way of cooking. Take Sandra Lee; she's trying to get us addicted to Ritz crackers, canned frostings and frozen veggies. To destroy our health, Lee purposely cooks meals that are brimming with processed foods. To throw us of track, Lee beguiles us with an appealing smile and mindless prattle. I'm not fooled. No amount of lip gloss and deceitful smiles can hide the fact that Sandra is a terrible cook.

As bad a cook as Lee is, she could not have learned this dark art on her own. She had to have been mentored by that Cruella Deville of cuisine—Rachael Ray. Ray is peerless; no one can out cook her and I don't mean that in a good way. She's a master at tricking us into believing she can cook. She accomplishes this by distracting us with her diminutive stature, chirpy personality and mindless yammering. But Ray deserves our kudos; she has managed to captivate and dupe an entire nation. Millions believe that she is actually a good cook.

Lee and Ray have teamed up to stamp out good cooking by any means necessary. Their nefarious tactics have been successful. They've succeeded at getting many unsuspecting home cooks to transform perfectly edible food into matter that is not fit for human consumption. And if they ever need reinforcements they can always haul out that old war horse, Paula Deen, who has waged a one-person war against good cooking for years now. Deen has made the use of short cuts into an art form, especially the use bouillon cubes.

Other top soldiers in the organization are Claire Robinson, Sunny Anderson and Nigella Lawson. These henchwomen are also willing to do whatever it takes to stamp out good cooking where ever it thrives. Every soldier in the Fool Network's Army (FNA) has vowed to not be taken alive. They've all sworn to eat their own cooking if they're captured. Each carries a highly concentrated form of one of her own dishes. More potent than the most powerful snake venom, one capsule of their food will bring merciful death within minutes.

Up until now, the Fool Network—the Klingon Empire of food networks—has succeeded in spreading its dangerous brand of culinary terrorism across the planet. It's infected unsuspecting homes throughout North America and has even begun to infiltrate the U.K., the E.U. and parts of Asia. Can this juggernaut be stopped? Everything good cooks hold sacred is under attack by the Fool Network. This villainous enterprise must be stopped at all costs. Our stomachs depend upon it.

Those of us who love good cooking must resist this global scourge. We're in a death struggle for the whole enchilada. Culinarians around the world must unite. It's imperative that we raise our spatulas and tongs in defense of the founding principles upon which modern cookery is built. The world looks to us for protection. Culinary academies from Vietnam to Denmark have responded to the call to arms. They're churning out well-trained cooks in record numbers to combat this global nemesis. Chef instructors work tirelessly to get trained cooks to the front lines as soon as possible. They're on a war footing. Our struggle is a noble one and must continue until we prevail!

Of course, this spoof of the Fool Network and is only meant to be a humorous parody. I kid the Fool Network. I love it. It's a constant source of humor in our house. I don't know what we would do in our house if we couldn't ridicule the Fool Network's show hosts. When I want, Marianna, my twenty-one year old daughter, to learn what not to do in the kitchen I force her to watch the Fool Network. When I want her to understand how processed foods can ruin a meal when combined with perfectly edible food I encourage her to watch Sandra Lee. When I want Marianna to hear someone who doesn't know what they're talking about half the time when it comes to cooking I encourage her to watch Rachael Ray. And so it goes.

A Dearth of Talent

ONCE THE FOOD Network suits decided to embrace *foodtainment* they seemed to have scoured America for the least talented cooks available. Apparently, they decided that it is more important for their hosts to be telegenically acceptable rather than possess culinary skills. Turns out they were correct. The Food Network has a stable of handsome thirty-something show hosts whose pretty smiles do little to disguise the fact that most of them are absolutely dreadful cooks. It has become wildly popular despite the fact that it has assembled a dearth of cooking talent and produced a lineup of deplorable cooking shows. The Food Network seems to set the talent bar lower with each new season. Evidence of this is Sandra Lee's return in 2011. There has been a steady stream of the unskilled show hosts for years now; Robin Miller, the Neelys, Sunny Anderson. Just when you think the Food Network can't get any worse it does. The Food Network's most recent addition to its pitiable lineup is Nigella Lawson. The Food Network offers what can only be described as "karaoke cooking"; unoriginal, uninspired, dumbed-down cooking that requires only rudimentary culinary skills. Sauce making is a hallmark of a well-trained cook. When did you last see a Food Network host make even a basic sauce (like beurre blanc, volute or crème Anglais) or discuss the differences between cereal and root-based thickening agents?

And I've never seen any of them demonstrate necessary skills like boning a chicken, filleting a fish or making a batch of pâte à choux or puff pastry. These are skills that many serious home cooks want to learn, but they won't learn them on the Food Network because the vast majority of its hosts lack these skills themselves. The sad part of all this is that the Food Network may be selling a segment of its audience short. Certainly, there are many serious home cooks out there looking to improve their cooking skills.

Change the channel to PBS and you'll find cooking show hosts—with a few exceptions—who have mastered their craft and are demonstrating advanced cooking techniques. Clearly, there is a market for cooking shows that are challenging. There are three exceptions, however; *Everyday Food, Cook's Country* and *America's Test Kitchen*. More on these shows later. Other than these duds all of PBS's cooking show hosts give us experienced professionals who impart useful culinary knowledge. For example, take *Mexico: One Plate at a Time* with host Rick Bayless. Viewers will learn advanced cooking skills from Bayless whether he cooks traditional Mexican cuisine or applies modern interpretations to classic dishes. This is possible only because Bayless has mastered a particular cuisine.

If you talk to working chefs, as I have, you'll discover that they have a different opinion of the Food Network. To them it's either an object of derision or a source pathetic entertainment. A restaurateur friend of mine put it like this, "The Food Network doesn't have a clue as to what's going on in the real world of cooking and its shows are a joke." And a pastry chef friend of mine said, "I've watched the *Ace of Cakes* and if one of my pastry cooks cooked like any those people we'd kick his ass out of the shop." The prevailing sentiment among professionals is that the Fool Network is a bad food joke.

Vannatizing the Food Network

IT MIGHT BE useful to take a closer look at a few show personalities, especially the Food Network. Let's begin with Rachael Ray. It annoys me to no end that Ray is referred to as a *chef*. She is not a *chef*. Not long ago I realized that Ray is a *chef* in name only. It also occurred to me that calling Ray a *chef* is not any more harmful than when Caligula, the demented Roman emperor, made his favorite horse, Incitatus, a member of the Roman senate. Like Ray, the horse did nothing to earn the title. But we ought to give the horse at least some credit; it occasionally attended Senate sessions. Has Ray ever spent any time in a working commercial kitchen? In other words, "A horse by any other name is still a horse!"

How does a person who has never worked as a cook in a commercial kitchen get to host not one but several cooking shows? Wouldn't knowing how to cook be a prerequisite to having a cooking show? If you read Ray's bio there is nothing in there telling us that she cooked except at home, but that doesn't count. We've all done that. Her only prior experience in the world of cuisine was as a waitress and a clerk in the gourmet section of a department store. These jobs hardly qualify her to teach us how to cook.

In Ray's defense, it's not fair to blame her for becoming America's queen of cuisine. She didn't ask for it, we coronated her. I've always struggled to find what Ray has done to deserve her celebrity status. I've thought about it and always come up empty handed. Ray is the love child of the Food Network and Wall Street who conceived her, packaged her and sold her to America as the cook who lives next door. More to the point, Ray is the creation of the American media. They took a waitress from upstate New York and transformed her into a culinary icon. How did this happen? The answer to that question is for people who are smarter than me to figure out.

Ray's rise to the top reminds me of an equally untalented personality who America fell in love with decades ago. This would be Vanna White who, in the early 1980s, became Pat Sajak's letter-turning associate on the *Wheel of Fortune*. Vanna's stardom is inexplicable, but the fact remains that she's still flipping letters, well, actually nowadays she just touches the screen and the letters illuminate. Ray's popularity is equally incomprehensible; I doubt that even Ray can figure it out. I guess it doesn't matter how it happened, Ray is a star and that's that. She's the cooking show version of game show Vanna.

A Rorschach Celebrity

MAYBE YOU'VE FIGURED it out, but I don't get why Ray is so beloved. I've thought about it and have come up with a few possible reasons. Perhaps, like Vanna, Rachael is a Rorschach celebrity whose devoted fans perceive her in any way necessary to justify their adoration. A segment of Ray's fans might actually see her as a talented cook while others might find Ray's girlish giggle and chirpy personality simply irresistible. Still others might view her as the popular girl in high school who allowed only a select few to sit at her table in the cafeteria. It doesn't really matter why Ray is so popular, she just is and naysayers, like me, have to accept her stardom.

One of the most annoying things about Ray is that she has a tendency to give wrong information. On one show she said that she was adding cumin "to give this dish that smoky flavor." Doh! Mmmm, that's weird; I never heard that in three years of chef school or at any time over my twenty-five year career. Maybe Ray should tell the rest of the world that cumin is smoky. Inane comments like that reveal Ray's utter lack of cooking knowledge. Even my teenage daughter knows that cumin isn't smoky. Chipotle is smoky, but cumin is not. Her uninformed comment would not be that big of a deal except for the fact that she misinforms people and she reveals how little she knows about cooking.

Ray committed a cardinal gaffe during her November, 2009 Thanksgiving dinner show. This one was very serious because it concerns fire safety in the kitchen. During this particular show Ray had too many dishes that required cooking in the oven. With the oven racks already full, Ray put a potato and cream casserole on the floor of a gas oven. This should *never, ever* be done under any circumstances. This is a fire hazard. The liquid can bubble violently and overflow onto the oven floor causing a fire or, at least, create an enormous amount of smoke. The floor of a gas oven gets extremely hot because the flame source is located directly underneath. (Statistics show that house fires are three times more likely to occur on Thanksgiving Day than any other day of the year. And cooking fires are the top cause of house fires and injuries, according to the National Fire Protection Association [NFPA]. With more than 377,000 house fires in 2009, cooking and fire safety are key factors to an incident-free Thanksgiving. Underwriters Laboratories [UL], the leading independent product safety organization, suggests that home cooks not place glass cooking container directly over heat sources as one of its safety precautions.) One of the main concerns of professional chefs is kitchen safety. Ray's incident provides more evidence that she is a complete amateur in the kitchen. Cooking badly is one thing, but to intentionally demonstrate unsafe cooking techniques is another matter entirely and a very serious one. I wonder how many kitchen emergencies happened as a result of Ray's unsafe demo.

Ray is a whirling dervish on the set, darting from the fridge to the sink to the oven. I get dizzy just watching this bundle of energy. As she cavorts around the set she chatters like one of those wind-up dolls where you pull the string and it just talks and talks and talks. Ray talks about things that have nothing to do with what she's cooking such as her husband's food preferences. Who cares? And Ray has even expanded America's culinary lexicon with words and acronyms like "yummo" and "e-v-o-o," which stands for "extra virgin olive oil". Why can't she just say "olive oil" like the rest of us? I don't mean to bust Ray's chops; it's just that I hold all cooking show hosts to a higher standard. After all, they are supposed to know more than we do. Actually, Rachael seems like a pleasant gal and I'm sure she'd be fun to hang out with. Maybe she'll invite me over for dinner one day and I'll show her how to use an oven.

Sundays with Sandra

PERHAPS THE EXPRESSION, "You can put lipstick on a pig, but it's still a pig." was invented for Sandra Lee. She is arguably the worst cook on television today. Lee is another example of Vannatizing the Food Network. Lee is a caricature of herself in that she presents an almost cartoonish distortion of relatively simple tasks—preparing home-cooked dishes. Her show could be interpreted as a satirical treatment of a real cooking show. Does Lee actual cook? If the definition of cooking is combining cans and boxes of highly-processed ingredients is considered actual cooking then she's cooking. Shakespeare once said, "All tragedies end in death and all comedies end in a marriage." All Sandra Lee's cooking shows end in heartburn.

There's no denying the fact that Sandra Lee has become a one-woman empire rivaling her girl friends, Paula Deen and Rachael Ray. Going into an impressive 14th season of *Semi-Homemade Cooking*, Lee is one of the premier show hosts in Food Network's pitiable lineup. Her new show initially aired Sunday on mornings, but that will change. The quality of ingredients doesn't matter; Lee still doesn't know what to do with them. Here's an example. During a recent show she mutilated a perfectly good piece of pork loin. She began the cooking process in fine fashion when she seasoned and pan-seared the meat. Things began to go south at that point. She placed the loin in a crock pot with canned chicken broth (naturally), dried fruits, celery and onions. After an unbelievably long eight hours of cooking time she dumped the overcooked offal onto a serving platter. I cringed as the once beautiful piece of pork loin had shrunk to half its original size. This indicated that all of the meat's natural juice had exuded into the surrounding liquid resulting in a wizened, dehydrated hunk of porcine flesh. I would have rather shared a burger with David Hasselhoff than eat that mess. Yes, it looked that bad.

If Lee knew the first thing about cooking meat she'd know that different cuts require different cooking methods. Pork loin—because it is low in connective tissue—requires a short cooking time. When cooked too long, the protein fibers become harder and harder and begin to crack, resulting in a grainy and crumbly product. Another problem with overcooking is moisture loss. Meat can be as much as 75 percent water, so when cooked too long the cell walls rupture and most of the interior moisture is lost. Plus, when meat is overcooked, the collagen—the *glue* that holds the meat together—is dissolved and the meat literally falls apart. This is why Lee's pork loin disintegrated into a dry, stringy mess. If Sandra was bent on slow cooking pork she should have selected the correct cut such as blade, butt or shoulder. These are tougher cuts that require moist heat cooking for extended periods, perfect for the slow cooker. But even these cuts can be over cooked. Depending on the cut and size of meat, two to four hours is usually enough time to render a tough cut tender without ruining it.

Slow cooking pork loin was the wrong cooking method for this particular cut of meat. Pork loin could have been seared, finished in the oven, sliced and served with pan juices. Another common technique would be to serve it Schnitzel-style where it is pounded thinly—using a mallet or rolling pin—then coated with seasoned flour or panko crumbs and sautéed for a minute or two on each side; longer than this will toughen the texture. True to form, Lee cooed over her creation and pronounced how scrumptious and tender the loin was. She always does this no matter how unappetizing her dish turns out.

There is one aspect of Sandra that I do admire—her devotion to social causes. Lee devotes more of her time to those in need than any of her other food celebrity colleagues. Sandra deserves our kudos for her support of Share Our Strength's Operation Frontline nutrition education program and the Food Bank. I have conducted cooking classes for this same organization and it's a worthwhile cause. Chefs and nutritionists around the country donate their time to teach disadvantaged people how to make inexpensive and nutritious meals. Lee should be congratulated for championing these noble causes. Now if she can just get the rest of the Fool Network gang to do join in the lives of many unfortunate Americans could be made better.

Paula, the Deen

TWO TYPES OF people watch Paula Deen's (who also answers to Old Yeller) cooking shows—people who are pushing three-hundred pounds and people who are over three-hundred pounds. Paula Deen is a back slappin' good ol' gal who knows how to cook country, well kind of. Bring on the biscuits, pork chops and sausage gravy. I rarely see a heart-healthy dish in her culinary repertoire. Don't get me wrong, I like Paula Deen. I enjoy her "aw shucks" style and I admire how she connects with her audience. It's this down-home image that makes us feel as if she's one of us. This is why she's so popular. It can't be for her cooking prowess. Fact is she's not a very good cook. Paula is a cool cucumber; she never becomes flummoxed no matter how many dishes she's a makin'. Even her hair remains perfectly coiffed.

Paula is a master of the culinary short cut. She's not above dumping in cans of mushroom soup or fried onion rings into the pot. And the woman worships bouillon cubes. I watched in disbelief as she tossed in a handful of beef bouillon cubes into a pot of gumbo. "These bouillon cubes will give it that nice, salty flavor . . ." she pronounced, in a rich country twang. I thought, *any cook who knows anything about gumbo is cringing right about now.* Gumbo rule No.1: Porcine products always; bovine products never (with one possible exception—smoked beef sausage). Clearly, Paula doesn't know the first thing about gumbo. If she, or any other Fool Network host, doesn't know how to make a particular dish they might want to consult with a professional chef before embarrassing themselves in front of millions. We chefs have an expression, "Don't cook beyond yourself." When you do this you're bound to get into trouble. A very limited use of short cuts and artificial flavor enhancers is acceptable. I use them myself on occasion, but they should be used judiciously.

On another show Paula made a feeble attempt at a fresh fruit tart. She began the process by making a good sweet dough paste for the bottom crust, but things went downhill from there. With little regard for aesthetics, she piled fresh fruit on top of some gooey cream cheese filling. Next, she slathered on an unidentified goop, that she called a "glaze," all over the fruit. (A good glaze for this dessert is warmed apple jelly. Just microwave the jar and liberally brush the melted jelly on the fruit.) Paula's tart looked absolutely appalling. She just heaped the fruit in a pile and painted it. It looked like a child threw it together. To be fair to Paula, this eyesore was not entirely her fault entirely. Clearly, the Paula has little or no training yet she's expected to produce dishes beyond her skill level. Doesn't the Food Network have a staff chef who can assist her? And she never did identify the glaze.

Paula seems to be a charming person and I bet she'd be a hoot to have a beer with. She comes across as down-to-earth and unpretentious. And don't get me wrong, I'm happy that she's succeeded. I love to see people succeed. It's just that it's so disappointing when someone in her position has the opportunity to show others how to cook and she can't be bothered to get it right. Her devoted fans deserve better. She gets paid a ton of money to get the food right. It's an insult to the audience that she can't be bothered to learn how to prepare a simple dish like a fruit tart correctly. Does she advance the art of cooking?

Partners in Crime

Of course, other inhabitants of Food Network's world bring us dumbed-down cooking; *Big Daddy's House, 5 Ingredient Fix, Quick Fix Meals with Robin Miller* and *Cooking For Real* to name a few. And I couldn't help noticing that Giada De Laurenttis, the granddaughter of legendary film director Dino De Laurenttis, has a couple of Food Network shows. I wonder whether her family name had anything to do with Giada getting these shows. Seems to me like Giada figured it was time to cash in on the family name and, of course, the Fool Network was more than happy to add this iconic name to its pantheon of *faux* chefs.

Although I don't feel the love for the Food Network, I must admit that there are a handful of exceptional cooks in an otherwise frighteningly bad lineup. Alexandra Guarnaschelli, Tyler Florence and Anne Burrell (her hair looks like she stuck her finger in a wall socket) are all accomplished cooks. I watch their shows regularly because I can learn from them. This is what a cooking show should be about. Why can't the Food Network give us more top notch pros like this trio? Instead, we get a steady diet of lame food competitions and brainless reality reality shows. Enough already!

For the most part the cooking shows on PBS are head and shoulders above the cable cooking shows. It would seem that PBS has different production criteria and standards. Except for a few, I've never seen a bad cooking show on PBS. Some are better than others, but I've never seen one that compels me to ask, *how did this person get a cooking show and why am I wasting my time watching?* My favorites are Hubert Keller, Lidia Bastianich, Steve Raichlen, Rick Bayless, Tommy Tang and Jacques Pépin. I've been a professional chef for twenty-five years and I still learn from good cooking shows. Cooking is a never-ending learning process.

There are a few PBS cooking shows that belong on the Food Network because they are more foodtainment than substance; *Everyday Food, Cook's Country* and *America's Test Kitchen.* On *America's Test Kitchen* and *Cook's Country*—which are nearly mirror images of each other—two cooks, Bridget Lancaster and Julia Collin-Davison, stumble through recipes while Christopher Kimball, their boss and the show's self-appointed quipster, does his darnedest to make himself relevant. He does this by shamelessly injecting stupid food anecdotes and lame jokes while he hovers over Lancaster and Collin-Davison as if he's scrutinizing their cooking demo. Lancaster and Collin-Davison—who lack the aplomb of experienced pros—perform like a pair of automatons who appear to have rehearsed their respective demos ad nauseam. A professional cook's performance would be a much more facile. The Kimball girls seem to be constantly looking to Kimball for approval.

I still don't understand why he's on the show. Lancaster and Collin-Davison reveal their lack of culinary acumen when they fail at basic cooking techniques. (If I hadn't mastered a particular cooking skill, I'd damn sure master it before I got in front of a camera.) A telling example is when either of them attempt to truss meat or poultry. They wound excess string every which way much like a five-year old would wrap a Christmas gift. (Correct trussing requires one continuous length of string that is strategically wound around the bird or roast to keep it bound during cooking.) This would not be a big deal except that trussing is a basic skill that every rookie cook should know. Kimball and his girls have no idea how to truss and couldn't be bothered to learn for the show. People watch cooking shows to learn how to perform new skills correctly. They have a right to expect this. Predictably, Kimball and his minions swoon over their creations. They blather on about how great their dishes turned out. What I don't get is why Kimball presumes that he and his assistants can teach us how to cook. Kimball's background is in food journalism and editing. He's never even a cooked for a living so where does he get off thinking he can teach us? *Cook's Country* is a clone of *America's Test Kitchen*. It features equally dreadful cooks and rates kitchen equipment. I don't get it.

On *Everyday Food*, one of Martha Stewart's endeavors, a collection of mostly novice cooks prepare ultra-easy meals. Easy-to-do meals are fine, but they should at least be demonstrated by people who can out cook the audience. The women—and it's an all-female cast except for the pastry guy, John Baricelli, who is actually quite good—on *Everyday Food* are all frightful cooks. Too often Martha's girl's reveal their lack of culinary expertise. They're painful to watch. On one show one of the hosts slow cooked lamb shanks. Either she couldn't be bothered or didn't know to season and brown the shanks in a skillet before placing them in the slow cooker. This is a prerequisite to slow cooking meat and poultry, this small step adds color and flavor and makes the dish more aesthetically appealing.

Not that demonstrating good cooking techniques is matter of concern for the Stewart girls. One of my ex-wives can cook better than any woman on *Everyday Food* and she's a Brit for crying out loud.

I would be remiss if I didn't mention an egregious act of misinformation that was committed by a Food Network veteran who should have known better, Ina Garten—who, by the way, comes across stiffer than Paula Deen's hair. Ina's error is proof positive that the woman has had little or no professional training or a chef is not reviewing the Food Network's cooking shows for technical accuracy. Here's an example of what I mean. On an episode of *Barefoot Contessa* entitled *All About Chocolate*, Ms. Garten bumbled through the procedure of tempering couverture chocolate, which is a very precise and unforgiving process. There is no room for inexactitude.

To illustrate my point it's necessary to explain why correct tempering is so important. Tempering couverture (French for covering or coating) chocolate—premium chocolate that has a percentage of cocoa butter in the 32-39 percent range and the total of the percentage of the combined cocoa butter plus cocoa solids must be at least 54 percent—is an exacting procedure with small temperature tolerances. Tempering requires many hours of practice to master. Tempering couverture correctly is critical to the appearance and texture of the finished product. It's painfully obvious that Ms. Garten does not understand the process. Cocoa butter, which is an important constituent of couverture, is a complex mixture of fats, each having a different melting and setting point. It is the presence of these different fats fractions that makes it so important that couverture is tempered correctly.

When melted couverture, which should be stirred frequently, has reached a temperature of 115-118°F (46-47°C) (milk couverture 110°F [43°C])—which is what Ms. Garten used during her show—it is removed from the heat, and the bottom of the bowl has been dried with a cloth, it is poured onto a dry marble slab where it is spread back and forth with a spatula until it begins to set. The chocolate must be returned to the bowl and very carefully taken to temperature of 88°F (31°C) (milk couverture to 84°F [29°C]). This juncture is critical because the residual heat in the bowl may be sufficient to take the couverture up to or beyond these temperatures. If the temperatures are exceeded, the tempering process must be started all over again.

The reason for tempering is not easy to explain and is beyond the scope of this book, but if tempering is not done correctly the couverture will not set quickly and molded figures will not leave the molds easily. There will also be fat and sugar blooms. Fat bloom is due to the fat (cocoa butter) fractions not being mixed so that they float to the surface and will present a grey film spoiling the chocolate's attractive glossy appearance. Sugar bloom is a result of dampness when the sugar on the surface dissolves and re-crystallizes in larger form upon drying.

During the episode in question Ms. Garten simply melted a batch of milk chocolate in the microwave and pronounced it "tempered." She completely disregarded the usual precautions as described above. Obviously, Ms. Garten isn't acquainted with the concept of tempering nor has she bothered to learn the process, yet she gives the impression to her audience that she knows what she's doing when she stated, "This is the easy way to temper without all those thermometers and things . . ." Clearly, she has no idea of what she is doing. Thermometers are a necessary tool in the tempering procedure.

When Ms. Garten's viewers follow her tempering process they'll be confounded when their *bonbon* don't turn out as Ina promised. Try as they might they will never achieve the desired results if they follow Ina's tempering process. It will be an expensive, failed experiment—couverture can cost around twenty dollars per pound or more. Erroneous information like Ms. Garten's is commonplace on the Fool Network. But misinformation and inaccuracies often go unnoticed because so few viewers possess the culinary expertise to recognize the mistakes. The Food Network understands. Apparently, professional chefs have no input on show content. Ina needs some serious cooking lessons.

F.O.R.C.

I THINK IT'S about time someone created a national organization whose members can only be *real* chefs. I've even thought of a name; the Fraternal Order of Real Chefs or F.O.R.C. for short. The whole purpose of the F.O.R.C. would be to weed out nonprofessional chefs. Just like any other professional organization, the F.O.R.C. applicants would have to present legitimate professional credentials to prove that they are a chef. But the F.O.R.C. would make it unbelievably easy. Prospective members only have to prove that they cooked professionally for one (1) day. They don't even have to be a graduate from a fancy culinary academy. No other credentials are required. They only have to have cooked for one day in a professional kitchen. That's it! With this singular requirement, 90 percent of the Fool Network's show hosts would not qualify to become F.O.R.C. members. But there are a few stipulations; running a catering operation out of your home (à la Paula Deen and Martha Stewart) doesn't count as professional cooking. And operating a food truck doesn't qualify you either. Somehow cooking in the back of a truck just doesn't seem to be professional cooking.

The F.O.R.C.'s creation is long overdue. America has had a belly full of imposters calling themselves chefs. It's high time for real chefs to rise up and put an end these phonies masquerading as professionals. The likes of Paula Deen and Martha Stewart give real chefs a bad name. It's a matter of professional pride. Would the American Medical Association grant membership to quacks? Would American Bar Association admit ambulance chasers? (Probably not, but then they can always run for Congress.) These organizations have professional standards to weed out the frauds and drum them out of the profession. It is high time real American chefs banded together and did the same thing. Enter the F.O.R.C.

The F.O.R.C.'s mission statement might read something like this: "To serve our members, our profession and the public by maintaining good culinary standards as the national representative of the culinary profession. The Order will play a key role in making sure that its members don't wind up on the Food Network. Our ultimate goal is to eradicate culinary imposters by exposing them wherever they exist." Like any other professional association, the F.O.R.C. would have a charter, bylaws, policies and procedures and standards of conduct.

Of course, the F.O.R.C would need a slate of founding officers. I've thought about a few possible candidates. First I thought of Emeril as President, but he talks too much, no one else could get a word in edge wise at board meetings. Then I considered Anthony Bourdain, but he's a New York chef and the only people who like New York chefs are other New York chefs. Jacque Pépin would be great except he's French, which wouldn't sit right with most American chefs who have ever worked with the French. Jamie Oliver would be acceptable except for the fact that he's a Brit and the world still believes that Britons can't boil water. Then, I thought of Bobby Flay, but most people find him obnoxious. I know I do. Come to think of it I just can't find suitable officers. I'd appoint myself president, but I don't have the time for the post. I'll be too busy autographing copies of this book. Oh, just forget the whole thing!

Chapter Eleven

A Cookbook

"I was 32 when I started cooking; up until then, I just ate."

Julia Child

ANYONE WHO COOKS for a living is bound to come across hundreds or thousands of recipes; some are keepers while others are not so good. Some just need a little modification others are fundamentally flawed and useless, but very occasionally professionals come across recipes that are, well, perfect. These are the ones chefs hang onto.. These are the ones they rely upon throughout their careers. Having multiple recipes for the same item is superfluous when a single, perfect one will do. Many professionals also cling to family recipes. I know I have. With a combination of professional and family recipes any pro is bound to amass a formidable repertoire. I thought I might share a few of my favorites with you. I've selected recipes that aren't beyond the average home cook's ability and that include ingredients that can be found at the neighborhood grocery store. I hope you try a few of these and have fun with them. Cooking should be first and foremost about having fun. Enjoy!

Entrées

Turkey Neck Gumbo

This is a variation on gumbo I learned to make in New Orleans. It's cheap, easy and tasty. I was introduced to turkey necks when I worked on an all-black crew in steel mill on the south side of Chicago. One of my coworkers generously made lunch for the crew once or twice each week. This was my first exposure to soul food, which I fell in love with. The cook's name was Castro. Everything he cooked was delicious, but I especially enjoyed the turkey necks.

Serves: 6-8 Time: 3 hours

Ingredients
1 pound smoked sausage, cut into ¼ "slices
4 pounds turkey necks
6 bay leaves
1 quart chicken stock
1 cup onion, diced
1 cup curly parsley, minced
1 cup green bell pepper, diced
¼ cup fresh garlic, minced
1 cup celery, diced
1 can tomato paste
2 tablespoons powdered time OR thyme leaves
3 tablespoons Worstershire sauce
½ cup vegetable oil or butter
½ cup all purpose flour
3 tablespoons hot sauce
1 teaspoon salt
1 teaspoon black pepper

Method
   In a heavy stockpot, simmer the turkey necks and bay leaves with the chicken stock. Simmer covered until tender, approximately 2 hours. When cooled, de-bone, reserving only the meat and stock, separately. Discard the bay leaves and bones. In a large, heavy pot combine the oil and flour and make a roux. Cook over low heat and stir continuously until dark brown. DO NOT burn roux. If it's burned, discard it and start over. To the roux add the sausage, onions, bell peppers, celery, parsley and garlic. Sauté until vegetables are softened, for about 15 minutes.
   Add thyme, tomato paste, Worstershire sauce, hot sauce, salt and pepper. Add turkey stock and bring to boil then reduce heat and simmer for one hour. Add chopped turkey meat and adjust seasoning. Serve with white rice.

Chicken and Smoked Sausage Jambalaya

Jambalaya is a quintessential Louisiana dish. Americans associate Louisiana cooking with jambalaya; and for good reason. It's as old Louisiana itself. Jambalaya is a perfect example of how a new dish is created when cultures meld together. In this case it happened when the French, Spanish and African cultures collided during Louisiana's colonial period. Each culture made a culinary contribution to the dish. Jambalaya's precursor is the traditional Spanish rice casserole, *paella*. When the Old World dish met New World ingredients—such as alligator and crawfish— *viola* a new dish was born. The commonly accepted version of how the dish got its name is that the word is derived from the combination of the French word *jambon* meaning ham, the French article *à la* and *ya*, thought to be of West African origin, meaning rice; hence, the name *jamb-à-la-ya*.

Jambalaya is a favorite among tourists and Louisianans alike. Unlike the classic *paella,* the combination of ingredients, vegetables and spices for making your favorite version of jambalaya is limitless. You can throw in vegetables, seafood, sausages, poultry and pork. It's sort of a Rorschach dish where it can be whatever you want it to be just by adding any of a wide variety of ingredients! I learned to make jambalaya at Chez Helene, a family-owned café with the reputation of serving some of the best Creole-Soul food anywhere. It's been closed of many years and, sadly, its owner, Austin Leslie, died from health complications brought on by hurricane Katrina.

Serves: 6-9 Time: 1½ hours

Ingredients
1 pound smoked sausage
½ pound bacon
1 cup tomato sauce
1 chicken, 2-3 pound fryer
1 cup each onion, celery, and bell pepper, course cut
1 cup chopped parsley
¼ cup garlic, minced
1 quart chicken broth, canned will suffice

2 cups converted rice
4 bay leaves
2 tablespoon Worstershire sauce and hot sauce
1 Tbsp dried thyme leaves
Salt and black pepper

Directions
Place cut up chicken in stockpot and cover with broth. Bring to boil the reduce heat to simmer. Cook for 10 minutes, chicken will be only partially done (cooking will be completed in the oven). Set aside chicken and stock. Cut bacon and sauté until fat is rendered. Slice sausage into ¼" slices and sauté with bacon until sausage becomes slightly crispy. Add celery, onion, peppers and garlic and sauté with bacon and sausage only until slightly softened. Combine ALL ingredients in a large baking pan or casserole dish. Add 5 cups of chicken stock and stir to distribute ingredients evenly. When all ingredients are combined, cover dish with aluminum foil and bake in 375ºF oven for 60 minutes or until rice is tender and chicken is fully cooked. Remove bay leaves and serve while still hot.

Turkey and Smoked Sausage Gumbo

Most Americans know that gumbo is a classic soup made famous by Louisiana chefs, but it also has African roots. The use of okra is commonly used as a thickening agent and for flavor. Gumbo came out of bayous of southwest Louisiana. There's no one recipe for gumbo, every family and every restaurant has its own. Here's one that I learned at Chez Helene restaurant near the Vieux Carré or old French Quarter. Try it, you'll love it.

Serves: 6-8 Time: 1½ hours

Ingredients
2 pounds smoked sausage, cut into ¼" slices
4 pounds turkey parts, thighs and legs (chicken, duck or pork is optional)
1 cup each parsley, bell pepper, celery and onion; chopped
¼ cup fresh garlic, chopped
6 bay leaves

4 tablespoons tomato paste
2 tablespoons thyme leaves
3 tablespoons Worstershire sauce
½ cup vegetable oil or butter
½ cup flour
Hot sauce, salt and pepper to taste

Directions

   In a stockpot, just cover the turkey parts with water or chicken stock. Simmer uncovered until tender, approximately 1 hour. When cooled, de-bone the turkey reserving the meat and stock. In a large, heavy pot combine the oil and flour and make a roux. Cook over medium heat and stir continuously with a whisk until the color of peanut butter. DO NOT burn the roux as this will impart a burnt flavor to the soup. If burnt, discard and begin again. To the hot roux add sausage, onions, bell peppers, celery, parsley and garlic. Sauté until vegetables are partially cooked. Add thyme, tomato paste, Worstershire sauce, hot sauce, salt and pepper. Add turkey stock and stir until mixture is homogenous. Bring to boil then reduce heat and simmer for one hour. Finally, add shopped turkey meat and adjust seasoning. Remove bay leaves. Serve with white rice

Shrimp Po' Boy

   Also called and "Shrimp Loaf", the shrimp po boy is one of the most popular varieties of this legendary New Orleans' sandwich. As mentioned earlier, the po' boy has its origins in the streetcar workers' strike of 1929. Po' boys can have a variety of fillings; oysters, soft shell crabs, roast beef, turkey, ham, chicken or egg salad . . . My favorites are the fried oyster and shrimp ones. Beyond the unparalleled flavor, the texture of the crunchy oysters takes this sandwich to another level. An oyster po' boy should be "fully dressed" meaning it has to be filled with shredded lettuce and tomato and basted with melted butter or mayo. Mayo may be substituted with tartar sauce or New Orleans' style *rémoulade* sauce—really doctored up tartar sauce. The foundation of this work of sandwich art is the bread. Common sandwich bread won't do. Any respectable po' boy must be made with an ample length of a crunchy French baguette. Preferably, the loaf should be toasted prior to building the sandwich. The crunchiness of the shrimp and warm bread are significant because they impart a perfect texture and mouth feel.

Serves: 4 Time: 20 minutes
Ingredients
16-20 raw shrimp, lg.
1 cup all-purpose flour
1 cup corn meal
2 eggs, beaten
1 cup milk
3 cups peanut oil
1 French baguette, sliced in 6-8" sections
Mayonnaise or melted butter
Shredded lettuce and tomato slices
Salt and pepper, to taste
Old Bay seasoning, to taste

Directions

Combine flour, corn meal and Old Bay. Add salt and pepper, to taste, to make seasoned coating blend. Whisk egg and milk in a separate bowl. Thoroughly coat raw shrimp in seasoned dry mixture then immerse in egg and milk mixture. One by one recoat each oyster in the seasoned dry mix and drop in hot peanut oil of 350°F. Submerge shrimp in hot oil and cook until golden brown. Shrimp will float when done. This should only take about two minutes. DO NOT overcook the shrimp. Shrimp are mostly water and will rapidly lose moisture when cooked too long. Drain on paper towel. Spread mayo or melted butter on the sliced, toasted baguette sections. Finally, arrange shrimp, lettuce and tomato in baguette and enjoy this uniquely American sandwich. Shrimp may be replaced with oysters or fish fillet. Place shrimp in a sliced crunchy baguette and serve with rémoulade sauce. Garnish with lettuce and tomato. Serve with hot French fries.

Deep-Fried Soft Shell Crabs

The soft shell crabs is one of the South's greatest contributions to American cuisine. Either way they are a mouth-watering delight. Soft shells are a delicacy in every sense of the word. They can be sautéed or deep fried. A soft shell is a common blue crab that's harvested, and cooked, during the early stages of molting, when the crab sheds its smaller shell and a new, larger shell forms. The crab should be cooked before the new shell begins to harden.

A bit of precooking preparation that needs to be done. The crab needs to be cleaned.

1. To clean soft-shell crabs, hold the crab in one hand, and using a pair of kitchen shears, cut off the mouth and eye parts.
2. Lift one pointed end of the crab's outer shell; remove the gills by pulling them out. Repeat on the other side.
3. Turn the crab over and pull off the small flap known as the apron. Rinse the entire crab well and pat dry. Once cleaned, crabs should be cooked immediately.

Only buy crabs that are alive. If they don't move when touched they're dead and you won't know when they expired. Smell the crabs. Like other seafood, soft shells should odorless or smell like the ocean. Avoid buying frozen crabs as they lose most of their body fluid when they thaw out and appendages tend to break off. Soft shells should only be consumed during the season, which varies with the latitude. Soft shells are great with French fries and cole slaw or in a po' boy sandwich.

Serves: 4 Time: 30 minutes

Ingredients
4 soft shells
2 eggs, lg
½ cup milk
1 cup all-purpose flour
4 cup frying oil, or as needed
Salt, pepper & seafood seasoning mix such as Old Bay, to taste

Directions
Combine the flour, salt, pepper and Old Bay. Whisk together the milk and eggs to make egg wash. To coat the crabs, dredge them thoroughly in

seasoned flour, then dip in egg wash and back into the flour mixture. The crab is now ready for frying.

Heat the frying oil to 350ºF in a sauté pan. Carefully place the crabs into the hot oil. Cook for at least 2 minutes, or until golden brown on one side. With tongs, carefully turn over and cook until golden on the other side. When crabs fry they tend to explode splashing oil on anyone standing nearby so cover with a frying screen or hold a lid a few inches over the pan. Drain on paper towel. Serve hot while they are still crispy.

Turkey Pot Pie

After Thanksgiving we can only eat so many turkey sandwiches. Why not turn those turkey leftovers into a filling dish that will get you through the chilly days ahead? Make a turkey pot pie. It's easy, inexpensive (you already have the main ingredient) and tasty. Americans are pie lovers. Pies are a vestige of our colonial past, especially here in the Mid-Atlantic region. The English are great pie makers, especially savory ones. In the middle ages the shell of a pie was referred to as a *coffin*.

The filling
1 stick salted butter
1 cup potatoes, peeled and cubed
1 cup celery, chopped
1 cup frozen peas and carrots
1 cup onion, diced
3 tablespoons flour
1 cup turkey broth or canned chicken broth
1 cup table cream
1 teaspoon thyme leaves
Salt and pepper to taste
2 cups leftover turkey, chopped

Serves: 8-10 Time: 3 hours

Directions
In a heavy-bottomed pot melt butter. Add potatoes, celery and onions and sauté until al dente. Add frozen peas and carrots, thyme leaves, salt and

pepper. Mix in flour until distributed, allow cooking for several minutes, but do not brown. Stirring continuously, add all cream and broth, only as needed, to achieve a thick stew-like consistency. Taste and adjust for seasoning. Transfer mixture to casserole of baking dish. Allow to cool before topping with pastry.

The pastry
2 sticks unsalted butter
½ tablespoon sugar
½ teaspoon salt
¼ cups very cold milk, as needed
2 cups sifted cake flour, all-purpose will suffice
1 egg, beaten

Directions
Mix together sifted flour, sugar and salt. Using a pastry cutter or fork, cut butter into the flour until pieces are pea-size. To form dough, add milk incrementally and mix until a dough ball is formed. Mix until just combined. Do not over mix. It should not be crumbly, but not sticky either. If too wet, add flour to compensate. Form dough into a flat disc, wrap with plastic wrap and refrigerate for at least 2 hours, preferably longer. On a lightly floured surface, use your hands to slightly flatten dough. Roll dough from center to outward to a size 1" larger than the casserole dish.

Food processor directions: Prepare as above, except place steel blade in food processor bowl. To bowl add flour, butter, sugar and salt. Pulse until most of mixture until butter is dispersed, but remains pea size. Add milk incrementally through feed tube and pulse until ball just begins to form. It is preferable to add too little milk when using a processor as dough can be formed by hand. Remove dough from bowl to plastic wrap, shape into a disc and refrigerate.

Assembling and baking
Rolled pastry will be transferred to cover filled casserole dish. To transfer pastry, dust with flour and wrap it around the rolling pin. Unfurl dough onto casserole. Crimp edge with fore finger and thumb to create a fluted edge. With a pastry brush, paint entire dough with beaten egg. Do

not prick pastry. Place pot pie on cookie sheet and bake at 400ºF until pastry is golden brown and cooked, about 45 minutes. Serve before pie cools.

Louisiana Shrimp Creole

Shrimp Creole is a dish of Louisiana Creole origin—French and Spanish heritage—consisting of cooked shrimp in a mixture of diced tomatoes or tomato sauce, onion, celery and bell pepper, parsley and garlic spice with condiments. Kit is served over steamed or boiled white rice. The shrimp may be cooked in the mixture or cooked separately and added at the end. Other "Creole" dishes may be made by substituting some other meat or seafood for the shrimp, or omitting the meat entirely and make an all veggie version. Nearly every restaurant in Louisiana has its own version of Shrimp Creole. Apart from the foundation ingredients of onion, celery and bell pepper, Creole dishes are commonly used as "improvisational" delight, as the basic recipe may be altered to include whatever ingredients the cook has readily available. The shrimp may be substituted with alligator, fried fish, chicken or pork. Smoked sausage may be added.

Serves: 8-10 Time: 1½ hours

Ingredients
2 pounds large shrimp with heads and shells
½ cup bacon, diced
1 cup bell peppers, chopped
1 cup onion, diced
1 cup celery, diced
1 cup curly parsley
2 bay leaves
2 tablespoons minced garlic
2 tablespoons dried thyme leaves
2 cups tomato sauce
Worstershire, hot sauce salt and cayenne and black pepper to taste

<u>Directions</u>

Peel the shrimp and use the shells and heads to make a shrimp stock. Simmer the heads and shells in two cups of water for 20 minutes. Reduce to one cup.

In a large heavy-bottomed skillet sauté bacon until fat is rendered out. Add celery, bell pepper, parsley, onion, bay leaves and thyme and sauté for 6 to 8 minutes. Add garlic, Worstershire and hot sauce, salt and cayenne and black pepper. Add shrimp stock, fresh shrimp and tomato sauce. Simmer entire mixture for 20 minutes, stirring occasionally. Remove bay leaves. Add the raw shrimp to the Creole mixture and cook a few minutes until done. Serve with white rice.

Chez Helene Stuffed Bell Pepper

Stuffed peppers are a dish which exists in various forms in a variety cultures around the world. In India peppers might be stuffed with mashed potatoes, onions and spices. An Arabic filling might be egg plant and zucchini. In Mexico *chili rellano* is made by stuffing a poblano chili with cheese, dipping it in egg batter and frying it. Eastern Europeans often fill bell peppers with minced meat and rice and bake them in a tomato sauce. The Polish immigrants of my childhood prepared them like this. Basically, peppers can be filled with any type of filling.

Here is the stuffed pepper a recipe I picked up at Chez Helene, the premier Creole-Soul restaurant in New Orleans. Sadly, Chef Leslie is no longer with us; he died from health complications brought on as a result of Hurricane Katrina. I'm sure Austin Leslie would be honored to know that one of his signature dishes lives on and one that food lovers are enjoying it still. He was honored with a jazz funeral in October 2005. Austin Leslie was known as the "Godfather of Fried Chicken". This might seem like a meaningless title until, that is, you ate his fried chicken. I go to know Austin fairly well when I worked at Chez Helene early in my career. The other cooks and I dubbed him "Big Funk" because he was a big man and he put soul in his food.

Serves: 8-10 Time: 1 hour

Ingredients
4-5 green bell pepper, halved
1 pound ground beef
1 pound small shrimp, peeled and deveined
1 cup each celery and onion, finely diced
½ cup curly parsley, finely chopped
6 Cloves fresh garlic, minced
1 tablespoon dried thyme leaves, heaping
2 tablespoon flour, heaping
1 cup plain bread crumbs
1 stick of butter, salted
Chicken stock, as needed
Salt and pepper to taste

Directions

Sauté ground beef in a large skillet for 10 to 15 minutes until it softens. Add celery, onion, garlic, thyme and parsley and sauté until softened. Stir in flour to combine with all ingredients. Add shrimp and chicken stock and stir until mixture binds together. Do not add so much stock as to make the mixture soupy, but just enough to moisten it. Continue to slow cook with lid on for 10 more minutes. Add a little stock as necessary to maintain moisture. Do not allow mixture to dry out. Halve peppers; remove stems, seeds and ribs. Immerse pepper halves in gently boiling water for 3 to 4 minutes to just soften them a bit. Once cooled, stuff each pepper with the filling.

In a large skillet, melt butter and stir in breadcrumbs. Arrange peppers in a shallow pan or casserole dish. Cover each pepper with the buttered breadcrumbs. Bake at 350ºF for 30 to 45 minutes or until peppers have softened and bread crumbs have browned. Serve as a main dish or with sides of choice.

Crawfish Etouffée

One of the best things about visiting New Orleans is that you have the opportunity to have food that you can't get anywhere else in America. Crawfish étouffée is one of those dishes. And even if you can get it in another city, it probably won't taste as good as when it's prepared by a

New Orleans' cook. This is because étouffée dishes are an integral part of Louisiana's culinary heritage. This dish is similar to gumbo with the same Creole seasonings, served over rice, and made with a dark roux.

In French, the word "étouffée" (pronounced eh-too-fey) means, literally "smothered" or "suffocated". For this particular dish this makes sense because the crawfish are literally "smothered" in a rich sauce. One of the main ingredients is the "Holy Trinity" of Louisiana cuisine, which is a combination of chopped bell pepper, celery and onions used as the staple base for much of the cooking in the Cajun and Creole dishes and regional cuisines of Louisiana.

If crawfish isn't available in your grocery store, shrimp, crab meat or chicken may be used. I learned to make this dish at Chez Helene Restaurant when I was an apprentice cook. Etouffée is an Old World cooking technique brought to Louisiana by the French and Cajuns when they fled Nova Scotia in the mid-18th century.

Serves: 6-8 Time: 2 hours

Ingredients
1 pound crawfish tail meat or fresh shrimp, peeled and deveined
½ cup lard, bacon grease of cooking oil
½ cup all-purpose flour
1 cup each of chopped green onions, parsley, celery, bell pepper and onion
3 tablespoon garlic, chopped
2 bay leaves
2 cups chicken stock
1 tablespoon Worstershire sauce
1 tablespoon dried thyme leaves
1 tablespoon tomato paste
Salt, hot sauce and cayenne pepper to taste

Directions
In a heavy skillet (preferably cast iron) melt fat or oil until it begins to smoke. With a long-handled metal whisk gradually mix in flour, stirring until smooth. Continue cooking and stirring until roux is dark brown,

about 3 to 5 minutes (be careful to not allow roux to scorch or splash on you). Remove from heat and add celery, onions, parsley, green onions, garlic, bell pepper and sauté until soft and golden brown. Return to heat and add tomato paste, thyme leaves, hot sauce, salt, Worstershire sauce, cayenne pepper and bay leaves. Gradually whisk in chicken broth until a thick gravy-like consistency is achieved. Finally, add crawfish tails or shrimp and allow simmering for 10-15 minutes. Remove bay leaves before service. Serve over white rice.

Mirliton Stuffed with Shrimp

The French call it "mirliton" (pronounced me-lay-taw), but this pear-shaped vegetable is also known as chayote, christophene, vegetable pear, choko, starprecianté, citrayota, citrayote (Ecuador and Colombia), chuchu (Brazil), chow chow (India) or pear squash is an edible plant that belongs to the gourd family Cucurbitaceae along with melons, cucumbers and squash. The word for chayote is Spanish, borrowed from the Nahuatl word chayotli. Chayote was one of the many foods introduced to Europe by early explorers, who brought back a wide assortment of botanical samples. The age of conquest also spread the plant south from Mexico, ultimately causing it to be integrated into the cuisine of many other Latin American nations.

Chayote is native to Mesoamerica where it is a very important ingredient to the diet. Other warm regions around the globe have been successful in cultivating it as well. The main growing regions are Costa Rica and Veracruz, Mexico. Costa Rican chayotes are predominantly exported to the European Union whereas Veracruz is the main exporter of chayotes to the United States.

Stuffed mirlitons are a traditional favorite in Southwest Louisiana. They are boiled, halved and filling with the cook's stuffing of choice, which can include crawfish, crab or shrimp. I prefer to use margarine for this recipe, but that's a personal preference.

Serves: 8 Time: 1½ hours

Ingredients
4 mirlitons, large
1 pound shrimp, peeled and deveined
½ cup each onion celery, parsley, bell pepper and green onion, chopped fine
¼ cup garlic, chopped
1 stick of margarine
½ cup curly parsley, chopped
1 teaspoon dried thyme leaves
1 stick of butter
1 cup plain bread Crumbs
1 teaspoon salt
1 tablespoon hot sauce
1 teaspoon pepper

Directions

Peel the mirlitons and slice in half. Boil them until fork-tender. Don't overcook them because if the skin gets too soft they will collapse when working with them. It's better to under cook the mirlitons at this point because they will be baked later. Once cooked, allow mirlitons to cool. When cool enough to handle, remove and discard the seed core and scrape the pulp into a dish, reserving it for later use. Remove as much of the pulp as you can without cutting through the walls.

If using shrimp, dice them up and refrigerate for later use. In a heavy skillet or Dutch oven sauté onions, green onions, celery and bell pepper in margarine for 10 to 15 minutes until soft, add garlic and cook for another 5 minutes. Add the chopped mirliton pulp, diced shrimp, pepper, salt and hot sauce and mix well. Cook over low fire for about 10 minutes. Taste to determine what seasoning adjustments are necessary. Heat the oven to 375°F.

In a skillet melt the butter and mix in the parsley and bread crumbs and season with salt and pepper. Liberally fill the miriton shell with the shrimp stuffing. Liberally sprinkle bread crumb mixture over the mirlitons and place them in a baking pan or casserole. Bake them on the top rack in the oven for about 20 minutes or until the bread crumbs begin to brown.

Red Beans and Rice with Smoked Sausage

Red beans and rice is one of New Orleans favorite dishes. It's one of those old dishes that has a history. It was traditionally served on Mondays because that was laundry day. Busy New Orleans homemakers needed a dish that was cheap, filling and didn't require a lot of attention. And *voila*, red beans and rice fit the bill.

Serves: 6 Time: 3 hours

Ingredients

1 pound dried red beans, rinsed and sorted over
3 tablespoons bacon grease
1/4 cup ham, chopped
1 1/2 cups chopped yellow onions
3/4 cup celery, chopped
3/4 cup chopped green bell peppers
1/2 teaspoon salt
1/2 teaspoon freshly ground black pepper
3 bay leaves
2 tablespoons chopped fresh parsley
2 teaspoons fresh thyme
1/2 pound smoked sausage, split in half lengthwise and cut into 1-inch pieces
1 pound smoked ham hocks
3 tablespoons chopped garlic
10 cups chicken stock, or water
4 cups cooked white rice
1/4 cup chopped green onions, garnish

Directions

Place the beans in a large bowl or pot and cover with water by 2 inches. Let soak for 8 hours or overnight. Drain and set aside.

In a large pot, heat the bacon grease over medium-high heat. Add the ham and cook, stirring, for 1 minute. Add the onions, celery and bell peppers to the grease in the pot. Season with the salt, pepper, and cayenne, and cook, stirring, until the vegetables are soft, about 4 minutes. Add the bay leaves, parsley, thyme, sausage, and ham hocks, and cook, stirring, to brown the sausage and ham hocks, about 4 minutes. Add the garlic and cook for 1 minute. Add the beans and stock or water, stir well, and bring to a boil. Reduce the heat to medium-low and simmer, uncovered, stirring occasionally, until the beans are tender and starting to thicken, about 2 hours. (Should the beans become too thick and dry, add more water, about 1/4 cup at a time.)

Remove from the heat and with the back of a heavy spoon, mash about 1/4 of the beans against the side of the pot. Continue to cook until the beans are tender and creamy, 15 to 20 minutes. Remove from the heat and remove the bay leaves.

Serve over rice and garnish with green onions.

Dirty Rice

Dirty rice has long-been associated with Cajun fare although no one seems to know its exact origins. Dirty rice received its name due to its dark appearance. A blend of white rice mixed and cooked with small pieces of meat such as gizzards or ground chicken liver, the browned meat imparted a dirty look to the dish. Over time, many variations of the dish have surfaced, using ground sausage or other meats in place of the ground chicken liver or gizzards. Choicer meats and poultry parts are usually favored in upscale restaurants that serve dirty rice or Cajun rice as a side dish. Aside from the meat ingredient, dirty rice will also be made with any variety of additional ingredients, the most common of which are celery, onion, green pepper, and various spices, seasonings, or garnishes. Dirty rice is typically served as a side dish in many restaurants in the Deep South, but can easily be a meal in itself.

Serves: 8 Time: 1 hour

Seasoning mix
1 teaspoon Cayenne pepper
1 teaspoon salt
1 ½ teaspoons black pepper
1 ¼ teaspoon paprika
1 teaspoon ground cumin
1 teaspoon dry mustard
1 teaspoon dried thyme leaves

2 tablespoons chicken fat, bacon grease of vegetable oil
¼ pound ground pork
½ pound chicken gizzards, ground
2 bay leaves
½ cup finely chopped diced onions
½ cup finely diced celery
½ cup finely diced green bell peppers
2 teaspoons minced fresh garlic
2 tablespoons unsalted butter
¾ cup uncooked converted rice
½ pound chicken livers, minced
2 cups chicken or pork stock

Directions

Combine the seasoning mix in a bowl. Heat chicken fat in a large skillet and add gizzards, pork and bay leaves cook over high heat until browned. Add seasoning mix onions, celery, bell peppers and garlic; stir thoroughly scraping pan bottom. Add butter and stock and continue to cook for 5 minutes continuing to scrape bottom of skillet. Stir in chicken livers and cook for 3 more minutes. Stir in rice and cover pan. Allow to cook 10-12 minutes covered. Remove from heat and leave covered on for 10 more minutes. Remove bay leaves and serve hot.

Chicken Paprikash

Aside from beef goulash, chicken paprikash may be the best known Hungarian dish. The world equates these dishes with Hungarian cuisine. I grew up making chicken paprikash. My grandparents were Hungarian immigrants so we made the authentic version of this classic. It's simple to make and inexpensive. Purists will serve this dish with tiny dumplings called spätzle, but egg noodles will suffice. When I owned my restaurant chicken paprikash was one of the menu favorites.

Serves: 8 Time: 2 hours

Paprikash
Ingredients
1 whole fryer, cut-up and washed

1 ½ cups sour cream
2 cups chicken broth
1 cup onion, diced
3-4 tablespoons Hungarian sweet paprika
2 tablespoon garlic, chopped
1 tablespoon salt
1 teaspoon ground black pepper
2 bay leaves
3 tablespoons olive oil
2 tablespoons of corn starch, as needed

Directions

Cut-up and wash chicken parts. In a heavy pot, heat olive oil and sauté the chicken parts until they are golden brown on all sides, about 10 minutes. Add onions and garlic and sauté with chicken. Stir in the paprika, salt, black pepper and bay leaves. Add chicken broth, cover and simmer to let the chicken and onions cook thoroughly, about 10 more minutes. Thicken broth with a slurry made from corn starch and water. Mix in the sour cream and taste final seasoning adjustment. Finally, remove bay leaves and it's ready to serve over warm spätzle.

Spätzle
Ingredients
½ cup milk
1 ½ cups all-purpose flour
1 teaspoon
3 eggs

Directions

Mix the milk, flour, and eggs in a bowl. Allow to stand for 30 minutes before boiling. In a pot with 3 quarts of boiling salted water cook spätzle. This can be done by forcing the batter through a colander with a large spoon or dropping small dollops of batter into the water with two small spoons, scraping of uniform size dollops into the hot water. If using the colander, do not pour all of the batter in at once, do this in batches. Remove the cooked spätzle with a slotted spoon before making another batch. Allow the spätzle to cook for 3 to 5 minutes. Taste a spätzle to determine doneness. When the batch is cooked remove from the water and drain. Serve immediately.

BBQ Pork Roast

First you need to select the correct cut of pork. You could use pork loin, but this is not the best choice because it's devoid of interior fat and collagen and only has a scant amount of surface fat. (One of the cruelest rules of nature I know is that animal fat equals superior flavor.) I would select pork shoulder or butt for this particular cooking method, dry radiant heat. A 5 to 7 pound roast should do nicely. It's better to cook a roast that is more than necessary because approximately one-third will be lost to shrinkage and there is that pesky bone. Preheat the coals as you would for any other BBQ procedure. If you have a gas grill, heat the chamber to 250°F.

Serves: 6 Time:

Dry rub
Ingredients
1 teaspoon salt
1 teaspoon brown sugar
1 teaspoon black pepper
1 teaspoon cumin powder
1 teaspoon paprika
1 teaspoon garlic powder
1 teaspoon chili powder

Directions
Combine all dry ingredients and hand-rub mixture over pork roast. Cover with plastic wrap and allow to marinate refrigerated for 2 to 4 hours. If there is any dry rub remaining, rub it on before cooking. Place a drip pan under the grill or, if this isn't possible, place roast in baking pan, with ½ cup of water, on the grill itself. A low constant cooking temperature is critical. The temperature must remain around 250°F during the entire cooking process. Replenish coals as needed to maintain heat level. The roast should remain uncovered at all times. Slow-roasting allows the interior fat and collagen to literally melt giving the roast that unctuous texture and flavor

that makes these particular cuts of pork ideal for roasting. Cook until the interior temperature reaches at least 145°F. Check the temperature with a meat thermometer (a tip-sensitive, instant-read digital thermometer is best). Cooking time will vary, but should be between 3 to 4 hours. Remove from heat and allow to rest for 10 minutes before slicing. The roast will exude natural juice as the muscle fibers relax. Save the juice for later use. The rest time is also important for food-safety reasons. According to the USDA, after meat is removed from a heat source, its temperature remains constant or continues to rise for a few minutes more, which helps to destroy harmful bacteria such as Salmonella or E. coli.

The Salsa

Ingredients

3 ears of fresh corn (drained canned corn is okay)
2 cans of black beans, strained to remove liquid (to get rid of preservatives and sodium)
1 teaspoon hot sauce
1 can diced tomatoes, including juice
½ cup yellow onion, diced
½ cup cilantro, chopped
½ teaspoon cumin
½ teaspoon chili powder
¼ teaspoon chipotle powder (optional)
½ teaspoon salt

Directions

With a paring knife, cut kernels off each corn cob. To do this, hold the cob vertically and shear off the kernels by slicing downward toward the cutting board. You might want to do this on a dinner plate as the kernels tend to fly everywhere. The plate will contain them. Cover raw kernels with water and simmer until tender, approximately 15 minutes. Strain cooked kernels and place them in a large mixing bowl. Combine all remaining ingredients with cooked kernels and mix thoroughly. Adjust for seasoning. Salsa does not have to be served warm. Corn tortilla chips would go well with this dish.

The Eating

Slice pork and display on a platter for service. The slices of the crispy exterior are wonderful. Dad gets first dibs on these. Sorry! Warm four tortillas over the grill or gas burner and keep warm with a cloth towel. Serve with sliced onion and avocado, chopped cilantro and tomato, shredded iceberg lettuce and sour cream. Dad can dress his taco the way he likes or he can even have it au naturale, without condiments. If dad chooses to go with just meat, he can drizzle some of the delicious warm pork juice on his taco. Sure it's messy, but who cares with eats this good? Dad can do whatever he desires, this is the only day of the year the man gets things his way. Dads rule!

Lamb Shanks

When we think lamb, most of think of that boneless roast or a bone-in leg, but why not try something different. Why not do lamb shanks? Of course, French cut lamb shops are wonderful, but expensive and lack flavor. Shanks are a great cut of lamb for several reasons—fairly inexpensive, bursting with flavor, soft texture and a high collagen (when heated, collagen dissolves to provide flavor and gelatinous texture). A meat shank or shin is the portion of meat around the tibia of the animal, the leg bone beneath the knee. Since this is a tough part of the animal's musculature, shanks must be braised or slow-baked in the oven. This recipe calls for the braising in the oven. As with any cut of lamb, the shanks are delicious with mint sauce. Please *don't* resort to mint jelly. Fresh mint sauce is a snap to make. You just add mint leaves to the natural juices. This is an easy recipe that you'll love. One caveat, the bone in lamb shanks can be large (this is a good thing because this means more flavor) so compensate for this when judging how many shanks to cook.

Serves: 4 Time: 3 hours

Ingredients
4-5 pounds of lamb shanks
¼ cup vegetable oil
1 teaspoon table salt
1 teaspoon black pepper
1 cup onion, diced

1 cup celery, diced
2 tablespoon fresh garlic, chopped
4 bay leaves
1 teaspoon thyme leaves
2 cups chicken broth, canned is fine
1 tablespoon Worstershire sauce
1 tablespoon tomato paste
6 sprigs fresh mint, finely chopped

Directions

In a heavy skillet or Dutch oven heat the oil over a high flame. Salt and pepper the shanks and sear in hot oil on all sides to form a brown crust. Remove and set aside browned shanks. Add the garlic, onion, celery, thyme leaves and bay leaves to the hot skillet. Cook over medium to high flame for 3 minutes. Add shanks back to the skillet. Add chicken broth and Worstershire sauce.

Either place covered skillet in a preheated 300ºF oven or simmer covered over low fire. Cook until shanks are fork tender, about 1 ½ to 2 hours. Remove shanks from skillet and set aside. Strain sauce into a separate container. Skim any oil from surface and discard.

Return sauce to skillet and reheat. Whisk in tomato paste. Add chopped mint leaves. Reduce sauce until desired consistency is achieved. If too thick add a small amount of chicken broth. Adjust seasoning to taste. Serve with oven-roasted potatoes or cous cous. Serve sauce in a separate container.

Mole Negro Qaxacqueño

While this sauce doesn't really belong in the Entrée category, I consider it so special that I wanted to share it with you. Mole negro is a classic Mexican sauce that goes with many types of meats and vegetable dishes. It's not an easy sauce to make by any means, but is well worth the effort. I usually make a quart when I make it and freeze what I don't need.

To Mexicans, *moles* are sauce royalty. Moles are a general class of sauces of which there are seven types. These are not sauces for the faint of heart; these are complicated and labor intensive concoctions that require many ingredients. Mole is commonly associated with holidays or special occasions. The state of Oaxaca—the ancient home of the Zapotec and Mixtec peoples—is famous for seven types of mole sauces. It can be served with chicken or pork, however, turkey is often the meat of choice for festive occasions in Oaxaca. *Mole negro* or *mole poblano* are probably the most popular and complex of the mole family of sauces.

But is mole really an ancient Mexican dish as commonly considered? Not really. Moles are a perfect example of fusion cuisine. The ingredients needed to make moles come from the Old and New Worlds. Tomatillos, chocolate and chilies are New World ingredients. But other ingredients come from other parts of the planet; almonds and lard from Spain, sesame seeds from Asia, peanuts from Africa and spices such as cumin, allspice and cinnamon from Arabic countries. Mexicans typically take the combined and cooked ingredients to a commercial *molino*, a grinding mill, where all is ground into a thick paste or they can buy the premade paste in bulk at a community market, *mercado publico*. Making the mole sauce at least a day ahead is recommended, to give the flavors time to meld together. The paste is thinned out to the desired consistency with broth before service.

I know there are a lot of ingredients to this recipe and it takes time to make, but it's worth the effort. The flavor is incomparable. You'll agree when you taste this sauce with its chocolaty, sweet and spicy overtones. This is definitely a world-class sauce. The ingredients can be purchased at Latino grocery store or most *supermercados*.

<u>Ingredients</u>
¼ pound each of dried mulato, pasilla and ancho chilies
¼ each almonds, raisins & sesame seeds
1 cup onion, chopped
¼ cup fresh garlic, chopped
1 teaspoon each cinnamon, dried oregano and thyme leaves
4 slices of stale bread, cut into pieces
1 cup lard
Mexican chocolate and salt to taste

<u>Directions</u>
Wipe off the dust from all dried chilies; remove seeds, stems and membranes. Place some lard in a cast iron skillet and blister chilies taking care to not burn

them. Adding additional lard as needed; fry almonds and the raisins until they plump and lighten in color. Also, fry the bread, onion, sesame seeds, cinnamon stick and garlic. Do not burn any ingredients when frying. Burnt ingredients will impart a bitter flavor. As each item is cooked, set aside.

Combine all fried ingredients and add cinnamon, chocolate (chopped into bits) and salt to taste. In a food processor, purée all ingredients to make a paste the consistency of cold pie dough. Refrigerate or freeze paste.

When mole is required, place desired amount of paste in a heated saucepan and slowly chicken broth to obtain the consistency of ketchup. Add chopped chocolate and a little melted lard to give it flavor and sheen. Add salt to taste. If sauce is too thin add dollops of paste to get consistency correct. Strain before serving. Serve warm with beef, pork, chicken or turkey, the classic meat of choice. This sauce can also be served as a base for a stew.

Desserts

Bûche de Noël (Yule Log)

Given New Orleans French connection it's only fitting that bûche de Noël, the traditional French Christmas dessert, would be popular in homes, hotels and restaurants around the holidays. A bûche is made by slathering butter cream on a sheet of flexible sheet cake called roulade, rolling it into a cylinder and decorating it to resemble a log ready for the fire. Making a bûche requires a bit of work, but it's worth the effort. Your guests will be impressed.

Serves: 8 Time: 2 hours

Roulade (Jelly roll)
Ingredients
4 egg yolks, from large eggs
1/3 cup white granulated sugar
1/3 cup all-purpose flour, sifted
2 tablespoons unsalted butter, melted and cooled
4 fresh egg whites, from large eggs

<u>Directions</u>

Grease a standard jelly roll pan (about 11 x 7 inches) and line it with parchment paper or waxed paper. Preheat the oven to 400°F. These tasks must be done prior making the roulade.

Whip the yolks and sugar on medium speed until the mixture turns pale yellow and ribbons form. This can be expedited by warming the bowl intermittently over hot water or a low flame on top of the range. Once ribbons have formed, incrementally fold the flour into the yolks and sugar mixture with a curved rubber spatula. Folding is best accomplished by turning the bowl whilst you fold in the flour in stages. This provides uniform distribution of the flour. If you have only one mixer, remove this mixture to another bowl then wash and dry the machine bowl for whipping the whites.

In a very clean and dry mixing bowl, whip the egg whites until stiff and peaks form. Whipping should be done on medium speed as this will result in firmer, more stable meringue. High speed will result in a meringue that collapses easily. Combine the whites with the egg, sugar and flour mixture. This is a very delicate procedure. This is best accomplished by combining half the whites with the mixture and gently folding the remaining whites into the mixture. Take care to turn the bowl as the whites are added incrementally.

With an off-set palette knife, spread the entire mixture over the prepared jelly roll pan. The batter should be spread to a depth of only ½ inches thick as the batter will rise when baked. Place pan in the middle of the oven and bake for 5 to 7 minutes or until the edges begin to turn light brown.

To check for doneness, insert a toothpick in the center and if it comes out clean the roulade is sufficiently cooked. Remove from oven and allow cooling before removing from pan. Remove the paper by beginning at a corner and gently pulling towards the opposite end.

Butter cream
<u>Ingredients</u>
1 cup water

3 cups white granulated sugar
9 fresh egg whites, from medium eggs
4½ cups unsalted butter, softened
2 tablespoons pure vanilla extract

Directions

In a clean, heavy-bottomed sauce pan combine sugar and water. Rapidly boil the syrup to precisely 240°F. A candy thermometer should be used to obtain the exact temperature. While the syrup is cooking whip whites on medium speed in a clean and dry machine mixing bowl. Once syrup has reached 235°F remove it from the fire. The temperature will continue to rise to the desired 240°F. With the mixer on high speed, slowly drizzle the hot syrup into the whites. Reduce mixer speed to medium and allow meringue to cool down to nearly room temperature, about 100°F.

With the mixer still on medium speed, slowly add dollops of butter to the meringue. Allow each addition to incorporate before adding the next. Add vanilla. Chocolate butter cream may be made by adding ½ cup of melted dark semi-sweet chocolate to the batch.

Assembling and Garnishing the Cake

Spread a thin layer of butter cream on the sheet of roulade and roll it into a cylinder. Wrap the cylinder in waxed paper or plastic wrap and refrigerate for 1 hour. Once thoroughly chilled remove to cutting board and slice each end at a 45° angle. Place the cylinder on the serving platter with which you intend to serve the bûche. This will obviate the need to transfer the finished log and possibly damaging it in the process.

With an off-set palette knife slather butter cream ½ inch over the entire cylinder including the ends. With a pastry comb or the tines of a dinner fork make textured lines to resemble tree bark. Make the bark design on the sides of the trunk only. The butter cream on the ends should remain smooth. The ends can be made to resemble tree rings by piping alternate concentric rings of melted dark chocolate and butter cream. Refrigerate cake until 1 hour before service.

New Orleans' Pecan Pie

There are few desserts that are as closely associated with the Deep South as is pecan pie. It's the quintessential Southern sweet treat. Food historians have found it difficult to pin down the origin of pecan pie, but legend has it that the French created this icon after settling in New Orleans and being introduced to the pecan by the Natives, the Quinipissa and Tangipahoa peoples who resided in present-day New Orleans.

As stated in an 1886 cookbook, "Pecan pie is not only delicious, but is capable of being made a 'real state pie,' as an enthusiastic admirer said. The pecans must be very carefully hulled, and the meat thoroughly freed from any bark or husk. When ready, throw the nuts into boiling milk, and let them boil while you are preparing a rich custard. Have your pie plates lined with a good pastry, and when the custard is ready, strain the milk from the nuts and add them to the custard. A meringue may be added, if liked, but very careful baking is necessary." While this recipe may be a departure from that which we are accustomed to it sounds mighty tempting.

Regardless of the folk lore, one fact is indisputable, the pecan pie originated in New Orleans. Any restaurant that serves traditional sin City fare is obligated to offer pecan pie. It's a natural. There are few better than a rich, unctuous wedge of pecan pie, especially when paired with a steaming cup of *café au lait* or strong chicory coffee. Bon appetite!

Serves: 8 Time: 4 hours

The pastry
Ingredients
½ stick unsalted butter, cold
½ cup vegetable shortening, cold
2 tablespoon sugar
¼ teaspoon salt
½ cup tablespoon very cold milk, or as needed
2 cups cake flour, all-purpose will suffice
½ cup chocolate chips, optional

<u>Directions</u>

Mix together sifted flour, sugar and salt. Using a pastry cutter or fork, cut butter and shortening into the flour until pieces are pea-size. To form dough, add milk incrementally and mix until a dough ball is formed. Mix until just combined. Do not over mix. Dough should be slightly crumbly, but wet enough to form a ball when compressed. Form dough into a flat disc, wrap with plastic wrap and refrigerate for at least 2 hours before rolling out.

On a lightly floured surface, use your hands to slightly flatten dough. Roll dough from center to edges into a circle about 12 inches in diameter. To transfer pastry, wrap it around the rolling pin. Unroll pastry onto a greased 9-inch pie plate. Ease pastry into pie plate, being careful not to stretch pastry excessively or puncture dough as this will allow filling to leak out when baking. Rim pastry to 1/2 inch beyond edge of pie plate. Fold under extra pastry. Crimp edge as desired. Do not prick pastry.

Food processor directions: Prepare as above, except place steel blade in food processor bowl. To bowl add flour, butter, sugar and salt. Pulse until most of mixture until butter is dispersed, but remains pea size. Add milk incrementally through feed tube and pulse until ball just begins to form. It is preferable to add too little milk when using a processor as dough can be formed by hand. Remove dough from bowl to plastic wrap, shape into a disc and refrigerate.

Filling
<u>Ingredients</u>
¾ cup sugar
¾ cup dark corn syrup
2 eggs, lg.
1½ teaspoons unsalted butter, melted
2 teaspoons vanilla extract
½ teaspoon
2 cups pecans halves or pieces
Semi-sweet chocolate chips, optional

<u>Directions</u>

Combine all ingredients except pecans a mixing bowl. Beat on slow speed of electric mixer until the batter is smooth about 2 to 3 minutes. Do not over beat as this will create froth and affect the appearance of the finished product. Strain mixture through a sieve.

Assemble and bake

Fill lined pastry-lined pie with pecans taking care to not puncture the pastry otherwise the hot filling will leak out. Place pie shell on baking sheet pan. Slowly pour the filling over the pecans (and chocolate chips, if desired) until they are completely covered. Fill tart shell ¼" from the top ridge. Bake at 300ºF for 1 hour or until the filling is set. This can be determined by moving the pie while on the baking sheet. If the filling is still liquid in center or does not move in unison continue cooking. Pecans will migrate to the top of the pie during baking.

Cool and serve with Chantilly cream, whipped cream with vanilla and sugar added to taste. Store pie at room temperature for the first 24 hours and refrigerate after that.

<u>Country Apple Tart</u>

What says autumn better than a home-made apple tart? When the apple harvest is in it's the perfect time to whip up everyone's favorite dessert, an apple dessert. Apple pies are fine, but here's a treat with a twist, a one-crust tart. This dessert is not only attractive it tastes great. You can't just use any apple for this tart. You need an apple that has the right sugar content and texture. The Granny Smith apple is the perfect choice.

Serves: 8 Time: 3 hours

Almond cream (Frangipane)
<u>Ingredients</u>
½ cup unsalted butter
1 cup confectioner's sugar
3 egg yolks
1 cup blanched almond slivers, ground
1 teaspoon pure vanilla extract

¼ teaspoon salt
Directions

In a food processor, grind the almonds to a consistency of corn meal. Set almond meal aside. Cream the butter and sugar until light and fluffy. This mixture will turn pale yellow. Mix in almond meal, salt and vanilla. Blend in egg yolks one at time until all is incorporated and smooth, creamy mixture is achieved. Refrigerate for later use.

Using the pastry recipe for the Pecan Pie, prepare pastry for a 9" tart pan.

Assembling

Peel, core and halve 4 Granny Smith apples. With a paring knife, thinly slice each half. Set all sliced halves aside. Line tart pan with rolled-out pastry. Fill tart pan half way up the sides with almond cream. With spatula, smooth-out the almond cream. Arrange apples around for an attractive appearance.

Baking and glazing

Bake tart in a 375ºF oven until apples begin to brown and pastry is cooked. This will take 30 to 45 minutes. Remove tart from oven and allow to cool. In a microwave melt ½ cup of apple jelly and brush on tart with a pastry brush. Serve warm with whipped cream with a dash of vanilla extract and a pinch of sugar.

Beignets

Beignets (pronounced *ban-yay*) means "fritter" in French. Most Americans consider beignets a New Orleans specialty and the most famous place to enjoy beignets is Café du Monde. This New Orleans landmark was established in 1862 and is still in business operating 24/7. Café du Monde is also famous for its café au lait, dark roast coffee and chicory served with an equal part of hot milk. Early in Louisiana's history chicory was added to coffee to stretch dwindling supplies. It was found to make for a richer, smoother brew. The addition of hot milk created one of the oldest and greatest coffee traditions in the world.

Enjoying coffee and beignets at Café du Monde is more than a great taste treat. Since Café du Monde is situated in the French Quarter, customers can take in the sights and sounds of tourism as they munch beignets and sip coffee. In 1986 beignets became the State Doughnut of Louisiana. This is testimony to the popularity of these "doughnuts that ain't go no holes" as I once heard beignets described by a French Quarter horse carriage driver.

Serves: 16-20 Time: 2 hours

Ingredients
1 cup lukewarm water
¼ cup sugar
½ tsp salt
1 egg, beaten
2 tablespoons butter, softened
½ cup milk
4 cup all-purpose flour
3 teaspoon instant dry yeast
4 cups vegetable oil, for deep frying
½ cup confectioners' sugar for dusting

Directions
    Dissolve dry yeast in a bowl with ¼ cup warm water. After yeast is dissolved add a Tbsp of the flour and a pinch of the sugar. Cover mixture with plastic wrap and allow it to "prove" itself by activating, which will be evident by foaming action. Using a table top mixer with the dough hook attachment, place remaining flour water, sugar, salt, egg, butter and milk in the mixing bowl. Add dissolved yeast mixture and to mixing bowl and knead until it's a smooth, plastic ball, about 5 minutes. Small amounts of flour or milk may be added to achieve the correct consistency. Once kneaded, cover dough with a cloth or plastic wrap and allow dough to rise in the bowl until it doubles in size. Roll the dough on floured surface to ½" thickness. Cut 2" squares and place on cookie sheet and allow rising again before frying. Do not omit second rising. If the second rising is omitted the beignets will be dense and heavy.

    In a deep fryer or large pot, heat oil to 350°F. Drop 6-8 beignets, one at a time. If the beignets don't float immediately when dropped into the oil, the oil is not hot enough. If this happens the oil must be heated to the correct temperature. Fry them for 2-3 minutes or until they are puffed and golden brown on both sides, turning them a few times with tongs so they brown on both sides. Remove to and drain on paper towel. Dust heavily with confectioners' sugar and serve while still warm.

Bread Pudding with Bourbon Sauce

If there is one dessert Americans associate with New Orleans its bread pudding. Bread pudding has its roots in Europe where thrifty cooks recycled stale bread in variety of dishes. In the Big Easy, bread pudding is thought of strictly as a dessert. It's usually served with an accompanying sauce with a hard sauce or one loaded with rum or whiskey. Additions to bread pudding can be pecans, chocolate chips or dried fruits such as raisins. It's inexpensive and easy to make, but bread pudding is quintessential comfort food.

Serves: 6-8 Time: 2 hours

Pudding
Ingredients
1 French baguette, stale
3 cups whole milk
6 eggs, lg.
½ cup sugar
1 tablespoon pure vanilla extract (never use imitation)

Directions
Slice baguette into 1" slices. Liberally grease a 9" cake pan (do not use a spring form pan). Arrange two layers of slices in pan making sure that they are packed tightly. Whisk and strain milk, eggs, sugar and vanilla. Pour custard into pan until bread is submerged. Wait a few minutes for bread to absorb custard and add more custard.

Place pan in a hot water bath and bake in a 350ºF oven until center is set and no longer liquid, approximately 1 hour. Check center with for doneness by making a small hole to make sure custard is no longer in a liquid state.

When done, allow to cool and turn it out by running a knife around the sides and placing a plate on top and inverting it; the placing another plate on the bottom and turning it over again. The topside will be up.

Whiskey sauce
<u>Ingredients</u>
1 cup white granulated sugar
¾ cup unsalted butter
⅓ cup bourbon or dark rum, if preferred
1 tablespoon vanilla extract
4 eggs, lg.

<u>Directions</u>
In a heavy saucepan melt butter over low heat, but do not brown. Mix in sugar, vanilla and bourbon. With a whisk stir until sugar is dissolved. In a bowl whisk eggs and slowly add hot mixture to eggs to warm them. Return all ingredients to the saucepan and heat over low fire, stirring constantly. Continue to stir until mixture just thickens. Strain and serve with pudding.

Appendix A

The Food, the Bad and the Ugly

WHAT DOES PUBLIC health have to do with a book about professional cooking and the restaurant industry? The short answer: Just about everything. Food safety is central to the job of a professional chef. America is awakening to a public health crisis in its food production system. The situation is exacerbated by unsafe imports that go largely uninspected, especially from China and Southeast Asia where government oversight is lax or nonexistent during the production or processing phase. With muckraking movies and books such as *Food Inc.* and *Fast Food Nation,* the curtain has been drawn back on the state of America's food production and processing systems. These critical analyses reveal how a handful of multi-national corporations are largely in control of the quality of the foods we consume. Moreover, these documentaries highlight the increasing impotence of government agencies that are responsible for oversight and intervention, but have been hampered by external political forces. In recent decades poor factory farming and meat processing practices have been the root causes of contaminated meat and poultry resulting in massive recalls. And unsafe agricultural practices have led to nationwide recalls of agricultural products such as lettuce, cilantro, spinach and alfalfa sprouts. Thousands have been sickened and many have died as result of contaminated food products. We have only to look at the enormous fresh egg recall of 2010 to understand that something is fundamentally wrong with our current food safety monitoring program. The post mortem analysis of this particular outbreak showed that the problem stemmed from a lax inspection program. The two Iowa egg farms at the center of the outbreak may have never been inspected by a government entity. More on this particular outbreak later.

On a smaller scale, there is potential for food-borne illness at your local restaurant. Many Americans contract food poisoning from eating unsafe food at the restaurant they trust to serve wholesome, safe food. A large part of a chef's job is—or should be—to make sure that the plate of food he sends to your table doesn't send you to the emergency room. A concerned and knowledgeable chef may well be the final layer of protection between you and food that is unsafe to eat. But the disturbing truth is that the food handlers, including the chef, at some of your favorite restaurants may not always be following accepted safe food handling practices. Restaurants may appear to be clean and sanitary in the dining area or bathroom, but the kitchen might be an entirely different story.

Americans are more concerned than ever about food safety. Distrust between the food industry and consumers is growing, according to a recent survey conducted by the National Restaurant Association. It sampled opinions from 1,050 consumers. One of the questions asked got directly to the misgivings many consumers have about the food they eat, "Are you more concerned than you were five years ago about the food you eat? Seventy-three percent of the respondents said "yes," up 8 percentage points from 2010, when 65 percent answered the same question affirmatively. Clearly, the public's apprehension about food safety and food-borne disease epidemics is on the rise.

This chapter contains food safety facts and need-to-know information that you can use to protect yourself and your family against food-borne diseases. Possessing an academic and professional background in environmental health and food safety in particular, and being a professional chef I am in a unique position to discuss food safety in the restaurant industry. As a former restaurant inspector, I have first-hand knowledge of the break-downs that can occur in America's food-service establishments. I want to share this important information with you so you can appreciate the magnitude of the problem and become a better informed consumer. Armed with this knowledge you will be better able to protect yourself and family. To accomplish this I thought it necessary to include a collage of facts and figures. Your eyes might glaze over at some point as you wade through the mountain of data presented here, but I saw no other way to do justice to these topics.

A Public Health Crisis

IN THE UNITED States food-borne disease affects one in six Americans each year according to the Centers for Disease Control and Prevention (CDC). There are approximately 48 million cases of food-related illness every year in the U.S. Of this number, 128,000 are hospitalized and 3,000 of the stricken die. The numbers are down from the 1999 CDC estimates. There has been a 20 percent decrease in food-related diseases in the past ten years. The reasons for this are largely unknown, but may be from improvements in data sources and methods used to develop the 2011 estimates; they cannot be compared with the 1999 estimates to measure trends. It is possible that food-borne illnesses have decreased through investments made on better detection, prevention, education and control efforts. The number of cases is difficult to pinpoint exactly due to under reporting, many case are clinically misdiagnosed and/or not reported to public health authorities. Because of under reporting the magnitude of the food-related illness problem may be much greater than estimated.

While the following section may seem like an introduction to microbiology and epidemiology, it isn't. It's merely an effort to acquaint the reader with some of the pathogenic organisms that commonly cause food-borne disease and to the role of epidemiology in epidemics. To do this, I have cited a few of the more significant outbreaks that have occurred in recent years. Having a basic understanding about how humans can become ill from consuming contaminated food will help to avoid contracting an illness yourself. It's important to know which pathogens can cause food-related illness. The most common ones are *Campylobacter, Salmonella,* Noroviruses and *Escherichia coli* O157:H7. This strain of E. coli burst into the public consciousness in 1993 when hundreds were sickened and four children died after eating tainted Jack in the Box hamburgers. While *Campylobacter* is the most common food-borne pathogen, *Salmonella* and *Listeria* remain the leading causes of death in the United States due to bacterial pathogens transmitted commonly through food. Most such deaths occurred in persons 65 years of age or older, indicating that this age group could benefit from effective food safety interventions. *Salmonella* and *Listeria* continue to be the leading cause of death from food-borne illness in the United States, according to a study published in the June 2011 edition of the Journal of Infectious Diseases. During 1996–2005, FoodNet ascertained 121,536 cases of laboratory-confirmed bacterial infections, including 552 (.5 percent) deaths, of which 215 (39 percent) and 168 (30 percent) were among persons infected with *Salmonella* and *Listeria*, respectively. The statistics come from an analysis of FoodNet data from 1996 to 2005. FoodNet is a CDC food-borne illness surveillance system in 10 states.

~~~

There is another illness-inducing pathogen that is second in terms of health care costs and mortality—*Toxoplasma gondii*. *Toxoplasma* is a parasitic infection caused by protozoa. Toxoplasmosis, the name of the disease, receives considerably less media attention than other food-related illnesses because it usually is not associated with large epidemics. In addition to disease caused by direct infection, some food-borne diseases are caused by the presence of a toxin in the food that was produced by a microbe in the food. For example, the bacterium *Staphylococcus aureus* can grow in certain foods and produce a toxin that causes intense vomiting. The rare but deadly disease botulism occurs when the bacterium *Clostridium botulinum* grows and produces a powerful paralytic toxin in foods. These toxins can remain potent and produce illness even if the microbes that produced them are no longer there.

The CDC estimates that 22.5 percent of the U.S. population over 12 years old has been infected with *Toxoplasma* at some point, with half of those infections coming from food. The parasite is typically transmitted to humans via raw or undercooked meats—historically pork and beef. In sheer numbers, Salmonella sickens far more people than *Toxoplasma*, but the mortality rate is lower. According to University of Florida's Emerging Pathogens Institute (EPI) there are an estimated 86,686 toxoplasmosis illnesses, resulting in 4,428 hospitalizations and 327 deaths. By comparison, *Salmonella* sickens 1.2 million, with 20,000 hospitalizations and 400 deaths annually. Clearly, the *Toxoplasma* organism is more virulent. Food poisoning caused by salmonella have increased by 10 percent in recent years, despite efforts to educate consumers and food producers about food preparation and handling practices to federal statistics released by the CDC.

The *E. coli* strain O157:H7 is one of the most common *E. coli* strains in food-related illnesses. The *E. coli* bacterium is part of the normal flora found in the intestines of humans and cattle and other ruminants. Fresh meat products can become contaminated through cross contamination at an abattoir where raw meat is processed for delivery to retail markets. *E. coli* O157:H7 is an enterohemorrhagic (EHEC) strain and is particularly virulent. The O157:H7 strain sickens more than 63,000, hospitalizes more than 2,000 and kills about 20 people every year in the United States according to EPI. The *E. coli* O157:H7 bacterium is different from other common food-borne pathogens in that it produces a powerful substance called Shiga toxin causing bloody diarrhea. As few as 50 bacteria can be infective. Shiga toxin-producing *Escherichia coli* (STEC) can progress to hemolytic uremic syndrome (HUS). The STEC serotype that causes most outbreaks and most cases of HUS in the United States is *E. coli* O157:H7. HUS brings death to 8 percent of its victims. While lives cannot be quantified in terms of money, there is an economic side to *E. coli* illness. The CDC estimates that a single fatal case of *E. coli* O157:H7 (another Shiga-toxin producing strain of *E. coli*) costs approximately $7 million dollars in medical expenses.

~~~

The life-threatening health effects of HUS became all too clear in a massive food-related epidemic caused by *E. coli* O104:H4 (EHEC) in Western Europe from early May through the late June 2011 when almost 4,000 people were sickened, nearly 900 were hospitalized due to kidney failure as a result of HUS. A total of 52 people died from the epidemic as of this writing. One fatality was an American from Arizona who had visited Germany during the outbreak. There may have been a large number of milder cases than was recorded, of people who were ill, but did not seek care. The "epicenter" of the outbreak was in Northern Germany, but it rapidly intensified spreading to sixteen other European countries according to World Health Organization. The majority of the patients were in Germany and the areas hardest hit were the Hamburg and Schleswig-Holstein states. The majority of the stricken were females; approximately 70 percent of the cases of HUS in Germany were females. There was no scientific explanation for overrepresentation of females.

Initially, German health officials blamed the outbreak on Spanish cucumbers because random samples showed that some were contaminated with *E. coli* O104:H4, but it was determined that the cucumbers were not responsible for the outbreak so they were dismissed as the sole vehicle for contamination. One month into the epidemic German health authorities indicated that bean sprouts were most *likely* the cause of the outbreak. This determination was made based purely on circumstantial evidence. Because initially public health officials had no idea of what was causing the epidemic they warned the public to not eat fresh produce of any kind. This resulted in the loss of an enormous amount of fruit and vegetables. Approximately 5,900 tons of cucumbers, over 3,200 acres of lettuce and 3,500 tons of tomatoes were destroyed according to Germany's Agriculture Minister. Ultimately, European public health authorities said the likely cause of the outbreak was a single lot of Egyptian fenugreek seeds imported to Europe and used to grow sprouts that were consumed in Germany and France. The European Union ordered a recall and temporary ban of fenugreek seeds. However, health officials feared further *E. Coli* outbreaks because the contents of original 10,500-kg shipment of fenugreek seeds that left Egypt on November 24, 2009 had been widely dispersed with the seeds divided into different lots had been shipped to distributors in different countries, who then repackaged the seeds before sending them to garden centers and stores throughout Europe.

European food safety officials appeared to have relied too heavily on high-tech laboratory analysis and microbiology of victims rather than traditional epidemiology. A microbiological approach to investigation has historically been shown to fall short of a detailed study of the epidemiology that characterizes food-borne illness outbreaks. An epidemiological investigation is a concerted effort by which "disease detectives" conduct interviews with outbreak victims, searching for common denominators and tracing to the source to find the culprit food(s). Epidemiologists rely on a number of scientific disciplines such as medicine, microbiology, biology, biostatistics and social science disciplines.

The inability to quickly identify the cause of the epidemic was a colossal failure of epidemiology on part of German public health officials. In any food-related disease outbreak the "window of opportunity" of finding the responsible food item(s) closes as time passes. It is imperative that suspect foods be traced as soon as possible especially if those foods are perishable such as fresh produce, which seemed to be the case in the German epidemic. It is critical in the early stages of any epidemiological investigation that a "common denominator" be ascertained. Typically, if the cause of an outbreak is not pinpointed within a week's time it's unlikely that the culprit will be ever be found. This was not accomplished in this particular outbreak. Instead chaos reigned rather than employing sound scientific and epidemiological techniques.

According to the World Health Organization, the bacterium responsible for the outbreak was a new strain that has "various characteristics that make it more virulent and toxin-producing" than the many *E. coli* strains people naturally carry in their intestines. Microbiological tests suggested a mutant form of two different *E. coli* strains was the casual agent. It is not uncommon for bacteria to evolve and swap genes. It is difficult to explain where the new strain came from, but bacteria from humans and animals easily trade genetic material. Chinese and German scientists analyzed the DNA of the *E. coli* bacteria that caused the outbreak and determined that it was "an entirely new, super-toxic" strain that contains several antibiotic-resistant genes, according to a statement from the Shenzhen, China-based laboratory BGI, "It's one that's never been seen before in an outbreak situation."

The massive outbreak inflicted horrendous economic damage on many of the affected countries. The U.S. Air Force banned the purchase of any E.U. fresh produce. In early June, Russia temporarily banned all shipments of fresh vegetables from the E.U. causing extreme financial hardship on European vegetable producers. The E.U. had to pay over two million Euros to farmers to reimburse them for their losses. Spain threatened legal action against Germany over the crisis. It wanted reparations for its farmers, who claimed lost sales amounting to $287 million a week and that 70,000 people were put out of work. This outbreak was considered the second-largest involving *E. coli* in recent world history, and the deadliest. Twelve people died in a 1996 Japanese epidemic that reportedly sickened more than 9,000 and 7 died in a Canadian outbreak in 2000.

~~~

While the most serious and widely publicized *E. coli* outbreaks are usually linked to the O157:H7 strain, other non-O157 strains of *E. coli* is becoming more widely recognized by food scientists as a threat to human health: *E. coli* O26, O45, O103, O111, O121 and O145. These various strains are distinguished by their unique *serotype*—distinct variations of subspecies of bacteria or viruses based on their surface antigens. An *antigen* is a substance/molecule that, when introduced into the body, triggers the production of an antibody by the body's immune system. The

Big Six serotypes, as they have come to be called, have been identified as responsible for 70 percent of non-O157:H7 *E. coli*-related illnesses in the United States. Little is known about the genetic differences between them, or what makes some types within each group more virulent than others. CDC has estimates that the Big Six strains cause approximately 113,000 illnesses and 300 hospitalizations annually in the United States.

E. coli infections can come from a variety of sources including seafood, raw field greens, certain nuts, raw milk, alfalfa sprouts and undercooked ground beef that gets contaminated during processing. Healthy people usually survive after a bout of diarrhea, but up to 500 people each year don't. They die a painful death and it is children, pregnant women, the elderly and the chronically ill who are the most vulnerable because of their compromised immune systems. Annual healthcare costs related to food-related disease amount to approximately $9 billion. Conducting epidemiological investigations of food-borne illnesses is a critical public health function in which CDC is deeply involved, but its involvement also dips into the national treasure.

Of the total number of food-borne illnesses, the CDC estimates that a significant number are caused by contaminated seafood. This is hardly surprising considering that as of 2008 there were approximately 13,400 domestic seafood processing establishments and the Food and Drug Administration (FDA)—in its 2008 Report to Congress—reported that it conducted only 2,456 inspections with only 195 laboratory test conducted on seafood when questionable processing practices were identified. More disturbing is that there were approximately 14,900 foreign seafood processing facilities and only 221 on-site inspections were conducted by FDA field investigators from 2004 through 2006. This is an enormous public health problem because it is the foreign aquaculture industry that routinely abuses the use antibiotics and chemicals. Approximately 80 percent of the seafood consumed in America comes from aquaculture—commercial facilities that raise fish and other marine species under controlled conditions by simulating their marine habitat.

With slightly more than 1 percent of imported seafood, vegetables, fruits and other foods undergoing any sort of inspection in the United States—the EU inspects about 20 percent of its food imports—there is a considerable chance that unsafe food can make its way into our food supply system. For example, salmon may infected with microscopic parasites and pathogens such as *Listeria monocytogenes,* an especially virulent infectious agent. (The mortality rate of *Listeria* ranges between 16 percent and 30 percent, extremely high for a food-related disease.) The only sure way to determine if imported seafood is safe is by laboratory examination. The consumption of raw seafood presents an even greater public health risk compared to seafood that is cooked. Raw oysters are known to carry the bacteria *Vibrio vulnificus* that causes septicemia in humans. Parasites are a special concern when we eat raw or lightly preserved fish such as sashimi, sushi, ceviche and gravlax. This is a concern because heat is not applied, which can destroy these pathogenic organisms. The popularity of raw fish dishes increases the risk of food-borne disease. With an expanding global marketplace, this problem may expand commensurately in the U.S. as our food imports increase. According to the National Oceanic and Atmospheric Administration (NOAA) the U.S. imports made up 83 percent of the seafood consumed in the U.S. and half of that is from aquaculture. The U.S. aquaculture industry supplies only about 5 percent of its seafood supply annually with the remaining coming from foreign operations.

A Public Health Crisis

THE MAGNITUDE OF the food-borne disease crisis may be grossly underestimated because most cases of food poisoning are not reported to the health authorities and/or clinically misdiagnosed by the afflicted person or health care professionals. For example, the CDC estimates that 38 cases of Salmonellosis—the illness caused by the *Salmonella* bacterium—actually occurs for every one case that is correctly diagnosed and reported to public health authorities. You may have experienced a bout of food-borne illness yourself and failed to recognize it as such. The symptoms are similar to other common infections like influenza; fever, diarrhea, nausea, vomiting and abdominal pain. Food-related disease can progress to a serious, even life-threatening illness. The *Salmonella* organism, for instance, can cause serious and sometimes fatal infections in young children, frail or elderly people, and others with weakened or compromised immune systems. *Salmonella* causes more food-borne illness in the U.S than another pathogen. Because many cases of Salmonellosis (sal-mohn-el-oh-sis) are milder cases they are not diagnosed or reported, the actual number of infections may be thirty or more times greater. There are many different kinds of *Salmonella* bacteria. The type of *Salmonella* usually associated with infections in humans is non-typhoidal *Salmonella*. Typically, a person with *Salmonella* poisoning experiences the onset of symptoms 12 to 72 hours after consuming the contaminated food. The illness usually lasts from 4 to 7 days, and most people do not require antibiotics or hospitalization in order to recover. The severity of the infection varies with dosage of the contaminating agent, the strain of the microorganism and the individual's ability to combat the infection. Salmonellosis is not only costly with regard to human suffering; it is also expensive in economic terms. The medical costs alone of one case of HUS costs approximately $7 million dollars. The USDA's Economic Research Service (ERS) "estimates that the annual economic cost of Salmonellosis is $2,649,413,401 (2009 dollars). This estimate is for all cases of Salmonellosis, not just food-borne cases. The estimate includes medical costs due to illness, the cost of time lost from work due to nonfatal illness and the cost of premature death."

A Classic Restaurant Breakdown. Breakdowns in the food delivery system often occur at the end source, the retail food-service establishment. In a March 2010 article, the Washington Examiner reported that hundreds of Washington, D.C. restaurants—which included several high-end establishments—were guilty of serious health code violations such as a bare handed cook observed to be "preparing desserts with cuts/sores on fingers" and other cooks were seen "using the same pair of tongs on raw and cooked food." Welcome to the restaurant world that I know all too well and have worked in for decades. Unhygienic food handling practices are commonplace in the nearly 1 million food service establishments in the U.S. Some common health code violations are unsafe food storage (unsafe temperature range, unapproved or unlabeled storage containers, etc.), food handlers not wearing hair restraints, smoking in the kitchen, coughing in their hands while preparing food, no hand washing after using the toilet and working while ill with an infectious disease. Unsafe food handling happens largely because the food service personnel lack a basic understanding of food sanitation. If they don't understand the concept of food safety and food-borne disease causation they're not likely to handle food safely simply because they're told to. Kitchen staffs are often comprised of individuals from third world countries who might not have been taught about the relationship between personal hygiene and safe food. So it normally falls to the head chef to monitor the staff, but he is not omnipresent. When the chef is absent the staff might not prepare food in a clean and safe manner. Even if the chef is present, food sanitation might not be a priority with him either. So why are we shocked at the estimated 48 million cases of food-borne poisoning in the U.S. every year? What is amazing is that there aren't more cases.

~~~

Restaurant employees who work while they're ill are a major factor contributing to the high rate of food-borne disease in the U.S. In a landmark study, *Factors Associated with Food Workers Working While Experiencing Vomiting or Diarrhea*, of restaurant food handling and food-related illness, about 12 percent of the servers and food preparers (Male food handlers are more likely than female food handlers to report to work sick.) interviewed told public health researchers they had worked while sick and exhibiting symptoms of vomiting and diarrhea. According to the findings, 11.9 percent said that during two or more shifts in the previous year they had served or prepared food while they were ill and their symptoms included vomiting and diarrhea. The busier the restaurant, the more reluctant the employees were to call in sick, the study found.

The study was a collaborative effort by universities, federal public health agencies and state and local Health Departments that participate in the Environmental Health Specialists Network. The EHS-Net states are California, Connecticut, New York, Georgia, Iowa, Minnesota, Oregon, Rhode Island and Tennessee. The study findings were published in the February 2011 edition of the *Journal of Food Protection*. About 20 percent of food-borne illness outbreaks involve pathogens that are transmitted to food by food handlers, the study noted. And while diarrhea and vomiting are common symptoms of some food-related infections, the study didn't mention that infected people are sometimes *asymptomatic*—an infected person may not exhibit clinical symptoms such as diarrhea and vomiting. The asymptomatic period is also called the *prodromal* period in the field of epidemiology.

The factor most associated with whether a food handler worked while sick was the restaurants' workload—restaurants that served more than three-hundred meals on their busiest days were the most likely to have had sick employees on duty. Based on this finding, it would seem that ill employees are reluctant to miss the opportunity to earn substantial tips even if it enhances the possibility of food-borne disease. The lack of a restaurant policy requiring workers to report their illness and the lack of on-call substitutes were also contributing factors. In other words, when a restaurant is extremely busy management will ignore the fact that an employee is ill and allow them to work regardless of their condition. The study showed those workers who had paid sick leave available were approximately half as likely to indicate they had worked while experiencing vomiting and diarrhea.

The result of this study was not exactly a news flash for those of us who have spent a career working in the hospitality industry. It is common knowledge that restaurant employees come to work when they're sick. This study merely fixed the prevalence rate of this phenomenon. Veterans in the business know from personal experience that restaurant employees are reluctant to miss work because they essentially live a hand-to-mouth existence; no work, no pay. This particular study not only quantifies the prevalence of restaurant employees working ill, it also states the obvious—the mode of transmission of pathogenic organisms to food. This crisis, and it is a crisis, is largely driven by two factors: the lack of paid sick leave and the absence health care benefits in the restaurant industry. Very few restaurants pay employees if they miss work due to illness and nor do they offer group health care insurance plans. If an ill employee seeks medical treatment he must pay for those services himself, which presents a financial hardship for many restaurant workers since they have low-paying jobs. Further, even if ill service staff were to receive paid sick leave it wouldn't amount to much since a large portion of their income is from gratuities.

The authors acknowledged the study had limitations: the food workers were not chosen randomly but selected by managers, information about their illnesses was self-reported, some of the interviews took place within the managers' hearing range and budget constraints prevented the use of translators, so everyone interviewed spoke English. The employees interviewed for the study may not have been completely truthful in their revelations out of fear of retribution from their employers. Based on the flaws in the study, the 12 percent prevalence rate reported may only be the tip of the iceberg and the actual rate may be far higher.

Contamination at the Source. The food we consume often becomes contaminated at its source—produce farms, livestock factory-farms and meat-processing facilities. This breakdown in our food production system was illustrated by the large-scale *Salmonella* poisoning outbreak during the spring and summer of 2010 that resulted from contaminated fresh chicken shell eggs. This was the largest such recall in U.S. history. Over 550 million eggs were recalled over a four month period. The epidemiological investigation of the outbreak led investigators back to the feed supplied at two Iowa chicken farms. The contaminated feed was produced at Wright County Egg and fed to chickens at both Wright County Egg and Hillandale Farms. Investigators found manure piled as much as eight-feet high as well as maggots and a rodent infestation. Records showed that neither farm had ever been inspected prior to this outbreak. According to the CDC, over 2,400 cases of Salmonellosis were associated with this outbreak.

In the wake of this historic egg recall the FDA stepped up plans to partner with local and state authorities to visit about 600 egg producers—those with 50,000 or more laying hens—to determine if their facilities are in compliance with the egg safety rules that went into effect in July 2010. Michael Taylor, FDA's deputy commissioner for foods, said, "The rule sets safety standards that are intended to prevent outbreaks of Salmonellosis like the one that has led to the recall of more than 550 million eggs." The U.S. might consider following the example of the U.K. and make vaccinating hens mandatory. "We have pretty much eliminated *Salmonella* as a human problem in the U.K.," said Amanda Cryer, director of the British Egg Information Service. In the U.S., 142,000 illnesses every year are caused by consuming eggs contaminated with the most common type of *Salmonella*. Routine inspections of egg production facilities are critical; Denmark and Sweden haven't had a *Salmonella* outbreak since the 1970s due mainly to routine inspections of egg production facilities.

The 2010 contaminated egg outbreak is a good example of what can happen when food production facilities are not routinely inspected. The absence of preventative measures and proper testing by the producers was the root cause for the Iowa outbreak. While the FDA is the government agency charged with oversight responsibility, it does not have the resources to adequately monitor every commercial agricultural operation in the U.S. The prospect of the FDA conducting routine inspections on all factory farm agriculture operations is becoming increasingly untenable. Factory farm operations increased by 20 percent between 2002 and 2007 and certain agricultural industries have become more concentrated. Nearly half of egg-laying hens are now located in just five states—Iowa, Ohio, Indiana, California and Pennsylvania.

Overall, total animals on industrial-scale farms grew by five million, or more than 20 percent over the same five year period. The increase in farming operations has meant an increase in the volume of manure produced. Commercial livestock operations produce half a billion tons of manure each year—more than three times as much as that produced by the entire U.S. population. Disposition of the waste products presents an environmental health hazard. Runoff from factory farms often finds its way into lakes, streams and rivers or seeps into ground water, polluting local drinking water supplies. Manure is often spread on crops as fertilizer. In other instances farmers cover their land with slaughterhouse waste and treated sewage. In measured amounts, that waste acts as fertilizer, but if the amounts are excessive, bacteria and chemicals can flow into the ground and contaminate local residents' drinking water. The waste products of some farm animals often contain antibiotics and growth hormones that affect the wellness of the at-risk human populations. Agricultural runoff is the single largest source of water pollution in the nation's surface water, according to the Environmental Protection Agency. An estimated 19.5 million Americans fall ill each year from waterborne parasites, viruses or bacteria, including those stemming from human and animal waste, according to a study published in 2008 in the scientific journal *Reviews of Environmental Contamination and Toxicology.* In addition, the Government Accountability Office reported that storing large quantities of livestock manure on factory farms can emit "unsafe quantities" of ammonia, hydrogen sulfide and particulate matter.

Antibiotics and Growth Hormones. In 2009, the Union of Concerned Scientists estimated that 50 million pounds of antibiotics had been used on farms in the two previous years, which accounted for about 80 percent of all antibiotics used in the U.S. Sub-therapeutic doses of antibiotics are routinely given to healthy farm animals as a prophylactic measure to prevent sickness, promote growth and compensate for unsanitary living conditions. (To keep the public in the dark, industry is attempting to make it illegal to take pictures of animal living conditions, which has been done by animal-rights group like PETA. At this writing, there were bills before the Florida and Minnesota legislatures to make it illegal to take video footage of a factory-farm operation.) The problem with routinely administering low doses of antibiotics to animals is that pathogenic microorganisms develop resistance to the category of drugs called *antimicrobials*. The resulting effect is that these antibiotic-resistant strains of bacteria are able to survive exposure to antibiotics that were once effective in fighting human diseases. Additionally, diseases can be spread to other animals and to humans by eating and handling meat and dairy products, along with other fruits and vegetables or by being exposed to water supplies that have been tainted by manure in the form of fertilizer and farm runoff. The primary cause of antibiotic resistance is genetic mutation in bacteria. The antibiotic resistant gene is transferred to succeeding generations of bacteria enhancing the ability to resist antimicrobials.

While widespread misuse of antibiotics in human medicine plays no small role in the problem, scientists have demonstrated that the misuse and overuse of antibiotics in poultry and livestock production is a major contributor to the global antibiotic resistance dilemma. Drug resistant bacterial infections among people can lead to higher medical costs and, in the worst cases, increased fatalities. The annual number of deaths from diseases that have become antibiotic-resistant is shocking and increasing world-wide. Every year in the U.S., there are 90,000 cases of invasive staph that are highly resistant to our most effective antibiotics, and can be life-threatening. More than 80 percent of the *E. coli* found in meat products is resistant to one or more antibiotics traditionally used as part of a treatment regimen. World-wide 150,000 people die each year from diseases that were antibiotic-resistant. The situation is rapidly becoming a crisis. In fact, the World Health Organization recently announced that we're quickly heading towards a post-antibiotic era, in which "many common infections will no longer have a cure and, once again, kill unabated."

In April 2011 researchers at Transnational Genomics Research Institute released results of a study conducted on the contamination levels of meat consumers typically purchase. The researchers analyzed 136 samples of beef, chicken, pork and turkey from 80 brands. The samples came from twenty-six grocery stores in five cities: Los Angeles, Chicago, Fort Lauderdale, Fla., Flagstaff, Ariz., and Washington, D.C. Forty-seven percent of the samples contained *Staphylococcus aureus*, part of the normal flora of human skin and mucous membranes. Of those bacteria, 52 percent were resistant to at least three classes of antibiotics. DNA testing suggested the animals were the source of contamination. "The fact that drug-resistant *S. aureus* was so prevalent, and likely came from the food animals themselves, is troubling, and demands attention to how antibiotics are used in food-animal production today," said Lance Price, lead author of the study and director of TGen's Center for Food Microbiology and Environmental Health, said in a news release. *S. aureus* can cause a number of problems from minor skin infections to more serious conditions including pneumonia, meningitis and sepsis. Methicillin-resistant staph, or MRSA, commonly called "superbug," which can be potentially fatal was found in three of the samples. *S. aureus* is not monitored by the USDA and the FDA does not routinely check meat products for it. About 11,000 people die every year from *S. aureus* infections, according to the CDC. The direct risk to meat consumers—a staph infection from the meat—can be reduced by cooking meat thoroughly and washing all foods or surfaces that come in contact with raw meat. But the wider danger to public health is that antibiotics will become increasingly ineffective in battling human diseases.

The overuse of antibiotics has long been a concern for those who follow the agricultural animal industry. The main concern with overusing antibiotics in the farm animal husbandry is that we have created a Catch-22 situation. It would be extremely difficult to reduce the amount of antibiotics without reducing the production of meat and poultry and consequently raising the cost of meat to the consumer. Because antibiotics serve to keep farm animals healthy there is an abundance of pork, beef and poultry moderating market prices. Americans consume more meat than ever and the rate continues to rise. As much as we may detest many of the practices and abuses associated with factory-farms and the overuse of antibiotics we seem to accept them as necessary evils. They have become economic necessities if we want to continue to produce of poultry and livestock required. This dilemma is not confined to the U.S., this is a global issue and with an ever-increasing world population the problem of antibiotic overuse may only worsen. Growth hormones are *not* given to all industrial livestock. Currently, cattle and milk cows are the only farm animals approved by the FDA for hormone injection in the U.S. Scientists have been able increase growth rates through selective breeding. For example, commercial broiler chickens—more than 8 billion broiler chickens are raised in the U.S. each year and 20 billion world-wide—are not given growth hormones because they have been bred to be slaughtered and processed at six to seven weeks of age. A 2003 study from North

Carolina State poultry researchers confirmed this phenomenon. The researchers discovered that because of genetic advancement, a 2001 broiler can reach the lower end of its target weight in about one-third as much time as a 1957 broiler—32 vs. 101 days—to reach four pounds. If you gained weight at that rate you could weigh about 175 pounds at five years of age. Chickens have been bred to gain weight that rapidly.

The vast majority of chicken meat we find in grocery stores and restaurants comes from "broiler" chickens intensively confined on factory farms. A broiler's life is not pleasant. They suffer both acute and chronic pain due to selective breeding, extreme confinement, transportation stress and slaughter methods. The leading health problem caused by rapid growth is the high rate of leg disorders causing crippling lameness. Broilers' bone growth is outpaced by the growth of their musculature and adipose tissue. Lameness causes many chickens to be unable to support their own weight. At six weeks, broiler chickens have such difficulty supporting their abnormally heavy bodies and they spend 76 percent to 86 percent of their time lying down. This, in turn, leads to breast blisters, burns and foot pad dermatitis. Contact dermatitis due to lameness has been shown to affect up to 20 percent of broilers. Because sheds are often not cleared of litter and excrement until chickens are taken to slaughter, the birds have no choice but to stand or lay in their own waste. As a result, bacteria often infect skin sores, leading to disease.

Some Sensible Solutions

THERE IS NO magic bullet to mitigate the public health crisis associated with America's food production and supply chain. There are too many players whose divergent political agendas impede sustained or adequate preventative measures. The playing field in this battle is not level; special interest groups have inordinate influence with their state and federal legislators and on Capitol Hill. For example, big agri-businesses have lobbied state legislatures to exempt agricultural animals from animal abuse laws. Politicians at the state and federal levels receive generous donations from the agricultural industry to protect their businesses interests from litigation. You would be in violation of animal welfare laws if you treated your house pet as most farm animals are treated. And agricultural animals have no protection from the federal government. Undercover investigations by animal-rights groups and industry whistleblowers have revealed incidents of heinous animal abuse on farms and in slaughterhouses. You have only to do a cursory search of the internet to view the grisly videos of actual animal abuse. You Tube is a good source for these disturbing videos.

Multinational agribusinesses such as Monsanto and Cargill, wield enormous power with the politicians at the state and federal level who craft the legislation that affects their business enterprises. Legislation is fashioned to maximize corporate profits. Clearly, this is one reason why routine inspections are lax or nonexistent in many agricultural operations. Government oversight is anemic because the agencies responsible for monitoring are routinely underfunded. As stated previously, the lack of oversight was determined to be a critical factor that led to the monumental fresh egg recall of 2010. In that particular recall the egg producers were left to monitor themselves. This is a real life example of the "fox watching the hen house." To make long-term improvements to America's food safety, a multifaceted approach must be embraced by all concerned parties—industry, government agencies and the public. Here are a few existing remedies and some possible solutions.

Industry/Government Partnerships. In the wake of nation-wide lettuce and spinach recalls in 2006, the producers formed the Leafy Green Product Handlers Marketing Agreement (LGMA) to partner with the federal government to have USDA-trained auditors conduct periodic inspections. The audits, both scheduled and unannounced, are independent third party inspections designed to protect public health by reducing potential sources of contamination in California-grown leafy greens. California produces approximately 80 percent of the nation's leafy greens. U.S. egg producers might consider emulating the model of California's leafy green vegetable producers and establish a similar self-monitoring program. This same partnering model could be applied to a range of food production industries, say, aquaculture and open ocean fisheries, for example. Reducing food recalls is smart business because it's more cost effective in the long run. It behooves businesses to come up with creative solutions to cooperate with each other and responsible government agencies to improve food safety in their respective industries. The LGMA is a good example of how this can work.

Federal Agency Consolidation. Food safety regulation is deeply fragmented. Although the FDA and the US Department of Agriculture (USDA) are the primary federal agencies responsible for regulating food, at least 14 different agencies and offices have some responsibility for food safety.[5] The FDA has broad authority over 80 percent of the US food supply, whereas the USDA regulates most meat, poultry, and egg products (but not eggs still in their shells, which are regulated by the FDA). This split often leads to bizarre regulatory results; for example, the FDA is responsible for frozen cheese pizza but the USDA is responsible for frozen pepperoni pizza. Moreover, the CDC, as well as state and local health agencies, play a large role in identifying and tracing outbreaks.

In a sweeping report on how to carve as much as $200 billion out of the federal government, the General Accountability Office (GAO) says there should be just one federal food safety agency, even if consolidating the now fragmented system does not save much, if any, money. The GAO, in its first annual report to Congress to identified federal programs, agencies, offices and initiatives that have duplicative goals or activities. As of March, 2011, there were fifteen federal food safety agencies. According the GAO, fragmented foods safety systems cause overlapping and inconsistent oversight, ineffective coordination, inefficient enforcement existing current food safety laws and inefficient use of resources. The Department of Agriculture's (USDA) Food Safety and Inspection Service and the FDA are the primary food safety agencies, but in all there are fifteen agencies involved in food safety in respect. The GAO said it takes fifteen federal agencies collectively to administer at least thirty food-related laws. With budget obligations for USDA's Food Safety and Inspection Service (FSIS) and FDA totaling over $1.6 billion in fiscal year 2009. This kaleidoscope of agencies could be streamlined into a monolithic entity under which all other food safety agencies would operate. This would reduce overlap and duplication of enforcement activities. The need to consolidate government efforts was echoed by the Journal of the American Medical Association who stated, "Although the FSMA seeks FDA-USDA collaboration in designing certain safety standards, it does not consolidate food safety functions into a single agency as the Government Accountability Office recommended."

Legislation. The nation's food recalls in recent years have resulted in pain, suffering and even fatalities. In response to these food safety emergencies the U.S. Congress passed landmark and wide-ranging legislation to address many of the food safety issues that have plagued U.S. consumers. In December 2010 the Congress gave President Barack Obama an early Christmas gift by passing—in a bipartisan vote—the Food Safety Modernization Act (FSMA), the biggest overhaul to the nation's food safety laws since the 1930s. The legislation requires larger farms and food manufacturers to prepare detailed food safety plans and tell the FDA how they are working to keep their food safe at different stages of production.

The Act embodies and requires the concept of Hazard Analysis and Critical Control Points (HACCP). (HACCP is a systematic preventive approach to food safety and pharmaceutical safety that addresses physical, chemical, and biological hazards. It's used in the food industry to identify potential food safety hazards, so that corrective actions can be taken to reduce or eliminate the risk of identified hazards.) The legislation updates the FDA's oversight of the nation's food supply, increases the frequency of FDA inspections and gives the agency the ability to issue a recall. Prior to passage of the Act the FDA had no authority to recall unsafe foods. They could only make recommendations to the private sector for recalls, but could not mandate one. With the passage of the Act, they were given that authority. With passage of the Act, they were given that authority. The Act also increases the rate of food processing plant inspections, boosts access to production and distribution records, and establishes a tracking system so if an outbreak does occur the source of the contamination can be quickly located and contained. For more information updates on FDA's Food Safety Modernization Act, visit www.fda.gov/fsma.

The legislation also gives the Health and Human Services (HHS) Secretary greater ability to track and trace foods to their source. U.S. manufacturers and food processors operating their own farms and plants overseas are also subject to the requirements of the Act. The legislation empowers the HHS Secretary to enter into agreements and arrangements with foreign governments to facilitate inspections of foreign facilities registered with the FDA and permits the Secretary to direct resources for inspection of foreign facilities, suppliers and food products determined to be high-risk. Foods from foreign factories, warehouses and establishments registered with the FDA where the owner or operator refuses inspections by U. S. inspectors or others designated by the Secretary will not be permitted into the United States.

Retailers selling private label food products governed by the Act will be required to perform risk-based foreign supplier verification indicating that the imported food is in compliance with new FDA requirements and is not adulterated or misbranded. Under the Act, private label retailers are required to provide the HHS Secretary with certification from an accredited certification entity or other assurances that their foreign-supplied food products are FDA compliant. The Secretary can refuse entry of imported foods whose certification or assurances are not deemed valid or reliable.

The Act exempts smaller food facilities from FDA oversight, including food facilities or farms with sales of $500,000 or less, or producers that sell half of their food to retailers, restaurants or consumers in the same state or within 275 miles. The Act does not apply to meat, poultry or processed eggs, which are regulated by the Agriculture Department. Those foods have long-been subject to much more rigorous inspections and oversight than FDA-regulated foods. (Although the Department of Agriculture failed to prevent the egg recall discussed earlier.) President Obama signed the bill into law on January 4, 2011, however, the Republican-controlled House threatened to not fund the Act in an effort to reduce the national deficit. This makes no sense. Deaths due to food-borne disease far outnumber those resulting from terrorism, yet the FY2011 budget for FSMA, $280 million (this represents one-fifth of the $1.4 billion the CBO estimates the Act will cost through 2015), is one-fortieth that of Homeland Security, $56.3 billion—requested by Secretary of Homeland Security. It would cost every American just ninety cents to fund the FSMA each year. This is a small price to pay for the quantum leap in the sustained food safety vigilance that FSMA would bring. The new standards take effect July 2011.

The FSMA fundamentally reforms an antiquated US food safety system and will significantly improve the public's health. Enhancing food safety requires not only effective government regulation, but also advances in regulatory science, industry accountability, and consumer education around safe food handling. In a globalized food environment, improving safety also requires non-US agencies, producers, and importers to meet uniformly high standards.

The FSMA laudably integrates these varied food safety components. Programs to build the capacity of domestic and non-US regulators and producers are essential to a robust food safety system. Yet they risk falling short, particularly because the act does not set firm targets for implementing such programs (unlike provisions setting numeric standards for inspections). Additionally, the FDA should fully engage partners in government and industry to improve global food safety. International cooperation is needed to regulate food contaminants, monitor food safety, and assist developing countries in establishing food safety systems. Through global cooperation, the United States can better ensure safe food for US residents while improving food safety throughout the world.

~~~

As of June 2011, The US Senate Committee on Commerce, Science and Transportation was considering a bill that would make it much easier for federal agencies to coordinate their response on seafood safety, seafood labeling and seafood fraud. This is an important first step in protecting our health, our oceans and our wallets from seafood fraud. (Recent studies have found that seafood may be mislabeled as often as 25 to 70 percent of the time, which means you could be feeding your family illegal, unsustainable fish.) This bill directs the Department of Commerce to enter into agreements with other federal agencies to strengthen cooperation on seafood safety, labeling and fraud. These agreements would include elements such as cooperative arrangements for examining and testing seafood imports; coordinated inspections of foreign facilities; standardized data on seafood names, inspection records and lab testing; coordinated collection, storage and analysis of information on imports, exports, trade, transportation, etc. of seafood; expedited imports of seafood from foreign countries and exporters that consistently adhere to the highest safety standards; enhanced labeling requirements; sharing information on foreign and domestic noncompliance with U.S. seafood requirements; and educating the seafood industry and the public on how they can help improve seafood inspection and detect and prevent seafood fraud and mislabeling. Annual reports on these and other efforts taken under the agreements would have to be submitted to Congress.

The Act, if enacted, would improve the protections afforded under Federal law to consumers from contaminated seafood by directing the Secretary of Commerce to establish a program, in coordination with other appropriate Federal agencies, to strengthen activities for ensuring that seafood sold or offered for sale to the public in or affecting interstate commerce is fit for human consumption. This legislation would strengthen Federal consumer product safety programs and activities with respect to commercially-marketed seafood by directing the Secretary of Commerce to coordinate with the Federal Trade Commission and other appropriate Federal agencies to strengthen and coordinate those programs and activities.

Publicize Food Safety Violators. In an effort to improve transparency and accountability in the food system, the FDA could launch a new policy to post information on its website regarding its compliance and enforcement activities. The FDA could periodically publish information on prosecution bulletins when a conviction was obtained against a company for violating the FSMA or other applicable regulations and information on its enforcement activities. The notices could include information on food imports that have been refused entry into the U.S.; federally registered food establishments whose licenses have been suspended, cancelled or reinstated; and notices of violations with warning and penalties, including identifying repeat offenders of animal transport regulations. In introducing this new policy, the FDA could make a concerted effort to work with the food industry in order to improve food safety. Just as the names of violators would be publicly released, those companies that come back into compliance would also be recognized. Exposing noncompliant companies would give FDA inspectors—and other agencies responsible for monitoring food safety—another tool to peel back the curtain of transparency on repeat offenders and companies that try produce unsafe food domestically or import unsafe food. A disclosure policy would enhance efforts to improve food safety, traceability, sustainability and accountability.

Certification Programs. In 1999 the seafood industry—in conjunction with World Wildlife Fund—voluntarily created the Marine Stewardship Council (MSC). The MSC is an independent non-profit organization with an "ecolabel" and a fishery certification program. Fisheries that are determined to meet the standard can use the MSC blue ecolabel. The MSC mission is to "reward sustainable fishing practices". When fish is bought that has the blue MSC ecolabel, it should indicate that this particular fishery operates in an environmentally responsible way and does not contribute to the global environmental problem of overfishing or bycatch. Essentially, the MSC, and other similar programs, is an industry self-monitoring body.

If this approach works for the seafood industry why can't other food production and processing businesses follow the seafood industries model and create a voluntary self-policing programs similar to the MSC? Why can't these programs apply to agribusinesses such as produce, poultry, egg, dairy and meat industries? Each industry could form an independent certification process conducted by an oversight organization such as the LGMA mentioned above. The certifying entity would have ombudsman authority and conduct periodic inspections and monitoring to ensure continued compliance. A seal of approval, or "ecolabel", could be awarded for individual businesses that meet established criteria for environmental impact of the operation, general health of agricultural animals and overall cleanliness of the facility. Production and processing businesses who qualify would be awarded an ecolabel to demonstrate their compliance with established standards. The ecolabel could also be awarded to retailers such as Whole Foods, Trader Joes, Costco and Walmart whose policy it is to purchase food products from responsible producers. Finally, the food service establishments in the U.S. could advertise that they purchase food products from "certified" agribusinesses, commercial fisheries or aquaculture operations.

Educate Producers/Consumers. One way to reduce contaminating the nation's agricultural food supply at its source is by teaching the producers about the potential for contamination and the mechanisms by which it can occur. Some institutions of higher learning now offer short courses to regional farmers about food safety. This effort is partially driven by demands of *locavores* whose preference is for locally sourced produce, meat and dairy products. Beyond consumer demand, the FSMA will establish minimum standards for the safe production and harvesting of fruits and vegetables based on known safety risks. Penn State University has responded by offering short courses for producers through its College of Agricultural Science.

Extension educators would teach Good Agricultural Practices (GAP), and develop a curriculum that delivers science-based, practical guidelines and materials for evaluating and documenting farm food-safety practices, at one-day workshops in different locations around the state. GAPs are voluntary guidelines established by the U.S. Food and Drug

Administration and the U.S. Department of Agriculture in the late 1990s. As the university notes in its announcement, "They were created with the intent of identifying potentially hazardous situations and taking preventive steps to avoid product contamination altogether, rather than having producers react to problems that occur, which could prove financially disastrous to a farm."

Instructors spend time focusing on the basics, but emphasis is placed on topics that growers have indicated they need more training on; irrigation water quality standards, traceability, container labeling, how to conduct a mock recall, proper use of sanitizers, recent developments in federal food safety legislation and the Produce Traceability Initiative. Of course, many restaurants and retail food establishments such as grocery stores have been moving toward their own GAP requirements, so even these smaller growers likely will be subject to the mandates of FSMA.

Consumers can be educated about what they can do to prevent food-borne illness. Too often consumers rely completely on the government agencies for food safety. While government does much to ensure that the public has a safe food supply, local, state and federal agencies cannot guarantee that food is prepared in a safe manner in the home. Consumers should take responsibility to learn about fundamental food safety and safe food handling procedures. Basic preventive measures such as cross contamination, time/temperature relationships in canning and cooking, proper food storage and the importance of personal hygiene in food safety. Public education is a key to reducing food-borne disease and one component of the overall effort to mitigate the problem. It will never be eliminated. While safe food handling information is readily available on various government websites, it seems that a public information program would be of significant value in promoting food safety at home.

Food safety should be taught as part of the core curriculum in middle school or high school. Most school curricula require classes on environmental or human health. Information could be included about basic food safety such as safe food handling procedures, cross contamination, safe storage temperatures and basic microbiology as it relates to food-borne disease. Environmental health specialists from the local and state Health Departments could participate by making guest appearances and distributing literature.

Test and Hold. Require meat producers to test meat products in the processing facilities before they can ship them to be sold in the market place. Many of the 8,600 USDA inspectors currently test beef, pork, poultry, lamb and egg products for pathogens at 6,300 production and processing plants nationwide. But companies are under no legal obligation to wait for test results before shipping the food to wholesalers and retailers. Testing procedures might have prevented the outbreak of *Salmonella* associated with the Jennie-O recall of 55,000 pounds of frozen raw turkey burgers sold nationwide through Sam's Club stores. According to USDA, forty-four Class I food recalls between 2007 and 2009 forty-four instances in which meat or egg products had to be recalled because laboratory test results showed they were contaminated with a pathogen likely to cause illness or possible death. (There are three classes of USDA food recalls, Class I representing imminent danger to public health.) The meat industry advocates the "test and hold" procedure not out of a sense of corporate responsibility but because recalls are expensive and damage the corporate public image. To corporate America, it isn't a matter of enhancing public health, but increased profits for share holders.

Enduring Gaps

DEPSITE THE STREGNTH of its reforms, the FSMA leaves regulatory gaps and no assurance of adequate funding and enforcement. Most obviously, the act does not cover USDA-regulated foods, including meat and poultry. Consequently, regulatory fragmentation continues, together with inefficiencies in the USDA regulatory system. Although the FSMA seeks FDA-USDA collaboration in designing certain safety standards, it does not consolidate food safety functions into a single agency as the Government Accountability Office recommended.[7]

Exemptions for small producers present another gap in the food safety system. An amendment to the FSMA, introduced by Sen Jon Tester (D, Montana), exempted small farms from requirements deemed too arduous for small producers. Under the FSMA, a small producer's exemption is lost only after a safety problem has been identified, undermining the act's prevention aims. Although small producers pose different challenges than multinational conglomerates, a robust food safety system requires regulation of all system participants to ensure both public health and public confidence.

Implementation of the law may also fall short of expectations. The act establishes new authorities and enforcement, but the FDA's ability to implement ambitious new programs will depend on adequate budget appropriations. Food safety is not an assured priority within a harsh political environment stressing spending restraints and less-burdensome regulation. Other goals, especially stepped-up inspections of foreign facilities, irrespective of funding, require other entities to cooperate with the FDA.

Had Those Crabs Long?

YOU'VE MADE A date to meet few friends for lunch on Monday at a restaurant none of you have ever tried. You're all sipping wine as the server rattles off the daily specials, the soft shell crab po' boy sandwich sounds tempting. Ah, but you might want to reconsider that crab sandwich. Why? Because it's Monday, the day when many chefs try their best to get rid of seafood that has seen fresher days. Most restaurants receive their fresh seafood deliveries at week's end in order to have plenty on hand for the weekend rush. I did the same thing when I owned my restaurant. But I intentionally ordered smaller quantities so I would run out by Sunday. What I didn't use, I served to the staff or froze if it was conducive to freezing. Not all restaurants do this. Many chefs over order (because they can get a better price by buying in volume), and come Monday, they're wondering how to get rid of all that not-so-fresh seafood before it begins to go off.

Certain seafood products present an even greater challenge. Take soft shell crabs. When they're in season, soft shells are supposed to be delivered to restaurants while they're still alive, but quite often they're delivered dead. This presents an opportunity for the restaurateur or chef to save a buck. The chef can buy them at discount because they're dead. The problem is he won't know when they expired so he's taking a chance that they haven't already been dead for days? But even if the dead ones do begin to go off, the chef can just spice them during cooking to mask the odor and flavor. One solution would be to freeze soft shells before they go bad, but chefs prefer to not freeze fresh crabs for two reasons; 1. The appendages get brittle and can snap off detracting from their presentation when served and 2. When the crabs thaw out they tend to exude bodily fluid rendering them less juicy when cooked. So what are customers supposed to do to ensure that they're always being served the safest seafood possible, even on Mondays? Unfortunately, little more than trust that the restaurant is serving safe seafood and its food service staff is adhering to best food safety practices. But this level of trust may only come with your dining experiences at particular restaurants. If you're eating a restaurant you've never tried, there is little trust level. You can also check with the local Health Department for any complaints about a particular establishment. There's no point in asking the server whether the seafood is fresh because you know what the answer will be.

Another major reason why Friday's delivery may not be fresh come Monday is improper refrigeration. Potentially hazardous foods such as seafood and poultry are stored in refrigerators, which are designed to maintain temperatures of 40ºF or below—just like your refrigerator at home. Temperatures between 40 and 140ºF are conducive to bacterial growth and a contributing factor to food-borne disease.

Seafood and poultry will remain safe and fresh if the refrigeration equipment is allowed to do its job and maintain the proper temperature range. This is fine in a perfect world, but actual restaurant conditions are far from perfect. The employees in the front and back of the house are constantly opening the refrigerator doors. The intermittent door opening allows outside air to enter the refrigerator raising the temperature to above the safe range. Refrigerator temps can remain at 55ºF or higher for prolonged periods. This has happened in every restaurant I've ever worked. Another common reason why refrigeration equipment might not operate at maximum efficiency is lack of proper maintenance. Sometimes the door gaskets are damaged or the door self-closing device is broken, allowing cold air to escape and preventing the equipment from maintaining a safe temperature. To beef up the bottom line, many restaurateurs don't spend cash on preventative maintenance of their refrigeration equipment. The result of this penny wise but pound foolish approach is that the equipment tends to break down more often and does not perform efficiently. When I had my own café I didn't skimp on preventative maintenance, it's always cheaper in the long run.

The profit motive is especially intense when restaurants are owned by a group of investors. Investors have one objective in mind—make a profit. This can mean throwing money at an expensive advertising campaign to get new customers at the expense of maintenance and employee benefits. Also, when business is slow—such as during a prolonged economic recession—a restaurant may not generate enough cash flow to pay for routine maintenance. A small restaurateur might have to choose between maintenance and paying the utility bills. It's a matter of rebalancing priorities.

Secondhand Food

LUNCHEON SPECIALS ARE not the only tool in a restaurateur's repertoire of cost-saving measures. What do you think happens to all that butter that's leftover on your table? Thrown out? Not on your life. Many restaurants recycle it by collecting all the used butter. They heat it up, use a cheese cloth to filter out the cigarette ashes and bread crumbs and use it to make hollandaise sauce or for sautéing food items. Leftover bread is recycled into croutons or bread pudding. High-end establishments and hash houses alike all have to make a profit and recycling food is one way to increase the bottom line.

Buffets are another way to reduce costs and increase profits. Many hotels and large restaurants offer these smorgasbords because they're a good way to get rid of leftovers or food that is not fresh. Got some shrimp that's beginning to smell a little rank? No problem. Just get rid of it on the buffet. All the chef has to do is spice up the smelly crustaceans and call it "Cajun Surprise." It's a surprise alright! The customers will be none the wiser. Got some bad ground beef? No problem, there are myriad dishes that require ground beef. Who'll know? Besides, if anyone does get sick it's up to them to prove what food made them ill.

Chefs are concerned about their food cost. Their salary or bonus may be tied to food cost. It's an inverse relationship; food cost high bonus low; food cost low bonus high. In extreme cases the chef's continued employment may depend upon his ability to keep food cost low. A chef who can't stay under budget won't be around long. Going over budget affects the bottom line of any business concern. Even if customers get sick, it might not be for up to twenty-four hours during which time they will have eaten other meals. Besides the evidence is long gone—the customers ate it. People rarely realize that they've contracted a food-borne disease; they usually think it's a virus since the clinical symptoms are very similar. It's very difficult to prove food poisoning without pinpointing the causative agent, the tainted food. An epidemiological investigation needs to do a lab analysis on the suspect food. The only conclusive indicator that an outbreak of foodborne illness emanated from a certain establishment is when multiple cases are reported to the public health authority and the tainted food is collected. Even with conclusive evidence it may be difficult to pinpoint the guilty establishment because the reports from the public might be made to multiple Health Departments who fail to communicate with each other.

~~~

Buffets also offer an opportunity for restaurants to serve *secondhand food.* Selling leftovers as if they are fresh is a common business practice in the restaurant and hotel industries. Here's a fantasy scenario to illustrate one way in which leftovers are sold to an unsuspecting client.

Let's say the ACME Hotel has contracted with Mr. and Mrs. Jones to host their daughter's January wedding reception. There will be two-hundred guests. It's scheduled for a Saturday afternoon, but there's a problem. That morning a severe snow storm paralyzes the entire city. Unfortunately, only fifty guests can get to the hotel. Per the contract, the ACME Hotel prepared food for two-hundred guests, but since only fifty guests show up, there are a lot of leftovers: thirty pounds of beef tenderloin, twenty-five pounds of Gulf shrimp, masses of risotto and two whole turkeys. Of course, because they paid for food to serve two-hundred guests, the Jones are entitled to take home the leftovers, but they don't. This would be awkward and even if they did take home the leftovers where would they store all this food? So what happens to all this leftover food? Easy! The ACME Hotel has several ways to use the Jones' leftovers: Sunday brunch, other clients' functions and/or ACME's employee cafeteria.

Sunday brunch buffets are an excellent opportunities to recycle and resell food. Leftovers from previous buffets or other private banquets can be reinvented to create as a variety of tasty-sounding dishes. The shrimp left over from the Jones' wedding can be combined with other random leftover seafood and a velouté sauce and *voila* the chef has a dish for the Sunday buffet. He gives it a fancy name like *Sauce de Fruits de Mer et Crème.* The unsuspecting customers will happily gobble it up. They have no idea that they're paying top dollar for other people's leftovers. This is pure profit for the hotel since another customer already paid for the food. Leftovers are not only served on buffets; they also appear at other private functions held at the ACME. The kitchen will freeze leftovers from one function and use them on another function days or even weeks later. The customers are none-the-wiser, but they're being had. They're paying for food they thought was made fresh for the ACME brunch or for their private party.

When the leftovers are not fit for recycling, they wind up in the employee cafeteria. I doubt many of the ACME customers would be amused to know that *their* food is served to the hotel's employees. Remember the Jones' wedding? Where do you think all that leftover wedding cake wound up; the employee cafeteria, of course. If the ACME Hotel's executive chef didn't re-serve some of the Jones' leftovers to the employees he would be forced to spend the hotel's money to feed the employees driving up his food cost. And it isn't only the main hotel kitchen who participates in the leftover scam. The pastry shop and *garde manger* kitchen also get in on the act. I've lost count of the number times I have re-served leftover Danish, croissants, cookies and desserts over the course my hotel career. When leftover Danish, baguettes or croissant are too stale to be re-served they make excellent bread pudding; another example of recycled secondhand food. One way or the other the ACME Hotel profits from the Jones' misfortune. These shady business practices are not confined to low-end establishments, it also happens at swank properties that you would never suspect. I know I've worked in them. To be clear, I'm not suggesting that all hotels or restaurants would re-serve food that is unsanitary or inedible, although I have no doubt that some would. Leftovers are also combined with fresh food and served on buffets. This practice is discouraged by Health Departments since the old food may have be contaminated with pathogens thereby rendering the fresh food unsafe as well.

If you must do buffets, avoid being the first in line when the buffet opens. The leftovers—either from the previous buffet or private banquet—are usually the first food items put out on the buffet. This is because chefs are trained to rotate food; oldest food and leftovers are served first; the freshly-made stuff is served once the leftovers are gone. They refer to this practice as FIFO (First In First Out). It's no different from what you might do at home. I know these food recycling practices actually happen; I've seen it and done it myself hundreds of times. Does this happen a lot? Yes and no depending the chef's and the management's approach to quality of food service and the importance attached to food cost.

Close Encounters of the Worst Kind

BUFFETS ARE ALSO questionable from purely an uncontaminated food standpoint. Rarely do we eat food that is sterile, but it only has to be sanitary to minimize the chance of contracting a food-related illness. Many things can contribute to buffet food becoming contaminated while it's sitting on the buffet. First of all, food sits in open containers for prolonged periods of time, depending upon how busy the buffet is. Customers are milling about, stirring up dust from the floor. This is more of a concern if the floor is carpeted, because carpeted floors harbor more allergens, dust, hair and bacteria. These airborne contaminants can settle on the unprotected food. Customers sometimes cough and sneeze in close proximity to the open containers of food. Of course, health codes require that the buffet is protected by sneeze shields, but these are more for affect than function. A human sneeze may produce an aerosol that contains up to 40,000 bacteria-laden droplets, which may be launched up to 15 to 20 feet at a speed of 35 to 40 mph. Obviously, sneeze shields will not completely prevent airborne microbes from a cough or sneeze from settling on the food you are about to eat. Of course airborne microbes are always present wherever we are, even at home, but the differences in basic sanitation between a bustling restaurant and your kitchen is clear.

Buffets can also pose a food safety risk. If raw egg products are kept on a buffet too long at an unsafe temperature—between 40 and 140ºF—there is an increased risk of food-borne illness because this temperature range is conducive to microbial growth. Food items such as Caesar salad dressing, hollandaise sauce, meringue-topped pies, mayonnaise, eggs Benedict, cold soufflés and mousses can present a health risk because they contain raw/undercooked eggs or egg products. Ask your server if the establishment uses pasteurized egg products. He probably won't know, so assume they do not.

Buffets also are a good mechanism to transmit infectious diseases. Certain bacteria are easily transmitted hand-to-mouth, which is why public health professionals emphasize hand washing by food prep staff. Other diseases, such as gastrointestinal illnesses, can be spread by this mode of transmission, which can occur when the ill person contaminates the buffet utensils. The infected person may not even know he is ill and unwittingly spreads the disease. This is known as the *asymptomatic* period of an infectious disease; when the person is infected but has not begun to exhibit symptoms. For obvious reasons this is an especially dangerous period in the cycle of an infectious illness. This mode of transmission is of special concern when huge numbers of people are partaking of a buffet. For this reason at least one cruise ship line has taken prophylactic measures. Holland America will not allow the guests to serve themselves at the buffets for the first forty-eight hours—again, the asymptomatic period for many infectious diseases—of any cruise. Only the staff is allowed to serve the food at buffets. While some guest might complain about not being able to pile their plates with food, the logic behind this measure is medically sound.

I am not suggesting that ALL buffets at ALL restaurants and hotels are ALWAYS a rip off or present a public health risk. I am suggesting that buffets may not be what they seem and the food may not be as wholesome or sanitary as food can be. So the next time the family wants to go out for that Mothers' Day buffet, you might want to reconsider. I avoid buffets because I know the risks associated with them and the quality of food that can be served at them. I've worked both sides of this issue, on the public health side as a restaurant inspector and the food service side as a chef. I believe my suggestions are grounded in real-life knowledge.

Use Your Noodle!

GOOD FOOD SENSE means understanding that all may not be as it appears when dining out. Have you ever gone to a restaurant where you were impressed by the enormous number of menu items; 14 appetizers, 12 salads, 22 entrees and 9 dessert choices? Unless that restaurant is an extremely busy one, you would do well to be suspicious about the quality of food they're serving. If a restaurant offering a huge variety of dishes and is not busy then a lot of food is sitting around in the refrigerator or freezer for far too long. It isn't being rotated fast enough to maintain freshness. Even frozen foods lose quality over time. They can get freezer burn. Prolonged storage is especially dangerous with protein-rich foods, such as dairy products, meats, seafood and poultry because protein is a good media for bacterial propagation. I stay away from "big menu" food establishments. I know how chefs operate. Too often they will only throw away bad food if they have no choice.

Many restaurants give a public impression that they run a sanitary operation, but this can be misleading. Take plastic gloves, for example.

We've all seen the food handlers in fast food service establishments wearing them. Seeing this, you feel better protected from food-borne illness because you presume the plastic gloves are more sanitary than bare hands. The gloves give you a sense of security in knowing that your food is more wholesome and safe because the food handler is wearing plastic gloves. This would be true *if* the gloves never became contaminated, but they do. It's unavoidable. Glove-wearing food handlers touch their hair and mouths and cough into their hands. Plastic gloves *do not* provide a greater level of personal hygiene compared to bare hands. Sure, a new pair of gloves would be more sanitary than human hands if the wearer walked like a surgeon just before a surgical procedure, but does not happen in a real-life situation. As soon as the gloves come in contact with any contaminated surface, they become just as contaminated as bare hands. I have seen food prep employees dumping garbage and handling cash while wearing gloves so what level of sanitation did the gloves provide? None. I've seen food prep employees come out of the bathroom still wearing plastic gloves so what use were the gloves? Their logic might have been that the gloves kept their hands clean.

Unless the employees are changing gloves every time a new pair gets contaminated—and they don't because it's too costly—the gloves provide little or no increased sanitation benefit. So don't let the plastic gloves lull you into a false sense of food safety. I contend that by using plastic gloves, food sanitation is further compromised because employees themselves believe their hands are more sanitary because they are wearing gloves. Hand washing by restaurant employees is by far the easiest, least expensive and most efficacious way to prevent the spread of communicable diseases and to ensure food sanitation.

Protect Yourself

AT THIS POINT you might be asking why the Health Department isn't protecting me. I pay my taxes; it's up to the Health Department to worry about this stuff. The fact of the matter is that your local Health Department isn't omnipresent. It doesn't have the resources to make sure that every restaurant you frequent is always practicing sound food safety practices. There are too many food-service establishments and wholesale food suppliers to monitor on a regular basis. In a former occupation I was a restaurant inspector. Most Health Departments do well to inspect every food-service establishment twice a year. The inspection frequency is often need-based, that is, if a restaurant is an especially bad sanitation history it might get inspected on a more frequent basis.

Chefs and restaurateurs know that inspectors don't normally inspect on the weekends. Yet this is when restaurants are the busiest and many of the food safety codes are violated. For example, on a busy Saturday a restaurant may run through all the fresh chicken breasts it had on hand. So the frozen breasts are yanked out of the freezer and given the "quick thaw" method by submerging the raw poultry in warm water. I know this happens; I did this myself a few times when I had my own restaurant. The chef knows this is a health code violation, but he's not going to take chicken breast off the menu when it's one his most popular menu items. How will he explain that to the customers and owner?

And restaurant inspectors can be bribed. Let's be realistic, they are under paid civil servants. When I was an inspector I was offered a bribe on several occasions. For a few hundred bucks an inspector might be asked to ignore serious sanitation conditions such as rodent infestations or contaminated food. It's worth it to the unscrupulous restaurateur to bribe the inspector because it makes his life easier and avoids costly physical repairs or having to hire a pest control service. Bribes are a fact of life in the restaurant industry, especially in urban centers. Of course, bribing is the exception rather than the rule, but it does happen and our public safety is worse for it.

So how can you be sure that your favorite restaurant has a clean operation and always serves the freshest and safest food possible? There is no way to be sure 100 percent sure all the time, but there are steps you can take to educate and protect yourself against food-borne illnesses and still enjoy eating out. Here a few suggestions to protect yourself and family.

Take Precautions. On its website the Communicable Disease Control and Prevention (CDC) offers some common sense suggestions to reduce the risk of contracting a food-borne illness when eating out, you can protect yourself first by choosing which restaurant to patronize. Restaurants are inspected by the local Health Department to make sure that food preparation area facilities meet minimum sanitation codes and that food service workers are following recognized safe food handling practices. You can find out how a particular restaurant did on their most recent Health Department inspections, and use that score to help guide your choice. A restaurants inspection history will be posted on the Health Department's website. In some jurisdictions, the latest inspection score is posted in the restaurant. Some restaurants have specifically trained their staff in principles of food safety. This is also good to know in deciding which restaurant to patronize.

Local/State Health Departments. While the Health Department cannot do it all, you will find they do offer resources to help you in your search for clean restaurants and safe meals. Many local Health Departments have their own website where you can register a complaint about a restaurant. You can also report problems to the state Health Department via their website. You can also contact the Food Safety Inspection Service (FSIS) which can easily be found by going to www.FSIS.usda.gov. The FSIS is a public health agency within the U.S. Department of Agriculture. On its site are links to the state Health Departments in every state.

These websites are useful because the Health Departments often post restaurant inspection histories. This makes it easy for you to see how your favorite restaurants have scored on their health inspections. Were they gigged for a rodent infestation, unhygienic employees, contaminated food? I routinely consult my local Health Department's website for the inspection history of restaurants I'm not familiar with as well as those I've frequented for years. No matter how long a restaurant has been in business, a change in personnel can result in sanitation issues. A clean restaurant requires constant vigilance.

No restaurant is perfect. It's difficult to comply with every Health Department ordinance and receive a perfect score. When I owned my café I never received a perfect score, and I know that my kitchen was cleaner than most. I've never met a health inspector who didn't find something wrong. They have to justify their existence somehow.

You may also want to discover if the restaurant has a Certified Food Manager (CFM) on site. It's the law; most Health Departments nationwide require this certification. Designated employees must attend a short course about food safety, basic food microbiology, kitchen sanitation and personal hygiene. They also have to pass one of the exams accredited by the Conference for Food Protection. Most Health Departments require that a CFM be present in the food-service establishment whenever food is being served. Theoretically, having employees with this certification provides an extra level of kitchen sanitation and food safety.

A number of local jurisdictions—Los Angeles County, St. Louis, Las Vegas and New York City—and only two states, North Carolina and Tennessee, require that food service establishments post a letter grade for the public to see. The food service establishment is assigned a grade of A, B or C based on how well (or poorly) they fare on their inspection by the local health authority. In some municipalities, such as New York City, the restaurant must display their grade placard in a conspicuous place for public viewing. In Las Vegas the restaurant must display its grade on the menu. This is of great benefit to the consumer because a grade indicates the level of compliance with applicable Health Department codes. An attractive decor and server's smile doesn't always indicate a sanitary establishment. Behind the scenes, in the kitchen is where the action is.

State and national restaurant associations are vehemently opposed to the public grading system. The industry worries that grade cards will serve as a "scarlet letter" taking a snapshot of performance and branding the restaurant with it for all eternity. That fear is unfounded. A 2003 study of the Los Angeles grade card system found that restaurants with an "A" grade saw an increase of revenue by almost six percent, and even revenues at "B" grade restaurants remained flat. So there was little difference in the level of business. Further, New York City has designed a clever re-inspection system that allows restaurants a grace period to protest a low grade without posting it. They are allowed a period of time to take corrective action before getting a second inspection. After the second inspection the grade is finally posted. Of course, the scored can be upgraded if the restaurant improves its performance on subsequent inspections.

Of course, just because a restaurant makes an "A" doesn't mean no one will ever contract a foodborne illness from that particular restaurant. A Health Department inspection is only a snapshot in time; unhygienic food preparation practices can resume once the inspector leaves and an "A" grade is assigned. This is why our food production systems needs the reforms of the Food Safety Modernization Act to implement preventive measures and require companies to identify and reduce the risks of their products, so that food can be made safe before it ever reaches the restaurant kitchen. Grade cards are just one tool in a working food safety system—the part that consumers can see and weigh when they are making their dining decisions.

Personal Observation. Many food-service establishments, especially fast-food outlets, have open food preparation areas. This is a good thing, because it allows you to observe the kitchen staff preparing your food. Do they appear neat and clean; are they wearing hairnets or hats; does anyone appear ill? You can also visually inspect the food prep area for cleanliness. Do the floors and walls appear to be clean; are there fly strips hanging; do you notice signs of rodents; does equipment appear unsanitary?

Not long ago I went to a fast-food outlet in Northern Indiana, where I'm from, to grab a few burgers from one of my favorite joints. This chain has been in around for decades. I love their burgers. I placed my order and, as I usually do, I began observing the staff as they prepared the food orders. I like to watch kitchens operate. It interests me. But in this case, I observed something that was not happy about; a pimple-faced teenager was preparing food orders *and* handling cash. He was wearing plastic gloves, but, as I said earlier, this does little good unless they're kept sanitary. I watched him move back and forth from the food prep area to the cash register. When he began to ring up my order I told him that I wanted to speak with the manager. The manager admonished the boy as if the transgression was his fault. It wasn't, it was her fault. She was the manager and ultimately responsible for food sanitation.

Unhygienic food handling practices are commonplace in the restaurant business for several reasons; the employees either haven't been trained, supervisors fail to monitor the kitchen staff or food safety isn't a priority with management. The problem is exacerbated when restaurants hire immigrants from developing countries where food sanitation is neither practiced nor understood. Many of these workers have no idea what causes a food-related illness or how to prevent it, yet they are preparing our meals. If a person doesn't understand the concepts behind safe food handling practices they are less likely to adhere to those practices.

The next time you have the opportunity to observe food being prepared in an open kitchen, say, at Subway Sandwiches, watch the food preparers. You don't have to be a Health Department inspector to notice when things are wrong. If you don't like what you see complain the owner or manager. You have a right to complain; your food is being prepared there. Owners and managers who are genuinely concerned want to know when performance is subpar so they can take corrective action. If you believe it is warranted, call the Health Department. By law, it must investigate complaints from the public. Sometimes this is the only recourse. The

Health Department wants to know about unsanitary restaurants because they may be able to intervene and prevent a full-blown food-borne illness outbreak.

Global Marketplace. The globalization of the food supply means new food safety and security risks such as cholera and contaminated food can be spread across greater geographic areas. Imported foods can present a health risk for a variety of reasons such as pesticides in fruits and vegetables, adulterated products, product mislabeling or unregistered processes for canned food products. A major concern with foreign produced agricultural animals is the overuse of antibiotics and growth hormones. Chickens produced domestically are not administered hormones and a "withdrawal" period is required from the time the last antibiotics are administered and before the bird can be slaughtered. This helps to ensure that no residual antibiotics remain in the bird's system. International bodies—including the World Health Organization (WHO) the Food and Agriculture Organization of the United Nations (FAO) and the World Organization for Animal Health (OIE)—have recognized that antimicrobial use in animals contributes to resistance problems in human beings. Antimicrobial-resistant bacteria can be spread from animals to human beings either by direct contact or, more importantly, through the food chain. Food-borne infections caused by these bacteria pose a particular risk to human beings owing to possible treatment failure. The overuse of growth hormones is also a public health concern since these materials can have a deleterious effect on humans. This topic is discussed in greater detail in Appendix B.

Educate Yourself. You have a personal responsibility to learn about and understand foodborne illnesses and what you can do to protect yourself. The FSIS website, www.fsis.usda.gov, is where we can learn more about food safety and what the federal government does to protect our food supply. When you go to the Food Safety and Information Service (FSIS) home page click on "Fact Sheets" at the top for a trove of consumer information related to the prevention of food-borne disease and material associated with food production and processing. The topics range from safe egg, meat and poultry preparation at home to the USDA's role in food production, inspection and labeling. You also can call the USDA's Meat and Poultry Hotline (1-888-674-6854) where you can ask food safety specialists about food sanitation and what you can do to protect yourself at home. A good source of information is www.FoodSafety.gov where you can find topics such as Safe Food Handling, News and Safety Alerts, Consumer Advice, Federal, State and Government Agencies, National Food Safety Programs and other topics. In May 2011 the FSIS made *Ask Karen,* its virtual food-safety adviser, available in mobile format, following the launch of a Web-based smartphone application. Using the Mobile Ask Karen, just like using Ask Karen from a desktop or laptop computer, consumers can search for nearly 1,500 answers by food-safety topic or by product. With an iOS (iPhone and iPad) or Android device, it's also possible to chat live with a food safety expert.

FDA Alerts. A good way to become aware of food safety issues and food recalls, in particular, is to sign up for the FDA for e-mail alerts. To do this, go to www.fda.gov. For example, there is currently an alert regarding mussels imported from Ireland. The alert provides the name of the producer and their specific products that are associated with public health problem and where the product has been distributed in the U.S. This site also provides information about safe food handling practices at home. It's a good source for basic food safety information. If you sign up for this service you will realized how many food recalls there are in the U.S. The vast majority never make it into the mainstream news.

~~~

This is stating the obvious, but we all know that life is fraught with risks and eating happens to be one. One way to protect ourselves from contracting a food-borne illness would be to never eat out, but even this wouldn't ensure 100 percent protection and it would deprive us of all the wonderful eating experiences there are in the world around us. When I go on vacation I want to eat local cuisine even if that means eating street food or in a restaurant that may not be in compliance with even minimal internationally recognized rules of food hygiene. I'm willing to take a reasonable risk for the pleasure I derive from eating. It's irrational to develop a food phobia because the possibility exists that we could become ill from eating contaminated food. If we all did that we would turn into a Howard Hughes-like character surviving on canned soup because it is thought to be safe to eat. I like canned soup as much as the next guy, but

I don't want to survive on it. I'm all for taking a common sense approach to food purchasing, preparation and consumption decisions and follow sensible food safety precautions. There is a wonderful world of eating experiences out there and I won't be denied because of the possibility of getting sick? A balance must be struck between the risk potential of food-borne illness and the desire for palatable and delicious food. It's a risk-benefit assessment. I'm willing to take the risk.

Appendix B

Green Food Matters

WHILE THIS BOOK is in many ways an exposé on the world of professional cooking, this world cannot be examined without discussing some aspects of the Green Revolution as they relate to gastronomy or, what I call, "Green Food" issues. Some of these green food issues include terrestrial agriculture, aquaculture, food safety, genetically modified food and the maltreatment of factory-farmed animals to name a few. Each of these topics warrants in-depth and extensive coverage which is beyond the scope of this book. My objective in this chapter is to offer a cursory treatment of these issues so you can at least become acquainted with them and appreciate how they are inextricably linked to cooking and other aspects of your world as well. I especially want to highlight the roles of chefs and restaurateurs in the larger green food narrative. The roles they play are absolutely critical to moving forward a whole host of green food issues. By way of example, chefs and restaurateurs are in a unique position to present consumers with *sustainable* seafood choices. Chefs can avoid serving seafood species whose wild stocks have been depleted from overfishing. Restaurateurs can make it a policy to serve only beef, pork and poultry that comes from agricultural operations where livestock are handled in a humane manner before being slaughtered. But more on these issues later.

Responsible restaurateurs can inform customers which seafood choices are "good" alternatives to threatened species, say, tilapia rather than swordfish or grouper. A major objective of this chapter is to present comprehensive overview of green food matters to enable you to make better informed decisions about the food choices you make in the restaurant and retail supermarket. Many of the topics discussed in this chapter impact the quality of our lives, what we eat and how we live—now and in the future.

This chapter is brimming with a plethora of mind-numbing statistics. I wanted to avoid inflicting this upon you, but I saw no other way to fully describe the green food issues without using them. Throughout my research I gleaned facts and much of the information from trusted and recognized sources such as the United Nations' Food and Agriculture Organization, Greenpeace and World Wildlife Fund. I also scoured a kaleidoscope of books, websites and periodicals to find the most current and accurate information available.

The Devil and the Deep Blue Sea

PART OF THE following section reads more like a eulogy than a discussion of a particular green food issue because it addresses one of the most tragic ecological stories of our time—the plight of the Atlantic bluefin tuna. As you will read, this species is being harvested into oblivion. Once eschewed by the culinary world, the Atlantic bluefin has become one of the most popular seafood delicacies around the world. Its desirability stems from its palatable flavor, delicate texture and the eye-appeal of its ruby-red flesh. Bluefin is especially prized by sushi and sashimi lovers, especially in Japan. These magnificent animals have commanded enormous sums in the marketplace. A single bluefin normally sells for between $2,000 and $20,000, but on January 5, 2011 a 745-pound Atlantic bluefin tuna sold for a record 32.49 million yen (nearly $396,000) a Tokyo's Tsukiji fish market. This works out to $531 per pound. Bluefin is too valuable for its own good and its unheard of value will be the cause its ultimate demise, which has been underway for decades. Seafood Watch, a program of the Monterey Bay Aquarium, asserts that the Atlantic bluefin population has declined by nearly 90 percent since the 1970s, in part because the massive fish are slow to mature and are captured before they have a chance to breed. The future of the bluefin is not hopeful unless the world can come together to save these pelagic denizens. Because of its extreme commercial value, the bluefin has become one of the poster children of exploiting the bounty our oceans have to offer.

Bluefin: The Last Gold Rush

MOST PROFESSIONAL CHEFS under estimate the significance of their role in protecting the oceans and vulnerable marine ecosystems or shirk their responsibility all together. This is unfortunate since culinary professionals can do much to mitigate the damage being done to wild and farmed fish populations. As a chef myself, I often wonder whether my culinary colleagues in the United States and abroad are aware that an act as simple as menu decisions can make a difference, however small, on the environment and the viability of threatened marine species. Culinary professionals have an important role to play. Chefs bring influence to bear on the choices made by the dining public. Their clout was illustrated in 1998 when the Natural Resources Defense Council launched its "Give Swordfish a Break" campaign. The campaign recruited more than seven hundred professional chefs who agreed to discontinue serving swordfish in their restaurants. Other businesses—hotel and supermarket chains, cruise lines and air carriers—soon joined the effort. The U.S. government agreed to close the swordfish breeding grounds to fishing. Within a few years the campaign produced dramatic results. Swordfish had gone from 10 percent to 94 percent of what biologists considered to be their historical population. This success story should prove to chefs that they can make a difference.

To be fair to my culinary brethren, they are most likely simply unaware—like the general public—that certain species of finfish are in real danger of being harvested into oblivion. Let's focus on Atlantic bluefin. The bluefin's predicament is one of the great ecological tragedies of our time and may presage the status of many seafood species of commercial value. While bluefin is now a much-loved menu item, it hasn't always been this way. In the early 1900s, bluefin was known as "horse mackerel" and its unappealing fatty, red meat was ground into cat food. But that has all changed. The current popularity of bluefin grew out of the North American sports fishing industry in the late 1960s and early '70s when Japanese entrepreneurs flew cheap electronics to the U.S. and returned to Japan with planes brimming with bluefin bought for pennies per pound. The Japanese soon developed a preference for bluefin over all other tunas and began using it in sushi and as sashimi. Eventually the Japanese penchant for bluefin spread to Westerners who also developed a taste for delicious tuna flesh. Within a few decades the demand for bluefin spiraled out of control and, as a consequence, this magnificent creature of the high seas inches towards extirpation with each passing year.

The situation has become critical. The bluefin's unbridled destruction is today's equivalent of the California gold rush; extract every bit of treasure until it's all depleted. The bluefin's very existence hangs in the balance in a classic struggle between commercial interests and those of conservationists. Commercial fisheries want to reap as great a profit as possible while supplies last and before environmental groups impose their will and catch quotas are drastically reduced or there is an outright international moratorium. Thus far, the commercial fisheries industry is winning the battle. They're backed by nation's whose fishing industries stand to be decimated if even quota reductions are enforced. The worldwide appetite for sushi coupled with a complete disregard for conservation and sustainable fishing means this fish will likely become extinct within the next few decades. Unless the wanton destruction of the bluefin is curbed it is sure to go the way of the North Atlantic cod, decimated to the point that it is on the verge of complete annihilation. In his illuminating and beautifully-written book, *Four Fish*, Paul Greenberg writes, "The passion to save bluefin is as strong as the one to kill them and these dual passions are often contained within the body of a single fisherman." Commercial fishermen seem to suffer a cognitive dissonance when their passion for bluefin collides with their reckless exploitation of it, which is leading to its collapse. Greenberg's book is a must read for anyone who wants to appreciate the history and, in some cases, the tragic demise of fish that are commonly appear, or used to, on our dinner tables—salmon, sea bass, cod and tuna.

~~~

Atlantic bluefin tuna are impressive physical specimens. They are the largest of the tuna species. These behemoths can grow to 15 feet in length, and weights of nearly 2000 pounds have been reported in various fisheries in the western Atlantic and Mediterranean Sea. As large predators, bluefin tuna play an important role in pelagic ecosystems. Juveniles prey primarily on fish, crustaceans, and cephalopods, and adults feed primarily on fish such as herring, anchovy, sand lance, sardine, sprat, bluefish, and mackerel. Bluefin been clocked at speeds of up 50 mph when chasing down its next meal. They possess enormous muscular strength which it channels through a pair of tendons to the crescent-shaped tail. Unlike many other fish, the bluefin's body remains rigid while the tail flicks furiously back and forth, increasing stroke efficiency. In the marine food chain, bluefin are apex predators. Except for humans and the occasional shark attack, bluefin have little to fear. Bluefin are ultra-efficient killing machines.

Think of these marine marauders as the Hells Angels of the high seas. Packs of these powerful bullies cruise the oceans devouring entire shoals of smaller fish they happen upon. When the blufin are in the neighborhood, the smaller fish often form into a fish ball in an attempt to "confuse" a predator species. Some prey might dive deeply in a futile escape attempt. This maneuver is useless; bluefin can effortlessly rocket down to 1,000 meters when necessary. A draft of small fish doesn't stand a chance against the relentless attack of ravenous bluefin.

Sadly, too many capture fisheries are catching the giant breeders and the younger tuna that have not had a chance to grow to reproductive size. By doing this, fisheries are removing the healthy adult breeders and the potential breeders ensuring the eventual collapse of the wild population. Bluefin do not breed until approximately eight years of age. In *Four Fish* Greenberg also cites Dr. Jeff Hutchings, Dalhousie University in Nova Scotia, who stated that removal of 70 percent to 80 percent of a fish population has a certain degree of reversibility. In a case where 20 percent or 30 percent of fish are still in the water, the population may be unstable but still has reasonable potential for recovery. But when removals dip to 90 percent or more, the chances of recovery diminish and it is possible that the genome—the sum of the genetic diversity of the population as a whole—itself may be affected. This may well be the future of Atlantic bluefin at the capture rate is stemmed or a global moratorium is imposed. Both the Western and Eastern populations are already on the verge of collapse. This will also mean the collapse of the Atlantic tuna fishing industry.

The demise of the Atlantic bluefin also spells the end of a time-honored Spanish fishing tradition, "almadraba." In the fishing method the Spanish call "almadraba," fishermen stretch maze-like nets from sandy beaches to catch the bluefin, a practice that dates from when Phoenician traders sailed to the Spanish shores 1,000 years before the birth of Christ. This laborious harvest includes lifting nets heaving with fish onto ships and is timed to coincide with annual tuna migrations from the Atlantic to warm Mediterranean waters where they spawn. The fish are captured and hoisted aboard ships. While hanging from their tails, they are drained of blood by slitting their gills. Supposedly, this practice concentrates flavor in their flesh. The churning sea water below turns red with blood. Most environmental groups say the almadraba technique does not represent a serious threat to the survival of bluefin tuna because so few are caught.

The continued depletion of bluefin is already taking its toll on this ancient tradition. In recent years there has been almost no fish for the almadraba fishermen to harvest. At the rate fleets of factory ships are decimating the bluefin almadraba will soon become nothing more than folk lore passed on through generations. This is another consequence of wonton overfishing.

Over the last few decades bluefin has become a popular menu item in many parts of the world, especially in Japan. The Japanese are voracious tuna eaters. Japan imports roughly 36 percent of the total world tuna and 80 percent of the total bluefin catch. The Japanese are especially partial to the part of the fish called the *toro*, the most tender part of the tuna that comes from the fatty, soft underbelly portion. Toro is a smaller area and a pricier part of the fish and can sell for $24 per morsel at high-end Japanese restaurants. It is rosy in color rather than the bright red *maguro* tuna flesh, the leaner and more plentiful part of the tuna that is commonly served. Bluefin's extraordinary flavor comes from a chemical. After death, insoinic acid (also called insosine monophosphate [IMP]) forms in the bluefin's flesh, which is thought to be associated with the "fifth" flavor the Japanese call *umami* or "tastiness." In the food industry, insoinic acid is used as a flavor enhancer in soups, sauces and seasonings for the intensification and balance of meat taste. The Japanese aren't the first to discover the virtues of bluefin, ancient Roman soldiers marched into battle with their kit bags and stomachs full of dried bluefin tuna.

~~~

To date, aquaculture is not a proven method for rearing bluefin from spawn. Apparently keeping tuna in tanks and cages complicates or prohibits their ability to reproduce. The massive fish are extremely active and naturally migrate great distances, so simulating their natural environment is impossible. Scientists hypothesize that when the fish are confined; a key hormone used in reproduction, gonadotroptin-releasing hormone (GnRH), is not produced or malfunctions. Bluefin "ranchers" simply capture the juveniles fish and fatten them like "foie gras ducks" until they grow to market size. In 2009, Clean Seas Tuna, an aquaculture operation in Australia, succeeded in breeding bluefin in captivity and keeping them alive through their development from larvae to fingerlings to young juveniles. Then in May 2011, Clean Seas Tuna reported a new milestone in its pioneering Southern Bluefin Tuna research, reporting a successful transfer of its young tuna into sea cages.

The piscivorous bluefin requires vast quantities of wild-caught forage fish such as pilchards to satisfy their energy demands. The reckless plundering of these feed stock fish is its own eco-disaster. Because bluefin are extremely active requiring more wild forage fish as feed than it yields in usable protein when harvested. Their "feed-conversion ratio" is roughly 16 to 1—that is, 16 pounds of forage fish is required to produce 1 pound of bluefin. Not a very efficient way to produce high-quality animal protein even if it has that desirable umami quality.

Harvesting wild bluefin stocks has been ruthlessly efficient. Although now illegal, fisheries in the Mediterranean still use spotter planes to direct capture ships to the bluefin. According to some estimates, the world wide bluefin population has plummeted 90 percent or so since the 1970s. According to some biologists this would suggest a "collapse" (*collapse* generally being defined as the depletion of at least 90 percent of the historical population). With annual catch estimates of bluefin exceeding the legal catch quota the outlook for the tuna is bleak indeed. Scientists already agree that the population has crashed and that quotas allocated to fishermen remain too generous to give any reasonable degree of certainty of a recovery. The extents to which illegal fishing can be brought under control will a have a huge impact on whether the fish population as a whole ever has a chance of recovering and regaining equilibrium. Imposing quotas on the production nations such as France, Spain, Italy and the consumer nations is politically radioactive so the delegates at the International Commission for the Conservation of Atlantic Tunas (ICCAT) choose to ignore their own scientist's recommendations of reduced quotas.

The plight of the bluefin came into sharp focus at a conference of the ICCAT who met in Paris in November 2010. The forty-eight member organization is an inter-governmental fishery organization responsible for the conservation of tunas and tuna-like species in the Atlantic Ocean and its adjoining seas. The fishing industry and environmentalists sparred over the future of the bluefin. Environmental groups such as Greenpeace fear that current guidelines for fishing the tuna are being ignored, and that the ICCAT is doing too little to stop this. Environmentalists also say quota violations is rampant in the Mediterranean Sea—the only place with significant remaining tuna stocks, since the Atlantic's supply of bluefin tuna has mostly been depleted. Environmentalist's contention of rules violations was supported by a report by the International Consortium of Investigative Journalists (ICIJ) that unveiled a culture of over-exploitation and cheating that was largely overlooked by government officials in the Mediterranean countries who aggressively harvest bluefin, primarily France, Spain and Italy. These same countries accuse ICCAT and European Union bureaucrats of needlessly tightening quotas and choking the bluefin fishing industry in their respective countries.

Environmental groups were disappointed with the outcome of the conference, especially at the miniscule reduction of bluefin quotas agreed upon by the delegates. They had hoped to see bluefin fishing slashed or suspended, claiming that illegal fishing is rampant in the Mediterranean and that scientists don't have good enough data to evaluate the problem. The commission agreed to cut the total allowable catches of bluefin in the eastern Atlantic and Mediterranean from 13,500 to 12,900 metric tons annually—a miniscule 4 percent reduction. ICCAT also agreed on measures to try to improve enforcement of quotas on bluefin. The delegates also renewed the total allowable catch of swordfish of 13,700 tons. This tiny quota reduction for bluefin makes no sense. In October 2009 ICCAT itself affirmed in that Atlantic bluefin tuna stocks have declined dramatically over the last 40 years, by 72 percent in the Eastern Atlantic, and by 82 percent in the Western Atlantic.

The World Wildlife Fund, Greenpeace, Oceana and the Pew Environment Group all strongly criticized the 2011 bluefin quotas set by ICCAT. Sergi Tudela, head of World Wildlife Fund Mediterranean's fisheries program, attacked the "measly quota reduction." Oliver Knowles, Greenpeace oceans campaigner, complained that "the word 'conservation' should be removed from ICCAT's name." Complicating the efforts for sustainable management of bluefin stocks within national exclusive economic zones, is the fact that these fish migrate long distances and hunt in the mid ocean (referred to as the "high seas" in nautical parlance) that isn't part of any country's exclusive economic zone and therefore have been vulnerable to indiscriminate overfishing by many countries' fishing fleets. Essentially, bluefin capture fisheries are allowed to catch as much bluefin as they like wherever they like.

There was one bright spot at the conference. The delegates moved to protect oceanic whitetip sharks and many hammerheads in the Atlantic, though they had hoped for more. Sharks were once useless bycatch for fishermen but have been increasingly targeted because of the growing market in Asia for their fins, an expensive ingredient used in soup. (The U.S. Congress gave sharks an early Christmas gift in December 2010 when it passed the Shark Conservation Act. Under the Act, sharks can only be landed with their fins attached. With the new changes to the existing Shark Finning Prohibition Act [passed in 2000], the U.S. not only has legislation that is actually enforceable now, but the bill also allows action against other countries who aren't doing their part to crack down shark finning.) Conservation measures for bigeye tuna, blue marlin and white marlin were extended through 2011. Finally, the parties agreed to develop an improved system for tracking Atlantic bluefin tuna to combat illegal, unregulated and unreported fishing.

In the Mediterranean, where bluefin tuna poaching runs rampant, the legal catch limits for bluefin arguably has a negligible impact on the total amount of fish harvested. A recent report by the ICIJ, a project of the Center for Public Integrity, found that the massive black market for bluefin tuna is driving the overfishing. "At its peak, between 1998 and 2007, more than one in three bluefin was caught illegally, creating an off-the-books trade conservatively valued at $4 billion," the report states. In the Gulf of Mexico, the only other spawning ground for Atlantic bluefin tuna, the problem is not the socioeconomically-entrenched poaching that plagues the Mediterranean; the problem is the ecological impact of the British Petroleum oil spill in April 2010 that threatened bluefin populations. Scientists estimate that 20 percent of juvenile bluefin were killed as a result of the oil spill.

The Atlantic bluefin tuna have caught a small break. National Oceanic and Aeronautics Administration Fisheries Service will require commercial fishermen who fish for yellowfin tuna, swordfish and other species with long-lines in the Gulf of Mexico to use a new type of hook, called a weak hook, designed to reduce the incidental catch of Atlantic bluefin. The weak hook is a circular hook constructed of thin gauge wire, and is designed to straighten when a large fish, such as bluefin tuna, is hooked, releasing it but holding on to smaller fish. The average size of bluefin tuna landed in the Gulf of Mexico long-line fishery is 485 pounds, while the average for yellowfin tuna is about 86 pounds. The hooks will be required starting spring 2011. Directed fishing for bluefin tuna in the Gulf of Mexico has been prohibited since the early 1980s, however, bluefin are caught incidentally by long-line fishermen who target other species. Many bluefin die from the stress endured in this incidental capture in warm water even if fishermen release them. By putting the weak hook rule into effect during the 2011 bluefin tuna spawning season, NOAA is also following a recommendation by the scientific committee for the ICCAT, to which the U.S. is a member.

Removing top predators from an ecosystem creates and imbalance. We have only to look at the removal of wolves and other top predators to understand why deer populations have proliferated in many states. Removing bluefin will result in the same ecological imbalance in a variety of marine ecosystems. Once the apex predators are removed commercial fisheries move onto another species further down the food chain—the next "link" in the chain. When we do this we are "fishing down" the food chain. It isn't just the large bluefin that are being removed. There has been a 54 percent of the decrease in large predator fish over the past 40 years. If we continue down this path the day will arrive when the "catch of the day" will be sardines. If commercial fisheries don't begin to adhere to strict capture quotas they will one day pull up empty nets and the delicious flavor of tuna many enjoy will be nothing more than a distant memory. If anyone believes that this prediction is far-fetched I would encourage them to review the history of the Atlantic codfish. The relentless overfishing of the Atlantic bluefin represents an ecological ticking time bomb.

Wild-Caught vs. Farm-Raised

THIS IS A no-brainer, right. Of course, you would choose to eat wild-caught seafood rather than farm-raised. Who wouldn't love have a meal of fresh fish or shrimp plucked straight out of the ocean? It seems everyone does. In 2010 the annual worldwide catch of wild fish in marine environments (off shore) measured 86 million tons, which is roughly the equivalent in weight to the entire human population of China. And the total production of seafood aquafarmed globally was 53 million tons. But there's a problem. The traditional marine fisheries have approached, and in many cases exceeded, sustainable levels. Some species, other than Atlantic bluefin, have been overfished to near extinction or are under severe pressure. We have only to look at the history of the Atlantic cod to understand that unrestricted fishing can lead to the collapse of a species.

It was only a few centuries ago that codfish was discovered by the European nation states. Scandinavian, English and European explorers discovered enormous codfish populations off the coasts of North

America. In 1497 Italian mariner John Cabot (Zuan Chabatto in Italy) was contracted by England's Henry VII to find the Northwest Passage to Asia that had eluded Columbus and others. Instead of a new trade route, Cabot found a land mass he named Newfoundland. Along the foreign shores he discovered a trove more precious than gold—Atlantic codfish. The word spread throughout Europe of this abundant food source ripe for the taking. In 1607, one of the most notable explorers of the period was the Englishman Henry Hudson who, hired by the Dutch East India Company, also made several failed attempts to find the short cut to Asia. He also failed, but did discover additional cod populations, which helped accelerate large-scale fishing. Upon returning from each of his three voyages he continued to trumpet the abundance of cod. His pronouncements set off a veritable "cod rush." Legend had it that shoals of cod off North America were so dense that "the passage of ships was slowed." The codfish population appeared to be an inexhaustible crop that magically multiplied as described in biblical lore, but this food source was superior to terrestrial farming. The codfish crop never required planting and never seemed to get depleted no matter how many fish were hauled in. The news of enormous cod stocks continued to spread throughout Europe. Nations built and dispatched entire fishing fleets for the sole purpose of harvesting and salting cod, beginning a relentless pattern of overfishing that would lead to its eventual collapse centuries later. The cod never stood a chance. The pressure of overfishing and not allowing the species to recover resulted in one to the greatest ecological catastrophes in modern times. Thousands became unemployed in the end when the entire industry collapsed.

Catching codfish during this early period was a dangerous undertaking. There was no industrial ship that corralled the cod with a purse seine or scooped them with a trawl net like today. There was no Occupational Safety and Health Act to protect fishermen from unsafe conditions. In those days cod were caught by hand-lining from dories lowered over the side of the mother ships to return only when full of fish. Often the dories got weighed down with so much cod they would sink taking the fishermen down with them or those who survived the sinking might be carried out to sea. Severe storms would also sink the heavily-laden crafts. Since the year 1716 more than 5,000 fishermen from the port of Gloucester, Massachusetts alone have died at sea.

Prized for its white, flakey flesh and limitless abundance, cod was one of the main reasons why Europeans migrated from the British Isles and Northern France to Canada's Maritime Provinces and the northeastern United States during the 18th and 19th centuries. Cod was a way of life in Massachusetts during its colonial period. Paul Revere used the image of a codfish, then a symbol of prosperity, when he designed currency plates for the Massachusetts Bay Colony in 1776. A five-foot wooden carving of a codfish still hangs from the ceiling in the Massachusetts State House, to celebrate the codfish's exalted place in the region's maritime history. But incessant overfishing of Atlantic cod continued unabated through most of the 20th century, leading to the abrupt and total collapse of the wild stocks. Recognizing that it was fishing the cod into oblivion and its fishermen out of jobs, the Canadian government imposed a moratorium on cod fishing in 1992. It was too little too late. Even this drastic measure couldn't save the cod. The breeding stocks of cod had fallen below the critical biomass scientists say is necessary to recover and re-grow. While the cod population has rebounded, it is still not a commercially viable resource. The story of the codfish is one of the most tragic environmental narratives of our time and one that should have taught commercial fisheries a lesson in practical conservation.

~~~

After World War II conservationists recognized a need for a multi-national organization to conserve the environment and promote sustainability. This led to the creation of the International Union for Conservation of Nature (IUCN) in 1948. In 1963, the IUCN created its Red List of Threatened Species. The red list is the world's most comprehensive inventory of the global conservation status of plant and animal species. A series of Regional Red Lists are produced by countries or organizations, which assess the risk of extinction to species within a political management unit. The IUCN red list is a set of precise criteria used to evaluate the extinction risk of thousands of species and subspecies worldwide. These criteria are relevant to all species and all regions of the world. The aim is to convey the urgency of conservation issues to the public and policy makers, as well as help the international community to try to reduce species extinction. The IUCN has nine categories of red listing set through criteria such as rate of decline, population size, area of geographic distribution, and degree of population and distribution fragmentation: NE-Not Evaluated, DD-Data Deficient, LC-Least Concerned, NT-Near Threatened, VU-Vulnerable, EN-Endangered, CR-Critically Endangered, EW-Extinct in the World and E-Extinct.

Since the "red list" criteria indicate the risk-status of a given species they are of great value to the consumer when deciding what to buy in the grocery store or order in a restaurant. For example, the consumer can avoid ordering, say, orange roughy in a restaurant because it is a threatened species and is currently red listed. Armed with this information, the consumer can order an alternative species of fish like catfish or tilapia that is not red listed. The main stream media has been virtually absent in publicizing the information consumers need to make an informed decision in the supermarket or restaurant. Environmental groups like Monterey Bay Aquarium make the status criteria available on its website and also suggest eco-friendly alternative species.

Dead in the Water

MANY OFF-SHORE or maritime fisheries capture marine species in addition to the targeted one. This so called "bycatch" is often thrown dead or dying back into the sea. In some trawl fisheries for shrimp, the discarded bycatch may be 90 percent of the catch. Other fisheries kill seabirds, turtles and dolphins, sometimes in huge numbers. Estimates vary as to how extensive the problem of bycatch is. Greenpeace estimates that between 6.8 million and 27 million tons million tons of fish alone are being discarded each year, reflecting the huge uncertainties and disparities in the data on this important issue. Also, according to Green Peace, the latest reports suggest that around eight percent of the total global catch is discarded, but other estimates indicate that around 30 percent might be tossed overboard, often dead. Because of intentional under-reporting, no one really knows the magnitude of the problem.

The Problem. National policies for bycatch globally run the gamut. Norway, Canada, Iceland, Norway and New Zealand, as examples, make discarding bycatch illegal while EU fishing vessels are subject to a complex set of regulations that require vessels to discard bycatch. As a result, an astonishing amount of fish is being wasted because they are either too big or too small or the skipper is over quota for a particular species. The

Scottish Government estimates that one million tons of fish is being wasted in this way in the North Sea alone every year. Of course, the quota system was introduced originally by the E.U. to protect threatened fish stocks. But no one predicted the unintended effects of so much waste of such a valuable resource.

There have been numerous studies on the scale of discarding. The Scottish government estimates that between 40 percent and 60 percent of fish caught in the North Atlantic is byctach. In the North Sea the total annual quantity of discards has been estimated at 800,000-950,000 tons or the equivalent of one-third of the total weight landed annually and one-tenth of the estimated total biomass of fish in the North Sea. Most bycatch is tossed overboard because they are too small, of the wrong species or will take fishing boats over their quotas, making it illegal to land them.

Professor Callum Roberts, University of York, a leading authority on fish stocks, told the Independent, a British newspaper, that as much as 50 percent of all fish caught in the North Sea are likely to be discarded as bycatch. "It could even be more," Roberts said. One species, for which there are firm estimates of the number of fish, rather than the weight, is North Atlantic cod. Scientists at the International Council for the Exploration of the Seas calculated that more than 60 percent are discarded in the North Sea, the figure rising to more than 90 percent for cod aged less than a year.

The Victims. Fish are not the only victims of bycatch; cetaceans, marine birds and sea turtles also become collateral damage as a result of irresponsible industrial fishery operations. Cetaceans, such as dolphins, porpoises and whales, can be seriously affected by entanglement in fishing nets and lines, or direct capture by hooks, used in long-line fishing, or in trawl nets. An estimated 300,000 cetaceans die as bycatch each year, because they are unable to escape when caught in nets. In some fishery operations, cetaceans are captured as bycatch but then retained because of their value as food or bait. Tuna fisheries, which in the past had high dolphin bycatch levels, are still responsible for the death of many sharks. It has been estimated that a staggering 100 million sharks and rays are caught and discarded each year. Of the 21 albatross species recognized by IUCN on their Red-List, 19 are threatened, and the other two are near threatened. Two species are considered critically endangered: the

Amsterdam Albatross and the Chatham Albatross. One of the main threats to albatross is commercial long-line fishing, because the albatrosses and other seabirds feed on the offal-baited hooks and drown. An estimated 100,000 albatross per year are killed in this manner. Unregulated pirate fisheries—an elusive potpourri of ocean-going flotsam—exacerbate the problem. Sea turtles, already critically endangered, have been killed in large numbers in shrimp trawl nets. Estimates indicate that thousands of Kemp's Ridley, loggerhead, green and leatherback sea turtles are caught in shrimp trawl fisheries in the Gulf of Mexico and the U.S. Atlantic annually. Sea turtles can sometimes escape from the trawls. In the Gulf of Mexico, the Kemp's Ridley turtles recorded most interactions, followed in order by loggerhead, green, and leatherback sea turtles.

Some Solutions. While there are no answers to completely eliminate the problem of bycatch, there are technical improvements that can help move us in the right direction. Turtle exclusion devices are used in some shrimp fisheries to avoid killing sea turtle species. In the case of long-line fisheries, the process of setting the hooks can be modified and bird-deterring devices employed, which can reduce the numbers of birds killed. Dolphins can be deterred from nets with pingers—sound-emitting devices attached to the nets. Escape hatches (consisting of a widely spaced metal grid, which forces the cetacean up and out of the net) have also been used with some success.

Although these devices may have a role to play, they cannot address the whole problem. Such devices need continual monitoring to check how well they work and assess any potential negative effects they may have. Realistically, they will probably only be used in areas with well-developed fishery management and enforcement agencies. Those who fish illegally will not bother with anti-bycatch devices. On a global level, probably the only effective way to address the problems of bycatch is to control the fishing effort. This will be best achieved through the creation of marine reserves. Nonetheless, in the case of highly mobile species such as seabirds and cetaceans, the only effective way of preventing bycatch is to discontinue the use of particularly damaging fishing methods.

What does bycatch have to do with professional chefs and the restaurant industry? Quite a bit actually. Ecologically-minded chefs can serve seafood that is harvested by certified fisheries that employ ecologically responsible harvesting or aquaculture practices. For example, chefs can purchase shrimp from Marine Stewardship Council (MSC) certified aquaculture operations that produce mollusks and shellfish. By purchasing seafood from certified vendors, chefs can have some assurance of traceability. Serving certified seafood is one important way chefs can contribute to saving our oceans and the creatures that inhabit them.

Many chefs don't understand the importance of their role in the seafood sustainability conversation. They don't understand the power they wield in the marketplace. Chefs can select and serve species of seafood that are not red-listed or associated with bycatch. Farm-raised tilapia is a good example of a "good" seafood choice. Tilapia is relatively eco-friendly because they eat a cereal or vegetable diet and are easy to raise making them one of the most profitable of the farmed fishes. There is a wealth of information for chefs to access if they desire to become informed about disastrous consequences associated with bycatch or seafood sustainability in general. Unfortunately, most chefs are oblivious to these issues. Seafood suppliers will continue to offer threatened or endangered species as long as restaurants continue to purchase them. Restaurants can also list on the menu the seafood selections that are red listed, if any. By doing this, consumers—the ultimate decision-makers in any overfishing scenario—can make better informed food choices and avoid eating species that are at risk.

Aquaculture

THERE ARE ESSENTIALLY two ways to harvest seafood—*capture* it in the wild or raise it in an *aquaculture* operation. Often referred to as aquatic barnyards, aquaculture produces seaweeds, mussels, oysters, shrimp and certain species of fish (primarily, salmon, trout, tilapia and catfish) under controlled conditions designed to simulate the natural marine environment. Kelp comprises about 17 percent of aquaculture production and is used as food product and as a source of various products used in the food industry. While aquaculture creates a simulated marine environment, commercial fisheries capture wild populations in their natural habitat by long-line, purse seine, drag nets or trawler. Aquaculture is growing about 6 percent annually and provides 5 percent of total food production worldwide, most coming from less developed countries. Aquaculture is used to raise 80 percent of all mollusks, 40 percent of shrimp and 75 percent of all kelp.

Man began to stop hunting animals for food on land about 7,000 BC when he began to domesticate cattle and swine. We realized that if we continued to relentlessly hunt terrestrial animals as a food source that we would eventually deplete the natural populations so we turned to animal husbandry to ensure a regular supply of livestock. We discovered that farming animals was a more efficient way to obtain meat, but also the other products that animals provided like eggs and dairy products. The future of the world's supply of seafood lies in aquaculture. Like land-based farming of livestock, aquaculture has the potential and capacity to satisfy the world's seafood needs. The parallels of aquaculture and terrestrial farming are obvious. The goal of both operations is to raise selected animal species for human consumption. An aquaculture operation is essentially a barnyard and the fish containment pens are aquatic feed lots.

Aquaculture offers a number of advantages over terrestrial farming agricultural livestock in that cold-blooded organisms convert more feed to useable protein. That is, the feed-conversion ratio is more efficient. For example, for every 1 million calories of feed required, a trout raised on fish farm produces about 35 grams of protein whereas a chicken produces 15 grams of protein and cattle produce 2 grams of protein. For every hectare of ocean, intense oyster farming can produce 58,000 kg of protein while natural harvesting of oysters produces 10 kg of protein. However, for aquaculture to be profitable, the species must be marketable, inexpensive to raise, trophically efficient, at marketable size within one to two years and disease resistant. Aqua-farming creates dense monocultures that reduce biodiversity within habitats and requires large levels of nutrients in the water.

Aquaculture is not exactly a modern method of farming marine species. The indigenous Gunditjmara people of Victoria, Australia may have raised eels as early as 6000 BC. The Romans bred fish in ponds and around 2,500 BC and the Chinese raised carp that became stranded in shallow lakes that were created when natural floods receded. In medieval Europe the "stew pond" was a common feature of large establishments such as monasteries.

Hawaiians constructed oceanic fish ponds. A remarkable example is a fish pond dating from at least 1,000 years ago, at Alekoko. Despite the long tradition of aquaculture practices in a few countries over many centuries, aquaculture in the global context is a young food production sector that has grown rapidly in the last 50 years or so. Capture fisheries as well as inland and marine aquaculture operations have advanced greatly. Since aquaculture is becoming an increasingly integral part of our lives, and many of us know so little about it, I thought it was important to have a short discussion about the benefits and risks of this burgeoning sector of food production.

According to the United Nation's Food and Agriculture Organization (FAO), aquaculture, probably the fastest growing food-producing sector, now accounts for almost fifty percent of the world's food fish and is perceived as having the greatest potential to meet the growing demand for aquatic food. Given the projected population growth over the next two decades, it is estimated that at least an additional 40 million tons of aquatic food will be required by 2030 to maintain the current per capita consumption. Did you know that as of there are over 44 million fishing vessels in the world and only 59 percent are motorized?

Also according the FAO, aquaculture remains a growing, vibrant and important production sector for high-protein food. The reported global production of food fish from aquaculture, including finfish, crustaceans, mollusks and other aquatic animals for human consumption, reached 52.5 million tons (88 percent coming from Asia) in 2008 valued at $98.4 billion. Production from aquaculture is mostly destined for human consumption. Globally, aquaculture accounted for 45.7 percent of the world's fish food production for human consumption in 2008.

If China's reporting is accurate, it was the world's biggest aquaculture producer with 80.2 percent (32.7 million tons) in 2008. China was followed by India, Viet Nam, Thailand, Indonesia and Bangladesh whose collective production accounted for 8.8 million tons of farmed seafood. Global marine and fresh water aquaculture provides jobs. As of 2008, 44.9 million people were directly engaged in aquaculture, with the great majority in developing countries. Adding those who work in associated aspects such as processing, marketing, distribution and supply industries, and the aquaculture supports nearly 180 million livelihoods worldwide. Aquaculture is feeding the world. Today, aquaculture accounts for 40 percent of the world's fish consumption and contributes 20 percent or more of average per capita animal protein intake for more than 3 billion people, mostly from developing countries.

Salmon

APPROXIMATELY 60 PERCENT (1.26 million metric tons) of the world's salmon comes from fish farms and Norway and Chili produce two-thirds of that supply. Other significant producers include the United Kingdom and Canada. The oceanodromous Atlantic salmon are usually grown in cages or pens in semi-sheltered coastal areas, such as bays or sea lochs. The cages, usually large, floating mesh cages, are designed to hold salmon but are open to the marine environment. Juvenile salmon are hatched and raised to become smolts in freshwater before they are transferred to the open marine systems to grow. Salmon is the most commonly farmed fish, but life is not all it's cracked up to be down on the farm if you're a "farmed" salmon.

Salmon are susceptible to debilitating parasites and deadly diseases. According to the Pure Salmon Campaign, a global project that partners with various nations to improve the way salmon is produced, salmon farms harbor two especially virulent parasites: sea lice and kudoa. Sea lice chew on salmon, creating open lesions. The second most prevalent parasite in farmed salmon is *Kudoa thyrsites*, commonly called "soft flesh syndrome." This microscopic insect breaks down muscle fiber in fish, causing post-mortem "myoliquefaction", a softening of the flesh to such an extent that the fish becomes jelly-like rendering it unmarketable. Kudoa is not infective to humans. Kudoa contamination is usually first detected when salmon are slaughtered and processed.

One of the most common diseases in large-scale fish farming is infectious salmon anemia (ISA). Symptoms include pale gills and swimming near the surface gulping air. In its more insidious form, fish may develop ISA without showing any signs of illness, even maintaining a normal appetite until they suddenly die. In salmon farms where this occurs, death rates may approach 100 percent. In 2008, the salmon farming industry in Chili was devastated by ISA resulting in layoffs of more than one-thousand workers from aquaculture operations. The outbreak occurred after a rash of nonviral illnesses in recent years that led to the use of high levels of antibiotics. To combat the plague, Chilean aquaculturists used almost 350 times more antibiotics in its farmed salmon than Norway its chief competitor and the world's largest salmon producer, according to official data from both countries. Researchers say the practice is widespread in Chilean salmon producers, which is a mélange of international and Chilean entrepreneurs. Some of those antibiotics, researchers say, are prohibited for use on animals in the United States. Many of those salmon still end up in American grocery stores, where about 29 percent of Chilean exports are destined. While fish from China have come under special scrutiny in recent years, in Chile regulators have yet to form a registry that even tracks the use of the drugs, researchers said. Salmon produced in Chile are sold in Costco and Safeway stores, among other major grocery retailers.

Furunculosis, another highly infectious disease caused by the bacteria *Aeromonas salmonicida*, primarily affects Atlantic salmon in both the freshwater and marine stages of their lifecycle, producing boils on their sides. This bacterium also persists in high concentrations in sediment under salmon pens. In early 2005, the disease killed 1.8 million Atlantic salmon smolts at a single commercial salmon hatchery on Vancouver Island. Like ISA, furunculosis has been spread around the northern hemisphere by the global salmon farming industry. Salmon farms, consequently, are ideal incubators for parasites and infectious diseases that are then spread to adjacent farms and to wild fish populations. These outbreaks are impossible to quarantine; mass escapes from salmon farms and the normal flow of tides and currents spread diseases and parasites to other fish over very wide areas.

There is also an escapement problem with salmon farms. Open at the top, salmon net pens allow thousands of fish at a time to escape easily when there are rough seas and high waves. Other small scale escapes (called "leakage" by the industry) routinely occur from poorly maintained pens. Together, these produce staggering annual losses. Globally, an estimated three million salmon escape from farms annually. Escaped salmon present an ecological disaster. Mass escapes of farmed salmon—which often out-compete wild fish because they are genetically superior—can result in interbreeding and competition with wild salmon for food, habitat and mates. Escaped fish over crowd natural spawning grounds and dilute the genetic pool of wild salmon species by interbreeding with them. They also transmit diseases and parasites to wild salmon populations and threaten related species such as steelhead salmon and sea trout. Hundreds of escapes have had a serious cumulative effect: more than 1.7 million farmed salmon escaped to the wild from farms in Scotland since 1998; between 9 million and 18.6 million escaped from Chilean farms since farming operations started there in the 1980s; more than one million Atlantic salmon escaped from farms in Washington State since commercial operation began there.

~~~

There are risks associated with consuming too much salmon. Polychlorinated biphenyls (PCBs) were banned in the U.S. in the late 1970s and slated for global phase-out under the United Nation's treaty on persistent organic pollutants. PCBs are highly persistent and have been linked to cancer and impaired fetal brain development. Salmon farming has made salmon the third most popular fish in America and comprises 22 percent of all retail seafood counter sales. Many consumers eat more salmon today as an alternative to poultry and red meat, and to benefit from anti-cancer and anti-heart disease properties of oily fish. However, analysis of U.S. government data found that farmed salmon are likely the most PCB-contaminated protein source in the current U.S. food supply. Approximately 800,000 U.S. adults have an increased cancer risk by eating PCB-contaminated salmon. Farmed salmon are fed ground fishmeal and fish oils that are high in PCBs. According to the U.S. Department of Agriculture, farmed salmon contains 52 percent more fat than wild salmon.

Farmed and Dangerous

SOME WOULD SUGGEST that fish farming is the world's answer to the growing demand for seafood, the perfect alternative to the problem of overfishing wild fish stocks. But aquaculture may not be all that it seems. Far from innocuous, aquaculture can have a ruinous impact on the environment and localized ecosystems. Fish waste, dead fish, uneaten food and antibiotics can contaminate the aquatic ecosystems around offshore aquaculture facilities. Concentrated *waste plumes* from fish farms can travel significant distances to reach coastlines, according to a study to be published in the May 2011 issue of *Environmental Fluid Mechanics*. Scientists from the Woods Institute for the Environment at Stanford University found that relatively high concentrations of dissolved waste from fish pens do not dilute consistently or immediately. Dissolved substances from feces, undigested food and other forms of discharge amass near fish pens. In multiple modeling scenarios in which these factors were varied to study how each one affected the behavior of such pollution; effluent was characterized by "plumes" of highly concentrated waste that remained cohesive over great distances from the source. The Stanford study is the first detailed look at how "real world" variables, such as tides, currents, the earth's rotation and the physical structure of the containment pens themselves, influence the flow of waste from fish farms. However, scientists have come with a partial solution to the waste problem. Growing seaweed in a fish farm can improve water quality by reducing nitrogen and phosphorous, both found in fish waste.

Aquaculture is not necessarily an efficient way to produce high-quality animal protein for human consumption. Fish farming is in itself a paradox because massive amounts of wild forage fish—anchovies, herring, sardines and menhaden—are required to produce market-size farmed fish, essentially converting one fish species into another. According to U.N. figures, capture fisheries and aquaculture produced 145 million tons of fish in 2009. Of this, 118 million tons was used as human food, much of the remainder being used as an ingredient in fish meal. While the feed-conversion ratio with marine species is more efficient than with agricultural livestock, there is room for improvement. Traditionally, Atlantic salmon, by example, requires 5 to 6 pounds of feed to produce 1 pound of useable protein. From purely a nutritional standpoint it is more efficient to consume the wild feed stocks directly, but this isn't likely to occur since affluent Westerners prefer a diet of apex predators such as salmon, tuna and other prized fin fish. The industry of farm-raising seafood in the West is a self-limiting one because the wild feed stocks are increasingly being depleted to levels at which they cannot reproduce fast enough to sustain viable populations. However, there has been some progress with regard to the feed-conversion dilemma. Through selective breeding, the Norwegian aquaculturists have been able to get the feed-conversion ratio down to 3 to 1 for their farmed salmon.

~~~

Many underdeveloped nations welcome a lucrative aquaculture industry. Costa Rica, Ecuador and Honduras have entered the exploding world tilapia market; however, China and Egypt remain the world's largest producers. Tilapias are ideally suited for aquaculture because of their adaptability and they are less costly to produce since they are vegetarians. And Vietnam has also become one of the world's major exporters of aquaculture products, in particular Pangasius fish, also known as *tra*, due to its edibility and low production costs. Tra is a freshwater member of the river catfish family. It is prized for its delicate white-meat and suitability for various cooking methods. Vietnam exported approximately $1.6 billion worth of seafood worldwide in 2010.

The food safety issue arises with the way in which tra is produced and processed in Viet Nam. While Vietnam's Ministry of Agriculture and Rural Development claims to have a robust aquaculture inspection program, there is scant evidence that routine inspections are carried out. A large portion of catfish and snapper produced in Vietnam is done by small, privately-owned fish farms in the Mekong River, primarily at the delta region. In Vietnam production is centered in 13 provinces around the Mekong Delta, especially Anyiang and Can Tho provinces. Having traveled through six countries (Tibet, China, Thailand, Cambodia, Laos and Vietnam), the Mekong River is one of the most polluted waterways in the world. Hundreds, perhaps thousands, of these small "mom and pop" fish farms are situated near the shoreline where the containment pens are physically attached to the farmers' floating homes. The fish are exposed to raw sewage expelled from these homes and to biological and chemical effluent spewed from the mechanized river traffic. Shrimp from South East Asia is also a concern. Shrimp farms are nothing more than fetid pools located in former mangrove swamps. The water is laced with antibiotics to keep the shrimp healthy.

Only a fraction of the millions of tons of seafood exported by other countries is inspected by the producer or consumer nations, the United States being a primary one. Consequently, the fish is produced, harvested, processed, shipped abroad and wind up on our plates without the benefit of having undergone even a visual inspection let alone laboratory testing for microbiological and chemical agents. As the world's population approaches 8 billion, and the aquaculture industry expands, the prospects for enhanced monitoring procedures seem tenuous at best. And in certain parts of the world fishermen continue to harvest wild fish illegally and restaurants in the West continue to serve red-listed species of fish—species whose wild populations are threatened. The vilest form of illegal fishing is pirate fishing—known by its less colorful name: illegal, unreported and unregulated fishing—is the scourge of the oceans. It leaves communities without a revenue stream and the marine environment decimated and barren.

For decades environmentalists have voiced a clarion call for stronger action by governments, private industry and the global retail sector to address the issue of overfishing. Too often their exhortations have been received with indifference by the commercial fisheries and ignored by the mainstream media. However, there is cause for hope. In recent years international concern for seafood sustainability has become a matter of importance like never before. Non-governmental bodies have been formed to develop, establish and implement acceptable certification guidelines at aquaculture facilities around the world. In October 2010 in Phuket, Thailand the first global guidelines for aquaculture certification were adopted by the Sub-Committee on Aquaculture of the Committee on Fisheries, part of the United Nations Food and Agriculture Organization. Over fifty countries attended the meeting of the sub-committee, which was the only global intergovernmental forum discussing aquaculture development.

~~~

The U. S. is a major consumer of aquaculture products—we import 84 percent of our seafood and half of that is from aquaculture—yet we are a minor producer. U.S. aquaculture (freshwater and marine) supplies about five percent of the U.S. seafood supply and U.S. marine aquaculture less than 1.5 percent. Inherent in the design of most aquaculture operations are environmental health concerns and public health risks. Since hundreds or thousands of farmed fish are crammed into containment pens, diseases and parasitic infestations tend to infect the entire population. Since they are often raised in coastal areas, farmed fish may be exposed to chemicals from farm and industrial runoff, causing physical abnormalities. An example of the harmful effects of anthropogenic pollutants is the abnormalities found in smallmouth bass in the Potomac River basin (virtually my own backyard) of Maryland and Virginia. For several years, scientists U.S. Geological Survey (USGS) and other organizations have conducted fish-health investigations to determine why so many male smallmouth bass in the Potomac River have immature female egg cells in their testes—a form of intersex. ("Intersex" characteristics, describes a range of abnormalities in which both male and female characteristics are present within the same fish.) Preliminary findings by the USGS show that a high incidence of intersex characteristics occurs in the Potomac watershed at sites where farming is most intense and where human population density is highest. Chemical contaminants include previously banned compounds, such as DDT and chlordane, natural and anthropogenic hormones, herbicides, fungicides, industrial chemicals, personal care products and pharmaceuticals that may act as endocrine disruptors in fish as well as other organisms. Other factors that may contribute to intersex characteristics are habitat temperature changes, lack of dissolved oxygen and water quality degradation, especially at the riparian zones. A prevalence of intersex is not unique to the Potomac River basin, nor is it restricted to wild bass stocks. It has been documented in other wild fish populations including spot-tail shiners in the St. Lawrence River, white suckers in Colorado, shovelnose sturgeon in the Mississippi and white perch from the Great Lakes.

Closed Containment Aquaculture

A VIABLE ALTERNATIVE to conventional open-cage salmon farming would be Closed Containment Aquaculture (CCA). Proponents of CCA tout it as the next generation in fish farming. Closed-containment, land-based recirculating systems for aquaculture are not new. However, the latest generation of this technology, highly integrated systems built from the ground up specifically for aquaculture purposes are distinct from land-based fish farms that employ tanks and pumps but have been assembled in an extemporized fashion and fail to reach the efficiency, scalability and profitability of next-generation systems. The latest next-generation closed-containment aquaculture systems represent a quantum leap forward, both as a lucrative and low-risk business venture as well as the most sustainable and efficient form of aquaculture today, with efficiencies more than 10 times conventional fish farms. Next-generation systems recirculate up to 99 percent of their effluent, have no discharge, use no chemicals or antibiotics, and can be sited close to market, resulting in a fresher product and dramatically lower transportation costs (food miles). The latest next-generation closed-containment aquaculture systems represent a quantum leap forward, both as a lucrative and low-risk business venture as well as the most sustainable and efficient form of aquaculture today, with efficiencies more than 10 times conventional fish farms. Next-generation systems recirculate up to 99 percent of their effluent, have no discharge, use no chemicals or antibiotics, and can be sited close to market, resulting in a fresher product and dramatically lower transportation costs (food miles). The latest next-generation closed-containment aquaculture systems represent a quantum leap forward, both as a lucrative and low-risk business venture as well as the most sustainable and efficient form of aquaculture today, with efficiencies more than 10 times conventional fish farms. Next-generation systems recirculate up to 99 percent of their effluent, have no discharge, use no chemicals or antibiotics, and can be sited close to market, resulting in a fresher product and dramatically lower transportation costs (food miles). Closed Containment Aquaculture has several eco-advantages over conventional aquaculture systems. It eliminates the waste problem by concentrating, treating and disinfecting all wastes and waste water, reduces feed requirements by 30-40 percent and there are zero mass escape events (eliminating the risk of disease and parasite transfer to wild salmon and polluting the wild gene pool) and eliminates algae and plankton blooms that can kill farmed fish by the thousands as well as protection from sea lice infestations and disease. Moreover, CCA can be as much as 20 percent cheaper than conventional salmon farming in open-net pens or cages. Because of these advantages, as well as advances in the technology itself over the last several years, closed containment has become widely regarded by scientists, conservationists, some salmon farming companies and the public as a more responsible alternative to open-cage aquaculture. Unfortunately, only a small percentage of salmon is currently farmed in closed containment due to industry's overall resistance to change and the profitability of externalizing costs. Externalized costs are currently borne by society or the environment and not by salmon producers, such as 'free' waste disposal from open net-cage farms into the marine environment.

Global Climate Change and Aquaculture

IN 1896, SWEDISH scientist Svante Arrhenius was the first to speculate that changes in the levels of carbon dioxide in the atmosphere—primarily by burning coal—could substantially alter the surface temperature through the "greenhouse effect." It wasn't until 1958 that measurements began to show that levels of carbon dioxide in the atmosphere were rising and temperatures shifting. Climatologists and marine biologists generally agree that the effects of climate change have caused profound changes to marine ecosystems. The Intergovernmental Panel on Climate Change projects that atmospheric temperatures will rise by 1.8 to 4.0°C globally by 2100. This warming will be accompanied by rising ocean temperatures and levels, increasing ocean acidification, altered rainfall patterns and river flows, and higher incidence of extreme weather events. Climate change will have a drastic effect on aquaculture operations worldwide. Global warming represents an additional pressure to the many others (overfishing, habitat destruction, pollution, escapements of farmed fish, etc.) that marine populations have been subjected to in recent decades.

Ocean Acidification. While global climate change continues to have a negative impact on the marine environment in general, there is one effect of climate change that portends a particularly dire consequence—ocean acidification. The earth's oceans are becoming acidic; that is, the pH levels are decreasing at an alarming rate. The pH scale, which measures acidity in terms of the concentration of hydrogen ions, runs from zero to 14. At the low end of the scale are strong acids such as hydrochloric acid that release hydrogen readily. At the high end are strong bases such as lye. Pure, distilled water has a pH of 7, which is neutral. Seawater should be slightly basic, with a pH around 8.2 near the surface. Thus far, CO_2 emissions have reduced the pH there by about 0.1. This may not seem like much of a reduction, but it is. Like the Richter scale, the pH is logarithmic, so even small numerical changes represent large effects. A pH drop of 0.1 means the water has become 30 percent more acidic. If current trends continue, surface pH will drop to around 7.8 by 2100. At that point our oceans will be 150 percent more acidic than they were in 1800. The acidification that has occurred so far is probably irreversible. Scientists estimate that more than 90 percent of anthropogenic green house gas emissions (especially atmospheric carbon dioxide, CO_2) are absorbed by the earth's oceans. This is of special concern since excess atmospheric CO_2 has the dual effects of increasing ocean water temperature and decreasing pH levels. This situation is caused by the 1 billion tons of carbon sent straight up into the atmosphere annually around the world.

Carbon dioxide absorption is even more pronounced at the earth's Polar Regions since cold water absorbs gases at an accelerated rate. This represents are particular problem for pteropods—tiny swimming snails that are an important food source for fish, whales and birds in both the Arctic and Antarctic regions. Experiments show that pteropod shells form at a slower rate in acidified seawater. The wild fisheries in the frigid waters around Alaska will be affected if the natural food source for the fish is affected.

Ocean acidity is major problem for the aquaculture industry. Some of the farm-raised species that will be adversely affected are mussels, shrimps, oysters, huge sectors of aquaculture. An abnormally low concentration of CO_2 retards the calcification rate of shell formation; the more acidic the water the slower the rate of formation. Some scientists estimate that by 2100 mussels are expected to calcify their shells 25 percent slower than currently and clams and oysters 10 percent slower. At lower CO_2 concentrations the mussel shell even dissolves. Decreased pH levels also affect the fertility levels of certain oyster species causing mortality levels to rise. If atmospheric CO_2 levels continue to rise the commercial mollusk and crustacean industries could be decimated.

Ocean Levels and Salinity. The predicted rise in mean sea level due to climate change is one of the more certain outcomes of climate change models, but it would take place over a relatively long time scale. It can be expected that this change will be accommodated within the normal operational cycles of an aquaculture facility. For example, as oceans rise, longer moorings will be required to anchor fish pens and aquaculture equipment will require increased maintenance due to damage from being battered by severe weather. Lake levels can and will vary at a faster rate than sea levels. Some scientists predict a rise of tens of feet within the coming decades, possibly leading to situations where relocation of fish-farming operations may be necessary. Some freshwater inland aquaculture facilities, which maintain their water levels artificially, will be largely impervious to the changes in the oceans due to climate change, but may experience difficulty with obtaining an adequate water supply.

Research based on satellite observations, published in October 2010, shows an increase in the flow of freshwater into the world's oceans, partly from melting Polar ice and partly from increased precipitation driven by an increase in global ocean evaporation. The increase in global freshwater flow, based on data from 1994 to 2006, was about 18 percent. Much of the increase is in areas which already experience abnormally high rainfall. One effect, as perhaps experienced in the 2010 Pakistan floods, is to overwhelm flood control infrastructures. As oceans become fresher, marine life that is sensitive to fluctuations in salinity will be harmed. The vast majority of seawater has a salinity of between 3.1 percent and 3.8 percent. As sea levels rise because of added fresh water, the salinity levels will decrease affecting sensitive ocean wildlife. Nearly 65 percent of aquaculture is inland and concentrated mostly in the tropical and subtropical regions of Asia, often in the delta areas of major rivers at the mid to upper levels of tidal ranges. Sea level rise over the next decades may increase upstream salinity, affecting inland fish farms.

Temperature Changes. The temperature of the water in which an aquaculture facility will operate is an important aspect of site suitability. In some cases the expected temperature ranges at a site may directly impact the decision to continue operating affected aquafarms. Subtle changes in water temperature can adversely affect marine life. For example, the temperature ranges in which a given species of fish can survive are, in general, more restrictive than those of farm animals on land, and an anticipated change of a few degrees may mean the difference between a successful aquaculture venture and an unsuccessful one. Temperature variations, again of a range of only a few degrees, can also have indirect implications for an aquaculture facility. A temperature rise can lead to aquatic plant proliferation that will cause oxygen depletion. Perhaps of even more serious concern would be an increased incidence of harmful algal blooms that release toxins into the water and precipitate fish kills. Penned fish are more susceptible to these types of occurrences than their free cousins that have a better chance of avoiding contaminated waters.

Extreme Weather Events. The frequency and severity of extreme weather events has increased over the past two decades. Severe weather events such as snowstorms, wild fires, tornadoes, droughts, hurricanes and catastrophic floods are projected by global climate models to increase. For example, we have only to look at the hurricane and torrential rains and subsequent flooding that hit Queensland, Australia in 2010 and 2011 to understand that climate change is driving the structural changes in global weather patterns. More evidence was the record flooding in the Midwest and the number of powerful tornadoes that swept through six states during April and May 2011. Nearly 500 people died and over 2,000 were injured by more than 850 twisters.

The last decade was the warmest on record and 2010 was the warmest year ever recorded. Instability in the climate system must be considered as one possible cause of these events and, therefore, the likelihood of even more unsettled and extreme weather in the future is all but certain. For the aquaculture industry, increased storm conditions would result in more physical damage to equipment with additional monetary losses resulting in higher prices for end consumers. Many coastal processes, such as sediment transport, take place mostly during high-energy events such as hurricanes and tornadoes. An increase in storm activity may therefore initiate ocean, river and lake bottom changes. Weather events can cause erosion or increased wind and wave activity. Increased violent wave activity can result in escapement of farmed-fish from the open containment nets. In the wild, as mentioned earlier, farmed fish out-compete their wild cousins for mates, habitat and food.

Associated Social Changes. Although not directly related to climate change, the public perception of the environment will be heightened by the perceived changes in climate. The realization that anthropogenic effects on the environment are real will be reinforced by the arrival of changes due to the greenhouse warming of the planet. It would be expected that this increased awareness of the interaction between society and the planet will lead to more stringent regulation and a more precautionary approach to management of the environment. At the same time, quota reductions in the capture fisheries are having major impacts on the economic viability of coastal communities outside major centers of employment. Aquaculture provides one on the few alternative sources of employment generally available. The interaction of these two factors in setting public policy has yet to play out. The impact of changes on the industry will be lessened by some foresight in the planning and selection of sites. Genetic manipulation of stocks may be able to offset the restrictions due to temperature rise. Similarly, advanced warning and precautions taken against new pests and diseases due to warmer waters will enable the industry to prepare for and guard against invasions.

Most Americans now agree that climate change is occurring, but still disagree on why, with opinions about the cause of climate change defined by political ideology, not based in scientific evidence, according to research from the Carsey Institute at the University of New Hampshire. Republicans most often point to natural causes of climate change while Democrats most often believe that the causes are anthropogenic. The greatest polarization occurs among people who believe they have the best understanding. Climate change is inevitably a challenge for commercial fisheries and aquaculture operations. Only through rigorous research on impacts can bring about mitigation and adaptation strategies. Research that involves resource users, builds strong partnerships and harnesses political will is crucial for making fisheries and aquaculture systems more resilient to the challenge of global climate change and securing a bright future for the billions of people that depend upon them.

Seafood Sustainability and Traceability

IT SEEMS THE term *sustainable* has come into vogue over the last few years. Unfortunately, the word has been bandied about to the point that it has become nothing more than a platitudinal buzz word often misconstrued by the media. So what does "sustainable" really mean? Simply put, it means a particular seafood product is sustainable if it comes from a fishery whose harvesting practices can be maintained indefinitely without reducing the target species' ability to maintain a viable population. In addition, it must not adversely impact any other species within the marine ecosystem by removing their food sources, accidentally killing them or damaging their environment. The term *traceability* has also been popularized in recent years and its meaning has also been distorted at times. Traceability means much more than merely tracing seafood food to its origin, it also means tracking seafood back to its source in order to verify that it was harvested legally and in an eco-friendly manner. Certifying organizations assist in this effort. Tracking the journey seafood takes from our oceans to our plates is a precondition for any serious sustainability effort. To guarantee a range of sustainable seafood retailers—restaurants, supermarkets and fish markets—need to know exactly which species they are sourcing. There is wide variability in colloquial and common names for seafood, so knowing the scientific name is vital. Theoretically, wild seafood species should be traceable back to the very boat that caught it to ensure that the correct stock and fishing method are known, and that the catch is legal. Farmed seafood should also be traceable back to the farm and the particular aquaculture practices being used, but this is not always possible since much of America's seafood comes from foreign producers whose record-keeping may inaccurate or nonexistent.

De-Coding Certification

CHOOSING THE BEST fish to eat can be a complicated and daunting task leaving the consumer bewildered as to which seafood choice is safe and eco-friendly. Which fish "good" or "bad" to eat? People browsing seafood counters or restaurant menus may wonder whether certain fish are both safe to eat and sustainable. In many instances, the more knowledgeable the consumer is the more questions arise: Is the species wild-caught or farmed-raised? Is it harvested locally or is it imported? Produced in an environmentally responsible way? Does it contain unacceptable levels of methyl mercury or other heavy metals? Is it tainted with antibiotics and chemicals? Does it contain a high level of pathogenic organisms? Theoretically, these fears are allayed if finfish, mollusks, crustaceans are harvested or processed by fisheries who subscribe to eco-friendly practices.

To address these concerns and other sustainability questions surrounding seafood, a number of certification programs have developed sets of standards and "ecolabels" to evaluate and then market "environmentally friendly" or "sustainably produced" seafood. While this is a step in the right direction, the problem of disparate standards has arisen. There is a mishmash of certification programs, accompanied by a veritable blizzard of acronyms, all claiming to be the quintessential certifying body. While the goal to raise awareness about sustainability among seafood suppliers and aquafarms is a laudable one, it is questionable whether these ecolabels are actually increasing sustainability in the marketplace. Moreover, they serve to make the selection of sustainable seafood more confusing for consumers.

Meanwhile, many seafood restaurants and retailers have begun sourcing their seafood predominantly or exclusively from fisheries or companies that have been "certified" by eco-labels in an effort to promote their environmental awareness about seafood sustainability to consumers. California's state government has committed to implement a seafood sustainability program that is based on the standards from some of these eco-labels. But what do these labels really mean? Food and Water Watch (FWW), an environmental watchdog group, reports that there are various seafood certification programs and, unfortunately, these labels do not always represent what consumers expect.

Research conducted by FWW reveals a variety of flaws and inadequacies associated with the eco-labels analyzed and suggest that private labels may not be the most appropriate means to convey neutral, credible information about seafood. A December 2010 report published by FWW proposes that in order to provide consumers with much-needed, unbiased and well-regulated information, the U.S. federal government should introduce and monitor standards for eco-labeled seafood. Until that time, FWW suggests that consumers can use its guidelines and recommendations on safer seafood choices.

Many restaurants and seafood purveyors claim to be serving or supplying products that come from "approved" sources, those that have been certified by the Marine Stewardship Council who claims to be the world's premier certifying body. The MSC is an independent non-profit organization that awards its ecolabel (also called the "blue-mark" label) to fishing operations suggesting that an independent, third party has verified that the seafood products come from a sustainable fishery. The MSC certifiers are accredited by Accreditation Services International (ASI), an independent accreditation body which delivers accreditation and other relevant services to the MSC and other certification schemes worldwide. The certification process is costly; the fishery operation can spend from $15,000 to $150,000 depending upon the size of the operation and complexity of the assessment. Restaurants can also display the ecolabel if they adhere to the MSC criteria for retailers. In other words, the ecolabel is a sign of approval that a restaurant, retailer or purveyor is not selling red listed seafood. However, MSC claims are inconsistent with the facts. For example, on its own website the MSC lists Costco as one of its certified retailers, but, according to Greenpeace, Costco currently sells fifteen of the twenty-two seafood species that are red-listed. Greenpeace is currently engaged in a campaign to publicize Costco's corporate policies regarding seafood sustainability.

Established in 1997 by the World Wildlife Fund and Unilever, the MSC has been helping consumers eat fish "guilt-free" by certifying commercial fisheries to ensure that they are employing environmentally responsible practices. Major North American grocery chains such as Wal-Mart, Whole Foods and Europe's Waitrose carry seafood bearing the blue-mark label as part of their sustainability strategy. Since its inception, the MSC has been the gold standard for certifying and monitoring aquaculture operations around the world to ensure that they are complying with best environmental practices. However, the MSC is not without its detractors. The MSC label was once the benchmark for fisheries based sustainable business. But recent comments by marine scientists suggest that some of the MSC certified sustainable fisheries may not be environmentally sound and that a review of the green certification process might be needed. "The MSC is supposed to be a solution, but a lot of what they do has turned against biology in favor of bureaucracy," said Jennifer Jacquet, post-doctoral fellow with University of British Columbia's *Sea Around Us Project* and lead author in an opinion piece in a September 2010 issue of *Nature* magazine. Jacquet also stated, "Unless MSC goes under major reform; there are better, more effective ways to spend the certifier's $13 million annual budget to help the oceans, such as lobbying for the elimination of harmful fisheries subsidies or establishing marine protected areas."

The MSC decisions to certify certain species as sustainable are questioned by others in the scientific community. For example, the largest MSC-certified fishery—with an annual catch of one million tons—is the U.S. trawl fishery for pollock in the eastern Bering Sea. It was certified in 2005 and recommended for recertification by the MSC during the summer of 2010. "Pollock has been certified despite a 64 percent decline of the population's spawning biomass between 2004 and 2009, with no solid evidence for recovery. This has worrisome implications for possible harmful impacts on other species and fisheries besides the viability of the pollock fishery itself," says Jeremy Jackson from Scripps Institution of Oceanography at the University of California at San Diego. "How is that sustainable?" Jackson added. The authors of the opinion piece in *Nature* also noted that the current certification system, which relies on for-profit consultants and could cost as much as $150,000, presents a potential conflict of interest and discriminates against small-scale fisheries and fisheries from developing countries—most of which use highly-selective and sustainable techniques.

The London-based Marine Stewardship Council isn't the only recognized certifying body in the world. According to a Food and Water Watch study there are at least five other certification programs in addition to the MSC;

◄ *Global Aquaculture Alliance* (GAA) was founded in 1997 by a wide range of international companies, food wholesalers, agribusinesses like Monsanto and Cargill and chain seafood restaurants. GAA claims that it is "the leading international organization dedicated to advancing environmentally and socially responsible aquaculture and a safe supply of seafood to meet growing world food needs." The GAA coordinates the development of Best Aquaculture Practices (BAP) certification standards for aquaculture facilities.

◄ *Friends of the Sea* (FOS) was established in 2006 in Italy by the creator of the dolphin-safe tuna label and has gained a sizable market share in central and southern Europe. FOS claims a wide range of certifications including fishmeal and oil.

◄ *Aquaculture Stewardship Council* (ASC) was founded in 2009 by World Wildlife Fund and the Dutch Sustainable Trade Initiative (IDH) to manage the global standards for responsible aquaculture. The ASC has plans to create standards for twelve species that "have the greatest impact on the environment." The ASC is not yet in full operation, but expects to be by mid 2011. ASC will take the approach of certifying just at the above-average level of environmental performance, similar to MSC, thus allowing products from less-than-sustainable operations to earn the same label as the most sustainable options carrying the same label.

◄ *Global Trust Certifications, Ltd.*, (GCT) the new name for IFQC Ltd., was established in 2007 to certify fish farms. On its website GCT states: "Global Trust Certification offers the most comprehensive range of recognized and accredited certifications and standards services to international seafood businesses." Its standards are not easily accessed by the public, raising suspicions about how rigorous GCT applies its standards.

To further complicate matters, there are other international oversight and monitoring bodies such as the ICCAT, IUCN and those operating under the auspices of the United Nations. What seems to be needed is one entity setting Best Aquaculture Practice standards and monitoring compliance worldwide? The current potpourri of standards is confusing and ineffectual. The consumers are not able to make informed decisions about sustainable seafood, which is the one of the goals of sustainability to begin with.

America's chefs and restaurateurs are largely misinformed or ignorant of the issues related to seafood sustainability. Too often chefs purchase seafood from a purveyor who sports an ecolabel without investigating what that "certification" actually means. Many chefs believe that they have done their part in the sustainability problem by merely choosing a supplier who possesses an ecolabel. Culinary graduates coming out of designer culinary schools might receive a small dose of then-current information about sustainability, but do they keep current with this constantly evolving subject? And what about the other culinary professionals who cook in the nation's nearly one million food service establishments? How is information about seafood sustainability disseminated to them?

Unfortunately, one of the nation's leading restaurant associations, the National Restaurant Association (NRA), does far too little to educate its members in any meaningful way about Green Food Revolution issues. As an industry leader, the NRA could assume a more proactive and aggressive posture on the seafood sustainability issue, for example. It is well for marine scientists and environmental groups to monitor the global seafood sustainability situation, but America's chefs and restaurateurs also play a critical role in the sustainability narrative. Unless the culinary community fully understands the magnitude of the global seafood crisis, the end goal of serving only sustainable seafood cannot be fully realized.

Genetic Engineering

THE SCOTISH-BORN American naturalist, John Muir, once warned, "When one tugs at a single thing in nature, he finds it attached to the rest of the world." It's certainly appropriate to call upon those prophetic words at this time in history. The highly controversial issue of genetically modified (GM) or engineered (GE) food remains a subject of heated public debate. Currently, there is at least one company attempting to get FDA approval to produce and sell genetically engineered salmon. In September 2010 the FDA convened public hearings pitting consumer groups and environmental advocates against industry proponents over the transgenic salmon issue or what has been dubbed the "Frankenfish" or "Frankensalmon". Even within the FDA, there has been a debate about whether the hybrid salmon should be labeled as GE (genetically engineered food crops are not labeled). The salmon's FDA approval would serve to open a path for companies and scientists developing other GE animals, like cattle resistant to mad cow disease or pigs that could supply leaner bacon. As of this writing FDA approval had not been granted.

The University of Guelph in Ontario, Canada has developed the "Enviropig" which has less phosphorus pollution in its manure. Their goal is to genetically alter a Yorkshire pig with specific DNA from mice and the E. coli bacteria, producing a pig that excretes about 50 percent fewer phosphates in its feces. This aspect is great for the environment because pig feces are used by farmers as fertilizer when it is sprayed on crops. This research is also important since pigs produce ten times more waste than humans. When it rains, the phosphates in pig manure find their way to underground water and pollute lakes, streams and ponds from farm runoff. Fewer phosphates in the water means less algae is produced allowing for increased levels of dissolved oxygen for fish and other higher aquatic life forms. Factory farms release hundreds of harmful toxins into the environment. Pig waste, which also contains high levels of nitrogen, is collected in lagoons (anaerobic cesspools) where it can contaminate local water supplies. Other harmful chemicals are released by sprays used to sanitize facilities.

~~~

The genetic engineering technology for salmon was developed by a Massachusetts-based company named AquaBounty Technologies who developed AquaAdvantage Salmon. According to the Center for Food Safety, "The genetically engineered Atlantic salmon being considered was developed by artificially combining growth hormone genes from an unrelated Pacific salmon with DNA from the anti-freeze genes of an eelpout. This modification causes production of growth-hormone year-round, creating a fish the company claims grows at twice the normal rate, allowing factory fish farms to crowd fish into pens and still get high production rates." These genes transfer the pout's ability to continually produce growth hormones allowing it to grow year-round. Normally, salmon only produce growth hormones during the warm weather months. Consequently, the AquaAdvantage Salmon, an advanced-hybrid salmon, can grow to market size in sixteen to eighteen months instead of the normal three years, though the company says the modified salmon will not end up any bigger than fish not manipulated genetically. Controversy has arisen, as some view the modified fish as a potential threat to the reproduction cycle of normal salmon if it is ever allowed to enter the wild. In fact, escapement is a chief concern among some scientists involved in the application review process.

Food and Water Watch, a nonprofit environmental watch dog group founded in 2005, recently made public excerpts of electronic communications from scientists weighing in on the current GE salmon debate. The information was made available through the Freedom of Information Act. Here are a few excerpts:

"I think the uncertainty of what will eventually happen to a species if genetically altered animals mix with "native" stocks, is reason enough to oppose this, at least until such times that controlled experimentation can take place . . . fish escape, and once they do, there is no closing that door . . . I think it is very bad precedent to set . . ."
Allan Brown, Program Supervisor for the Service's Southeast Region FWS to FWS listserve!
(congencopleads@lists.fws.gov) (9/28/10)

"[Fish and Wildlife Service Region 5] has concerns that approval of the proposal is premature, given the unknowns and uncertainties regarding the possible ecological and environmental effects of these fish. The proposal also presents a situation where FDA, whose jurisdiction is not focused on natural resources, is entrusted with the authority to approve an application which poses such a threat to the country's natural resources."
Jeff Adams, Branch Chief of Region 5 Fisheries and Habitat Restoration, Fairbanks Fish and Wildlife Field, Office to several FWS employees (10/4/10)

" . . . the Environmental Analysis is overly simplistic and does not adequately capture the actual risk of environmental damages to wild Atlantic salmon or the ecosystem. Additional studies will be necessary to assess this risk . . ."
Letter from FWS Conservation Genetics Community of Practice (COP), 10/6/10

Apparently, many scientists who are knowledgeable about the issue of GE salmon have real concerns regarding potential escapement and environmental impact. As of early 2011, some scientists believe that FDA approval would be premature. Another big problem is that seafood is not always labeled properly making it impossible for consumers to make an informed choice. If approved, the salmon would represent the first genetically engineered animal sold as food to unsuspecting consumers—currently there are no national labeling requirements in place to assist consumers in identifying and avoiding GE foods. However, this may be changing. In January 2011 it was announced that the California State Assembly is considering landmark legislation that would require all future GE salmon sold in California to contain clear and prominent labeling.

~~~

Proponents of AquAdvantage Salmon contend that the carbon footprint associated to GE salmon is much less severe. They contend that salmon can be grown economically closer to population centers, thus reducing the need for long distance transportation, a huge benefit to the environment. Further, proponents say that in an era of ever-shrinking wild fish stocks, AquAdvantage Salmon should be applauded by environmentalists and those concerned about food security. AquaBounty is also developing hybrid trout and tilapia.

GE food raises a whole host of questions about creating food that is safe for public consumption and about the monopolies manufactured by multinational corporations. For example, global agribusinesses, such as Monsanto and Cargill, have engineered seeds with so called "terminator technology," which means plants produce sterile seeds after only one season, forcing the farmers to purchase more seed for each succeeding harvest. While has nothing to do with GE seafood, it does demonstrate how science can be subsumed by the corporate world to monopolize a particular industry. This revolutionary technology has a sinister side. This corporate seed technology has wreaked tragic social consequences in agricultural communities worldwide, contributing to extraordinarily high suicide rates among farmers. The genesis of the problem is that GE seeds are twice as expensive as regular ones, increasing farmers' personal indebtedness. The high cost of seed every growing season coupled with others costs like pesticides often create an untenable situation in many cases. An already precarious situation is made even worse by disastrous weather events such as droughts and floods. As debts increase and become insurmountable, farmers are compelled to sell kidneys to pay expenses. In extreme cases, farmers commit suicide since they see no way of escaping their plight. America is not immune to this problem. The suicide rate among farmers in America's Midwest is twice the national average. The situation is more critical in India where more than 17,500 farmers took their lives between 2002 and 2006.

The multi-national corporations seem to have a choke hold on the world's farmers, which is also a concern even for the Catholic Church. In January 2011 WikiLeaks, the whistle blower website, made public transmissions that revealed the concerns of the Holy See. An excerpt from the transmission reads: " . . . *the main issue for the Church will continue to be the economic angle of biotech food. Many in the Church fear that these technologies are going to make developing-world farmers more dependent on others, and simply serve to enrich multi-national corporations,*"

Despite the fact that the Vatican has also remained neutral regarding GE crops in its public communiqués, the Pontifical Academy of Sciences has given tacit approval. In a memo WikiLeaks uncovered a transmission from Christopher Sandrolini, a U.S. diplomat to the Holy See that demonstrates the Vatican's clandestine approval of genetically modified crops: *"Recent conversations between Holy See officials and USAID and EB representatives visiting the Vatican confirmed the cautious acceptance of biotech food by the Holy See. Vatican officials asserted that the safety and science of genetically modified foods would eventually be non-issues at the Holy See"* read the memo.

In February 2011 Congressional lawmakers in both chambers introduced bills to ban GE salmon. Sens. Begich and Murkowski—a bipartisan team from the salmon-rich state of Alaska—are determined to keep the AquAdvantage Salmon off the market. "Frankenfish threatens our wild stocks, their habitat, our food safety, and would bring economic harm to Alaska's wild salmon fishermen," said Begich, adding that he believes the modified fish are "risky, unprecedented and unnecessary." AquaBounty insists the technology is safe. "We believe the economic and environmental benefits of our salmon will very effectively help to meet the demand for food from the growing world population," said Ronald Stotish, president and CEO of the company. In September 2011 eleven senators, mostly from the Pacific Northwest, where wild salmon fishing is an important part of the economy, asked FDA to halt its consideration of the GE fish. In a letter, lawmakers blasted FDA's approval process. "One of the most serious concerns regarding AquaBounty's application is the FDA has no adequate process to review a [genetically engineered] animal intended as a human food product," an excerpt from the letter read. "FDA is considering this [genetically engineered] fish through its process for reviewing a new drug to be used by animals, not for creation of a new animal, especially one intended for human consumption. Clearly, this is inappropriate." It remains to be seen whether the FDA moves forward with the approval process.

~~~

If you are skeptical about consuming GE food because it's unnatural, how would you feel about eating meat grown in a petri dish? Ridiculous you say? Don't look now, but it's already on the drawing board. A South Carolina scientist is attempting to do exactly this. At the Medical University of South Carolina, Vladimir Mironov, M.D., Ph.D., has been working for a decade to develop the process of growing meat tissue in a laboratory. A developmental biologist and tissue engineer, Dr. Mironov, is one of only a few scientists worldwide involved in bioengineering "cultured" meat. It's a product he believes could help solve future global food crises resulting from shrinking amounts of land available for growing meat the old-fashioned way—on the hoof. Growth of "in-vitro" or cultured meat is also under way in the Netherlands, but in the United States, it is science in search of funding and demand. The new National Institute of Food and Agriculture, part of the U.S. Food and Drug Administration, won't fund it, the National Institutes of Health won't fund it, and the National Aeronautics and Space Administration funded it only briefly, Mironov said.

Dr. Mironov has taken myoblasts—embryonic cells that develop into muscle tissue—from turkey and bathed them in a nutrient bath of bovine serum on a scaffold made of chitosan (a common polymer found in nature) to grow animal skeletal muscle tissue. But how do you get that juicy, meaty quality? Scientists want to add fat and a vascular system so that interior cells can receive oxygen will enable the growth of steak instead of just thin strips of muscle tissue. "Thirty percent of the earth's land surface area is associated with producing animal protein on farms." Generally, animals require between 3 and 8 pounds of nutrient to make 1 pound of protien. It's fairly inefficient. Animals consume food and produce waste. Cultured meat doesn't have a digestive system so there are no waste products. People of the Ethical Treatment of Animals advocate the project. They see this as a way to reduce factory-farming of agricultural animals and the abuse they are subjected to. Here's a question. If beer is produced in a brewery and wine in a winery, would a meat-producing lab be called a "carnery"?

Power of the Marketplace

WALMART AND COSTCO represent a tale of two mega-retailers. Walmart—not known for its green corporate policies—has embraced the sustainable seafood movement while Costco is being dragged kicking and screaming into the green revolution. As the world's largest retailer of seafood, Walmart knows that by offering sustainably harvested seafood at affordable prices it can impact consumer buying habits and help shape the entire seafood industry. In February 2006 Walmart pledged to source all wild-caught fresh and frozen fish for the U.S. market from fisheries that meet the MSC's independent environmental standards by 2011. For farm-raised aquaculture products like shrimp, Walmart requests the producers and processors obtain certification from the ACC who ensures that processors comply with acceptable aquaculture practices recommended by the GAA. Certification guidelines will bring harmony to the aquaculture market. Even Target has agreed to discontinue the sale of farm-raised salmon. This decision was made in response to pressure from Greenpeace and other environmental groups.

On the other hand, Costco currently rejects the seafood sustainability movement. Costco's intransigence has resulted in the continued sale of fifteen of the twenty-two red-listed seafood species; Alaskan pollock, Atlantic cod, Atlantic salmon, Atlantic sea scallops, Chilean sea bass, grouper, monkfish, ocean quahog, orange roughy, red snapper, redfish, South Atlantic albacore tuna, swordfish, tropical shrimp and yellowfin tuna. Greenpeace has waged an ideological war with Costco over this issue. Since 2008 Greenpeace has repeatedly asked Costco about its seafood sales practices and purchasing policies, but the company has refused to respond. Greenpeace has brought pressure to bear on Costco by continuing to publicize the retailer's failure to modify its seafood sustainability policies.

Fortunately, a handful of national chains—such as Wegmans, Target, and Whole Foods—are deeply invested in making better decisions and providing safer, more sustainable seafood choices for their customers. Trader Joe's has become a bit greener, thanks to pressure from Greenpeace—who dubbed the chain "Traitor Joe's"—and thousands of consumers across the country who demanded change. Trader Joe's is crafting a sustainable seafood policy and redesigning its labeling. The parent company, the German mega-grocer, Aldi, has agreed to discontinue selling its red-listed marine products by 2012.

A few months before World Oceans Day 2011, McDonalds announced that it would be serving sustainable fish at its restaurants in Europe. The fast-food behemoth's Filet-o-Fish sandwiches will bear the blue eco-label of the Marine Stewardship Council. McDonalds uses four species of wild fish for the sandwiches: cod (Pacific), haddock, Alaska pollock and New Zealand hoki and sells 100 million fish-wiches. Beginning in October 2011, the blue eco-label of the MSC will appear on the wrappers of McDonald's Europe's Filet-o-Fish sandwiches, which are made from fried white fish, tartar sauce and a slice of cheese served on a steamed bun. The European arm of McDonald's, faced with persistent criticism from environmentalists who accuse it of destructive practices, has in recent years sought to burnish its image with the rollout of Rainforest Alliance-certified coffee and sustainable agriculture programs.

Private Sector

A PARADIGM SHIFT is occurring in the U.S. retail market place with regard to selling sustainable seafood. Large retailers are embracing the green movement. Not only does this make good economic sense, but it enhances their public image. But is it too little too late? Clearly, it's too late for the North Atlantic cod, but is it too late for the bluefin tuna? The catch size of bluefin continues to decrease indicating that the breeding size fish are being harvested, assuring further reduction in wild stocks. As mentioned above, bluefin do not reproduce until approximately eight years of age. If this trend continues unabated the bluefin is destined for virtual extinction.

Many in the E.U. business community do not believe that International Commission for the Conservation of the Atlantic Tunas (ICCAT) is doing enough to save tuna stocks. Therefore, some businesses are taking matters into their own hands. Giant retailers like Carrefour, Ikea and several sushi chains have signed a Tuna Market Manifesto—pledging not to sell or buy bluefin tuna until a proper recovery plan is implemented. The World Wildlife Fund has also reported that French supermarket chain Auchan, French food services giant Sodexo and British restaurant chains Pret A Manger and Moshi Moshi have pledged to stop serving Atlantic bluefin tuna until the situation for the fish improves.

Had efforts toward sustainability begun, say, forty years ago the world might not have found itself in the current crisis, but hindsight will not get us out of the fix we're in. Moving forward, and on a global scale, regular seafood summits are needed in an effort to bring together global representatives from the seafood industry and conservation community for in-depth discussions, presentations and networking with the goal of finding a balance between sustainability and the marketplace.

In the long-term, bludgeoning industry into submitting to the green movement will only result in sporadic or short-term improvements. Industry will only create novel ways to circumvent the system. Only by incentivizing cooperation by the seafood industry and encouraging it to partner with the environmental community will there be long-term solutions to a seafood sustainability problem facing the global community. For example, governments can offer tax credits to seafood producers and processors who certify—which must be verified by an independent and trustworthy third party—that they harvest wild-caught seafood in an environmentally responsible manner. Government-funded, low-interest loans can be made available to aquaculture entrepreneurs when they adhere to eco-friendly certification guidelines. Foreign seafood producers and processors should be made to prove that they too adhere to best certification guidelines before they are allowed access to U.S. markets. In the future, certification guidelines must become more stringent and made mandatory. Only with the collaboration of government, industry and environmentalists can we turn the tide from wanton environmental degradation to a harmonious balance with nature to preserve the planet's aquatic and terrestrial resources. The seafood sustainability issue is of paramount importance and must be addressed sooner rather than later.

The business community must be convinced that providing sustainable seafood is good business. A Marriott hotel in Canada understands this. In November 2010 the Halifax Marriott Harbourfront Hotel announced that it has begun serving sustainable seafood in the hotel restaurant. According to the press release, this Nova Scotia hotel is committed to providing guests with an environmentally-responsible menu. The hotel has partnered with Ocean Wise, the Vancouver Aquarium's conservation program. Hopefully, more small and large businesses will go green and discontinue serving red-listed seafood. This particular situation could not be more ironic since Nova Scotia was part of the epicenter for the obliteration of the wild cod stocks in the North Atlantic beginning in the18th century through the early 1990s. Nova Scotia was home base for a large part of the Atlantic cod fishing fleet. This Marriott's decision to not serve red-listed seafood gives reason for optimism and makes a strong statement. And enough statements can become a trend and a trend can become a movement. As we move into the 21st century the marketplace will respond to the desires and needs of customers world-wide. Some retailers such as Costco might be reluctant to embrace the green movement, but they will have little choice if they want to maintain their market share.

Kiss My Apps

HOW DO CONSUMERS find sustainable seafood in the marketplace whether it is a restaurant, retailer location or a fresh seafood market? Enter the latest version of iPhone application called the "Project Fish Map" that was specifically created to work in conjunction with the Monterey Bay Aquarium Seafood Watch program. The free app also has enhanced search functions that help people find seafood quickly and easily by its common market name, or, in the case of sushi, by its Japanese names, making it an invaluable tool for a sushi night out. And for those consumers craving fish on the Seafood Watch "Avoid" list, the app provides some healthy and more sustainable seafood alternatives. According to industry analysts, food and health apps will be the one of the biggest trends in 2011. These tools will help people make healthful and environmentally friendly choices and can potentially improve overall lifestyles.

Because of consumer demand to know where their seafood comes from and whether it was harvested or produced in an ecologically responsible manner innovative ways of securing information about sustainability. Seafood Watch raises consumer awareness through their pocket guides, website, mobile applications and outreach efforts. On the Monterey Bay Aquarium website (www.montereybayaquarium.org) consumers can discover which restaurants participate in its Seafood Watch program.

Participating restaurants pledge to not serve items from the Seafood Watch "Avoid" list and train service staff about their seafood choices. Seafood Watch assists consumers in these efforts, providing materials, answering questions and helping with staff training.

In our quest for easy answers to living sustainably, it is natural to want to know the one, correct decision, like changing our light bulbs to fluorescents, so we can move on. But sustainability is not that easy, it is a goal; with each decision we take a step toward or away from that goal. What should I eat, buy or wear in pursuit of the goal? Sometimes the choice is obvious (Use mass transit instead of driving?), but often it is not (Organic corn from far away or local corn treated with pesticide?) The difficult truth is that there is no single or perfect answer to embracing a greener life style. Make no mistake, being green is a life style change no different from modifying our approach to life in general. It is acceptable for us to make such a change incrementally as long as we constantly strive towards the goal.

Welfare of Factory-Farmed Animal

ANIMAL HUSBANDRY HAS long been associated with mistreatment of agricultural animals. The welfare of factory-farmed animals has come into sharp focus in recent years, largely through the efforts of animal-rights groups. This movement has had a discernable impact in society and the marketplace. For example, agricultural animal abuse has compelled local and state legislative bodies to ban certain animal products as I will discuss later. These actions were the direct result of instances of animal abuse that were exposed in the media. Because of the perceived ethical dilemma in modern society associated with the abuse of agricultural animals many consumers have reduced their consumption of farm animals or eliminated them from their diet all together. Many have become vegetarians or even embraced veganism, shunning all animal products. Big agribusiness has put pressure on state legislatures in New York, Iowa, Florida and Minnesota to make it illegal for anyone to go undercover to film or record animal abuses. These laws include provisions for civil recovery and equitable relief, so that corporations can force activists to compensate them for any revenue lost due to the exposure of their violence. Animal-rights groups maintain that these laws have it backwards because they seek to criminalize someone who is an eyewitness to a crime. This section is only meant to touch upon the disturbing issue of factory-farmed animal abuse. This section is not intended to persuade you to modify your food choices, only to inform and enlighten.

Fowl Play?

WHILE THERE ARE many forms of agricultural animal abuse, one of the most controversial practices (relative to the maltreatment of other factory-farmed animals, the level of abuse of foie gras ducks is a matter of degree) involves with the production of foie gras (pronounced fwah grah). Foie gras is the fatty liver of a duck or goose that becomes enlarged ten to twelve times its normal size by inserting a tube down the animal's esophagus to force feed it corn mash. In the U.S. (Almost all foie gras produced in the U.S. comes from Moullard ducks, which is a hybrid of a male Muscovy and a female Pekin.) Foie gras production has come under fire in recent years by animal-rights groups making it one of the most visible forms of agricultural animal abuse. Whether it is the most heinous and represents to greatest level of suffering inflicted upon agricultural animals may be a matter of opinion. The life of a broiler or egg-laying chicken is no picnic either.

The foie gras industry is small in contrast to the beef, pork, eggs and poultry industries. In 2009, U.S. production was 9,000 ducks per week, which resulted in 350 tons of foie gras for the year (each liver weighed an average of 1.5 pounds). This might sound like a lot of liver, but fatty duck liver is a luxury item within a tiny niche market. So why do animal-rights activists focus on the foie gras industry when there are other industries that treat agricultural animals worse than foie gras ducks are treated and on a grander scale? The reasons are clear; opponents have targeted the industry partly because the industry is so small that unfavorable press exposure can actually impact the industry. While the poultry or cattle industry might abuse animals on a greater scale, these industries are much less vulnerable to attack. They also have the financial and political clout to oppose animal rights advocates. Activists view the foie gras industry as a gateway to impacting other agricultural animal business sectors. Animal-rights groups are also concerned because foie gras consumption is on the rise due to the demands of more sophisticated North American diners. The activists' ultimate goal is the prohibition of future production and sale of foie gras nationwide. They have made headway. In 2006 the

Chicago City Council voted to ban foie gras sales in the city and effective July 1, 2012 the production and sale of foie gras is banned in the entire state of California.

~~~

There is a special role for celebrity chefs to play in the agricultural animal welfare narrative. They have a vested interest. This is their planet too. Sadly, few food celebrity chefs take a stand on agricultural animal welfare. But there are a few celebrities who are willing speak out. Charlie Trotter, Chicago's mega-celebrity chef, banned all forms of aquatic bird liver from his restaurants. After years of serving foie gras, Totter saw the light. He understood that by selling foie gras he was only contributing the appalling abuse of ducks and geese raised to produce foie gras. Because he dared to take an ethical stand he was vilified by some of his fellow chefs and in the media as if he had committed religious blasphemy. He wasn't telling other chefs to not serve foie gras; he just made it known that he came to realize that to serve it was immoral for him. He has that right. In his 2009 book, *The Foie Gras Wars,* Mark Caro makes this point very clear.

As a chef in the early 1990s I felt that by serving foie gras I was promoting the mistreatment treatment of foie gras ducks and geese. I decided to never serve the product in my café, which opened in 1993. Before chef Trotter decided to take a stand against serving foie gras, I felt it was ethically wrong to serve the stuff. Apparently, even God is against the foie gras industry. In 2002 then-Cardinal Joseph Ratzinger, the future Pope Benedict XVI, said of the industrial fattening of geese: "This degrading of living creatures to a commodity seems to me in fact to contradict the relationship of mutuality that comes across in the Bible." If God is not your side, you just might be in the line of work.

Even a few Hollywood types have championed the anti-foie gras cause. Most notably, Sir Roger "007" Moore has been an outspoken critic of the foie gras industry for years. In an undercover on-line video Moore solemnly narrates over grisly footage on a foie gras duck farm. The footage is moving and should be required viewing for foie gras devotees everywhere. Consumption might plummet. From the point of view of the foie gras producers, animal-rights activists are guilty of a form of nihilism because they are bent on obliterating the industry. They also take umbrage with activists who judge the foie gras industry by the worst run farms—those where deplorable living conditions and animal abuse has been documented—rather than the best run operations where ducks are not mistreated, that is, until the gavage procedure begins, which I'll discuss later in the chapter.

Everything but the Quack

OH, IN CASE you're wondering what happens to the remainder of the duck once he's sacrificed his hefty liver, nothing goes to waste. Everything is used but the quack! The carcasses are sold whole or sold off in parts and processed further. Breast (the *magret*) is standard fare in many high-end restaurants where they are usually sautéed in duck fat and served rare. The breasts are also smoked and often served with salads. The legs and thighs can be cooked confit-style (slowly cooked in duck fat with salt and pepper) and served in various ways. The lobes of fresh liver can be sold fresh and whole to restaurants or the liver can be made into pâté or mousse at the production farm or at restaurants. The drummettes can also be cooked confit-style then shredded and made into rillettes, a paste that can be spread on slices of baguette or crostini. Rendered duck fat is another valuable product. Unless he's a total quack, any chef will tell you that duck fat is the epitome of cooking fats. The flavor it imparts to sautéed foods is incomparable. If you've ever tasted hash browns sautéed in duck fat you'll know what I'm talking about. It's not heart healthy, but who cares with flavor this good?

These Little Piggies Go to Market

FOIE GRAS DUCKS aren't the only agricultural animals whose life is not a bowl of cherries. Ducks and geese have only to look at their porcine pals to see farm animals who really have it tough. In December 2010 the Humane Society of the United States (HSUS) released footage, secretly taken by an undercover employee, of the living conditions at Murphy-Brown, a subsidiary of Smithfield Foods, the world's largest pork producer. The footage revealed disturbing and gruesome evidence of maltreatment of farmed hogs; an issue that must be included any discussion of modern pig farming. The video showed pregnant and nursing sows confined behind bars that were covered in their own blood and trying to bite their way out through the bars. It also showed live piglets being thrown in with heaps of pig corpses, piglets were found having fallen through holes in the floor into manure pits. Pigs were denied veterinary care for open wounds and abscesses.

Murphy-Brown presents itself as an "industry-leading" animal welfare program on its website. The company claims to "subscribe to the animal welfare position put forth by the National Pork Producers Council." Murphy-Brown's actions belie its claims of humane treatment of hogs. Female breeding pigs were crammed inside "gestation crates"—individual, metal enclosures that prevent pregnant sows from turning around—so small the animals could barely move for virtually their entire lives. In 2007 Smithfield announced that it would phase out its use of gestation crates within ten years. The HSUS applauded this move as an important step toward improving animal welfare in the industry. However, despite the company's 2007 pledge, Smithfield revealed that while it intends to discontinue the use of gestation crates, due to economic concerns it has removed its deadline for doing so. Translation: Smithfield does not intend to phase out the use of gestation crates. Citing the inherent cruelty of gestation crates, the E.U. and seven U.S. states have outlawed their use. And major companies like Burger King, Wendy's, Sonic, Carl's Jr., Hardee's, Quiznos and Safeway have taken steps to increase purchases of gestation crate-free pork products. Other companies—like Whole Foods and Chipotle and chefs such as Wolfgang Puck—don't use any pork produced using gestation crates. Farmed animals currently have no federal protection from abuse on factory-farms. The cruel and violent nature of hog farming is ignored by state legislatures who are under the control of the hog industry in their respective states.

It would seem that companies like Smithfield Foods are interested in profits first and animal welfare last. The cognitive dissonance that is required to kill animals by the thousands while at the same time claiming to be concerned about the animals' welfare is illustrated every time that they implement some new "animal welfare" initiative. The HSUS applauded this move as an important step toward improving animal welfare in the industry. Policies like the phasing out of gestation crates for sows or battery cages for hens are meaningless publicity stunts, even when they are implemented as promised. Moves like these are not designed to change the lives of animals, but to placate consumers who feel guilty about the treatment of the animals they eat.

Between April and June of 2011 an undercover investigator for Mercy for Animals, an animal-rights group, shot video of disturbing video at one of the nation's largest pork producers—Iowa Select Farms in Kamrar, Iowa. At this factory-farm, mother sows and their piglets are forced to suffer brutal abuse and lives of unrelenting confinement and misery at the hands of Select Farms' employees. The employees seem to be inured to the pain and suffering they inflict. One segment of the video shows piglets being castrated and having their tails cut off without the benefit of anesthetic. Workers are shown tattooing hogs by striking them with one-inch metal spikes affixed to metal mallets. Hogs' ears are tagged by driving a large spike through the ear to create a large hole. Hogs are shown to have open sores and abscesses that go unattended by a veterinarian. The hog industry has much to answer for, but is never castigated by the press for its willful and blatant transgressions. The mainstream media largely ignores animal abuse stories.

~~~

In her muckraking 2009 documentary, *Pig Business*, director Tracy Worcester chronicles the consolidation of pig production from small farms into a handful of large agribusinesses such as Smithfield Foods, the subject of the documentary. It is a feature documentary exposing the huge hidden costs behind the pork and processed meat products on our supermarket shelves, and shows viewers and consumers how they can use their buying power to help create a more compassionate world.

"During the 90s, large scale meat processors bought up livestock farms (in the U.S. and Europe). This allowed them to control the whole process, from raising to packaging," according to Worcester. Through her job as an ecologist, the more Worcester learned about the impact of pig farm consolidation, the more she became concerned about the environmental effects of the industry. Worcester's concerns compelled her to make this documentary chronicling pig farming industry's odious effects in terms of deteriorating public health, environmental degradation (a pig defecates ten times more than a human) and the devastation of local economies.

In the documentary, Worcester highlights the fact that Smithfield Foods has expanded its operations from North America into Europe, especially in Poland, the focus of the documentary. Poland is one of the largest pork producers in Europe. Worcester shows footage of Robert

Kennedy, Jr. (son of Robert Kennedy) testifying before the Polish Environmental and Agricultural Committee. He warned the Poles of the harmful environmental and economic effects of hog farm consolidation and factory-farming. Kennedy stated, by way of example, that twenty years ago in North Carolina (the most prolific hog-producing state in the U.S.) there were 27,500 privately-owned hog farms and today there are 2,200 with 1,500 owned or operated by Smithfield.

The documentary reveals video shot in 2006 of ghastly conditions on one of Smithfield's pig farms in Poland. Gruesome images of piglet's corpses floating in the farm's waste collection lagoon were shown. Other footage shot at the same farm showed thousands of pigs—on a U.S hog farm, a single barn may hold up to 10,000 pigs—in an overcrowded barn where pigs were feeding on the carcass of a dead pig. Another video showed caged pigs chewing on the bars of its cage; indicating a heightened level of emotional distress.

Cargill, another global agribusiness giant, also gets in on the act of factory-farmed pigs. Cargill provides the pig food. One of the main ingredients in pig feed is soya. Enter Brazil, one of the world's largest producers of soya. To meet rising demand of pig feed, millions of acres of Amazon rain forest has been denuded and transformed into soya farms. The largest soya producer in Brazil is Erai Maggi who owns a 494 thousand acre soya plantation. According to environmentalists, Maggi knows how to accelerate deforestation of the Amazon, at least indirectly. By buying up the savannah for soya cultivation, he has forced cattle ranchers north into the rainforest where they slash and burn, releasing millions of tons of carbon dioxide into the atmosphere, said Paulo Adario, the Amazon director of Greenpeace in Brazil. "It is an indirect but fundamental impact."

Pig Business was originally developed as a tool that Non-Governmental Organizations (NGOs) could use to illustrate the problems associated with industrial farming, says Worcester. The film was created with an eye towards raising awareness among consumers of the role they play in contributing to agribusiness, and what they can do to promote environmentally friendly, humane pig-raising processes. She hopes the film will reach a wider audience than the materials an NGO is usually able to disseminate. *Pig Business* is available on YouTube. Perhaps we should heed the words of Mahatma Gandhi, "To my mind, the life of a lamb is no less precious than that of a human being. The more helpless the creature, the more that it is entitled to protection by man from the cruelty of man."

Of course pigs aren't the only large farm animals to suffer horrific abuses. In June 2011 the Australian government suspended the export of live cattle to eleven abattoirs in Indonesia, after a TV documentary showed brutal treatment of animals at the facilities. The footage, broadcast on ABC, showed Brahman cattle being flogged, beaten and kicked before having their throats slashed. In some cases the animals took up to thirty minutes to bleed to death. The Australian live-export industry has shipped more than 6.5 million head of cattle to Indonesia for slaughter over the last 20 years. The obvious question is why has it taken so long for Australia's Ministers of Agriculture, past and present, to discover the wanton maltreatment of cattle at Indonesian slaughter houses?

~~~

At least one retail giant is putting its program where its mouth has been. Whole Foods Market is providing shoppers with a new level of transparency about how farm animals are raised by now offering beef, pork and chicken certified under 5-Step Animal Welfare Rating system. The rating system is the signature program of Global Animal Partnership, Global Animal Partnership is a nonprofit organization that facilitates and encourages continuous improvement in the welfare of animals raised for food.

Independent, third-party certifiers audit farms and rate animal welfare practices and conditions using a tiered system that ranges from Step 1 (no crates, no cages, no crowding) to Step 5+ (animals spend their entire lives on one farm). The system provides a way to engage and reward producers by promoting continuous improvement in farm animal welfare. For shoppers, the rating system provides a way to make more informed choices when purchasing meat at a Whole Foods Market.

More than 1,200 farms and ranches providing the company's 291 U.S. locations with products have received incremental "Step" certification through independent, third-party certifiers. Color-coded signs and stickers throughout Whole Foods Market meat departments identify these ratings. All meat sold at Whole Foods Market must meet the company's stringent quality standards, which require that animals be raised on a vegetarian diet without being administered antibiotics or added growth hormones. Step-rated options are available at all U.S. Whole Foods Market stores and all beef, pork and chicken products carried in the fresh and pre-packaged cases will be rated according to 5-Step Animal Welfare Rating standards. The chain promises that additional species (turkey, lamb, etc.) will be rated as Global Animal Partnership standards are completed. Other retail giants might follow Whole Foods Market example and adopt an agricultural animal welfare rating system. Make no mistake, Whole Foods and other retailers are not adopting welfare standards because of some deep sense of altruism, they are doing this because their customer base demands that they do so.

The Debate

I HAVE ONLY cited the abuse of ducks and pigs as examples of maltreatment to factory-farmed animals when other farmed animals may suffer a similar fate; geese, turkeys, cattle, goats, sheep . . . One of the most well known books in the genre of animal welfare is, *Animal Liberation*, written by Australian philosopher Peter Singer. The 1975 book is widely considered within the animal liberation movement to be the foundation of philosophical statement because of the ideas and concepts espoused. Singer himself rejected the use of the theoretical framework of rights when it comes to human and nonhuman animals: he argued that the interests of animals should be considered because of their ability to feel pain and that the idea of rights was not necessary in order to consider them. Singer introduced and popularized the term "speciesism" in the book to describe the exploitative treatment of animals.

There is an ancient philosophical debate about mistreatment of farmed animals versus the perceived need for humans to consume them. The debate hinges upon the level of suffering endured by the creatures relative to their contribution to the dietary needs and/or taste preferences of their human consumers. If a little pain and suffering is acceptable at what level do we decide that an animal has suffered enough or too much? Some would argue that no level of suffering is acceptable; that animals were not put on earth to become part of the human diet and that humans should eschew all forms of animal products and embrace veganism. While the vast majority of humans do not feel this way, many feel uneasy or even guilty about consuming agricultural animals that have been subjected to any level of mistreatment. This debate was crystallized in the 2010 HBO movie *Temple Grandin*, which focused on the cattle industry. In 2002 Dr. Grandin—currently an associate professor of animal sciences at Colorado

State University—delivered a paper entitled *Animals Are Not Things*, which was a view of animal welfare based on neurological complexity. While the paper primarily discussed the physiological reasons why higher life forms feel pain, it also presented philosophical undercurrents about animal abuse and, by implication, the role factory-farming plays in animal welfare. Today, at least half of all cattle in the United States and Canada, as well as many in other countries, are handled in more humane slaughter systems designed by Grandin. Her animal welfare guidelines have become the gold standard in the $80 billion meat-packing industry.

Let us turn to foie gras production one last time. The average American foie gras duck lives for a relatively blissful 12 weeks roaming free outdoors or in a climate controlled barn before the two-to-four-weeks of gavage begins. The practice of gavage itself has a long history. The technique dates as far back as 2500 BC, when the ancient Egyptians began keeping birds for food and deliberately fattened them through force-feeding. Is gavage painful or just uncomfortable? The gullet of most aquatic birds is designed to accommodate an elongated or disc-shaped, scaly fish as it is swallowed whole. Is the quality of life of a foie gras duck less than that of, say, a broiler or egg-laying chicken who are denied freedom of movement for their entire lives and never get a glimpse of natural light? Broilers are crammed wing-to-drumstick with thousands of other broilers destined to meet an identical fate. And what about egg-laying chickens that are crammed together in battery cages so tightly that they cannot even flap their wings? Did you know that the male layers are deemed "expendable"—they can't lay eggs and are not meaty like their broiler cousins because they are a different genetic strain—and gassed with carbon monoxide as hatchlings? This all begs the question, which bird species, ducks vs. chickens, is treated less humanely or are both, but to varying degrees and in different ways. Do humans misapply anthropomorphic emotions to factory-farmed animals as we are so prone to do with house pets? (We intend to bury our cat, Snowball, behind our house when she meets her maker.) The issue of agricultural animal welfare is a bit like holding a "wolf by the ears," do you control the wolf or risk letting it free? It's a delicate balance between ethics on the one hand and human self-preservation on the other.

To their credit, two of the three domestic foie gras producers are more transparent than their counterparts in the chicken and turkey industries. In his book, *The Foie Gras Wars*, Mark Caro says that he was denied access to visit Butterball as well as several chicken producers. However, Caro was given a tour of two foie gras producers; Hudson Valley Foie Gras, in New York, and Sonoma Artesian Foie Gras, in California. The owners of Hudson Valley and Sonoma were eager to give Caro their points of view regarding the ethics of foie gras production and for him to see their operations. He was denied access to LaBelle Farms, located near Hudson Valley, the only other U.S. foie gras producer who also happens to raise chickens commercially. This raises the obvious question; if foie gras production is so heinous then why do two of the producers allow a reporter (Caro writes for the Chicago Tribune) to visit their operations? Perhaps the animal-rights groups are judging the industry by the worst producers. Or perhaps the reputable foie gras producers found guilty vicariously because they are lumped together with commercial chicken and turkey operations—notorious for exposing poultry to horrid conditions. Where ever you come down on the foie gras issue, it will not be settled anytime soon; U.S. production of foie gras is up 10 percent since 2005. Production in France, Hungary, Bulgaria and China dwarf domestic output. As of 2005, U.S. output was less than 2 percent of production worldwide.

Where's Bourdain When We Really Need Him?

DON'T GET ME wrong, I love Anthony Bourdain. I like his snarky attitude and the fact that he's a real chef who came up the hard way in the restaurant business. He's all over the place, he talks and talks, but never says a word (at least not that I've heard) about any green food issues. Couldn't he at least give a nod to cod or a shout out to bluefin? Bourdain exemplifies celebrity chefs who do little or nothing to advance the conversation about eco-gastronomy or the humane treatment of factory-farmed animals. Where are the mega-celebrities like Martha Stewart, Rachael Ray or Paula Deen on any green food issues? We never, at least not that I've noticed, hear these people discussing anything other than their upcoming show, their next cookbook or their newest line of cookware. Do we really need to learn how to make another kitchen craft or cupcake recipe from Martha Stewart? One would think at this point in her career she might want to champion an issue that doesn't expand her empire. Why can't she do for green food issues what Betty White has done animal-rights? Is it possible for food celebrities to devote a little time talking about issues such as sustainable agriculture, locavorism, abuse of factory-farmed animals or red-listed seafood? And the same goes for chefs such as Mario Batali, Bobby Flay, Alton Brown and Rick Bayless. Instead of popularizing and promoting a culinary carnival act, *molecular gastronomy*, Ferran Adriá could champion the plight of bluefin tuna or rail against bycatch. Adriá is from Spain, along with France and Italy; Spanish fishermen are notorious for illegally fishing bluefin. Apparently, Adriá would rather fiddle with culinary alchemy than champion something that impacts the world we live in. Perhaps some of these folks are doing what I advocate and if they are their efforts are not well publicized. Jamie Oliver has latched onto childhood obesity. Why can't the others devote themselves to doing something other than self-promotion?

It's bad enough that food celebrities disregard or are callously indifferent towards eco-gastronomy issues, but some have gone in the opposite direction and aligned themselves with agribusinesses that do harm to the environment and/or destroy local economies. Take Paula Deen, for example. A few years ago I was doing some grocery shopping for our Christmas dinner when I noticed Paula Deen's image plastered on the wrappers of a whole pile of Smithfield hams. Apparently, Deen felt no compunction about associating herself with a food company that has a history of swallowing up small, independent pig farmers so it can monopolize the agribusiness in a given locale. Once Smithfield acquires the small farms it can contaminate the environment and devastate the local economy. For example, for every factory farm that Smithfield builds it eliminates approximately ten traditional family farm jobs and replaces them with two or three minimum wage ones. If Deen had known the destructive effect Smithfield can wreak on a community would she have allowed them to use her image to sell hams? Would she still have lent her star power to a company who puts profits before peoples' lives and their environment? Deen gives the word "pork butt" new meaning.

What food celebrities fail to understand is that they are missing an historic opportunity to do a vast amount public good. They can give voice to issues largely ignored by mainstream media. The current flock of food celebrities will not be in vogue forever so they might want to take advantage of their current popularity and put it to good use rather than do what they usually do—make mindless cooking shows or hawk their latest cookbook or line of cookware at a Sur La Table. Why is it left to Hollywood celebrities, and other media personalities, do the heavy lifting when it comes to correcting injustices and supporting worthwhile causes?

Fortunately we have concerned citizens like Ted Danson to champion the critical issues. Mr. Danson has been a tireless activist in the conservation movement. He is famous for his work as a passionate ocean advocate and Oceana spokesman. Mr. Danson doesn't even come from the world of cooking yet he seems more interested in eco-gastronomy issues than food celebrities themselves. Why can't popular food personalities become celebrity activists too? Are they living in a bubble? Have any of them bothered to watch *Pig Business, Food, Inc., Fast Food Nation, Temple Grandin* or *The Cove*? By not getting involved in green food issues they're lowering the bar that we've come to expect from, say, professional athletes. There are so many worthwhile issues food celebrities can get behind; obesity, world hunger, protecting our oceans, food safety and factory-farmed animal welfare. Isn't it about time food celebrities strived to make a difference? They have skin in the game; it's their earth too.

Appendix C

Stock Pot

Every kitchen has—or should have—a stock pot bubbling away when meals are being prepared. The reason for a stock pot is to make broth from all the miscellaneous food scraps that can't be used elsewhere, but are too useful to toss away. That's what this section is for. An addendum really, *Stock Pot* is where I decided to put food-related items that didn't seem to fit elsewhere in the book. Consider this section a little something extra or as they say in New Orleans, a *lagniappe*.

Food in Cinema

FOOD HAS BEEN depicted in art ever since modern humans felt compelled to express themselves through media. The oldest example of food in art would be the cave paintings, or pictograms, at Chauvet Cave near Vallon-Pont-d'Arc in Southern France. These Upper Paleolithic (also called the Late Stone Age) artists drew renderings of animals they hunted for food such as horses, cattle, buffaloes and megaloceros, a type of giant prehistoric deer. At 32,000 years old, the paintings at Chauvet Cave are by far the oldest ever discovered. Were the artists attempting to interpret the world around them or communicate with future generations? In any event, it would seem that the modern human soul was awakened. And Egyptologists have found drawings of food on chamber walls of pyramids. Known as funerary art, these paintings depicted food to assist the decedents during their trip through the afterlife. The ancient Romans and Greeks also used food as *objets d'art*. And we've all seen still life paintings of food-related subjects by the European masters of 15th and 16th centuries. One of the most famous works of art with food or eating as a subject would be Leonardo da Vinci's *The Last Supper*. (I've always wondered why everyone is sitting on the same side of the table.)

Fortunately for us food in art survived long enough to make the transition to more contemporary media—movies. Since Hollywood's early days, food and flicks have gone together like mashed potatoes and gravy. Countless celluloid food scenes are forever immortalized, even romanticized, in movie history. Great movies help us explore the rich connotations of food in our lives; food brings us together (for better or worse), comforts us and elicits past memories. I was eating lunch with my mother when I heard that JFK had been shot. She began to sob. With so many films dedicated to food or at least featuring singular, powerful scenes involving food, it's difficult to decide which movies depict food and eating most eloquently, but here are few that stand out in my mind.

Departures (2009) A recently unemployed, young cellist Daigo (Masahiro Motoki) trains for a new professional role as a *nakanshi*, the ritual of preparing a corpse for burial. Daigo works at the NK Agency with the owner, Mr. Sasaki (Tsutomu Yamazaki) and the one other employee Yuriko (Kimiko Yo). Daigo has a hard time at his first day at work, being made to act as a corpse himself in an instructional DVD explaining the procedure and symbolism of *nakanshi*. Initially, he's sure this job just isn't his cup of tea, but he slowly comes to embrace his new line of work and even develops friendships with Mr. Sasaki and Yuriko. The delicious food scene arrives when the trio shares take-out as a sort of an office Christmas party. The three have only each other with whom to celebrate the holiday. They attack a heaping platter of extra crispy fried chicken. No lines are spoken. We only hear eating sounds as they crunch crispy skin and chomp the juicy meat. Dialogue would detract from this powerful and sensual scene. Their obvious pleasure does the talking.

Babette's Feast (1988) This elequent Danish film is the story of Babette (Stéphane Audran), a former Parisian chef, who is forced to take a job as housekeeper for twin spinster sisters (Bodil Kjer, Birgitte Federspiel) in a Danish seaside village. The year is 1871. As luck would have it, Babette wins the French lottery and she generously offers to prepare a sumptuous banquet in honor of the twins' birthday. A handful of the townsfolk are invited. But the God-fearing villagers have a problem; they regard the feast as a flagrant display of hedonism and excess. They are loath to partake in the earthly pleasure of enjoying food, which should be regarded as mere sustenance. To enjoy the feast would belie their quasi-monastic lifestyle of austerity and self-denial. Babette returns from Paris with the various and never-before-seen ingredients. The sisters begin to worry that the meal will be, at best, the cardinal sin of sensual ecstasy, and at worst some form of witchcraft. But it's too late to refuse Babette's offer; the chef's preparations have already begun. At an impromptu conference, the sisters and the villagers agree to eat *Babette's feast*, but to forego any pleasure they might derive, and to make no mention of the food during the entire meal no matter how much they enjoy it. As the evening progresses, and the wine flows, inhibitions melt away like sorbet in the August sun and by dessert everyone is having a rollicking good time. Prior to the feast the film shows drab, wintery grays, but gradually picks up more and more colors as the collective mood of the diners elevates. The film portrays the undeniable power of food to transcend class barriers and break down even the most rigid social mores.

__The Godfather__ (1972) Food scenes are sprinkled throughout this flick, one of the greatest in Hollywood history, but for my money there are two exceptionally powerful ones. The first scene is when Clemenza (Richard S. Castellano), a long-time capo for the Corleone family, participates in the assassination of Paulie (John Martino), a soldier under Clemenza, who has somehow egregiously breached Cosa Nostra etiquette. Mafia protocol dictates that punishment must be meted out, which, unfortunately, means sometimes getting whacked. As a ruse, Clemenza tells the unsuspecting Paulie that he has to relieve himself and to pull off the highway. While Clemenza is urinating his confederate pumps three bullets into Paulie's head. As they prepare to leave the crime scene Clemenza instructs his minion to: "Leave the gun, take the cannolis." Apparently, Clemenza didn't want to upset his wife who had previously instructed him to pick up the pastries when he left the house earlier that day.

The other magnificent scene was when Michael (Al Pacino) assassinates the crooked police chief, Captain McCluskey (Sterling Hayden), and the evil Solatso (Al Lettieri), who is in league with the archrival Tattaglia family. The trio meets a restaurant to reconcile differences, but they don't make it to dessert because Michael puts a slug into Solatso's brain and two into McCluskey just as he's enjoying a plate of veal, the house specialty. What a waste of good meat. But hey, Fuhgetaboutit!

Ratatouille (2007) This charming, computer-animated comedy doesn't have food "scenes";the entire flick is about food and cooking. At its center is a young rat named Remy (voice of Patton Oswalt) who finds that his dream of culinary superstardom stirs up controversy in the kitchen of an elegant French restaurant. It's hard being a rat with culinary aspirations, but Remy is convinced he has what it takes to break the stereotypes and follow in the footsteps of star chef Auguste Gusteau (voice of Brad Garret). As fate would have it, Remy is situated in the sewers directly beneath Gusteau's elegant restaurant. Soon Remy teams up with a young human chef with little cooking talent named Linguini (voice of Lou Romano). Remy and Linguini are able to create some fabulous dishes with Remy sitting under Linguini's tall chef hat and controlling his limbs by pulling tufts of his hair and turning Linguini into a virtual marionette. Remy's passion for cooking turns the pretentious world of French cuisine upside down. He passes final muster when the much-feared food critic, Anton Ego (voice of Peter O'Toole), visits the restaurant. Filled with trepidation, Remy outdoes himself and Ego writes a glowing review of the meal the next day, declaring Remy "nothing less than the finest chef in France."

Big Night (1996) Secondo (Stanley Tucci) and Primo (Tony Shalhoub) are immigrant brothers who own a small café during 1950s New Jersey. Business is slow, but they're hoping a visit by Louis Prima will put them on the map. The brothers spend the entire day preparing a magnificent feast for the "big night." But there's a problem; Prima and his band is a no show. Worse yet, a ferocious argument between the brothers takes place over long-festering business issues. While the premise of the film is food, the most poignant food scene is also the movie's last. Crestfallen Secondo cooks an omelet for himself and their waiter, Cristiano (Mark Anthony). As he's dividing the omelet Primo tentatively enters the kitchen. Secondo forgivingly gets him a plate. They eat in silence, but lay their arms across each others' shoulders as they do so. This is a powerful, uninterrupted scene that makes us wish movies had more eating and cooking, less talking.

The Man Who Shot Liberty Valance (1962) This is one of John Ford's greatest films in my opinion. Not only is it one of the very best of the western movie genre, it gives one of the most memorable food scenes of any Hollywood production. The scene takes place in the town of Shinbone's only restaurant. Liberty Valance (Lee Marvin) is the sadistic town bully who finds pleasure in humiliating Ransom Stoddard (Jimmy Stewart)—the tinhorn lawyer from back East—who is earning his keep by working as a waiter and dish washer. As Stoddard is delivering a steak dinner, Valance trips him. Tom Doniphon (John Wayne), whose steak it is, commands Valance to pick up the meat. Just then, Floyd (Strother Martin), one of a pair of Valance's despicable minions, attempts to pick up the steak for his boss, but Doniphon kicks him squarely in the face as he bends over. The stalemate is resolved when Stoddard picks it up the meat and pronounces, "Nobody fights my battles," to Doniphon, who rejoins, "Well, that was my steak that he ruined." This scene has it all; great acting, high-intensity and a good piece of meat. My only beef with this movie is the title song. The Top 10 Hit, *The Man Who Shot Liberty Valance,* by the enormously talented Gene Pitney was not used. Ford opted for a song from one of his previous productions.

Cooks Who Changed World History

UNDOUBTEDLY, SOME WHO read this book will have occasionally wondered what role cooks and bakers have played in world history. While doing research for this book I came across two remarkable individuals who impacted world events. One was Ho Chi Minh, whose real name was Nguyễn Sinh Cung, the famous, or infamous depending upon your perspective, Vietnamese Marxist revolutionary. Cung was one the most distinguished and controversial political figures of the 20th-century. In 1911, Cung signed on as cook's helper with a French steamship company. After visiting ports in Europe and Africa, Cung eventually made his way to the United States. From 1912 to 1913, he lived in New York's Harlem neighborhood and eventually made his way to Boston where he worked as a baker at the Parker House Hotel. Cung also claimed to have worked as a cook for a wealthy family in Brooklyn between 1917 and 1918. During this period, Cung might have been influenced by Marcus Garvey in Harlem. It is believed that, while in the United States, he also made contact with Korean nationalists, an experience that helped mold his radical political philosophy. Cung left America for Western Europe. From 1919-1923 Ho Chi Minh lived in Paris where he embraced communism and was transformed into a Marxist revolutionary. Ho Chi Minh's culinary skills allowed him to earn a living while he developed a fervent anti-colonial posture and embraced Marxist ideology. Ho Chi

Minh formed the Democratic Republic of Vietnam and led the Việt cộng during the Vietnam War until his death in 1969.

Culinarians have also played diabolical roles on the stage of world history. Consider the part played by Christopher Columbus' personal cook and valet, the evil Espinoza. The turncoat cook was complicit in the plot, with the Court-appointed Francisco de Bobadilla, to have Columbus arrested. Most likely inspired by some long-held ill feeling toward Columbus, Espinoza volunteered testimony against the great mariner. Espinoza's testimony was instrumental in Columbus' apprehension and incarceration. Clearly, he was a Judas who betrayed his supeior. The dirty deed was committed in the year 1500 in Santa Domingo, the newly established capital of Hispaniola, when the Columbus was Viceroy and Governor of the Indies. Along with his two brothers, the 48 year old Admiral of the Seas had manacles placed on his arms and chains on his feet. The trio was cast into prison until their return to Spain six weeks later. As a consequence of the arrest and imprisonment, Columbus was forced to restore his reputation at Court, which consumed valuable time delaying the planning and execution of his last voyage. Finally, eighteen months after his arrest Columbus set sail for his fourth and final voyage. The date was May 11, 1502. Had the arrest not occurred Columbus' quest to explore beyond the Indies, further west and south of the equator, might not have been impeded. More territory in the New World could have been claimed by Spain rather than by its colonial rivals, England, France and Portugal. The world will never know how this singular event changed the course of maritime exploration and world history.

~~~

While they might not have affected world history, the cooks who fed our founding fathers are important figures in American history. George Washington's personal chef was a slave named Hercules (1755-?), familiarly called Uncle Harkless by the house domestics. Hercules was the enslaved African cook of the Washington family, both in Mount Vernon and in Philadelphia, the new nation's first capital. He was said to be one of the best chefs in the land. Hercules and another enslaved African traveled to Philadelphia by stage coach from Mount Vernon, the Washington's home and plantation in Northern Virginia. When Hercules arrived in Philadelphia in 1790, he was already in his late 30s.

He stayed in Philadelphia for nearly all of the seven years the President lived here. He had been married while living in Virginia but his wife had died, leaving him to raise their three children. At the end of Washington's presidency, the family was preparing to return to Mt. Vernon. Rather than face continued enslavement, Hercules decided to run away. His daily contact with Philadelphia's large Free African population may have had an influence on his decision to seek his freedom. His escape caused the President much distress. Uncle Harkless virtually vanished. Hercules remained in hiding. The first reference to him is in a January 15, 1798 letter from former-President's House steward, Frederick Kitt, indicating that the fugitive was living in Philadelphia. Washington died on December 14, 1799, and through his will Hercules was freed on January 1, 1801, along with Washington's other 124 enslaved. There is no evidence that Hercules knew he had been manumitted, and legally, was no longer a fugitive. A December 15, 1801 letter by Martha Washington indicates that the now-freedman Hercules was living in New York City. Nothing more is known of his whereabouts or life in freedom. He was never seen or heard from again.

Thomas Jefferson's chief cook was an American slave named James Hemings (1765-1801) who was owned and eventually freed by Jefferson. He was an older brother of Sally Hemings (the slave woman with whom Jefferson purportedly sired at least one bastard child) and is said to have been a half-sibling of Jefferson's wife Martha Wayles Skelton Jefferson because their father was John Wayles. As a young man Hemings was selected by Jefferson to accompany him to Paris when Jefferson assumed the post of Minister to France. Hemings was 19 years old when he made the journey to France. While in France, Hemings became adept at cooking French cuisine and learned to speak the French language. Jefferson became concerned that Hemings might learn that he could be free when France had abolished slavery in 1789. He returned to America with Jefferson, likely because of kinship ties with the large Hemings family. Jefferson paid Hemings wages as his chef when he worked for the president in Philadelphia. A French chef eventually replaced Hemings as chef to the President. Hemings negotiated with Jefferson for his freedom, which he gained in 1796. Said to suffer from alcoholism, James Hemings committed suicide at age 36.

Cirque du Olé

SINCE THE 1980s culinary art and science has merged to create the science of "molecular gastronomy" or, to put it in understandable terms, "food Science." It's the study of the chemical composition of food and food ingredients; their physical, biological and biochemical properties and how they interact with each other and their environment. The term "Molecular and Physical Gastronomy"—eventually shortened to "Molecular Gastronomy"—was coined in 1992 by Hungarian physicist Nicholas Kurti and French physical chemist Hervé This. One thing is clear; this scientific discipline is in vogue. This is the attempt of scientists and chefs to bring science into the kitchen.

Food science is not exactly new. It's always been part of the cooking process. It's just that now it's being explained scientifically by *gastro-geeks*. We have only to watch a cake rise in the oven to witness the natural principles of chemistry and physics working synergistically. The cake can rise through the use of chemical leavening agents (baking powder) or by the expansion of bubbles in the batter. Most people don't care how it rises; they just want it to rise. They don't care to know the scientific explanation. Whether the general public embraces food science or the new dishes created by "food scientists" is another matter entirely. Some would call the food science "culinary alchemy" while others might consider the discipline "culinary evolution."

I'm all for integrating culinary art and science, but does this move the art of cooking forward in a way that it touches the life of the average home cook or diner? A few celebrity chefs have moved out of the kitchen and into the lab. Take three Michelin star El Bulli, for example, the renowned Spanish restaurant owned by Spanish chef, Ferran Adriá—self-described food revolutionary who is widely credited with popularizing molecular gastronomy—whose creations have included irresistible dishes such as monkfish liver and barnacles with tea foam. Adriá is often described as the world's greatest chef. Adriá is an international celebrity chef and every gastronome wants to get into his restaurant along with the legions of *faux* foodies who wouldn't the difference between a mousse and foam. Nevertheless, they can tell their friends that they ate a thirty something course meal, which included a vodka and vermouth martini imbibed through an atomizer.

Is Ferran Adriá a food science genius or merely a chef who is bored with traditional cooking methods? Few seem to care as it's difficult to get a reservation at El Bulli. About two million people each year try to book a table in the fifty seat restaurant. The odds of getting in are made even more insurmountable since El Bulli is open only six months each year.

Ah, but not everyone has drunk the Kool Aid. Traditionalist chef and former El Bulli cook, Santi Santamaria, criticized Adrià's cuisine as unhealthy, alleging: "Adrià's dishes were designed to impress rather than satisfy and used chemicals that actually put diners' health at risk." The criticism has split top Spanish chefs into pro and anti Adrià camps. And German food writer, Jörg Zipprick, has accused Adrià of more or less poisoning his customers with the additives he uses in his "molecular gastronomy". Zipprick said that: "Adrià's menu should carry health warnings." There is bad news for Adrià's fan club. In September 2010 he announced that he is closing his restaurant at the end of the 2011 season. But El Bulli devotees ought not to despair; El Bulli is scheduled to reopen in 2014 albeit under a different format, one that will not accommodate paying customers. It will be more of a think tank, a nonprofit foundation to dabble in gastronomic experimentation and education.

And Adrià took his food circus on the road. In the September, 2010 he and other chefs appeared as guest speakers as part of an undergraduate course at Harvard called: *Science and Cooking: From Haute Cuisine to the Science of Soft Matter.* The course was extremely popular; 700 students applied for 300 spots. The course promised to, "illustrate the bond between science and cooking, students used physics, chemistry, and biology to manipulate recipes and create foods that stretches the imagination." I wish someone would tell me why this is supposed to be interesting, necessary or even relevant. I get it that some useful creations can come from this; especially recipes for people with food allergies. For example, Chef Barbara Lynch asked the students to create a recipe for gluten-free pasta. Without flour is it still pasta? It might resemble pasta, but is it pasta?

~~~

The most recent contribution to the "food science" movement is *Modernist Cuisine: The Art and Science of Cooking*, an epic culinary tome of encyclopedic magnitude, and the newest holy grail of foodie geekdom written by 21st century Renaissance man Nathan Myhrvold, Ph. D., and two accomplished experimental chefs, Chris Young and Maxime Bilet. This may be the most talked about food book since Julia Child released *Mastering the Art of French Cooking* in 1961. *Modernist Cuisine* is a comprehensive and excruciatingly detailed discussion of the application of scientific research principles and new techniques and technology to cooking. Apparently, *Modernist Cuisine* was born out of Myhrvold's desire to explore utility of cooking *sous vide*—a method of cooking at steady low temperatures in sealed vacuum bags. Sous vide translates to "under vacuum." While the six-volume, 2,400-page set ranges from a primer on food history and safety to how an ultra sonic bath makes crispier French fries to a collection of chef inspired recipes. For example, there is a recipe for a magnificent cheeseburger. According to Dr. Myhrvold: "The cheeseburger requires the meat to be cooked sous vide. Freezing with liquid nitrogen ensures that the crust will stay crispy while the center stays perfectly medium rare once it is deep fried. The heirloom tomato is vacuum compressed. The cheese must be melted first, then restructured. The bun is made from scratch and toasted in beef suet. The crimini mushroom ketchup includes honey, horseradish, fish sauce, ginger and allspice." This is not a burger that most of us will or can cook at home so what is the point. Most of us will never taste a burger prepared like this. While I should imagine *Modernist Cuisine* is useful in explaining the science behind what we cook, it is largely useless to the everyday cook or most professional chefs. What is the point of it all? The handful of celebrity chefs regards this surge in food science as a culinary revolution. But is it? This is not an organic movement craving the esoteric knowledge of food science. It appears to be nothing more than a cadre of celebrity chefs—who move in a rarified atmosphere—and a media that has bought into the premise that has popularized this *revolution*. Is the movement about them or science?

I get it that chefs want to distinguish themselves from their peers and make a culinary statement, but shouldn't it be done by applying sensible modern interpretations to traditional dishes—like what Rick Bayless does with Mexican food? I haven't seen Bayless creating tamale foam or *mole verde* ice cream. He wouldn't waste his time or embarrass himself. The Adriàs of the food world come across as precocious and bored lads in chemistry class whose silly experiments led to a menu of useless creations.

Call me old fashioned, but this stuff sounds just plain silly. How do we know what chemicals are used in these teas, foams, bubbles and sprays?

Even if the ingredients are safe to eat why should this matter? Because a few bored celebrity chefs and well known food writers deem it so isn't good enough. What's the point of it all and does molecular gastronomy move the art of cooking forward for the masses? Does this have social worth? These are a few questions that have to be answered before I would be convinced that this aspect of "food science" is worth pursuing. Remember when the much anticipated chemically-reconfigured Olestra hit the store shelves? And how did that work out?

Appendix D

Delicious Food Moments

OUR LIVES ARE can be defined by extraordinary moments, those special memories that remain with us throughout our lives. For some of us, many of these snapshots in time often involve food in one way or another. You might recall where you were the first time you tasted a flakey croissant or who you were with when you discovered the unctuous flavor of high-quality European chocolate. But not all food memories are pleasant ones. You might remember the row you had with your husband when he criticized you're pie crust or the Thanksgiving dinner at which your mother-in-law turned her nose. I recall the time I mistook black caviar for blackberry preserves. I was a busboy at a country club in Terre Haute, Indiana and decided to make a sandwich with what I thought was blackberry preserves. Sturgeon row and Wonder bread doesn't pair very well. We've all got a kaleidoscope of special food memories tucked away in our minds. I thought I'd share a few of my more entertaining food moments.

Hot Pepper "Mon"

IN THE MID 1970s my then-girl friend, Tessa, and I vacationed in Jamaica. Being a Briton, Tessa was excited to visit one of England's former colonies and the home of reggae that we both love so much. We stayed at a small seaside resort with a whimsical name, Strawberry Fields. With white beaches and swaying palms, Strawberry Fields was an idyllic spot situated on a cove in an undeveloped part of Jamaica. A soothing breeze constantly caressed our little hideaway. A dozen or so thatched huts surrounded the small cove where the locals dived for lobsters. They sold them to the tourists. We bought a few ourselves for dinner one night.

They were excellently prepared by the resident chef. There was always plenty of rum and, of course, "ganja", the Sanskrit word for cannabis.

Our resort wasn't far from Ocho Rios, a popular tourist destination on the north side of the island. The natives couldn't have been more welcoming or hospitable. Tessa's nationality seemed to confer a special tourist status upon us. Jamaicans seemed to hold the legacy of the British in high regard for the infrastructure they established on the island during the colonial days—roads, educational system and governance. Our special relationship allowed us an entrée into the local society, which resulted in an intimate glimpse of their culture rarely seen by most tourists.

One fellow, who called himself Bogart, took us on a tour of his farm. It was small plot situated on a hillside; it couldn't have been larger than half an acre. Bogart grew okra, plantains, tomatoes and bananas. But mostly he grew marijuana. He had well over one hundred plants each of which was over ten feet tall. They were so bushy they provided shade for his chickens. I asked him if the pot was his main cash crop.

"Me sell some, but dis ganj' be mostly for me."

Smoking reefer is at the core of Jamaican culture. It's a normal part of daily life for many islanders, at least in that part of the island. Day and night large joints, or "spliffs" as they called them, were never far from their lips. Spliffs are enormous joints. They use bakery paper to roll them. The Jamaicans we came to know smoked pot the first thing in the morning and the last before they turned in at night.

After befriending a few of the locals, one of our new acquaintances invited us to a private party. We considered it an honor and eagerly accepted. They even offered to provide round trip transportation. At the appointed time a van full of dread-locked locals collected us and off we went. The party was at some guy's house a short ride from our lodging. The house was thick with marijuana smoke when we arrived. No one seemed to have any difficulty getting into a party mood. Lithe bodies swayed like supple palms to a steady Reggae beat. Wolf Man Jacques, the DJ, worked a dilapidated portable record player. As the party grew, the guests spilled out into the backyard where we noticed a man stirring a five-gallon pot bubbling of what looked to be some type of stew or soup. He was doling out bowls to the guests. I asked him his soup.

"Dis be goat head soup mon, it be da national soup of Jamaica. It be a bit spicy, but me tink you gonna like it mon."

Not wanting to offend him, we accepted his offer. He ladled the soup into hemispheres of hollowed out calabash—a type of gourd common to the Caribbean basin. It was tasty and more than a little piquant. As I ate I felt something soft and mushy in my mouth. Thinking it might be a goat's eyeball and wanting to get it out of my mouth I gave it a quick chew and swallowed. That would prove to be a huge mistake.

My mouth felt like someone had just shoveled hot BBQ briquettes into my mouth. The 5-alarm feeling would turn out to be only the beginning of what would be one of the most memorable food moments of my entire life. It turned out that I had ingested one of just several peppers added to a five-gallon caldron of soup. I later discovered that I had eaten a dreaded "Scotch Bonnet", a habañero on steroids. The "Scotch" is commonly found in Caribbean cuisine and is the hottest chili in all the West Indies.

While far from the being world's hottest chili, the Scotch Bonnet has earned a very respectable ranking on the Scoville Scale, a sort of Richter scale for measuring the heat in chili peppers. Peppers contain a chemical called capsaicin, which gives chilies their heat. Most of the capsaicin is concentrated in the seeds and ribs of a pepper, not the fleshy wall. The Scoville scale measures the hotness or piquancy of a chili pepper by the amount of capsaicin it contains. The amount of a chili's *capsaicin* is measured and the pepper is assigned a score expressed in numerical units. Based on its relative score, a chili is ranked against all other chilies on the scale. For example, regular bell peppers are so mild they merit zero units while law enforcement grade pepper spray is near the top with a maximum of 5,300,000 units, toward the high end of its range. The highest rating is 16 million units for pure *capsaicin*. Jalapeño peppers, thought to be only mildly hot, score anemic 2,500-8,000 units while a Scotch Bonnet comes in with at a fiery 100,000-350,000 units. This might not sound formidable, that is, until you eat one. But the king of heat—the Naga Viper—was crowned the world's-hottest-pepper, outdistancing its predecessor, the Bhut Jolokia, or "ghost chili," by more than 300,000 points on the scale. In November 2010 researchers at Warwick University tested the Naga Viper and found that it measured in at a tongue-scorching 1,359,000 units. You might think the Naga Viper would hail from some part of the world with a strong demand for spicy food, such as India or Mexico, but it doesn't. The Naga Viper is actually the handiwork of Gerald Fowler, a British chili farmer and pub owner, who crossed three of the hottest peppers known to man—including the Bhut Jolokia—to create his Frankenstein-monster of chilies.

Within a few minutes I began to suffer the full effects of the chili. My entire mouth and upper throat were completely numb. It felt like I had just numbed-up for oral surgery. Then I began to feel faint. I collapsed at the base of a nearby coconut palm. Perspiration oozed from every pore. I believe even my feet were sweating. I could only sit there, lifeless. Within a few minutes the Hawaiian shirt I was wearing became completely saturated. Recognizing what had happened to me, one guest barked.

"Hey, Chuck got da pepper mon." His comment alerted the other guests who began to file by. I soon became a source of entertainment. Passersby giggled. A few party-goers just stood in front of me silently sipping frosty Red Stripe beer. Even Tessa joined the onlookers. Most people seemed to derive a perverted sense pleasure from my suffering. The Germans have an expression for this, *schadenfreude*—taking pleasure in another's pain or misfortune. All I could do was sit there, miserable.

Nothing extinguished the fire; beer, water, soda. Nothing squelched the pain! I remained planted under the palm for the remainder of the evening. By the time the chili's lethal effects began to subside the party was winding down. We returned to Strawberry Fields where I spent a fitful night. The pepper wasn't done with me. I would suffer the residual effects the next morning. Thirty plus years later, and the memory of that night can still elicit a physical reaction. I'm beginning to perspire as I'm typing this. You might say that night was "burned" into my memory.

Jacques Pépin, A Chef's Chef

AFTER DECADES OF enjoying Jacques Pépin's cooking shows I finally got to see him in the flesh. I'm a cooking show fanatic. I regard well done productions as tutorials and Jacques' shows are some of the best ever done. Watching him cook is like having Rembrandt give painting lessons. Pepin is an anachronism or sorts. He learned his craft in a different era in culinary history. He began cooking before the food processor and microwave oven were invented. Everything was done by hand. There was no gas ranges, fire were stoked in the oven chamber. Few living chefs can cook at Pépin's level. I've learned more about cooking by watching his shows than from any other.

During the autumn of 2009 my lovely friend, Barbara Sadek, and I had the opportunity to see Jacques at the Smithsonian Institute where he appeared with the Travel and Food Editor for the Washington Post. We had great seats, just a few rows from the stage. The audience greeted him with thunderous applause as he walked on stage. He was calm and controlled just as I knew he would be. He was impeccably dressed. Even his hair was perfect. I'm not fond of European chefs. Most of them are real dicks, but Jacques is different. He's a prodigious talent, but has never forgotten his roots. Pépin's resume is the stuff of legend. He's been chef to three French heads-of-state; Felix Gaillard and Pierre Pfimlin and Charles de Gaulle. He's a humble person and his blue-collar upbringing comes through in his autobiography, *Jacques Pépin*.

It's a slight overstatement to say that Jacques Pépin is to American gastronmy what the Marquis de Lafayette was to the American Revolution. America has benefited from the efforts of both men. There have been other great French chefs who became famous on American soil, Pierre Franey, Paul Bocuse and Jean Louis Paladin, but none have had Pépin's impact. Through his cooking shows, cookbooks, textbooks and personal appearances he's elevated the art of cooking in American. Through hundreds television productions Pépin's been a guest in our homes for decades. His rich culinary legacy has been surpassed only by Julia Child, the undisputed matriarch of modern American cuisine. Jacques and Julia became a true tour de force years ago when they teamed up on *Julia and Jacques Cooking at Home*. It was a match made in heaven for us gastro-geeks.

During the presentation Jacques reminisced about working in his mother's café as a boy and how much she influenced him. He also talked about doing the PBS productions and working with Julia Child. Although he always deferred to Julia on the set he was far more skilled than her. She helped to launch his career and he never forgot it. He also discussed his stint at Howard Johnson's where he worked with his friend, Pierre Franey, who had his own cooking show on PBS in the early 1990s. Sadly, Pierre passed away in 1996.

Following the presentation they opened it up for some Q & A. Hands stabbed the air throughout the auditorium, including mine. I recall thinking, *Jacques pick me, pick me.* as if I were some fifth-grader trying to get the teacher's attention. He didn't even look in our direction. After answering a half dozen or so questions Jacques said, "I'll take one more."

But he still hadn't looked my way. I was desperate and had to act fast. I knew that I'd never have this opportunity again. I had to do something.

"Jacques," I screamed spontaneously.

I probably shouldn't have yelled, but had no choice. Jacques was startled. His head whipped around in my direction; he even repositioned his chair so he was facing us. He had to have been thinking, *who is this maniac*. It didn't matter; I wouldn't be denied. After taking a second to regain my composure, I calmly asked,

"Chef, who had the greatest influence on your culinary career?" Professional etiquette demanded that I address him as "chef." The moment seemed surreal. I couldn't believe this was happening. I was actually talking with Chef Pépin, someone I've admired my entire career. I would have felt the same sense of euphoria had I put a question to another one of my heroes—John Lennon.

"Mr. Lennon, when did you first discover that you had musical talent?"

To me, Jacques Pépin is the gastronomic equivalent of a rock legend. Few cooking show hosts, if any, have reached a larger audience or influenced as many American cooks as has Pépin. He has remained at the forefront of the American culinary scene since the late 1960s. None of today's celebrity chefs are in Pépin's league, not Eric Ripert, not Anthony Bourdain, not Mario Batali, not even Emeril. Pépin is a chef's chef and in a class by himself. Other celebrity chefs might be better known, but none are better cooks. I know it sounds as if I'm gay for the guy. I'm not really, it's just that we all have, or should have, professionals we admire and want to emulate. It never hurts to aim high.

"Without question", he responded, "My mother had the greatest influence on me. She taught me all the basics in our family restaurant, Le Pelican. After school I would help out in the kitchen, doing odd jobs like peeling vegetables and washing pots. Eventually, she let me help her at the stove."

And that was it; the Q & A was over. I got to ask the last question. As he rose to walk off the stage the audience gave him a standing ovation. Pépin is the last of the great cooking show celebrities. Do they make screen savers of this guy?

Oaxaca de Vacaciones

IN OCTOBER 2007 my friend, Barbara Sadek, and I traveled to Oaxaca, Mexico. Oaxaca is one of Mexico's largest states and is located in the Valley of Oaxaca. Oaxaca is the historic home of the Zapotec and Mixtec peoples, and contains more speakers of indigenous languages than any of Mexico's thirty-one states. Oaxaca's most notable favorite son would be Benito Pablo Juárez Garcia, who was a five term president of Mexico and instrumental in ousting the French in 1866.

We stayed in Oaxaca City, the state capital, at a charming B & B called La Casa de Mis Recuerdos or "House of My Memories". Fortunately, we were located only a few blocks from the *zocalo,* or town square. The zocalo is surrounded by grand restaurants and romantic cafes all of which serve some of the best south-of-the-border fare I've ever tasted. It was not the faux Mexican fare or Tex Mex most Americans are used to; this was the real deal, authentic *comida Mexicana.* It was at one the restaurants at the town square where we were introduced to *chapulines*—tiny grass hoppers that are sautéed and served with salt a squirt of fresh lime. Chapulines are served as a snack or used as a crunchy garnish to dishes. This pre-Columbian taste treat can be purchased at any of the local markets the largest of which is the sprawling *Central de Abastos* **walking distance from the city center. The** *Abastos* is an ordered confusion of baskets and crafts, piles of tropical fruits; bleating goats, live chickens and turkeys, mounds of dried chilies and herbs such as epazote, which has both culinary and medicinal uses. Oaxaca has other open-air markets that are only open certain days of the week.

During our stay in Oaxaca we were able to sample several of the mole sauces for which the state capital is famous. Oaxaca is known as the Land of the Seven Moles although Puebla disputes this claim and regards itself as home to the moles. The most popular are the black, red and green versions. The true story of how mole developed may never be truly known as the first recipes did not appear until after the Mexican War of Independence in 1810. But the Nahuatl origin of the name probably defines its Mesoamerican origin. While chili pepper sauces existed in pre-Hispanic Mexico, the complicated moles of today did not. Most likely what occurred was a gradual modification of the original sauce, adding more and different ingredients depending on the location. This diversified the resulting sauces into various types. Ingredients that have been added into moles including plantain, cilantro, spices, garlic, herbs, raisins, pumpkin and sesame seeds, dried chilies, potatoes, vanilla, tomaotes, cacao, tomatillos, almonds, onions, chocolate, lard, bread . . . The combination of ingredients and cooking methods vary to create a variety of types.

While at the Casa de Mis Recuerdos we particpated in a cooking class offered by one of the co-owners, a lovely and charming woman named Nora. The class was conducted in the B & B's open garden, a tranquil courtyard complete with a gurgling fountain and hanging baskets of tropical plants. Nora set up a make shift kitchen right in the courtyard. I volunteered to be her sous chef during the class. My sole assignment was to fry the ingredients in the order Nora decided. To do this, we used a *comal*—a sort of shallow wok made of metal or fired clay used for frying and toasting.

Four types of chilies, raisins, onions and the almonds were toasted in smoking hot lard in the camal. Even the stale bread needed to be fried to a crisp according to Nora's recipe. The frying generated a plume of smoke, but it's necessary to give the sauce that distinctive flavor mole negro is famous for. All ingredients were combined and dumped into in a bucket, which we hauled to the local *molino* (the Spanish name for grinder) where the mixture is finely ground into a thick paste. Some families are purists and will only use a *metate* (a mortar or grinding stone), which they believe provides a smoother more velvety texture allowing the flavors to intensify. When the class returned to the B & B, Nora mixed the fresh paste with homemade chicken broth to obtain the desired consistency. She finished the sauce by adding some melted lard and chocolate to give it sheen and a flavor that is crucial in this particular sauce. Our mole negro was served with chicken that Nora had poached earlier. It was delicious. The sauce was a complicated amalgam of flavors; sweet, bitter, nutty and salty.

~~~

The next day we were off to another cooking class, which was conducted at the Seasons of My Heart, a combination cooking school and B &B. The owner is Susana Trilling who has established a respectable reputation through her cookbooks and exposure on television. It was a long drive to get there since it's quite a ways outside the city of Oaxaca.

The day began with a visit to the Etla market. Etla is a small town outside of Oaxaca City en route to the cooking school. The market was a bustling bee hive of activity. The sights, sounds and smells were sensory overload. There was and enormous assortment of fresh produce and meats, Mexican chocolate and unrefined sugar, dried chilies and sweets as well as locally-made crafts. One of the specialties was the string cheese for which Oaxaca is famous. Roaming the market were the tiniest people I have ever seen in my life. They were full-blooded Zapotec Indians. (The Zapotec civilization was an indigenous pre-Columbian civilization that flourished in the Valley of Oaxaca.) These Latino Lilliputians couldn't have been more than four feet tall, many were shorter.

While at the market, the class enjoyed a tasty lunch of pork tamales with *mole verde* and rice. Oaxacan tamales are rectangular or square and made of smoothly ground cornmeal wrapped in a dark green banana or plantain leaf, which imparts a distinctive flavor and slight color to the absorbent cornmeal masa. Traditional Mexican tamales is meat-filled masa wrapped in corn husks. Our market tour guide was one of Trilling's staff. The market experience itself was easily worth the cost of the class. In fact, the market visit proved to be the high point of the day.

Loafing in France

DURING THE SUMMER of 1989 my then-wife, Anne-Marie, and her mother, Anna Dalier-Gordon, and I visited France. After a short stay in Paris we traveled south to visit their relatives who lived in and around the small farming village of Arcizac-Adour. The town takes its name from the nearby Adour River. Arcizac is situated between the city of Tarbes and world-famous Lourdes. The area is in the Hautes-Pyrénées region in the south sector of the country. Roman armies used the Adour as a water source when they occupied Gaul over two thousand years ago.

Arcizac-Adour is a sleepy hamlet that modernity seems to have forgotten. Farmers still drive their dairy cows through town and few have a computer. They like it this way. Arcizac boasts a population of about one hundred permanent residents. However, during the summer months the population may swell to one hundred and fifty or so. Arcizac features its own grain mill and bakery, which provides assorted breads and basic pastries for the town's people and residents from the surrounding countryside. Unlike Paris, where there is a bakery on every corner, a country bakery provides baked goods for the inhabitants of several small communities.

Unfortunately, Arcizac's bakery was closed for summer vacation while we were there. This wasn't a problem because another bakery that served a neighboring community was open so we headed there. It seems that French country bakers coordinate vacations so their customers never go without fresh bread. The French are adamant about having fresh bread daily.

Joseph Dalier, Anna's cousin, and Arcizac's favorite son, drove us to the neighboring bakery. Joseph was a gregarious and chatty fellow whose youthful appearance belied his actual age. Joseph seemed to be somewhat of a local celebrity; he was on a first name basis with everyone we encountered en route to the bakery. As we wound our way through the country side in Joseph's vintage Citroen he tooted the horn as we whizzed by his neighbors. Occasionally, he'd pull off the road to chat up an aquaintance and proudly introduce his relatives from America. These down-to-earth country folk were a breath of fresh air compared to the haughty and condescending Parisians I was happy to be rid of.

The bakery itself was nothing more than a rudimentary cinder block structure located at the end of a dirt road situated between wheat fields. It was a simple operation with a large brick oven, worktables, a dough mixer and a few racks for storing baked goods. There was no proof box (A proof box is a climate controlled chamber for proofing bread.) These bakers simply allowed their various bread products to rise naturally at room temperature.

Anna and Anne-Marie, who both speak fluent French, interpreted while I took notes, but, of course, Joseph wasn't going to be left out of the conversation. He jumped in with a few questions of his own. He could have queried the bakers anytime he visited the bakery, but apparently he felt it necessary to pepper them with questions at that particular moment. I thought it amusing that he suddenly developed a keen interest in bread production. I had a list of prepared questions. I was curious to discover things like the varieties and quantity of breads they produced and whether they also made pastries. The bakery staff seemed to take pride that an American chef took such interest in their work.

The room smelt of yeast and flour and warm bread. The smell was delicious. There were huge baskets of baguettes, ficelle and boules. Their bread was beautiful, golden brown split crusts, different shapes and sizes. I purchased an assortment. I couldn't resist ripping into a still warm baguette. It was the best bread I'd ever eaten. It was the perfect combination of texture and flavor. The thick crust crackled, it had a nutty flavor while the inside was tender yet substantial with a yeasty flavor and aroma. No need for butter as it would only mask the flavor. No bakery in Paris, Washington, D.C. or New Orleans can produce bread as good as that unpretentious, simple country operation.

The bakers could see that I was enjoying myself as I devoured their fresh bread. Through Anna, I told them that their bread was the best I'd ever had. They were flattered. I asked them why they thought their bread was so good. They thought it was because they used locally grown and milled wheat and the pure water from the Pyrenees. These were the key ingredients, but I was curious about something else I noticed. On bottom of each loaf there was fine grit. I knew that it wasn't corn meal—which is what most commercial bakeries use. They told me that the meal was finely ground olive pits imported from Spain. This imparted a distinctive flavor and created a sort of barrier and allowed the loaves to easily slide on and off the *planche* or peel without sticking. (A peel is a flat, broad with a long handle used for to load and unload a deck oven.)

These humble bakers certainly taught this big city chef what good baking is about. Neither baker had ever attended any sort of culinary program yet they produced magnificent breads. Formal schooling has its place, but its technique and experience that are irreplaceable. They were just simple country boys who took enormous pride in their craft. They did one thing and they did it to perfection. I really admired these guys. I find it amazing how a few simple ingredients—flour, water, yeast and salt—can be transformed into a thing of beauty.

St. Maarten

IF YOU HAPPEN to be driving around St. Maarten/St. Martin and spy a plume of white smoke head straight for it. At its source you'll most likely find a local grilling baby back pork ribs and chicken. Smokey and cloyingly sweet sauces aren't necessary; they would only mask the deliciousness of the pork. The natives just lightly season the ribs with salt and pepper. Dispersed over the island are food trucks whose owners serve up succulent barbeque chicken and ribs and other dishes such as fried plantains and a seasoned rice and beans combination similar to *congris* found in Puerto Rico. These road side chefs offer generous portions for only a few dollars.

It's only fitting that this island specialty be prepared by the local inhabitants since it is thought that *barbque*, as a cooking method, was introduced to the island by their ancestors, the Caribs and Arawaks—Indian tribes who migrated from the Oronoco River basin in Venezuela to the Caribbean archipelago in approximately 1200 CE. It is also thought that the word *barbque* is derived from the word *barabicu* found in the language of the Taíno people who preceeded the other tribes in the Caribbean basin. The word *barabicu* translates to "sacred fire pit." The word suggests a grill for cooking meat, consisting of a wooden platform resting on sticks.

My friend Barbara Sadek and I spent ten sunshine-drenched days on the island of St. Maarten. The island divided into approximate geographical halves; roughly 60/40 between France and the Netherlands Antilles; it is the smallest inhabited sea island divided between two nations, a division dating back to 1648. The southern Dutch half comprises the Eilandgebied Sint Maarten (Island area of St. Martin) and is part of the Netherlands Antilles. The northern French half comprises the Collectivité de Saint-Martin, an overseas collectivity of France.

The Island has become synonymous with fine cuisine and has earned a reputation of being the gastronomic Mecca of the Caribbean, but is primarily renowned for French cuisine. After all, it is a little slice of France. The French side, as one might expect, also features a handful of boulangeries and patisseries, bakeries and pastry shops, all of which are exceptional. We enjoyed dunking our pain chocolate in our morning coffee while we watched the waves lap the shore from our balcony.

Marigot, the capital of the French side, offers quaint cafés and first class restaurants on the sea promenade, Grand Case features "lolos", open-air barbeque joints where lobster, ribs and chicken is grilled before your eyes. Grand Case was our favorite place to dine and for good reason; it is commonly regarded as the culinary capital in all the Caribbean although other island towns might take issue with that.

The Dutch side also offers excellent cuisine although French fare is only one component of the food scene. The Dutch are open to a variety of cuisines. In Philipsburg, the capital on the Dutch side, food lovers will be delighted to find Indian, Indonesian, Thai and Chinese eateries. Generally, the chefs cooking in the ethnic restaurants hail from the country which dishes they prepare, ensuring that what they prepare is authentic. It's best to avoid Philipsburg when the cruise-ship hordes descend upon the town. This deluge of humanity tends to diminish any pleasant dining experience and makes getting around more difficult. Fortunately, most of the tourists head straight for the beaches so they can gawk at nude sun bathers as if they are circus acts. It was sort of embarrassing to watch my fellow countryman lead the pack.

In addition to the traditional European-style and ethnic restaurants, St. Maarten offers many obscure diners owned and operated by the local black residents. These little places offer traditional Caribbean fare such as tripe, bull foot and goat soups, Jamaican meat patties and Johnny cakes. The food in these eateries is usually good a good value.

Our culinary experiences in St. Maarten were memorable ones. We were pleasantly surprised by the quantity and quality of the restaurants at such a small venue. With more than four hundred restaurants situated on this tiny rock St. Maarten surely offers more places to eat per capita than any other Caribbean destination. We can't wait to get back.

Sin City

WHAT HAPPENS IN Vegas doesn't always stay in Vegas. I'm referring to the weight I gained during a long weekend we spent in Vegas in January 2010. Other than New Orleans, I don't usually gush over the food scene of any American city, but Las Vegas is an exception. Today's Las Vegas is definitely not your parent's Las Vegas. The days of the Rat Pack and fried chicken buffets are long gone. It's been well known for years that Las Vegas' culinary scene has evolved to the point that it doesn't have to play catch up or apologize for its food scene. It ranks up there with any city in America; Chicago, New York and LA. So why am I so late to the party?

I was astounded at the sheer number and variety of fabulous restaurants and cafés. But what was equally amazing was the level of quality. While Las Vegas seems to have a limited number of ethnic restaurants, there are enough of other marvelous places to eat it that isn't an issue. Each hotel houses its own selection of restaurants, coffee shops and bistros, but it might not have a restaurant to your liking. No problem, just hop in cab and zip over to one that suits your mood. The City Center—a collection of hotels, residences, restaurants, spas and shopping—itself has more great places to eat than many cities in America. It was still under construction during our visit.

I knew that la Vegas' gastronomic metamorphosis began in the early 90s, but I knew serious change was afoot when renowned French chef Jean-Louis Palladin left Washington, D.C. for Sin City. Many top notch chefs followed. We had a burger at Hubert Keller's Burger Bar located in Mandalay Bay. I thought how good can a burger be? Keller answered that with one of the best burgers I've ever had. We enjoyed a beef burger and a buffalo burger. Both were unctuous and perfectly seasoned and with house-made bread. Even the fries were perfect. We were tempted to split the signature burger; a ground beef filet topped with pan seared foie gras. But $60 is a little much for a burger no matter how good it is. I'm too cheap.

Clearly, many of the new Las Vegas chefs are doing awesome food. Las Vegas has become one of the premier food venues in North America and the best part is that most of the chefs are Americans. For the food bargain seekers there are still plenty of hotel buffets. The Rio Carnival World Buffet is a good example of great value. Like Las Vegas itself, the World Buffet is a larger-than-life spectacle. It's a football field-size smorgasbord that offers more than two-hundred dishes. It serves a whopping half ton of fresh shrimp daily.

It's worth a trip to Vegas just to stuff your face for a few days. There are cheap vacation packages and the shows are world class. But keep in mind that Las Vegas is not an inexpensive place to eat out. In fact, it's the most expensive city in the nation with an average meal cost $47.53 in 2010 beating out New York ($41.76) and Miami ($39.86) according to the Zagat's Survey.

Viet Nam, The Ascending Dragon

IF YOU THINK Vietnamese food is identical to its neighbors', you would be mistaken. You would also be wrong if you believe that Vietnamese food is vastly different from its neighbors. The culinary lines are definitely blurred in Southeast Asia where nations butt up against one another. Boundaries on a map do little to prevent the melding of cultures including and especially their culinary traditions and styles. There are subtle differences between the cuisine of the northern and southern regions of the country just as there are influences derived from the neighboring countries; China, Laos, Cambodia and Thailand. To complicate things even more, Vietnamese cuisine still retains a measure of French culinary influences as a result of French colonialism. But the French influence seems to have waned since they pulled out in the early1950s. Chinese culinary influences continue to pervade Vietnamese gastronomy, especially in the north where the two countries share a common border.

There are two Viet Nams. The modern one has its foot in the 21st-century while the ancient Viet Nam has the other foot firmly planted in 16th-century. Modern Viet Nam holds membership in sixty-three international organizations. In August 2010 Viet Nam conducted joint military exercises with the U.S., tangible evidence that it's fast becoming a full-fledged member of the global community. Ancient Viet Nam is determined to cling to its old culture and traditions. Farmers wearing cone-shaped hats still toil in rice paddies as their ancestors did a hundred generations ago.

An important way the Vietnamese remain connected to their past is through their food. Vietnamese gastronomy has changed little over the centuries. Cooking and eating has always played an important role in Vietnamese culture. The word *ăn* (eat) is included in a great number of ancient proverbs. They value balance and harmony in the food they eat. This can be achieved by incorporating the "five elements" into their cooking; five spices, five nutrients and five colors all appealing to the five human senses.

On a recent trip to Southeast Asia I had the opportunity to visit Viet Nam and get a taste of this surging nation's amazing cuisine. So now when I think of Vietnamese food I think of intense fermented sauces, fresh vegetables and herbs such as lemon grass, Thai basil, mint and coriander. From Saigon (Ho Chi Minh City) to Hanoi, the capital, in the north, Vietnamese cuisine offers many regional variations and specialty dishes, but there is one dish that is common to all reaches of this slender, hour glass-shaped nation. It's a noodle soup called *phở* (pronounced *fer*). *Phở* is usually served with thinly-sliced semi-cooked beef in a natural broth (*phở bo*) or chicken pieces in its own broth (*phở ga*). Since rice was not cultivated in Louisiana during the colonial period Europeans imported rice from Asia and Africa. *Phở* broth isn't just plain meat stock; it's typically flavored with dried star anise, cinnamon sticks, coriander seeds, lemon grass, black pepper, salt and sugar. The condiments may be placed in a cloth bag and immersed in the broth for several hours to attain the distinctive flavor. The soup is typically enjoyed with Thai basil, fresh lime, bean sprouts and sliced hot chili peppers that are added to the bowl by the consumer.

The Vietnamese eat *phở* just about any time of day or night; at breakfast, lunch, dinner or as snack.

Viet Nam is also a great place for street food. Street food might be a hot trend in America right now, but we're a little late to the party. The Vietnamese have been enjoying street fare for centuries. Street vendors are usually found in the open markets of the large urban centers where they simply crank up a charcoal fire in a hibachi or any metal container that suffices. They just grill away without being bothered by those pesky health inspectors like we do in the U.S. They grill marinated beef, pork, chicken or shrimp on a stick called *satay* (pronounced *sa-tay*)—this meal on a stick originated in Indonesia—that is eaten with rice or added to a bowl of *phở*. Every city has an open air market where the locals make daily food purchases of fresh produce, meat, poultry and seafood. It is in these markets where you'll find most of the street food vendors.

The Vietnamese take their food seriously. They eat everything from fried insect pupae to deep-fried swallows to pig anuses. Mmmm, I don't know how you would have felt about it, but I couldn't wait to get to Viet Nam and dive into a pile of pig anuses. They also eat something called the Thousand-Year Egg, which are eggs preserved for several months in a mixture of lime, salt, clay, ash and rice hulls. A chemical reaction occurs causing the yolk and white to become a black, gelatinous substance. I sampled one and it tasted pretty much like black, egg-flavored Jell-O. It was pretty weird. I didn't see any of the Vietnamese eating these either.

The Vietnamese love intense, bold flavors. Enter the fermented sauces. These are strong sauces the Vietnamese use as condiments either added during cooking the cooking process or at the table by the consumer or both. The most popular sauces are *nước mắm*, a concentrated fish extract, a staple in many Asian cuisines, and *tương* is a type of mild soy sauce. The Vietnamese are partial to curries, hoisin sauce, shrimp paste called *mắm tôm* and chili sauces that range from mild to eye-tearing hot.

Viet Nam has always been on the wrong side of history. For more than one thousand years it was occupied by the Chinese, its monolithic overlord to the north, and at war from time to time with it ancient enemy, the Khmer Empire (what is now Cambodia). For more than a century the French occupied Viet Nam and brutalized its people. The Americans picked up where the French left off, but were eventually expelled in April 1975. However, in 1996 President Bill Clinton normalized relations with America's former adversary resulting in an explosion of tourism.

For example, during the first seven months of 2010 nearly 3 million international tourists visited Viet Nam representing a 51 percent increase over the same period in 2009.

Mother Nature has not been kind to the Vietnamese. Because of its geographic location, Viet Nam has been battered by countless typhoons and seasonal monsoons throughout its 2,700 year history. But the Vietnamese are indomitable. In spite of all the hardships there are two constants in Viet Nam; the resilience of the people and their culinary tradition. Both endure, always. Outside of Viet Nam, Vietnamese cuisine is widely available in countries with strong Vietnamese immigrant communities, such as Australia, the United States, Canada, and France. It's only a matter of time before the rest of the world rediscovers Viet Nam and its culinary treasures. If you have a bucket list add the Ascending Dragon to it; it's only a matter of time before the Starbucks and KFCs spoil it.

Giraffic Park

DURING OCTOBER 2010 Barbara Sadek and I went on a wildlife safari in the heart of East Africa, zoo to the world. The main reason for our trip was to visit the magnificent game preserves in Kenya and Tanzania; Tarangire National Park, Ngorongoro Conservation Area, Serengeti National Park and Masai Mara National Reserve—a Kenya preserve famous for an abundance of wildlife. We were treated to the greatest show on earth. The sheer amount and variety of wildlife was truly staggering. Lions, cheetahs, zebras and wildebeests dart around like so many house pets. We blew through several memory cards taking photos of nearly every plains animal I've ever seen on National Geographic and then some. We were fortunate to snap shots of two of the rarest cats in all of nature, the caracal and serval.

A secondary reason for the trip was to experience the cuisine of East Africa. Africa has given the world a variety of foods and spices that we take for granted; tilapia, okra, peanuts, seeds, various greens, yams and other tubers, cereal grains . . . One of the lodges where we stayed offered a buffet that featured wild-caught tilapia from Lake Victoria. The fish were enormous, easily eight to ten pounds. Another lodge offered Nile Lake Perch served with fresh sage, which was absolutely delicious. Throughout our trip we were treated to a variety of legume dishes; curried black lentils, spicy red beans in tomato sauce, black beans simmered in coconut milk. A staple was mashed yams. They were delicious when mixed with only butter and seasoned with only salt and pepper. We also ate an African version of Southern pecan pie but made with peanuts instead. It was delicious.

While in Nairobi we took the opportunity to enjoy some Indian cuisine for which the city is famous. We dined at a restaurant called Haandi where we had one of the finest Indian meals we've ever had. Indian cuisine is special. Most knowledgeable foodies would agree that Indian culture has taken the use of spices to an art form. But there's more to Indian cuisine whose cooks have also applied a philosophy to their gastronomy, *ayurveda*. Ayurveda (Sanskrit for "science of life") is the science of life or longevity and is the holistic alternative approach to medicine in Indian culture. Since eating and nutrition is inherent in good health and well-being, ayurveda, quite naturally, applies to gastronomy. Only ancient Asian cultures seem capable of applying philosophical thought to their cuisine in order to achieve balance and mind-body harmony. And we have KFC.

One of our guides was Patrick Angugo, a safari director for the luxury outfitter Micato Safaris—an extraordinary man who is a true polyglot; he spoke Italian, Spanish German, Swahili and English. Patrick can talk at length about a number of topics; the migratory habits of wildebeest, the history of the Maasai and social hierarchy of the Marsh Pride—a pride of lions that inhabit the Masai Mara game preserve and one that is often the subject of nature shows such as *Big Cat Diary.* Patrick introduced me to *machalri*, braised beef with plantains in a spicy tomato sauce. This is traditional fare of the Chaga Tribe of the Kilimanjaro region. He also explained the importance of *ugali* or *kimyet*, as it's often called in Kenya, in the East African diet. Ugali is made from cornmeal cooked with water to a dough-like consistency and usually eaten by rolling it into a lump or a ball with the right hand and then dipping it into a sauce or stew of vegetables or meat.

Acknowledgements

IT TOOK ME nearly four long years to write *Accidental Chef*. It required this length of time for several reasons. This is the first book of this type I've written. I'd only done cook books, restaurant reviews and food articles before. The constant rewrites impeded my progress, but this continual self-editing made *Accidental Chef* a better piece of literature in the end. I never expected that writing a book would be easy, but I also didn't expect that it would be as laborious as it was. I now have immense respect for professional authors. My task was made easier with the help of several people. First and foremost I am indebted to Barbara Sadek for her unwavering encouragement throughout the process. Barbara was involved in the creative process from conception to the conclusion of formal writing process. She also assisted by offering useful ideas and concepts regarding subject matter. Barbara assisted with the editing and taking images of the food for the recipe chapter. I also want to thank my good friend Frank Gordon, the photographer who selected and shot the photographs in New Orleans. Frank Gordon is a consummate professional who has owned a photography business in New Orleans for many years. I also want to thank Frank's associate, Mae Lizama who was instrumental in technical aspects of the image production. Finally, I want to thank Cullen Wade who helped edit *Accidental Chef*. Cullen's contribution made *Accidental Chef* a more polished work.

I sincerely want to thank you all.

Selected Bibliography

Books

Attwater, Donald and Catherine Rachel John. *The Penguin Dictionary of Saints*. 3rd edition. New York: Penguin Books, 1993.

Bourdain, Anthony. *A Cook's Tour*. New York: Bloomsbury USA, 2001.

Bourdain, Anthony. *Kitchen Confidential*. New York: Bloomsbury USA, 2000.

Cambridge World History of Food (2000), 2 vol. editors Kiple, Kenneth F. and Coneè Ornelas

Casey, Susan. *The Wave*. New York: Doubleday, 2010.

Charles Hrh The Prince of Wales; Juniper, Tony; Skelly, Ian. *Harmony*. London: Harper Collins, 2010.

Child, Julia. *My Life In France*. New York: Alfred A. Knopf, 2006.

Danson, Ted; D'Orso, Michael. *Oceana*. New York: Rodale, 2011.

Eric Schlosser. *Fast Food Nation: The Dark Side of the All American Meal*. New York: Harper Perennial, 2001.

Garavini, Daniela. *Pigs and Pork*. Cologne: Konemann, 1996.

Greenberg, Paul. *Four Fish*. New York: Penguin Press, 2010.

Gregory N.G. *Animal Welfare and Meat Science.* Oxon, U.K.: CABI Publishing, 1998.

Kurlansky, Mark. *Salt.* New York: Walker and Company, 2002.

Pauline Nguyen; Luke Nguyen; Mark Jensen (2007), *Secrets of the Red Lantern: Stories and Vietnamese Recipes from the Heart.* Australia: Murdoch Books.

Pépin, Jacques. *Jacques Pépin.* Boston: Houghton Mifflin Company, 2003.

Prudhomme, Paul. *Chef Paul Prudhomme's Louisiana Kitchen.* New York: William Morrow and Company, 1984.

The New International Confectioner, 5th edition. edited by Wilfred J. Fance F. Inst. B.B., London and Coulsdon, England: Virtue & Company Ltd. 1981.

The Picayune Creole Cook Book. The Times-Picayune. The Sesquicentennial Edition. Edited by Marcelle Bienvenu.

Caro, Mark. *The Foie Gras Wars.* New York: Simon and Schuster, 2009.

Thị Chơi Triệu, Marcel Isaak, *The Food of Vietnam: Authentic Recipes from the Heart of Indochina.* Vermont: Tuttle Publishing, 2001.

Periodicals and Newspapers

Calnek BW, Barnes HJ, Beard CW, McDougald LR, and Saif YM (eds.), *Diseases of Poultry*, 9th edition, (Ames, Iowa: Iowa State University Press, 1991), pp. 293-9.

Demaster, DJ; Fowler, CW; Perry, SL; Richlen, ME (2001). "Predation and competition: the impact of fisheries on marine mammal populations over the next one hundred years". *Journal of Mammology* (82): 641–651.

Editorial. "Blue Fin Slaughter" *New York Times,* November 17, 2007.

Hall, M; Alverson, DL; Metuzals, KI (2000). "By-Catch: Problems and Solutions". *Marine Pollution Bulletin*. 41. pp. 204–219.

M.L. Tasker; C.J. Camphuysen, J. Cooper, S. Garthe, W. Montevecchi & S. Blaber (2000). "The impacts of fishing on marine birds". *ICES Journal of Marine Science* 57: 531–547.

N. Daan; P. Bromley, J. Hislop & N. Nielsen (1990). "Ecology of North Sea Fish". *Netherlands Journal of Sea Research* **26**: 343–386.

Rogers, Paul. "Economy of Scales". *Stanford Magazine*. Stanford Alumni Association.

Walsh, Bryan. "Code Blue" *Time Magazine,* September 23, 2010.

Weeks CA, Danbury TD, Davies HC, Hunt P, and Kestin SC, "The Behaviour of Broiler Chickens and Its Modification by Lameness," *Applied Animal Behaviour Science* 67 (2000): 111-25.

Web Sites

Accreditation Services International: www.accreditation-services.com

Animal Protection and Rescue League: www.aprl.org

AquaBounty Technologies: www.aquabounty.com

Aquaculture Stewardship Council: wwwacsworldwide.org

Blue Ocean Institute: www.blueocean.org

British Broadcasting Corporation: http://news.bbc.co.uk

Care2: www.care2.com

Center for Disease Control and Prevention: www.cdc.gov

Center for a Livable Future: www.liviablefutureblog.com

Chicken Industry.Com: www.chickenindustry.com

Compassion Over Killing: www.cok.net

Corporate Social Responsibility Newswire: www.csrwire.com

CorpWatch: www.corpwatch.org

Deutsche Welle: www.dw-world.de

Eco-Business: www.eco-business.com

Fish Source: www.fishsource.org

Fish Update: www.fishupdate.com

Food and Water Watch: www.foodandwaterwatch.org

Food-borne Illness: www.foodborneillness.com

Food Safety News: www.foodsafetynews.com

Friend of the Sea: www.friendofthesea.org

Global Animal Partnership: www.globalanimalpartnership.org

Global Aquaculture Alliance: www.gaalliance.org

Global Trust Certification: www.gtcert.com

Greenpeace USA: www.greenpeace.org/usa

International Commission for the Conservation of Atlantic Tunas: www.iccat.int

International Fishmeal and Fish Oil Organisation: www.iffo.net

International Seafood Sustainability Foundation: www.iss-foundation.org

José Made In Spain: www.josemadeinspain.com

Kitchen Project: www.kitchenproject.com

Leafy Green Product Handlers Marketing Agreement: www.caleafygreens.ca.gov

Mercy for Animals: www.mercyforanimals.org

Monterey Bay Aquarium: www.montereybayaquarium.org

National Fire Protection Association: www.nfpa.org

National Geographic: www.nationalgeographic.org

National Marine Fisheries Services: www.nmfs.noaa.gov

National Fish and Wildlife Foundation: www.nfwf.org

National Oceanic and Atmospheric Administration: www.nwfsc.noaa.gov

National Restaurant Association: www.restaurant.org

Northwest Fisheries Science Center: www.nwfsc.noaa.gov

Oceana: www.na.oceana.org

Organic Center: www.organic-center.org

PR Newswire for Journalists: www.media.prnewswire.com

Pure Salmon Campaign: www.puresalmon.org

Restaurant Report: www.restaurantreport.com

Safety At Home: www.safetyathome.com (An Underwriters Laboratories' web site)

Seafood Choices Alliance: wwwseafoodchoices.com

Science Daily: www.sciencedaily.com

Scientific American: www.scientificamerican.com

Scottish Environmental Protection Agency: www.fwr.org/fisheries/sr9705. html.

SiamCanadian: www.siamcanadian/vietnam-seafood/exports.htm

Stop Force Feeding: www.stopforcefeeding.com

Sustainable Fish Partnership: www.sustainablefish.org

Sustainable Table: www.sustainabletable.org

Take Part: www.takepart.com

The Economist: www.economist.com

The Fish Site: www.thefishsite.com

The IUCN Red List of Threatened Species: www.iucnredlist.org

The Nibble: www.thenibble.com

Underwater Times: www.underwatertimes.com

U.S. Geological Survey: www.usgs.org

Accidental Chef

USDA: Food Safety: www.foodsafety.gov

USDA: Economic Research Service: www.ers.usda.gov

Wikipedia: www.wikipedia.com

World Wildlife Fund: www.worldwildlife.org

Technical Reports and Papers

Gulf of Mexico Red Snapper: Assessment Summary Report. Southeast Data Assessment, and Review (SEDAR) Stock Assessment Report of SEDAR. 2005.

Clucas, Ivor (1997). *Discards and bycatch in Shrimp trawl fisheries*. Food and Agricultural Organization of the United Nations.

Estevez I, "Poultry Welfare Issues," *Poultry Digest Online* 3 No. 2 (2002): 1-12.

Grandin, Temple, *Animals are Not Things*, Paper presented at a discussion on whether or not animals should be property, with Marc Hauser, Dept. of Psychology, Harvard University, 2002.

Scottish Environment Protection Agency, "Collection and treatment of waste chemotherapeutants and the use of enclosed-cage systems in salmon aquaculture," SNIFFER/SEPA, 1998.

Will Concrete Keep Farmed Salmon Home?, Short Takes, International Foundation for the Conservation of Natural Resources, Fisheries Committee, April 9, 2004.